Handbook of Culture and
Consumer Behavior

FRONTIERS OF CULTURE AND PSYCHOLOGY

Series Editors
Michele J. Gelfand
Chi-yue Chiu
Ying-yi Hong

Books in the Series

Culture and Group Processes
Edited by Masaki Yuki and Marilynn Brewer

Handbook of Culture and Consumer Behavior
Edited by Sharon Ng and Angela Y. Lee

Handbook of Culture and Consumer Behavior

EDITED BY SHARON NG

AND

ANGELA Y. LEE

OXFORD
UNIVERSITY PRESS

Oxford University Press is a department of the University of
Oxford. It furthers the University's objective of excellence in research,
scholarship, and education by publishing worldwide.

Oxford   New York
Auckland   Cape Town   Dar es Salaam   Hong Kong   Karachi
Kuala Lumpur   Madrid   Melbourne   Mexico City   Nairobi
New Delhi   Shanghai   Taipei   Toronto

With offices in
Argentina   Austria   Brazil   Chile   Czech Republic   France   Greece
Guatemala   Hungary   Italy   Japan   Poland   Portugal   Singapore
South Korea   Switzerland   Thailand   Turkey   Ukraine   Vietnam

Oxford is a registered trademark of Oxford University Press
in the UK and certain other countries.

Published in the United States of America by
Oxford University Press
198 Madison Avenue, New York, NY 10016

Library of Congress Cataloging-in-Publication Data
Handbook of culture and consumer behavior / edited by Sharon Ng and Angela Y. Lee.
pages cm. — (Frontiers of culture and psychology)
Includes bibliographical references and index.
ISBN 978-0-19-938851-6 (hbk.) — ISBN 978-0-19-938852-3 (pbk.)
1. Consumer behavior—Cross-cultural studies.   2. Consumers—Cross-cultural
studies.   3. Consumption (Economics)—Cross-cultural studies.   I. Ng, Sharon.
II. Lee, Angela Y.
HF5415.32.H3635 2015
658.8'342—dc23
2014025871

9 8 7 6 5 4 3 2 1
Printed in the United States of America
on acid-free paper

CONTENTS

LIST OF CONTRIBUTORS

Nidhi Agrawal
Foster School of Business
University of Washington
Seattle, Washington, USA

Rohini Ahluwalia
Department of Marketing
Carlson School of Management
University of Minnesota
Minneapolis, Minnesota, USA

Hans Baumgartner
Department of Marketing
Smeal College of Business
Penn State University
State College, Pennsylvania, USA

Russell Belk
Department of Marketing
York University
Toronto, Ontario, Canada

Tonya Williams Bradford
Department of Marketing
Mendoza College of Business
University of Notre Dame
Notre Dame, Indiana, USA

Cathy Yi Chen
Department of Marketing
Singapore Management University
Singapore

Shirley Y. Y. Cheng
Department of Marketing
Hong Kong Baptist University
Kowloon Tong, Hong Kong

Louise Chim
Department of Psychology
Stanford University
Stanford, California, USA

Chi-yue Chiu
Nanyang Business School
Nanyang Technological University
Singapore

Zeynep Gürhan-Canli
Neely School of Business
Koc University
Istanbul, Turkey

Michael J. Houston
Department of Marketing
Carlson School of Management
University of Minnesota
Minneapolis, Minnesota, USA

Ryan P. Jacobson
Department of Organizational Studies
Anderson School of Management
University of New Mexico
Albuquerque, New Mexico, USA

Minkyung Koo
Department of Business
Administration, College of Business
University of Illinois at
Urbana-Champaign
Champaign, Illinois, USA

Robert Kreuzbauer
Nanyang Business School
Nanyang Technological University
Singapore

Virginia S. Y. Kwan
Department of Psychology
Arizona State University
Tempe, Arizona, USA

Angela Y. Lee
Kellogg School of Management
Northwestern University
Evanston, Illinois, USA

Dongmei Li
Hang Seng Management College
Hong Kong

Yexin J. Li
Department of Psychology
Arizona State University
Tempe, Arizona, USA

Durairaj Maheswaran
Department of Marketing and
International Business
Stern School of Business
New York University
New York, New York, USA

Sharon Ng
Division of Marketing and
International Business
Nanyang Business School
Nanyang Technological University
Singapore

Akshay Rao
Department of Marketing
Carlson School of Management
University of Minnesota
Minneapolis, Minnesota, USA

Gülen Sarial-Abi
Department of Marketing
Universita Commerciale Luigi
Bocconi
Milan, Italy

Prashant Saxena
Associate Director
Agility Research & Strategy
Singapore

Sharon Shavitt
Department of Business
Administration, College of Business
University of Illinois at
Urbana-Champaign
Champaign, Illinois, USA

Tamara Sims
Department of Psychology
Stanford University
Stanford, California, USA

Carlos Torelli
Department of Marketing
Carlson School of Management
University of Minnesota
Minneapolis, Minnesota, USA

Jeanne L. Tsai
Department of Psychology
Stanford University
Stanford, California, USA

Jie Wei
Department of Marketing
National University of Singapore
Singapore

Bert Weijters
Vlerick Leuven Gent Management
School
Ghent University
Gent, Belgium

Andrew E. White
Department of Psychology
Arizona State University
Tempe, Arizona, USA

Robert S. Wyer, Jr.
Department of Marketing
Chinese University of Hong Kong
Shatin, N.T., Hong Kong

History of Culture and Consumer Behavior and Future Research Directions

SHARON NG AND ANGELA Y. LEE ■

Research on the influence of culture on consumer decision making and consumption behavior has witnessed tremendous growth in the last decade. Rigorous investigations that make important theoretical advances and offer managerial relevance are being presented at major conferences and appearing in top marketing and psychology journals. These are exciting developments and signal a broad-based recognition that culture matters—that new theories should be forged and existing frameworks revalidated with the awareness and sensitivity that norms, values, and thinking styles may differ across different cultures and, in turn, drive different psychological processes and consumption behaviors.

This increased momentum in culture and consumer behavior research can be attributed to two factors. First, industry concerns and interests are driving the need for more rigorous research that is motivation and process driven rather than phenomenon based. With increasing globalization, managers are becoming increasingly aware that operating in multiple markets is crucial for firms' survival and growth. As the world's growth engine shifts from Europe and North America to Asia and Latin America, it has become apparent that an inward looking and domestic focus strategy would not be sustainable in the long run, and success in foreign markets requires marketers to understand not just what consumers in these markets need, but also how they think, behave, consume, and purchase. The popular press is laden with stories of firms failing to enter a foreign market, with many of these firms being important players in their domestic markets, including major multinational conglomerates. Despite their dominance in the domestic market, they did not manage to transfer their success to the emergent markets. For example, eBay was not able to make significant inroads into China. It remained a distant second in the global marketplace to its China-based competitor Taobao, and eventually was forced to relinquish its operations in China. Although part of the reason for the lack-luster performance of many foreign companies may be attributable to unfavorable regulatory constraints imposed by these emergent markets, a major reason for the failure is the lack of insight by these foreign investors into the local consumers' psyche.

A second factor that contributes to the recent surge in cross-cultural consumer behavior research is the approach advanced by scholars conducting cross-cultural research. Earlier cross-cultural research was characterized by the documentation of differences in consumers' cognition and behavior patterns across different countries as evidence of cultural differences (e.g., Mueller, 1987). While the demonstrations of differences across consumers residing in different nations provide strong external validity for cultural effects, critics were quick to point out that the findings were confounded by other country-specific differences that may or may not be relevant to the theoretical constructs under investigation (see Chapter 8 by Baumgartner and Weijters for further discussion on this topic). Each country has its idiosyncratic differences (e.g., types of stores and brands available, income, geography, climate, population size, political system, social norms, history, culture, language, etc.) that may lead to differences in product judgments and brand-choice decisions. Thus, what truly underlies cross-country differences could be rather elusive. Then toward the end of the 1990s a paradigm shift occurred, followed by significant advancements in our understanding of how culture affects cognition and behavior. Instead of relying on country borders to examine cultural differences and assuming that culture exerts a constant and consistent influence on people's cognition and behavior, researchers started to examine cultural differences from a psychological perspective, studying psychological constructs and processes as potential mechanisms that may be underlying cultural differences (e.g., Gardner, Gabriel, & Lee, 1999). Researchers were also adopting an accessibility perspective to understand the influence of culture. Departing from prior beliefs and practices, researchers argue that cultural knowledge is neither omnipotent nor always at work (Hong, Morris, Chiu, & Benet-Martinez, 2000). Rather, culture exerts its influence only when the set of cultural knowledge is activated or primed. This new paradigm allows researchers to examine culture in a more controlled environment, which helps to address the criticisms of cross-country comparisons. This new approach that encourages the systematic investigation of cultural effects as psychological processes and consequences has injected renewed energy and enthusiasm into cross-cultural research.

Fueled by the interests of the practitioners and academics, research in culture and consumer psychology has progressed from simple cross-country comparisons of consumer behavior to more in-depth analyses with the objectives of understanding how, when, and why culture matters. While we are excited to see heightened interests and increased activities in cross-cultural research, we also note the infrequent occurrences of conversations, debates, and dialogues among researchers. Thus, one objective of this handbook is to provide some perspectives on how culture research in consumer psychology has evolved, how it contributes to our understanding of the consumer psyche across different continents, and where it is heading. Another objective of the handbook is to provide a forum for researchers to come together and engage in thoughtful debates and stimulating conversations. A third objective is to provide an overview of the current state of research and identify avenues for future research.

The remaining fourteen chapters in this handbook are organized into four sections. Part I of the handbook focuses on the impact of knowledge accessibility on consumers' processing and emotion. The first two chapters in this section discuss how people's view of the world and how it operates is profoundly influenced by their cultural experiences. Members of a hunter-gatherer society necessarily have a very different worldview from those of an agrarian community, and people living in land-locked regions do see the world through a different lens as compared to those inhabiting coastal areas. In Chapter 2, Kwan and her colleagues discuss the consequences and implications of different worldviews on how people view the self, how they view change and balance, and how they view death. This is followed by a thorough discussion by Wyer on how culture may influence goal-directed processing. In particular, Chapter 3 focuses on how culture influences the tendencies of people to process information holistically versus analytically, to consider relationship between versus within entities, and to differentially weight positive versus negative features of choice alternatives. Chapter 4 follows with an in-depth discussion by Tsai and her colleagues on how culture shapes emotions and, in turn, impacts decision making and consumer behavior. The next chapter in this section (Chapter 5 by Shavitt and Koo) examines how variations in cultural values are reflected in consumers' motivation and attention toward advertising appeals and, in turn, influence persuasiveness of the appeals.

Part II of the handbook focuses on how culture affects the elicitation and measurement of attitude. First, Chapter 6 in this section by Agrawal examines how consumers' perception, attitude, and behavior may reflect the values consistent with their self-view. At the heart of the discussion is the recognition that individuals' attitudes and behavior may be influenced by a self-view that is culturally encouraged and hence chronically accessible, or by a self-view that is temporarily made salient through situational cues. This chapter raises the important question of when consumers will rely on their culturally encouraged versus situationally primed self-view in decision making. But consumer decision making as a function of self-view is not limited to the values associated with the distinct way in which people view the self. Self-view can influence motivation, perception, attitude, and behavior through a match with self-regulatory orientation, construal level, temporal perspective, or what signifies success in life. The chapter by Lee and Bradford discusses how self-construal fit may influence consumers' motivation, engagement, and empathic experiences and, in turn, impact product judgment, brand choice, and charitable giving behaviors. The final chapter in this section by Baumgartner and Weijters issues the caveat that comparisons across different cultures may be clouded by culture-specific response scale biases rather than a substantive difference in the constructs of interest. This chapter reviews the most common response biases and provides guidelines for researchers to handle these biases.

Part III of the handbook focuses on branding and brand relationships. The first chapter in this section (Chapter 9 by Chen and colleagues) presents the case that people perceive nations in a similar way as they perceive brands, and that the equity of a nation, whether it is positive or negative, can have significant impact on how consumers evaluate products from that nation. However, independent of the valence of a nation's equity and the quality of the products, consumers may feel their own heritage cultural identity threatened by the influx of foreign brands and hence develop exclusionary reactions toward these brands. In Chapter 10, Li and her colleagues discuss how exclusionary reactions to globalization efforts may lead to xenophobic behaviors with the objective of protecting their own heritage. These authors further describe conditions under which these culturally motivated exclusionary responses may be facilitated or attenuated. The remaining three chapters in this section take a deep dive into the cultural meaning of brands. The authors describe how culture influences the way that consumers think about and form relationships with brands, how culture impacts consumers' evaluation of brand extensions, and the corresponding effects of these extensions on the parent brand and on culture. These discussions provide a rich understanding and appreciation for how domestic brands may serve to fulfill the consumer's cultural identity needs, while foreign brands threaten one's cultural identity. Together, these chapters provide a comprehensive overview of the culture and branding literature.

Finally, Part IV of the handbook examines the impact of culture on consumption. In particular, Belk in Chapter 14 discusses how culture may define certain aspects of materialism but not others. For instance, whereas different cultures have different expressions for the social aspects of materialism such as keeping up with the Joneses, social comparison, conspicuous consumption, or status seeking, the manifestation of individual traits that are closely related to materialism such as acquisitiveness, possessiveness, envy, avarice, compulsive hoarding, and compulsive buying are invariant across different cultures. In Chapter 15, Rao offers a neuropsychological perspective on the link between culture and self-regulation and impulsive consumption behaviors.

Collectively, the chapters present an excellent overview of the most recent research in culture and consumer psychology, with most of the investigations focusing on three broad categories of cultural differences—substantive variations (e.g., beliefs, values, respect for tradition, motivational orientations, etc.), processing differences (e.g., holistic versus analytic), and differences in emotional experiences (e.g., excitement and enthusiasm versus calm and peacefulness). We expect the burgeoning trend to continue and hope that the discussions presented in this handbook will serve as the platform and inspiration for future research.

APPLIED SIGNIFICANCE

Going through the chapters, one will come across different theorizing as to why cultures differ and how they differ. Different antecedents are presented and consequences discussed. While it is clear that the various frameworks make significant theoretical advancements, one question that is raised time and time again is whether the findings from academic research has any merits that warrant managerial attention. This is a fair and important question that deserves an answer—"Yes!"

While it is not our intention to provide a complete list of all the possible applications of the findings, we highlight below a few research areas that are relevant to practitioners.

As noted above, substantial research has been conducted to examine how people from different cultures perceive local versus global brands and develop brand relationships. One finding shows that consumers from a collectivistic culture or those with a more dominant interdependent self-view are more accepting of relational extensions (see Chapter 11). The implication is that companies can strategically leverage their core brands for branding purposes when entering markets in countries like China, Korea, or Japan. The tendency of consumers from collectivistic cultures to engage in relational processing allows companies to extend their brands into product categories that do not necessarily have a strong link with their core products and market them under the umbrella of the more established brands. The finding that consumers from collectivistic cultures are more forgiving when new products introduced by their favored brands fail suggests that firms may be at lower brand equity dilution risk when product extensions fail. This may help explain why big corporations in Korea and Japan (e.g., Chaebol in Korea) have traditionally been able to extend to a more varied mix of businesses than companies in Western countries.

Another line of research examining consumers' impulsivity and self-regulation suggests that Western consumers are more impatient compared to Eastern consumers. The implication is that Westerners would find financial products with a long maturity period less appealing. Being more short-term focused, Westerners are more attracted to products or services that provide immediate gratifications and faster rewards. This is particularly relevant in loyalty program design. For example, in designing loyalty programs, companies may have to decide on the number of points customers have to accumulate before they can redeem in exchange for a gift. Bigger prizes require more points to redeem and take longer to accumulate, whereas smaller prizes require fewer points and less time and effort to accumulate. Extant literature would suggest that the former would be more attractive to consumers with an Eastern orientation, whereas the latter should be more attractive to consumers with a Western orientation.

Other practical implications can be gleamed from the research reviewed in the various chapters and it is not our intent to repeat them here. It suffices to say that for firms expanding to overseas markets, a good understanding of how consumers may differ in terms of the way they process information, the basis on which they form brand preferences and make brand choices, as well as their worldview and affective sensitivities would be invaluable in their efforts. This handbook should provide managers with the necessary background information and strategic insights.

DIRECTIONS FOR FUTURE RESEARCH

In reviewing the literature, it becomes apparent that there are substantial gaps in the literature that warrant further investigation. In the spirit of promoting cultural research in the domain of consumer psychology, we highlight some potential avenues for fruitful research. This is by no means a comprehensive list of research topics; rather, it is a reflection of our thoughts and observations in the course of editing this handbook.

Taking a broader perspective of cultural differences

First, most cross-cultural consumer behavior research conducted so far views the world in a binary fashion—East (epitomized by China) versus West (epitomized by United States). Whereas the Eastern culture is typically seen as collectivistic, group-focused, and context dependent, the Western culture is typically seen as individualistic, self-focused, and content independent (e.g., Aaker, 2000; Bolton, Keh, & Alba, 2010; Chen, Ng, & Rao, 2005). The whole world is conceptualized as falling into either category, and comparisons are made by contrasting one versus the other. This binary worldview is reflected in the multiple chapters in this handbook. While consumers within an Eastern or Western culture do share many similarities, within-cultural differences as well as cross-cultural similarities have also been observed. In particular, individualism–collectivism is only one of six dimensions along which cultures may differ; other cultural dimensions include power distance, masculinity–femininity, uncertainty avoidance, pragmatism, and indulgence (Hofstede Centre, 2014). For example, India and China are both Asian countries and would typically be considered to belong to a collectivistic culture; yet they differ in many aspects. In fact, while India and China share similar scores along the dimensions of power distance (77 vs. 80), masculinity–femininity (56 vs. 66), uncertainty avoidance (40 vs. 30), and indulgence (26 vs. 24), they are rather different along the individualism–collectivism (48 vs. 20) and pragmatism (51 vs. 87) dimensions (http://geert-hofstede.com/countries.html). While some researchers have ventured to examine time orientation (Park, Chung & Woo 2013) and power distance (Zhang, Winterich, &Mittal 2010), these are few and far in between. Thus, it is imperative that researchers go beyond the individualism–collectivism dimension to examine other cultural differences.

Culture is a complex concept. In investigating cultural differences along some of the other dimensions, researchers are well advised to focus on identifying the underlying psychological constructs, similar to how people's independent versus interdependent self-view has been identified as the construct underlying the individualism–collectivism difference across cultures. As a construct, self-view is much more clearly defined than culture, and focusing on self-view has helped make important theoretical advancements in our understanding of cross-cultural consumer psychology, cognition, and consumption. In the same spirit, examining psychological constructs that underlie other dimensions of culture will continue to push the boundary of the field.

We note that focusing on an East–West difference also ignores the heterogeneity among consumers within a country or a culture. In some instances, the within-country deviation may even be greater than the deviation across countries. Again, using China as an example, consumers in first tier cities like Shanghai and Beijing may be more akin to consumers in major US cities such as New York and Los Angeles than to consumers in rural China. Greater affluence, exposure to foreign brands, and parenting styles that encourage independence and creativity under the one-child policy may have led to a more independent self-view. Thus, simplifying the classification of consumers into an Eastern versus Western bloc ignores regional differences within a country and may cloud our understanding of consumption behaviors.

We would also like to make a call for cross-cultural investigations beyond making comparisons between China, India, and the United States. Currently, we have very little knowledge about how consumers in say, Thailand, Saudi Arabia, Brazil, or South Africa think and behave. Although China and India are the world's biggest and fastest growing markets, firms do not operate only in these countries. Many multi-nationals are thirsting for knowledge on consumers in other countries—what motivates them, how they make decisions, what emotional experiences are more intense, and so on. For instance, some financial institutions are beginning to provide special Islamic banking services for Muslim consumers who have specific needs and requirements that traditional financial instruments are not able to fulfill. Yet the consumption practices of these consumers are not well understood or documented. Chapter 14 by Belk is a good start in this direction, but we need more.

Beyond pricing and advertising effects

A vast majority of the literature on culture and consumer psychology is devoted to investigating the impact of culture on brand definition, brand extension, brand feedback effect, brand iconicity, brand relationship, and preference for local (versus foreign) brands (see Chapters 9 to 13). Prior research has also examined how consumers across cultures respond to different forms of advertising appeals and persuasion attempts (see Chapter 5). While the field definitely benefits from advancements in these areas, we also like to see more research activities in other marketing and consumer behavior domains. One potential avenue of research is to better understand how culture may affect consumers' processing of price information and their responses to different pricing strategies. Price is an important marketing tool. Yet with the exception of Bolton et al. (2010) examining how culture-evoked emotions affect consumers' perception of price fairness, there is almost no cross-cultural investigations of how consumers process price information. More needs to be done. For instance, do Asian consumers who adhere to the teachings of Confucius and hence are more frugal pay more attention to price information? Do Westerners who tend to be more promotion-oriented pay more attention to benefits (versus costs) and hence are less price-sensitive? How may discount rates differ as a function of long-term orientation and pragmatism? Answers to these and other questions would make important contributions to both the culture and pricing literatures.

Other areas of consumer research that could benefit from a deeper understanding with a cultural perspective include consumer religiosity and well-being, risk perception and financial decision making, savings and over-spending, materialism and compensatory consumption . . . the list goes on. For the field to progress, it is important that cultural researchers go beyond the traditional topics and expand their scope of enquiries.

CONCLUSION

We would like to convey our sincere gratitude to all the contributors of this handbook for their wisdom, time, and efforts. Together, the chapters in this handbook offer a unique, integrative perspective on recent research in culture and consumer psychology. We believe that the chapters will initiate interesting dialogues and spark new, exciting research, and hope that readers will find the reviews useful and inspiring.

REFERENCES

Aaker, J. L. (2000). Accessibility or diagnosticity? Disentangling the influence of culture on persuasion processes and attitudes. *Journal of Consumer Research, 26*(4), 340–357.

Bolton, L. E., Keh, H. T., & Alba, J. W. (2010). How do price fairness perceptions differ across culture? *Journal of Marketing Research, 47*(3), 564–576.

Chen, H, Ng, S., & Rao, A. (2005). Cultural differences in consumer impatience. *Journal of Marketing Research, 42*(3), 291–301.

Gardner, W. L., Gabriel, S., & Lee, A. Y. (1999). "I" value freedom, but "we" value relationships: Self-construal priming mirrors cultural differences in judgment. *Psychological Science, 10*(4), 321–326.

Hofstede Centre. (2014). *Country comparison.* Retrieved from http://geert-hofstede.com/countries.html

Hong, Y. Y., Morris, M. W., Chiu, C. Y., & Benet-Martinez, V. (2000). Multicultural minds: A dynamic constructivist approach to culture and cognition. *American Psychologist, 55*(7), 709.

Mueller, B. (1987). Reflections of culture: An analysis of Japanese and American advertising appeals. *Journal of Advertising Research, 27*(3), 51–59.

Park, S. B., Chung, N., & Woo, S. C. (2013). Do reward programs build loyalty to restaurants? The moderating effect of long-term orientation on the timing and types of rewards. *Managing Service Quality, 23*(3), 225–244.

Zhang, Y., Winterich, K. P., & Mittal, V. (2010). Power distance belief and impulsive buying. *Journal of Marketing Research, 47*(5), 945–954.

PART I

Worldview, Knowledge Structure, and Emotion

Cultural Worldview and Cognition

VIRGINIA S. Y. KWAN, YEXIN J. LI,
ANDREW E. WHITE, AND RYAN P. JACOBSON ■

INTRODUCTION

A universal property of humans is the attempt to understand how the world operates. Before the Renaissance, people subscribed to the geocentric view that the Earth is the center of the universe and the Sun and other planets revolve around it. In 1543, Nicolaus Copernicus presented the heliocentric model of the universe, launching the Copernican Revolution. In 1616, Galileo Galilei published his telescopic observations to support the heliocentric model, paving the path for Isaac Newton's discovery of the fundamental laws of motion. Along with other scientists of the Copernican Revolution, Copernicus, Galileo, and Newton instigated dramatic challenges of doctrines that had prevailed since the Ancient Greeks.

Scientists are not the only ones to educate us about how the world operates. Cultural psychologists assert that worldviews are often products of personal experiences and the socialization process. Worldviews pass from generation to generation. Children learn how to navigate the world within the realm of their cultural systems. Supporting this assertion, previous research shows that people from different cultural groups tend to hold distinct beliefs or views about how the world operates (see Hofstede & Hofstede, 2005; Moore & Lewis, 1952; White, 1947). Culture, by way of providing a context for cognition, serves as an important influence on building representations of a meaningful reality (see Kashima, 2008; Nisbett, Peng Choi, & Norenzayan, 2001).

Shweder (1990) affirmed that "cultural psychology is the study of intentional worlds." An intentional world is one in which the people who compose it are the ones who infuse their world with meaning. "Realities are the products of the way things get represented, embedded, implemented, and reacted to" (Shweder, 1990, pp. 4–5). The cultural environment is an intentional world. Every object is there for a reason and every event happens for a reason. As Toelken (1996) put it, "*worldview* refers to the manner in which a culture sees and expresses its relation to the world around it" (p. 263).

Cultural differences in worldviews may reflect the adaptations that different cultural groups develop to handle the specific problems they face. Nisbett and his colleagues argued that contemporary differences in cultural worldviews stem from the original differences in thought expressed by the ancient Greek and Chinese cultures (see Nisbett et al., 2001). Ancient Chinese civilization was based on agriculture, which would promote visual emphasis on the greater context of nature and natural relationships (e.g., the entire field of crops, the climate, and predators). On the other hand, research on Greek ecology suggests the Greek economy might have been largely based on hunting, fishing, and trading, which would have promoted greater visual emphasis on the objects being hunted or traded. The need to visually attune to particular aspects of the environment, based on their distinct mode of production, may have influenced each culture's social organization of the world (Masuda & Nisbett, 2001). Furthermore, these cultural differences implicate cognitive organization and structure of brand information (Ng & Houston, 2006).

Worldviews align with values in some ways. There has long been a values tradition in psychology that examines how cultural values influence social behavior. Values tell us what is important, desirable, and appropriate. Values serve as guiding principles of life. In contrast to values, worldviews are beliefs about how the world operates. For example, some worldviews reflect our vulnerability to the unpredictable environment and in turn serve the purpose of making the unpredictable world more predictable. Views like "good luck follows if one survives a disaster" and "fate determines one's successes and failures" immediately imply a sense of unscientific irrationality and helplessness. Nonetheless, these worldviews are often assumed to be true and continue to affect most individuals within their culture. In short, worldviews represent beliefs about how the world *actually* operates while values represent desires for how the world *should* operate.

While we know that cultural worldviews encourage certain ways of thinking and behaving, relatively little research has been done to understand the impact of cultural worldviews on consumer behavior. Therefore, the major goal of this chapter is to review the current state of the research on this topic. Our hope is to spark ideas for future research that advance an interest and enthusiasm in the dynamic nature of cultural worldviews and their impact on consumer behavior. Specifically, we will begin our discussion with a review of the research on cultural worldviews and their links to social cognition and behavior. We then discuss the conditions that lead to changes in cultural worldviews and their effects on consumer behavior. Finally, we discuss future directions for research on cultural worldviews and consumer behaviors.

POWER OF CULTURAL WORLDVIEWS ON SOCIAL COGNITION AND BEHAVIOR

A large body of research suggests that Easterners and Westerners think about the world very differently from each other (for a review, see Fiske, Kitayama, Markus, & Nisbett, 1998; Lehman, Chiu, & Schaller, 2004; Nisbett et al., 2001). One aspect of cultural worldviews that has been studied most extensively is how people see themselves in relation to others in the social environment. Markus and Kitayama (1991) postulated that there is no one universal construal of the self. There are two divergent kinds of self-contrual—interdependent and independent views. The interdependent view, often found in collectivistic countries, focuses on the connectedness of the self to others, whereas the independent view, common in individualistic countries, stresses the separateness of the self from others. These different self-construals pervade the ways in which independent and interdependent individuals think, feel, and behave.

Effects of cultural differences in self-construal emerge in the connotation attached to human behavior, which is often judged on the basis of social comparison with the majority. That is, any given behavior is evaluated on the basis of whether it is the same or different from what most others are doing, particularly if they constitute a dominant cultural group in that society. In particular, the interpretation for a given individuating behavior (i.e., one that makes the actor stand out and appear different from others) varies in terms of the cultural emphasis on "self-in-relation-to-other" (Markus & Kitayama, 1991, p. 225). The judgments attached to those individuators who choose to act differently from others can be either positive or negative (Kwan, Bond, Boucher, Maslach, & Gan, 2002). Whether individuation connotes "the squeaky wheel gets the grease" or "the nail that stands out gets pounded down," depends on the nature of the individuating behavior and the social context in which it is enacted. Being different from others is praised as unique and independent in individualistic cultures like the United States. In stark contrast, the same individuating behaviors invite criticism in collectivist cultures like East Asia (Kwan et al., 2002). The positive social impact of individuating behaviors may be diminished or negative in collectivistic cultures, where such behaviors are regarded as showing oneself off to draw attention from the public.

Evaluations of human behaviors may be parallel to evaluations of objects. Culture affects our basic likes and dislikes and our evaluations of option alternatives. In a series of studies, Kim and Markus (1999) showed that East Asians prefer objects that are alike, as well as themes that emphasize harmony, while Westerners prefer unique objects, as well as themes that emphasize individuality. For example, American travelers overwhelmingly choose a uniquely colored pen among those offered, whereas East Asian travelers opt for the pen in the majority color.

Cultural preferences for uniqueness also predict the common themes of advertisements. In a content analysis of popular magazine ads, Kim and Markus (1999, p. 793) identified differences in print advertisements between Korea and the United States. Overall, Korean advertisements emphasize conformity, whereas the US. advertisements emphasize uniqueness. More specifically, Korean advertisements highlight (a) respect for collective values and traditional social roles (e.g., "Our ginseng drink is produced according to the methods of 500-year-old tradition" and "Bring a fresh breeze to your wife at home"); (b) harmony with group norms (e.g., "Seven out of ten people are using this product"); and (c) following trends (e.g., "Trend forecast for spring: Pastel colors!"). In contrast, US. advertisements feature (a) rebellion against collective values and traditional roles (e.g., "Ditch the Joneses" and "Princess dream, pony dream. Ready for a kick butt dream?"); (b) choice and freedom (e.g., "Possibilities are endless" and "Freedom of vodka"); and (c) individual uniqueness (e.g., "The Internet isn't for everybody. But then again, you are not everybody").

Consistent with this cultural emphasis on "self-in-relation-to-other," the research of Han and Shavitt (1994) demonstrates that East Asians, in comparison to North Americans, find advertising appeals that highlight in-group benefits, harmony, and family integrity more persuasive, and appeals that highlight personal preferences or benefits less persuasive. Furthermore, the work of Aaker and Schmitt (2001) illustrates that North Americans are more likely to make consumption choices that highlight personal distinctiveness and individuality while East Asians are more likely to make consumption choices that enhance in-group benefits or status.

Another set of cultural worldviews that have been studied extensively is how people approach contradictions. Compared with Westerners, Easterners are more comfortable reconciling seemingly inconsistent claims (e.g., Miller, 1984; Morris, Nisbett, & Peng, 1995; Morris & Peng, 1994; Nisbett et al., 2001; Peng & Nisbett, 1999). Notably, Americans resolve conflicting viewpoints by selecting the one that best represents their view of the world. Conversely, East Asians use a dialectical approach to synthesize propositions and counter-propositions that Americans may deem inconsistent. For example, given two contradictory research findings (one more plausible than the other), Peng and Nisbett (1999) provided evidence that American participants tended to rate the stronger argument as more plausible when they were presented with both findings than when presented only with the stronger argument. In contrast, Chinese participants tended to rate the weaker argument as being more plausible when presented with both findings—indicating that they may have felt obligated to find merit in the weaker argument when presented with both findings. Thus, Americans tend to anchor on a particular perspective whereas East Asians are willing to entertain the possibility that multiple apparently inconsistent approaches or outcomes are valid.

These cultural differences in logical reasoning also emerge in consumer behaviors. Briley, Morris, and Simonson (2000) asked European Americans and East Asians to make a series of choices from among three consumer objects that varied on two dimensions. The first object was always superior to the second and third on one of the dimensions, the third object was always superior to the first and second on the other dimension, and the second object was always intermediate on both dimensions. When not asked to justify their choices, the likelihood of choosing the intermediate consumer object did not differ between the two cultural groups. However, when asked to provide reasons for their choices, East Asians became more likely and European Americans less likely to choose the intermediate object. Critically, the justifications provided in this condition were consistent with hypothesized cross-cultural differences in the use of rule-based logic (i.e., avoidance of contradiction) versus dialectical reasoning (i.e., acceptance of contradiction). When asked to justify their preferences, European Americans were more likely to report the use of simple rules emphasizing the importance of one dimension over the other whereas East Asians were more likely to report reasons emphasizing a compromise between dimensions. Thus, a European American preference for avoiding contradiction appears to have led to more extreme consumer decisions whereas an East Asian acceptance of contradiction appears to have led to less extreme (i.e., compromising) consumer decisions.

Another difference in worldviews involves how cultures interpret the nature of change and balance. Eastern cultural views emphasize the inevitability of change and balance. The *I Ching* is a principal text of Taoist philosophy (see Ritsema & Karcher, 1994). The first character "I" means "change" in Chinese. The second character "Ching" means "a book." *I Ching* states that all forces in the universe have both Yin and Yang states. The Yin and Yang represent two opposing but complementary forces. The interplay of Yin and Yang brings about the inevitability of change and transformation between extremes. For example, "winter can turn into summer," "what goes up must come down," and "night changes into day." According to the Taoist worldview, change is constant and nonlinear. In contrast, Western cultural views emphasize continuity and linear changes (Logan, 1956). For example, ancient Greek thinkers, such as Parmenides (born 510 BC), argued that all things that existed in the present had always existed, and nothing could emerge from nothingness (see Ji, Nisbett, & Su, 2001). As such, change is a rare and unnatural occurrence, and balance is irrelevant to the natural order. Even philosophers who recognized the existence of change argued that it is linear and progressive, moving in one particular direction rather than oscillating between two endpoints (e.g., Heraclitus, ca. 540–480 BC). Supporting Nisbett's hypothesis about East and West differences, previous research has found that Chinese and Americans predict change differently. Americans anticipate less change from an initial state than do Chinese (Ji et al., 2001). Specifically, Americans are more likely than Chinese to anticipate linear continuity. In contrast, Chinese people are more likely to predict change in a different direction.

IMMEDIATE CULTURAL ENVIRONMENT AND SALIENCE OF WORLDVIEWS

Different worldviews do coexist within the individual. Which worldview influences behavior and decision making depends on its accessibility in mind. Accessibility could be chronic (socialization over extended periods of time) or temporarily primed (cues in the immediate environment). For example, conflicting cultural worldviews exist within bicultural individuals, who have internalized two distinct cultural constructs. According to the cultural frame-switching paradigm (Hong, Morris, Chiu, & Benet-Martínez, 2000), the two internalized cultures take turns (i.e., switch frames) in guiding bicultural individuals' thoughts and behaviors. Frame switching results from cues such as contexts (e.g., home or school) and symbols (e.g., language or cultural icons) that are psychologically associated with one specific culture and not the other (Hong et al., 2000; Ross, Xun, & Wilson, 2002). For example, bicultural Chinese Americans make typically Chinese judgments when primed with a Chinese dragon icon, and typically American judgments when primed with an American flag (Hong et al., 2000).

Furthermore, the power of cultural worldview transcends geographical boundary. According to traditional views of culture, people from different cultural groups hold distinct beliefs or views about how the world operates, and cultural change happens slowly and infrequently (see Moore & Lewis, 1952; Hofstede & Hofstede, 2005; White, 1947). In a sense, the traditional approaches to culture assume that cognition is *intracultural,* or situated within a particular cultural context.

However, affordable international travel, globalized commerce, and the Internet have enabled people to interact and live on a global scale. People are increasingly exposed to different cultures, both at home and abroad. There is good reason to expect that their cognitions and behaviors may be affected by their immediate cultural context. Our recent research found supportive evidence for *extracultural* cognition in European Americans (Alter & Kwan, 2009). That is, cultural worldviews could be temporally malleable to the extent that the environment conveys alternative cultural worldviews. Previous research has shown that European Americans tend to anticipate linear continuity in the environment, whereas East Asians are more likely to anticipate change in existing patterns (Ji et al., 2001). If cultural contexts dictate behavioral patterns, European American participants would predict change more often in the presence of Chinese context. Indeed, when asked to forecast the weather or create a stock portfolio, New Yorkers in the Upper East Side of Manhattan made different weather predictions and investment decisions from New Yorkers in Chinatown. Visitors in Chinatown predicted more changes in the weather and invest less heavily in previously appreciating stocks than did people in the Upper East Side (Alter & Kwan, 2009). These findings are consistent with cultural interpretations of change.

Furthermore, Alter and Kwan (2009) examined the effects of cultural symbols on consequential decisions and behaviors. Culturally and ideologically laden symbols are ubiquitous in our environments. These symbols serve as subtle yet constant primes of the entities they signify. Specifically, European Americans recognize that the Chinese Yin–Yang symbol implies change. They invest less heavily in previously appreciating stocks and predict less continuity in the weather when primed with that symbol than with symbols unrelated to change. Importantly, European Americans who are primed with a Yin–Yang symbol make similar judgments to Chinese participants, suggesting that the Yin–Yang symbol influences European Americans' judgments because it primes a different cognitive frame from the one they traditionally adopt (Alter & Kwan, 2009).

These findings have important theoretical and practical implications for foreign trade, investment, advertising, and Internet-based exposure to foreign cultural worldviews. Theoretically, culture appears to express itself more changeably than researchers previously believed. Even so-called monocultural individuals sometimes adopt cognitive mindsets typically associated with familiar and temporarily salient foreign cultures. Furthermore, the growth of international travel, trade, and the Internet suggest that culturally laden stimuli will increasingly influence commerce and transcultural relations, sometimes counter to naïve intuitions. Researchers and businesspeople who work across international boundaries should assume that people from one culture behave predominantly according to their own cultural worldview, although they also may adopt salient foreign worldviews.

An interesting direction for future research is to examine how strongly foreign cultural stimuli (e.g., imported cultural symbols) influence cognition among different populations. Thus far our findings show that people from one culture temporarily infuse their judgments with the tenets of a second salient culture, as long as they recognize the meaning embodied in that culture. The biculturalism literature suggests that immigrants rapidly become competent with their adopted culture, implying, for example, businesspeople who live for an extended period of time in a foreign culture may be more susceptible to foreign cultural primes than their counterparts who visit that culture for a short period of time.

Research on self-construal priming illustrates another powerful way to alter cultural worldviews (see Gardner, Gabriel, & Lee, 1999). This line of research provides evidence that cultural worldviews are malleable to the extent that alternative modes of thinking can be primed. The strength of independence versus interdependence varies both between and within cultural groups (Oyserman, Coon, & Kemmelmeier, 2002). Importantly, the salience of an interdependent self-construal at a given situation may influence worldview-consistent behaviors. In one study, participants from the US and Hong Kong were primed to adopt an independent mindset by circling words like "I" or "Me," or an interdependent mindset by circling words such as "Us" or "We". Then, in a later phase of the study, participants from both cultural groups showed prime-consistent shifts in values, endorsing either the individualistic or collectivistic values expressed by the words they had circled in the earlier word search task (Gardner et al., 1999).

This has important implications for marketers. The salience of these different self-views could be manipulated to vary across contexts and thus influence subsequent decisions and behaviors. For example, advertisements that depict interdependent self-views might be more effective or appealing when delivered to individuals for whom interpersonal concerns are chronically or acutely activated, whereas advertisements that highlight independent self-views might be more effective when delivered to those for whom intrapersonal concerns are chronically or acutely activated. Furthermore, research found that the two types of self-views are closely linked to preferences for promotion versus prevention strategies (Aaker & Lee, 2001; Lee, Aaker, & Gardner, 2000). When individuals focus on getting ahead and achieving independence, they focus on approaching and promoting goal-oriented strategies (i.e., promotion focused). In contrast, when individuals focus on fitting in and getting along with others, they focus on avoiding and preventing loss (i.e., prevention focused). Consumers with independent self-views find promotion-focused information more appealing, whereas those with interdependent self-views find prevention-focused information more attractive.

Mortality salience

Cultural worldviews remind us that our beliefs are shared and that we are valuable members of our cultural group. According to Terror Management Theory, individuals are likely to engage in worldview-consistent behaviors as a means to defend against the fear of death when they are reminded of their mortality (see Arndt, Solomon, Kasser, & Sheldon, 2004; Solomon, Greenberg, & Pyszcznski, 2000). This has implications for consumer ethnocentrism. The proclivity of buyers to buy domestic products and shun foreign products irrespective of price or quality considerations may be due in part to ethnocentrism and patriotism. To cite support for this implication, Arndt et al. (2004) mention the boycotts of French foods following France's opposition to the war in Iraq as an example (p. 207). Additionally, Nelson et al. (1997) found an increased likelihood for US participants who were reminded of their mortality to blame a Japanese versus an American car manufacturer for an accident. Similarly, Jonas, Fritsche, and Greenberg (2005) showed increased preferences for German products when mortality was made salient to German participants. Finally, Jonas Schimel, Greenberg, and Pyszczynski (2002) showed an increase in donations to national but not foreign charities following mortality salience.

A number of products and services (e.g., life insurance, funeral services, estate planning) deal directly with death and one might expect mortality salience to be particularly likely when consumers are contemplating purchase decisions in these domains. Thus, worldview-consistent marketing campaigns might be especially successful for these products. However, because cultural worldviews differ, worldview enhancement as a reaction to mortality salience should sometimes lead to different forms of behavior across cultural groups. For example, a member of an individualistic group might engage in more autonomous/independent behaviors as a reaction to mortality salience whereas a member of a collectivistic group might engage in more interdependent behaviors under these same conditions. Thus, highlighting the opportunity to express one's individuality might be a particularly effective way to market funeral-related products/services in an individualistic culture but not a collectivistic culture. An implication of this is that marketing campaigns that have been shown to be equally effective across cultural groups for certain products might not be equally effective for products that evoke mortality concerns.

GENDER DIFFERENCES IN WORLDVIEWS

Masculinity versus femininity

Thus far, we have reviewed worldviews of groups from different geographic locations and ethnic backgrounds. Gender is the largest social group in which a person can be a member. Countries differ in in the extent to which gender roles are distinctly separated. Hofstede (1980) identified national differences in the values they attach to uphold traditional gender roles (masculinity–femininity). Masculine countries, such as Venezuela, Italy, Jamaica, and Japan, tend to value competitiveness, success, and materialism. Feminine countries like Sweden, Norway, Netherlands, and Thailand value caring, modesty, and quality of life.

Masculinity–femininity is associated with a variety of organizational outcomes, including the percentage of female managers in a company (Hofstede & Hofstede, 2005) and the level of organizational commitment among employees (Gelade, Dobson, & Auer, 2008). However, until recently few studies have examined the link between masculinity–femininity and consumer behavior. Marketing researchers have begun studying how the concept of masculinity and femininity relates to brand personality. For example, Grohmann (2009) developed a scale measuring masculine and feminine brand personalities and found that the congruence between brand personality and consumers' sex role identity increases positive brand evaluations and purchase intentions. A fruitful direction for future research is to pinpoint how countries that vary along the masculinity-femininity dimension differ in the types of brand personalities that are popular in those countries.

Gender and fundamental social goals

Considering the evolutionary approach to fundamental social goals provides another way to discern sex differences in worldviews. Fundamental social goals are a set of motivations that are linked to adaptive problems that have confronted humans throughout history (Kenrick, Maner, Burner, Li, Becker, & Schaller, 2002; Kenrick, Griskevicius, Neuberg, & Schaller, 2010). These goals can lead to a set of adaptive worldviews aimed at enhancing survival and procreation. Below, we focus on the fundamental social goals of mating, status acquisition, and self-protection. Each of these goals is characterized by specific problems and opportunities, and likely to operate according to different arrays of worldviews. When it comes to consumer behavior, different worldviews should lead to distinct yet predictable variations in preferences and choice.

We are alive today because our ancestors were successful at obtaining high-quality mates. When thinking about acquiring mates, the two sexes may endorse different worldviews. According to the theory of differential parental investment, females often invest more in offspring care and are thus choosier in selecting mates than males (Trivers, 1972). In mammals, for example, females carry developing young inside their bodies and nurse them after they are born. Females are thus more selective in their choice of mates. Males, due to the low parental investment necessary to pass on their genes, can benefit biologically by being more sexually unrestricted. Within a species, the sex investing less in offspring faces more keen competition for mating. Therefore, a mating motivation may lead to a worldview that promotes competition and impulsivity in men, but caution and vigilance in women.

The success of mating lies in one's ability to attract the opposite sex or to compete with one's own sex. Darwin's (1871) idea of sexual selection explains that one sex (usually the male) is often larger, more colorful, and more competitive than the other. This has implications for consumer behavior. Previous research shows that men who are mating-minded become less conforming, preferring to stick out by going against the grain when giving their opinions to a group (Griskevicius, Goldstein, Mortensen, Cialdini, & Kenrick, 2006). This suggests that men, but not women, would be more likely to be persuaded by products that are marketed as "unique and limited edition" rather than "tried and true" (Griskevicius, Goldstein, Mortensen, Sundie, Cialdini, & Kenrick, 2009). This worldview also leads men to purchase more conspicuous items, like expensive watches or flashy cars, in order to impress potential mates (Griskevicius, Tybur, Sundie, Cialdini, Miller, & Kenrick, 2007). Another study showed that, given a choice between a smaller cash award available immediately and a larger award available in the future, male participants were more likely to choose the smaller, immediate award after being exposed to photos of highly attractive women—an effect that is clearly relevant for marketing tactics such as "buy now, pay later" and "pay as you go" (Wilson & Daly, 2004). In line with differential parental investment and sexual selection theories, such behaviors are not found in women who are thinking about mating. Together, these findings seem to support the age old adage "sex sells"—but with some important caveats: sex does sell, but mostly unique and ostentatious products, and only for men.

Status acquisition is another fundamental goal that has the potential to influence consumer decisions. People who are motivated to achieve status are often careful about selecting products that allow them to self-present in certain ways.

The corresponding worldview to this motivation may be "all the world's a stage." A bruised ego can lead to the purchasing of high status goods, presumably to help restore one's self-esteem (Sivanathan & Pettit, 2010). Other research finds that both men and women who are motivated to gain status tend to buy environmentally friendly products that send a prosocial signal to others, broadcasting that they are both willing and able to expend resources to help the environment. The desire to self-present, in this case, has been linked to the popularity of hybrid cars such as the Prius, despite the relatively high price tag and somewhat less than ideal features (Griskevicius, Tybur, & Van den Bergh, 2010). Importantly, previous literature indicates that men and women are not equally concerned about acquiring status. Across cultures, men who are high in the status hierarchy tend to have more mating opportunities, while the same is not necessarily true for women (Betzig, 1986; Buss, 1989). This can lead to sex differences in consumer-relevant behaviors when men and women are concerned about status. For example, one study found that men (but not women) who were motivated to gain dominance became more risky with money, but only in situations where increases in the social hierarchy were possible (Ermer, Cosmides, & Tooby, 2008). This would lead to the prediction that men and women would be differentially persuaded by, say, advertisements that focus on the increased social standing that may be available through consumption of a product or service.

Finally, self-protection, which is the goal of protecting oneself and one's family members from physical danger, may lead people who are motivated by this goal to view the world as a dangerous place, and feel that it is important to be cautious of interactions with others who may pose a physical threat. They are likely to endorse such views as "it's better to be safe than sorry" rather than a more naïve or innocent view of the world.

A number of cognitive biases illustrate that people are especially alert to possible threats under certain conditions predicted by an evolutionary perspective. Ancestral humans frequently confronted dangers from members of other groups and were more defenseless in the dark. Supporting an evolutionary perspective, ambient darkness increases threat-related prejudices against stereotypically dangerous groups (Schaller, Park, & Mueller, 2003). People are also biased to perceive intention of threat more readily in members of out-groups than in-groups, and particularly good at remembering angry males from threatening out-group (Ackerman, Shapiro, Neuberg, Kenrick, Becker, Griskevicius, Maner, & Schaller, 2006).

A view of the world as a dangerous place, which arises from a self-protection motivation, appears to lead people to lay low and avoid sticking their necks out too far. For example, when people are primed with a self-protection motivation, they tend to be more conforming (Griskevicius et al., 2006) and to be more strongly persuaded by social proof (e.g., "most popular") than by scarcity (e.g., "limited edition") heuristics (Griskevicius et al., 2009). People with a worldview that the world is a dangerous place also make more pessimistic risk judgments than people who do not have this worldview, and are thus less financially risk taking (Lerner & Keltner, 2001). Together, the above research suggests that an effective way to advertise to people possessing a "dangerous world" worldview is to employ social proof rather than scarcity heuristics.

SOCIOECONOMIC STATUS AND CULTURAL WORLDVIEWS

Economic infrastructure shapes human cognition and behavior (Marx, 1844). One way to define one's control over resources is their socioeconomic status (SES). Socioeconomic status has been operationalized in various ways, such as household income, parental education, or subjective feelings of relative wealth (see Adler, Boyce, Chesney, Folkman, Kahn, & Syme, 1994). Despite differences in operationalization, each of these measures ultimately captures the extent to which individuals have control or perceived control over material resources.

Although socioeconomic status is a common variable that is included in a number of research studies, its effects are most often statistically controlled for rather than investigated in their own right. Behavioral scientists are just beginning to understand how socioeconomic status shapes a great deal of our material lives—from the foods we eat, the arts we enjoy, the schools we attend, and to the activities in which we engage (Bourdieu, 1985; Snibbe & Markus, 2005). In the following section, we will explore how control of resources, as indexed by SES, influences cultural worldviews, and, in turn, how these worldviews shape consumer behavior. It is our hope that the research outlined below provides a starting point for future research on this topic.

One of the primary ways in which SES shapes a person's cultural worldview is by influencing one's dependence on others. In nearly every aspect of everyday life, as control of resources increases, individuals are less and less dependent on others (Johnson & Krueger, 2006; Lachman & Weaver, 1998). Upper SES individuals have enough resources to live comfortably, whereas lower SES individuals have to pool resources with others to fulfill even their basic needs. Moreover, these differences in dependence on others are reinforced at the workplace. Upper SES workers often have occupations that involve a higher degree of individual autonomy, control, and choice than lower SES workers (Browne, 2005). Similarly, differences in dependence on others can be seen in interactions with family members. Upper SES individuals are less reliant on family members for emotional and financial support and tend to spend less time with their families compared to lower SES individuals (Argyle, 1994; Markus, Ryff, Curhan, & Palmersheim, 2004).

Upper and lower SES individuals have different experiences of how much an individual can depend on others and these differences foster distinct worldviews. Compared to lower SES parents, upper SES parents spend less time participating in hands-on care giving with their children and seek to instill a different set of values in their children (Argyle, 1994). While upper SES parents promote the belief that "it's your world" and emphasize developing a unique identity and interests, lower SES parents promote the belief that "it's not just about you" and emphasize the importance of taking others into consideration (Wiley, Rose, Burger, & Miller, 1998).

These different worldview perspectives on dependence are reflected in the types of moral judgments that people make, the types of products people desire, and the extent to which people prefer to be similar to or different from others. Moral judgments are innate intuitions of right and wrong and have the potential to guide subsequent decisions and behaviors (Graham, Haidt, & Nosek, 2009). Upper SES individuals, compared to lower SES individuals, prioritize individual rights as a realm of moral judgment to the exclusion of other realms (Haidt, Koller, & Dias, 1993). In contrast to the emphasis on individual rights by upper SES individuals, lower SES individuals are more likely to support and conform to community norms and reach consensus in moral dilemmas (Rusbult, Verette, Whitney, Slovik, & Lipkius, 1991; Stephens, Markus, & Townsend, 2007; Wieselquist, Rusbult, Foster, & Agnew, 1999).

This preference for conformity by lower SES individual may influence consumer behavior. A series of recent studies show exactly this (Stephens et al., 2007). In one study, participants were given the opportunity to make a series of choices between various consumer products, but before making their selections the participants saw the choices of previous participants. Compared to upper SES individuals, lower SES individuals made choices that were more similar to those of the previous participants, essentially conforming to the choices of the previous participants. In a related study, participants made product choices, but before they could rate the products they selected, a confederate chose either the same product as the participant or a different product. Compared to lower SES participants, upper SES participants were more upset that the confederate had made the same choice as them and actually liked their choice less when someone else made the same choice (Stephens et al., 2007). Taken together, these findings reveal that differences in dependence on others, created by differences in control of resources, foster distinct cultural worldviews in which upper SES individuals value independence and individuality whereas lower SES individuals value interdependence and conformity.

Furthermore, Snibbe and Markus (2005) showed that upper and lower SES individuals prefer products that match their own cultural worldview. While upper SES individuals prefer rock music, a genre that emphasizes uniqueness, controlling the environment and influencing others, lower SES individuals prefer country music, a genre that emphasizes adjusting the self to the situation and community values. As Stephens et al. (2007) demonstrated, some companies are already aware of the different worldviews held by upper and lower SES individuals and are actively adjusting their marketing strategies accordingly. For example, print advertisements in magazines that target upper SES individuals contain relatively more messages promoting the product's uniqueness, whereas advertisements in magazines that target lower SES individuals contain relatively more messages appealing to relationships and connections with others.

An interesting direction for future research is to compare how the differing values of independence and individuality versus interdependence and conformity influence consumer behavior. It may be that upper SES individuals are more persuaded by appeals that emphasize a product's uniqueness, such as "limited edition" products or "exotic" products, whereas lower SES individuals may be more persuaded by appeals that emphasize how popular or common a product is, such as "social proof" products.

Another potential area of research could examine how the opinions of significant or close others sway those of upper and lower SES individuals. Because lower SES individuals are more dependent on those around them for resources, lower SES individuals may rely more on the consumer opinions of their friends and family compared to upper SES individuals. If true, businesses may need to adopt different strategies for influencing consumers depending on their SES. For instance, "word-of-mouth" marketing campaigns may be more effective among lower SES individuals than upper SES individuals.

In addition to fostering worldviews that differently emphasize individuality and conformity, SES can influence how individuals interact with others by creating divergent worldviews concerning power and authority. Lower SES individuals have greater feelings of powerlessness and are more likely to value obedience in others and obey authority figures, compared to upper SES individuals (Mirowsky & Ross, 1986; Kusserow, 1999). One could argue that lower SES individuals would want to change their existing social conditions to create more equity in the distribution of resources. However, to the contrary, previous findings show that lower SES individuals are more likely to support their current social conditions and agree that inequality is necessary (Jost, Pelham, Sheldon, & Sullivan, 2003). These findings suggest that lower SES individuals tend to show deference to those in power and inevitably support the hierarchy of power. This sentiment is closely related to power distance, which is the extent to which people accept that power is distributed unequally (Hofstede, 1980). Given that the cultural worldviews formed by upper and lower SES individuals relating to power and authority are so distinct, future research could continue to investigate how these worldviews affect consumer behavior. For example, advertising pitches from authority figures or experts may be more persuasive to lower SES individuals compared to upper SES individuals.

As a whole, psychological studies suggest that that there may be a connection between socioeconomic status and cultural interdependence—a dimension that has received much attention in the consumer literature. Individuals of lower socioeconomic status have fewer resources at their disposal and as a result they are necessarily more interdependent with those around them (Argyle, 1994; Kraus & Keltner, 2009). Those of lower socioeconomic status seem to display many of the psychological and behavioral characteristics associated with cultural interdependence. Correlational and experimental findings suggest that both lower socioeconomic status and cultural interdependence are related to greater contextual attributions and fewer dispositional attributions (Kluegel & Smith, 1986; Kraus, Piff, & Keltner, 2009; Morris & Peng, 1994; Oyserman & Lee, 2008), more empathic accuracy (Graziano, Habashi, Sheese, & Tobin, 2007; Kraus, Côté, & Keltner, 2010; Stinson & Ickes, 1992), and greater orientation toward others (Kraus & Keltner, 2009; Markus & Kitayama, 1991).

Currently, it is not clear whether low SES fosters cultural interdependence as it is typically defined in cross-cultural research, or if there is merely a similarity between lower socioeconomic status and cultural interdependence on some dimensions. Regardless of which of these possibilities is correct, it would be fruitful for market researchers to begin examining whether consumer preferences and decision making that are influenced by cultural interdependence can also be influenced by socioeconomic status. For example, in culturally interdependent countries, advertisements tend to have more interdependent themes, including an increased number of people, more contextual attributions, and increased appeals to the collective (see Morling & Lamoreaux, 2008 for a review). Given the evidence reviewed above, these types of advertisements may also influence those of lower socioeconomic status.

LIMITATIONS AND FUTURE DIRECTIONS

In this chapter, we have discussed how cultures can influence individuals' worldviews and the implications this may have for consumer behaviors. However, it is also important to acknowledge the fact that individual-level consumer behaviors (inspired by aspects of worldview) can lead to the emergence of new or modified worldviews at a shared, cultural level. In other words, existing worldviews may influence individuals' consumer behaviors and, in turn, patterns of individual behavior may give rise to new or modified worldviews (e.g., increased acceptance of "materialism"). Thus, a more complete understanding of the relationship between cultural worldviews and consumer behavior requires recognition of the dynamic interplay between psychology (i.e., individually held worldviews and associated behaviors) and culture (see Lehman, Chiu, & Schaller, 2004). The reciprocal dynamic between these influences are interesting, but have not been studied in much detail. A fruitful direction for future research is to address the ways in which worldviews and worldview-consistent consumer behaviors influence cultural emergence and change.

Our review of the literature suggests that current research on cultural worldviews focuses on how worldviews influence social and consumer behaviors. However, cultural worldviews could themselves also be seen as consumable goods. For example, marketing approaches often link products and services to specific worldviews or aspects of worldviews, and, over time, these products and services can become emblematic representations of these aspects of culture (e.g., Marlboro cigarettes as an emblem for the rugged individualism of the American frontier). Penaloza's (2001) analysis of consumer behavior at a large annual stock show and rodeo illustrates this process by demonstrating how stock show visitors can achieve desirable associations with the idealized culture of the American West through attending the show's parade and rodeo, visiting promotional booths, viewing animal auctions, and participating in the show's various other events and activities. Although Penaloza (2001) did not specifically state the process in these terms, one could view this as selectively consuming (associating with) worldviews as a means to create and maintain a desired personal identity. A key contribution of Penaloza's research is to illustrate how these behaviors are to some extent motivated by a desire to be associated with a Western cultural worldview. Another contribution of the research is to suggest how the motivated consumption of another culture can affect how that culture is subsequently perceived and what elements of that culture become widely available for future consumption. For example, while cooperation and interdependence were important strategies in the American West, individuals may be more strongly motivated to associate with elements of the culture that emphasize independence and personal freedom. Thus, over time, the less desirable elements become somewhat hidden from public perception.

An impressive diversity of worldviews has emerged over time. There are universal beliefs as well as culture-specific worldviews. We have discussed some cultural differences in worldviews. Leung and Bond's (2004) social axioms may serve as a good starting point for understanding universal domains of cultural worldviews. Their basic idea is that there exists a central processing mechanism or cognitive framework that is universal for all peoples across all contexts. These authors proposed five pancultural beliefs (they called them social axioms): social cynicism, social complexity, reward for application, religiosity, and fate control. The authors arrived at these five axioms inductively, by compiling a list of beliefs from proverbs, newspapers, stories, and interviews based on the Hong Kong Chinese and Venezuelan cultures, asking members of these two cultures to rate their agreement with the statements, and deriving these five axioms from factor analyses on their responses. These axioms are broad, nonevaluative, and context-free beliefs which relate to a wide range of social behaviors. Data from the social axioms are now available from more than forty countries, and cultural groups show difference levels of endorsement of these beliefs. These five axioms represent the universal structure of beliefs, thus providing a unifying paradigm for analysis on worldviews and consumer behavior across cultures.

CODA

In conclusion, there is no such thing as a small undertaking in contributing to the field of cultural psychology. Nisbett et al. (2001) make it clear that it would be a mistake to assume that it would be an "easy matter to teach one culture's tools to individuals in another without total immersion in that culture" (p. 307). Fortunately, the culmination of cross-cultural studies has provided insights into how cultural worldviews may influence social and consumer behavior. We hope that the research outlined above illustrates some of the exciting areas and directions for future research on cultural worldviews.

REFERENCES

Aaker, J. L., & Lee, A. (2001). I seek pleasures and we avoid pains: The role of self regulatory goals in information processing and persuasion. *Journal of Consumer Research. 28*, 33–49.

Aaker, J., & Schmitt, B. (2001). Culture-dependent assimilation and differentiation of the self. *Journal of Cross Cultural Psychology, 32*, 561–576.

Ackerman, J. M., Shapiro, J. R., Neuberg, S. L., Kenrick, D. T., Becker, D. V., Griskevicius, V., Maner, J. K., & Schaller, M. (2006). They all look the same to me (unless they're angry): From out-group homogeneity to out-group heterogeneity. *Psychological Science, 17*, 836–840.

Adler, N. E., Boyce, T., Chesney, M. A., Cohen, S., Folkman, S., Kahn, R. L., & Syme, S. L. (1994). Socioeconomic status and health: The challenge of the gradient. *American Psychologist, 49*, 15–24.

Alter, A., & Kwan, V. S. Y. (2009). Cultural sharing in a global village: evidence for extracultural cognition in white Americans. *Journal of Personality and Social Psychology, 96*, 742–760.

Argyle, M. (1994). *The psychology of social class.* New York, NY: Routledge.

Arndt, J., Solomon, S., Kasser, T., & Sheldon, K. M. (2004). The urge to splurge: A terror management account of materialism and consumer behavior. *Journal of Consumer Psychology, 14*, 198–212.

Betzig, L. L. (1986). *Despotism and differential reproduction: A Darwinian view of history.* Hawthorne, NY: Aldine.

Bourdieu, P. (1985). The social space and the genesis of groups. *Theory and Society, 14*, 723–744.

Briley, D. A., Morris, M., & Simonson, I. (2000). Reasons as carriers of culture: Dynamic versus dispositional models of cultural influence on decision making. *Journal of Consumer Research, 27*, 157–178.

Browne, K. (2005). *An introduction to sociology* (3rd ed.). Malden, MA: Polity Press.

Buss, D. M. (1989). Sex differences in human mate preferences: Evolutionary hypotheses tested in 37 cultures. *Behavioral and Brain Sciences, 12*, 1–49.

Darwin, C. (1871). *The decent of man and selection in relation to sex.* New York: D. Appleton and Company.

Ermer, E., Cosmides, L., & Tooby, J. (2008). Relative status regulates risky decision making about resources in men: Evidence for the co-evolution of motivation and cognition. *Evolution and Human Behavior, 29*, 106–118.

Fiske, A., Kitayama, S., Markus, H., & Nisbett, R. (1998). The social matrix of social psychology. In D. T. Gilbert (Ed.), S. Fiske, (Ed); et al. *The handbook of social psychology,* Vol. 2 (4th ed.). (pp. 915–981). New York, NY, USA: McGraw-Hill.

Graham, J., Haidt, J., & Nosek, B. A. (2009). Liberals and conservatives rely on different sets of moral foundations. *Journal of Personality and Social Psychology, 96*, 1029–1046.

Gardner, W. L., Gabriel, S., & Lee, A. Y. (1999). "I" value freedom but "we" value relationships: Self-construal priming mirrors cultural differences in judgment. *Psychological Science, 10*, 321–326.

Gelade, G., Dobson, P., & Auer, K. (2008). Individualism, masculinity, and the sources of organizational commitment. *Journal of Cross-Cultural Psychology, 39*, 599–617.

Graziano, W. G., Habashi, M., Sheese, B., & Tobin, R. M. (2007). Agreeableness, empathy, and helping: A person X situation perspective. *Journal of Personality and Social Psychology, 93*, 583–599.

Griskevicius, V., Goldstein, N., Mortensen, C., Cialdini, R. B., & Kenrick, D. T. (2006). Going along versus going alone: When fundamental motives facilitate strategic (non)conformity. *Journal of Personality & Social Psychology, 91*, 281–294.

Griskevicius, V., Goldstein, N. J., Mortensen, C. R., Sundie, J. M., Cialdini, R. B., & Kenrick, D. T. (2009). Fear and loving in Las Vegas: Evolution, emotion, and persuasion. *Journal of Marketing Research, 46*, 384–395.

Griskevicius, V., Tybur, J. M., Sundie, J. M., Cialdini, R. B., Miller, G. F., & Kenrick, D. T. (2007). Blatant benevolence and conspicuous consumption: When romantic motives elicit strategic costly signals. *Journal of Personality and Social Psychology, 93*, 85–102.

Griskevicius, V., Tybur, J. M., & Van den Bergh, B. (2010). Going green to be seen: Status, reputation, and conspicuous conservation. *Journal of Personality and Social Psychology, 98*, 392–404.

Grohmann, B. (2009). Gender dimensions of brand personality. *Journal of Marketing Research, 46*, 105–119.

Han, S. P., & Shavitt, S. (1994). Persuasion and culture: Advertising appeals in individualistic and collectivistic societies. *Journal of Experimental Social Psychology, 30*, 326–350.

Haidt, J. Koller, S. H., & Dias, M. G. (1993). Affect, culture, and morality, or is it wrong to eat your dog? *Journal of Personality and Social Psychology, 65*, 613–628.

Hofstede, G. (1980). *Culture's consequences: International differences in work-related values,* Beverly Hills, CA: Sage Publications.

Hofstede, G. Hofstede, G. J., (2005). *Cultures and organizations: Software of the mind.* New York: McGraw-Hill.

Hong, Y.-Y., Morris, M. W., Chiu, C.-Y., & Benet-Martínez, V. (2000). Multicultural minds: A dynamic constructivist approach to culture and cognition. *American Psychologist, 55*, 709–720.

Ji, L.-J., Nisbett, R. E., & Su, Y. (2001). Culture, change and prediction. *Psychological Science, 12*, 450–456.

Johnson, W., & Krueger, R. F. (2006). How money buys happiness: Genetic and environmental processes linking finances and life satisfaction. *Journal of Personality and Social Psychology, 90*, 680–691.

Jonas, E., Fritsche, I., & Greenberg, J. (2005). Currencies as cultural symbols—An existential psychological perspectives on reactions of Germans to the Euro. *Journal of Economic Psychology, 26*, 129–146.

Jonas, E. Schimel, J., Greenberg, J., & Pyszczynski, T. (2002). The Scrooge Effect: Evidence that mortality salience increases prosocial attitudes and behavior. *Personality and Social Psychology Bulletin, 28*, 1342–1353.

Jost, J. T., Pelham, B. W., Sheldon, O., & Sullivan, B. N. (2003). Social inequality and the reduction of ideological dissonance on behalf of the system: Evidence of enhanced system justification among the disadvantaged. *European Journal of Social Psychology, 33*, 13–36.

Kashima, Y. (2008). A social psychology of cultural dynamics: examining how cultures are formed, maintained, and transformed," *Social and Personality Psychology Compass, 2*, 107–120.

Kenrick, D. T., Griskevicius, V., Neuberg, S. L., & Schaller, M. (2010). Renovating the pyramid of needs: Contemporary extensions built upon ancient foundations. *Perspectives on Psychological Science, 5*, 292–314.

Kenrick, D. T., Maner, J. K., Burner, J., Li, N. P., Becker, V., & Schaller, M. (2002). Dynamical evolutionary psychology: Mapping the domains of the new interactionist paradigm. *Personality & Social Psychology Review, 6*, 347–356.

Kim, H., & Markus, H. (1999). Deviance or uniqueness, harmony, or conformity? A cultural analysis. *Journal of Personality and Social Psychology, 77*, 785–800.

Kluegel, J. R., & Smith, E. R. (1986). *Beliefs about inequality: Americans' views of what is and what ought to be.* Hawthorne, NY: Aldine de Gruyter.

Kraus, M. W., Côté, S., & Keltner, D. (2010). Social class, contextualism, and empathic accuracy. *Psychological Science, 21*, 1716–1723.

Kraus, M. W., & Keltner, D. (2009). Signs of socioeconomic status: A thin-slicing approach. *Psychological Science, 20*, 99–106.

Kraus, M. W., Piff, P. K., & Keltner, D. (2009). Social class, the sense of control, and social explanation. *Journal of Personality and Social Psychology, 97*, 992–1004.

Kwan, V. S. Y., Bond, M. H., Boucher, H. C., Maslach, C., & Gan, Y. Q. (2002). The construct of individuation: More complex in collectivist than in individualist cultures? *Personality and Social Psychology Bulletin, 28*, 300–310.

Kusserow, A. S. (1999). De-homogenizing American individualism: Socializing hard and soft individualism in Manhattan and Queens. *Ethos, 27*, 210–234.

Lachman, M. E., & Weaver, S. L. (1998). The sense of control as a moderator of social class differences in health and well-being. *Journal of Personality and Social Psychology, 74*, 763–773.

Lee, A., Aaker, J. L., & Gardner, W. (2000). The pleasures and pains of distinct self-construals: The role of interdependence in regulatory focus. *Journal of Personality and Social Psychology, 78*, 1122–1134.

Lehman, D. R., Chiu, C-y., & Schaller, M. (2004). Psychology and culture. *Annual Review of Psychology, 55*, 689–714.

Lerner, J. S., & Keltner, D. (2001). Fear, anger, and risk. *Journal of Personality and Social Psychology, 81*, 146–159.

Leung, K., & Bond, M. H. (2004). Social axioms: A model for social beliefs in multicultural perspective. In M. P. Zanna (Ed.), *Advances in experimental social psychology, 36*, 119–197. San Diego, CA, USA: Elsevier Academic Press.

Logan, R. F. (1956). *The alphabet effect.* New York: Morrow.

Markus, H., & Kitayama, S. (1991). Culture and the self: Implications for cognition, emotion, and motivation. *Psychological Review, 98*, 224–253.

Markus, H. R., Ryff, C. D., Curhan, K. B., & Palmersheim, K. A. (2004). In their own words: Well-being at midlife among high school-educated and college-educated adults. In O. G. Brim, C. D. Ryff, & R. C. Kessler (Eds.), *How healthy are we? A national study of well-being at midlife* (pp. 273–319). Chicago: University of Chicago Press.

Masuda, T., & Nisbett, R. E. (2001). Attending holistically vs. analytically: Comparing the context Sensitivity of Japanese and Americans. *Journal of Personality and Social Psychology, 81*, 922–934.

Miller, J. G. (1984). Culture and the development of everyday social explanation. *Journal of Personality and Social Psychology, 46*, 961–978.

Mirowsky, J., & Ross, C. E. (1986). Social patterns of distress. *Annual Review of Sociology, 12*, 23–45.

Morling, B., & Lamoreaux, M. (2008). Measuring culture outside the head: A meta-analysis of individualism-collectivism in cultural products. *Personality and Social Psychology Review, 12*, 199–221.

Moore, O. K., & Lewis, D. J. (1952). Learning theory and culture. *Psychological Review, 59*, 380–388.

Morris, M. W., & Peng, K. (1994). Culture and cause: American and Chinese attributions for social and physical events. *Journal of Personality and Social Psychology, 67*, 949–971.

Morris, M. W., Nisbett, R. E., & Peng, K. (1995). Causal attribution across domains and cultures. In D. Sperber, D. Premack, & A. J. Premack (Eds.), *Causal cognition: A multidisciplinary debate* (pp. 577–612). Oxford, England: Clarendon Press.

Nelson, L. J., Moore, D. L., Olivetti, J., & Scott, T. (1997). General and personal mortality. *Personality and Social Psychology Bulletin, 23*(8), 884–892.

Ng, S., & Houston, M. (2006). Exemplars or beliefs? The impact of self-view on the nature and relative influence of brand associations. *Journal of Consumer Research, 32*, 519–529.

Nisbett, R. E., Peng, K., Choi, I., & Norenzayan, A. (2001). Culture and systems of thought: Holistic vs. analytic cognition. *Psychological Review, 108*, 291–310.

Oyserman, D., & Lee, S. W. S. (2008). Does culture influence what and how we think? Effects of priming individualism and collectivism. *Psychological Bulletin, 124*, 311–342.

Oyserman, D., Coon, H., & Kemmelmeier, M. (2002). Rethinking individualism and collectivism: Evaluation of theoretical assumptions and meta-analyses. *Psychological Bulletin, 128*, 3–73.

Penaloza, L. (2001). Consuming the American West: Cultural meaning and memory at a stock show and rodeo. *The Journal of Consumer Research, 28*, 369–398.

Peng, K., & Nisbett, R. E. (1999). Culture, dialectics, and reasoning about contradiction. *American Psychologist, 54*, 1–12.

Ritsema, R., & Karcher, S. (Trans.). (1994). *I ching*. Rockport, MA: Element Books.

Ross, M., Xun, W. Q., & Wilson, A. E. (2002). Language and the bicultural self. *Personality and Social Psychology Bulletin, 28*, 1040–1050.

Rusbult, C. E., Verette, J., Whitney, G. A., & Slovik, L. F., & Lipkius, I. (1991). Accommodation processes in close relationships: Theory and preliminary empirical evidence. *Journal of Personality and Social Psychology, 60*, 53–78.

Schaller, M., Park, J. H., & Mueller, A. (2003). Fear of the dark: Interactive effects of beliefs about danger and ambient darkness on ethnic stereotypes. *Personality and Social Psychology Bulletin, 29*, 637–649.

Shweder, R. A. (1990). Cultural psychology—What is it? In J. W. Stigler, R. A. Shweder, & G. Herdt (Eds.), *Cultural psychology*. Cambridge, UK: Cambridge University Press.

Sivanathan, N., & Pettit, N. C. (2010). Protecting the self through consumption: Status goods as affirmational commodities. *Journal of Experimental Social Psychology, 46*, 564–570.

Snibbe, A. C., & Markus, H. R. (2005). You can't always get what you want: Educational attainment, agency, and choice. *Journal of Personality and Social Psychology, 88*, 703–720.

Solomon, S., Greenberg, J., & Pyszczynski, T. (2000). Pride and prejudice: Fear of death and social behavior. *Current Directions in Psychological Science, 9*, 200–204.

Stephens, N. M., Markus, H. R., & Townsend, S. S. M. (2007). Choice as an act of meaning: The case of social class. *Journal of Personality and Social Psychology, 93*, 814–830.

Stinson, L., & Ickes, W. (1992). Empathic accuracy in the interactions of male friends versus male strangers. *Journal of Personality and Social Psychology, 62*, 787–797.

Toelken, B. (1996). *Cultural worldview*. Dynamics of Folklore (revised and expanded edition, pp. 263–313) Logan: Utah State University Press.

Trivers, R. L. (1972) Parental investment and sexual selection. In B. Campbell (Ed.), *Sexual selection and the descent of man, 1871-1971* (pp. 136–179). Chicago, IL, USA: Aldine.

White, L. A. (1947). Culturological vs. psychological interpretations of human behavior. *American Sociological Review, 12*, 686–698.

Wieselquist, J., Rusbult, C. E., Foster, C. A., & Agnew, C. R. (1999). Commitment, pro-relationship behavior, and trust in close relationships. *Journal of Personality and Social Psychology, 77*, 942–966.

Wilson, M., & Daly, M. (2004). Do pretty women inspire men to discount the future? *Proceedings of the Royal Society, 4*, 177–179.

Wiley, A. R., Rose, A. J., Burger, L. K., & Miller, P. (1998). Constructing autonomous selves through narrative practices: A comparative study of working-class and middle-class families. *Child Development, 69*, 833–847.

3

Cultural Differences in Procedural Knowledge and Their Impact on Consumer Behavior

ROBERT S. WYER, JR. ∎

Knowledge of cultural differences in consumer judgment and decision making is essential for understanding communication and advertising effectiveness in the global marketplace, and several recent reviews have been concerned with these differences (Shavitt, Lee, & Torelli, 2009; Wyer & Hong, 2010). A conceptual framework that integrates research and theory in cultural and consumer psychology has yet to emerge, however. The present chapter does not pretend to provide such a framework. However, it reviews an important subset of phenomena that the framework would need to address.

Many approaches to an understanding of culture have focused on differences in content, that is, the norms and values that distinguish various cultural and national groups. Hofstede (1980, 2001), for example, identified a number of dimensions along which these norms and values vary (see also Schwartz, 2009; Triandis & Gelfand, 1998), and cultural differences among several of these dimensions can influence consumers' responses to information and the judgments and behavioral decisions that they base upon it. This chapter, however, concerns the *processes* that underlie the use of information, that is, the cognitive procedures that are used to interpret information and to construe its implications for a judgment or decision. The effect of these processes cannot always be dissociated from that of the content on which the processes operate. However, research in a number of areas has identified cultural differences in thinking styles that generalize over a wide range of content domains and influence both responses to social stimuli and cognitive task performance. This chapter reviews this research and discusses its potential implications for consumer behavior.

An understanding of cultural differences in information processing requires a distinction between two types of processes. First, well-learned sequences of behavior are often elicited spontaneously by situational and cognitive stimuli with which it has been associated and are performed without awareness of any goal to which it might be relevant. Second, procedures can be applied consciously and deliberately in pursuit of a goal to which they pertain but without awareness of the reason why the procedures have been selected. Thus, when more than one procedure is relevant to attainment of a goal, differences can exist in the one that is used.

The procedures that bear on judgments and decisions are governed in part by principles of knowledge accessibility (Förster & Liberman, 2007; Higgins, 1996; Wyer, 2008). That is, concepts and knowledge become accessible either because they have been applied frequently in the past or because they have been recently used in the course of pursuing a task that requires them (Higgins, Bargh, & Lombardi, 1985; Srull & Wyer, 1979). Moreover, this knowledge has similar effects regardless of the reason for its accessibility (Bargh, Bond, Lombardi, & Tota, 1986). Consequently, the effectiveness of individual and cultural differences in the "chronic" accessibility of concepts and procedures can be verified in the laboratory by situational manipulations of the recency with which they have been activated. This possibility becomes important in drawing conclusions about cultural differences in consumer information processing.

In the remainder of this chapter, I consider the role of both automatic and deliberately chosen procedures in judgment and decision making and review cultural differences in the likelihood of employing these procedures. In doing so, I draw largely on comparisons between Asian and Western cultural representatives, as most of the research conducted to date has focused on these differences. In discussing each type of procedure, I first review the cognitive processes that underlie the activation and use of the procedure and then consider its effects on consumer behavior.

AUTOMATIC PROCEDURE ACTIVATION

To reiterate, individuals acquire well-learned responses to stimuli in a situation that are performed automatically with little, if any, cognitive mediation under conditions in which these stimuli are encountered. These responses, which can consist of a single act or a sequence of cognitive and motor behaviors, can be represented in memory as "*if* [X], *then* [Y]" *productions* (Anderson, 1982, 1983), where [X] is a configuration of both external stimulation and internally generated stimulus features and [Y] is a sequence of cognitive and motor actions that are elicited automatically when this configuration of features is experienced. Not all of the features of [X] need to be consciously articulated. Therefore, the behavior activated by a production can sometimes occur without awareness of either the behavior itself or the conditions that elicited it. Several avenues of research in both social psychology (Bargh, Chen, & Burrows, 1996; for reviews, see Bargh, 1997; Dijksterhuis & Bargh, 2001) and consumer behavior (e.g., Shen & Wyer, 2008, 2010; Shen, Wyer, & Cai, 2012) exemplify these effects. In the present context, the construct of a production is particularly useful in conceptualizing the role of language in comprehension and inference, and the use of verbal and visual information processing strategies.

Influences of language on consumer information processing

Whorf (1956) postulated that the language individuals speak leads them to acquire different concepts, and that these concepts determine their perception and interpretation of their physical and social environment. Although the validity of many of Whorf's speculations have been questioned (Chiu & Hong, 2007; Hunt & Agnoli, 1991), more general implications of his observations are undoubtedly correct. Social cognition research (Carlston, 1980; Higgins & Lurie, 1983; Sherman, Ahlm, Berman, & Lynn, 1978; Srull & Wyer, 1980, 1983) provides evidence that once information with multiple implications has been interpreted in terms of a concept that happens to be accessible in memory at the time, this interpretation is later recalled and used as a basis for judgments of its referent independently of the original information about it. Considered in the present context, these findings suggest that if individuals have applied a particular set of linguistic concepts to the stimuli they encounter, they may later retrieve and use these concepts and their implications as a basis for judgments without considering features of the stimuli that are not captured by these concepts. Thus, their judgments may be influenced by implications of the concepts that were not explicitly mentioned in the stimulus information, whereas relevant information that *was* mentioned may have little impact.

In fact, the encoding of information in terms of language-specific concepts influences its recall. Evidence of this was obtained by Hoffman, Lau, and Johnson (1986) where Chinese bilingual participants read personality descriptions in either Chinese or English. Some descriptions had a name in English but not Chinese, and others had a name in Chinese but not in English. Participants had better memory for details of the descriptions that could be related in terms of a concept that had a name in the language in which they were read which they were presented than if they could not. Thus, individuals from different cultures may not differ in their perception of the physical stimuli they encounter (Chiu & Hong, 2007). Nevertheless, the language-specific concepts they apply to these stimuli may have features associated with them that are unique. If these concepts are later recalled and used as a basis for judgment rather than the original information to which the concepts were applied, these associated features could later bias their responses.

An indication of this bias was obtained by Schmitt and his colleagues (Pan & Schmitt, 1996; Schmitt, Pan, & Tavassoli, 1994; Schmitt & Zhang, 1998). Nouns in the Chinese language, unlike English or European languages, are preceded by "classifiers" that convey more general characteristics of the class to which the referent belongs. For example, *zhang* is used to classify flat, extended objects (table, paper, etc.) and *ba* is used to classify objects that can be held in one hand (e.g., umbrella). These classifiers may sensitize Chinese to attributes of the object that Westerners do not think about (e.g., functionality). In a series of studies, Schmitt and Zhang (1998) found that Chinese were more likely than English speakers to identify classifier-related features of objects. Furthermore, they judged objects that were typically assigned the same classifier (e.g., paper and cartoons) to be more similar to one another than English speakers did.

The importance of these differences for consumer behavior arise from the fact that many objects can potentially be assigned more than one classifier and the implications of these classifiers can differ. "Lipstick," for example, could be preceded by either *zhi* (which refers to long, thin objects) or *guanr* (which refers to pipe-like, thick objects). In such cases, Schmitt and Zhang (1998) found that participants made different inferences about the attributes of a product, depending on the classifier that was applied. Thus, in the preceding example, they inferred that a lipstick was thinner and was of less quantity if *zhi* was used as the classifier than if *guanr* was used.

In construing the implications of this research, it is important to keep in mind that language may not affect individuals' perceptions of physical stimuli at the time the stimuli are presented. Moreover, consumers may not spontaneously assign labels to the products they encounter unless there is some reason to do so, and may simply retain a visual image of them in memory. (For evidence that individuals do not spontaneously assign verbal labels to information that is conveyed in pictures, see Wyer, Adaval, and Colcombe, 2002.) However, if the products described in an advertisement or commercial are referred to by name, or if consumers have a reason to label the products spontaneously at the time they view it, these labels may be retained in memory and may later be recalled and used as a basis for a purchase decision independently of the products' features. Furthermore, this tendency may increase over time (Carlston, 1980; Srull & Wyer, 1980). Consequently, to the extent the labels are in different languages and different attributes are associated with these labels, the effects of the languages on later recall and judgments may have an increasing effect as time goes on.

Linguistic determinants of visual and verbal information processing

The effects described in the preceding section could be attributable to differences in content rather than in the procedures that individuals employ. More important in the present context, however, are cultural differences in the *structure* of the language that people apply independently of its content and implications. In English and European languages, for example, there is a close relationship between the physical characteristics of a word and its phonetic character. Thus, individuals can pronounce a word by looking at it. Learning to read in these languages often involves subvocally "sounding out" the various syllables that compose the words one encounters. In Chinese, however, there is little or no relation between the visual representation of a word (i.e., its ideograph) and its sound. As a consequence, relatively greater emphasis is placed on how a word looks. In short, the languages that are typically used in Chinese and Western cultures can affect the relative tendency to focus on visual and auditory features of information and, therefore, can influence the processing of this information. For example, European Americans' processing is likely to be facilitated by presenting verbal information acoustically as well as in writing, whereas Chinese, if anything, are likely to be distracted by the acoustic stimulation.

Differences in the processing of verbal material when it is conveyed in different modalities were identified by Schmitt and et al. (1994). Chinese and Westerners were shown a series of products along with fictitious brand names that were conveyed either acoustically or in words. Chinese had better recall of the brand names when they were conveyed in writing than when they were spoken, whereas English speakers recalled the names better if they were spoken than if they were written.

Evidence that these effects are localized in the language that individuals use to process information and not in other culture-related factors is provided by research using Chinese bicultural participants. This research also indicates that biases in the use of auditory and visual processing styles generalize to complex stimuli. In a study by Tavassoli and Lee (2003), for example, bilingual Chinese participants received an advertisement that was written in either Chinese or English and that was accompanied by either distracting auditory stimulation (music) or distracting visual stimuli (irrelevant pictures). Participants who read the advertisement in English were expected to process the written components of the advertisement subvocally. Consequently, the auditory distraction was expected to interfere with this processing, whereas the distracting visual material was largely irrelevant. In contrast, participants who read the advertisement in Chinese were assumed to process written material visually. In this case, the irrelevant pictures should be distracting and the auditory stimulation should be irrelevant. Recall data confirmed this difference. That is, when the advertisement was read in English, participants had poorer recall of the advertisement content if it was accompanied by auditory distraction than if it was accompanied by visual distraction. When the advertisement was read in Chinese, the reverse was true.

Further evidence of a language-induced bias in the processing of visual and auditory information was obtained by Pan and Schmitt (1996). Chinese and American participants evaluated brand names of products that were either used by men (i.e., a power drill) or used by women (e.g., lipstick). In *auditory presentation* conditions, the products were conveyed orally by either a male or female speaker. In these conditions, American participants evaluated brand names more favorably when the sex of the speaker matched the type of product being described, whereas Chinese participants' evaluations were unaffected by the speaker's sex. In *visual presentation* conditions, the brand names and products were written in a type face that was normatively either masculine or feminine. In this case, Chinese evaluated the brand name more favorably when the script matched the product being described whereas Americans' evaluations were unaffected.

The aforementioned research converges on the conclusion that Chinese are disposed to process information visually whereas Westerners are inclined to process information verbally. Moreover, the evidence that bilingual Chinese participants' information processing depends on the language they are asked to use suggests that both general processing dispositions exist in memory and that the effect of these dispositions depends in part by situational factors that influence their relative accessibility. If this is so, insight into chronic cultural differences in the disposition to process information visually or verbally may be obtained from the effects of situational variables that induce these dispositions.

Two series of studies by Yuwei Jiang, Yael Steinhart and myself (Jiang & Wyer, 2009; Jiang, Steinhart, & Wyer, 2008; for a review, see Wyer, Hung, & Jiang, 2008) may be worth noting in this context. In some studies, we experimentally induced a disposition to process information either verbally or visually by asking participants to perform a task that required this processing (either a task that required the identification of figures that were embedded in a picture, or the identification of words that were embedded in an array of letters). In other studies, chronic differences in processing were assessed using Childers, Houston, Heckler's and (1985) Style-of-Processing scale. Results were virtually identical in each case.

In one experiment, for example (Jiang, Steinhart, & Wyer, 2008; see Wyer et al., 2008), participants received verbal information about a product that they believed to be either familiar (a standard computer mouse) or unfamiliar (a trackball mouse). Individuals with a disposition to process information visually (*visualizers*) presumably had a previously formed mental image of the familiar product that they could use in organizing the verbal attribute descriptions. When the mouse was unfamiliar and a picture of it was unavailable, this was not the case, and a visual image of the product was difficult to construct on the basis of the attributes alone. Consequently, visualizers evaluated the unfamiliar product less favorably than the familiar one. However, presenting a picture of the unfamiliar product increased visualizers' evaluation of it to a level similar to that of the familiar one. In contrast, individuals with a disposition to process information verbally (*verbalizers*) based their evaluations on the semantic implications of the product-attribute descriptions, which were the same regardless of the product's ostensible familiarity. Therefore, they evaluated the familiar and unfamiliar products similarly even in the absence of a picture.

Other studies (Steinhart et al., 2010) demonstrated the effects of processing at different stages of processing. For example, verbalizers' difficulty of processing an advertisement was an increasing function of the number of visually coded items of information presented and, therefore, the number of recodings that had to be made in order to transform these items into verbal terms. Visualizers' ease of processing, on the other hand, depended primarily on whether the items of information could be integrated into a coherent representation of the product as a whole. Thus, these participants found it more difficult to process the information in a hotel advertisement if items elicited images that could not easily be integrated (e.g., the exterior of a hotel versus the interior of a room), and evaluated the hotel less favorably in this condition. Verbalizers, on the other hand, were unaffected by the compatibility of the images elicited by the information items.

These studies did not consider cultural differences in processing. However, if Chinese are chronically disposed to process information visually, whereas Westerners are disposed to process it verbally, the studies suggest that verbal descriptions of an unfamiliar product are likely to have less effect on Chinese than on Westerners. Furthermore, advertisements that describe features of a product that cannot easily be integrated into a coherent visual image may also be less effective.

The role of procedures in nonverbal communication

Although individuals' verbal behavior is governed to a large extent by productions, this may be even more true of their nonverbal behavior. Individuals are often quite unaware of their facial expressions, body posture, and tone of voice, and are even less conscious of the situational factors that give rise to these mannerisms. Yet, others are sensitive to these behaviors and make inferences on the basis of it (DePaulo & Friedman, 1998). An understanding of these inferences can become particularly important in interactions in which the meaning that participants attach to one another's nonverbal behavior is likely to differ.

Nonverbal behaviors may be responded to configurally. Moreover, the elements that compose the configuration may vary over cultures. Evidence of this is suggested by Ambady's research on the impact of "thin slices" (e.g., 30 second segments) of behavior on person impressions (Elfenbein & Ambady, 2002; Marsh, Elfenbein & Ambady, 2007; for a review, see Ambady, Krabbenhoft & Hogan, 2006). In Marsh et al.'s (2007) study, for example, Australians and Americans watched film clips of members of either their own or the other culture walking or waving. Individuals could identify the nationality of the actors at an above-chance level. Furthermore, they made trait judgments of the actors that were consistent with cultural stereotypes. For example, walking Americans were seen as more dominant than walking Australians, and waving Australians were seen as friendlier than waving Americans.

When cultural differences exist in the nonverbal behavior that individuals express, misinterpretations can arise. For example, people can more accurately identify the emotions conveyed by the facial expressions of members of their own culture than those conveyed by members of a different culture (Elfenbein & Ambady, 2002). Other evidence that facial expressions, eye contact, physical proximity and gestures vary over cultures in the meaning they convey has been obtained by Smith, Bond, and Kagitcibasi (2006). Although these studies were not performed in a consumer context, it is easy to imagine that the effect of cross-cultural transactions in the marketplace can often be misconstrued as a result of such differences.

Cultural differences can also exist in the *intensity* of the emotions expressed in a given situation. As Wyer and Hong (2010) point out, the overt expression of emotion is more likely to be accepted in societies that encourage individuality and uniqueness. Collectivist societies that foster interdependence may discourage the public expression of feelings which might threaten interpersonal harmony and cohesiveness (Matsumoto, Yoo, Fontaine, Anguas-Wong, Ariola, & Ataca, 2008). Chinese apparently believe that a restrained emotional demeanor promotes social harmony (Bond, 1993). To this extent, facial expressions of emotion may be less common in Chinese and East Asian cultures than in Western societies.

The difference in the cultural norms about the social appropriateness of expressing feelings might lead to different rules of nonverbal communication. Smiling, for example, could convey not only happiness but also amusement, sympathy and understanding, or reassurance that everything is not as bad as it seems. Thus, a salesperson who smiles when a customer is complaining about a service failure might intend to convey reassurance and understanding, but the customer might interpret it as an indication that the salesperson considers the complaint to be amusing and is not taking it seriously. Expressions of dissatisfaction or disagreement are especially likely to be misinterpreted (Bond, Zegarac, & Spencer-Oatley, 2000).

Cultural differences in eye contact can also have an impact. As Patterson (1966) notes, there is an optimal level of eye contact at which individuals feel at ease, and either more or less contact than is optimal can lead to discomfort. Cultural differences may exist in the level that individuals consider to be optimal. Europeans, for example, habitually maintain more eye contact than Americans. Thus, suppose an American and European interact, and the European's eye contact exceeds the level at which the American considers appropriate. In such an event, the American is likely to feel uncomfortable and to interpret the European as coming on too strongly. In contrast, the European might consider the eye contact manifested by the American to be less than optimal and may interpret it as aloofness and unfriendliness. These nonverbal behaviors are likely to be governed by productions, and parties to the interaction may not consciously isolate them from other behaviors that occur. Consequently, neither party to the interaction may be aware of the source of their negative reactions, and their misperceptions could have a negative impact on the parties' perceptions of one another and their desire for future interaction. Cultural differences in physical proximity, or in the amount of touching behavior that is considered normative, can likewise give rise to misunderstanding (Smith et al., 2006).

THE ROLE OF PROCEDURES IN GOAL-DIRECTED ACTIVITY

Productions of the sort described in the previous section are often applied automatically. Other procedures are goal directed and may be applied intentionally in the course of attaining an objective to which they are relevant. When more than one such procedure is potentially applicable, however, the one that is chosen can depend on its accessibility in memory, or how quickly it comes to mind. This, in turn, is determined by the frequency and recency of its use in the past (Higgins, Bargh, & Lombardi, 1985; Srull & Wyer, 1979). Thus, cultural differences in the behavior that individuals perform in a particular situation can be the result of socialization practices that influence the chronic accessibility of not only the goals that the individuals pursue in a given situation but also the procedures they use to attain these goals. Furthermore, these procedural differences may be evident in a remarkably diverse number of situations.

In this regard, the same procedure can be involved in the pursuit of quite different goals. (For example, determining which of two animals is larger and deciding which of two products to purchase both involve making a comparison.) The generalization of procedures over situations is evidenced in part by research on the impact of behavioral mindsets (for a review, see Wyer & Xu, 2010). This research shows that inducing individuals to use a procedure in one situation can increase their likelihood of reapplying it in a later, quite different situation in pursuit of a goal that is unrelated to the purpose for which the procedure had been applied earlier (Shen & Wyer, 2010; Xu, 2010; Xu & Wyer, 2007, 2008).

These considerations suggest that the socialization processes that distinguish different cultural groups can give rise to chronic behavioral dispositions that influence behavior in not only social situations, but also situations to which social motives are quite irrelevant. This is evident in comparisons of Asian and Western cultures. It can be misleading to lump all East Asians (Koreans, Chinese, and others) and all Westerners (Americans, French, Scandinavians, and others) into two categories, as the countries within each group obviously differ in many respects (Hofstede, 1980; Schwartz, 2009; Rhee, Uleman, & Lee, 1996). Furthermore, there is substantial variation in norms and values within a given country (Triandis, 1995). Nevertheless, Asian and Western societies appear to differ along three general dimensions, each of which has implications for the processing of both social and nonsocial information.

1. Members of Western societies are likely to be individualistic and to pursue personal goals, whereas Asians are more inclined to perceive themselves as part of a group and perceive the group to which they belong as the unit of analysis in making behavioral decisions (Hofstede, 1980; Triandis, 1995).
2. Western cultural representatives tend to think of themselves as independent of others, whereas Asians tend to think of themselves in relation to others (Markus & Kitayama, 1991).
3. Westerners emphasize the positive features of an actual or anticipated situation in making judgments and decisions, whereas Asians tend to focus on negative features (Aaker & Lee, 2001).

As we point out in the next section, these characteristics may all be traceable to a common set of socialization practices. However, there are important differences in their implications. For example, a chronic focus on the group to which one belongs rather than on its individual members could give rise to a more general disposition to think of stimuli as a whole rather than to consider its individual components. A focus on oneself in relation to others could lead to a more general disposition to think of elements in a stimulus configuration in relation to one another or to the context in which they are embedded. In the next section, I consider the antecedents of these dispositions. I then discuss the implications of each for social and nonsocial behavior and decisions.

CULTURE-RELATED ANTECEDENTS OF INFORMATION PROCESSING

Compelling analyses of the social and anthropological antecedents of cultural differences in values and behavior are provided elsewhere (e.g., Diamond, 1997; Nisbett, 2003). To oversimplify, social and physical needs that are necessary for survival at the time a society is formed may give rise to behavioral norms and dispositions that are useful in fulfilling these needs. In early agrarian societies, for example, cooperation and mutual dependence were required in order to overcome natural and social obstacles (Diamond, 1997). The development of group cohesiveness and cooperation in the course of defending against external threats to survival and well-being is quite evident in war time, and was demonstrated empirically in the classic "Robbers' Cave" study conducted by Sherif (1966) and his colleagues many years ago.

Strong in-group cohesiveness gives rise to a feeling of responsibility to other group members, a need to consider others' interests as well as one's own, and a tendency to conform to the standards established for members of the group as a whole. To this extent, it can have two effects. First, it can foster a tendency to think of oneself in relation to other persons rather than as an independent individual. Second, it can induce a motivation to subordinate one's own interest to the needs of the group as a whole, and avoid behaving in ways that are likely to have negative consequences for other members or to incur their disapproval.

Although these tendencies and the motivation that underlies them may initially be necessary for group survival, they can become functionally autonomous of the goals that led to their development. As a consequence, they can become part of the traditions of the society and may continue to be reinforced by socialization practices that are common in this society. As a result, they persist independently of the objectives for which they were originally established.

Effects of early child rearing

Research by Peggy Miller (1995) and her colleagues (Miller, Fung, & Koven, 2007; Miller, Fung, & Mintz, 1996; Miller, Sandel, Liang, & Fung, 2001; Miller, Wiley, Fung, & Liang, 1997) suggests that the differences in information processing dispositions of the sort of concern in this chapter are traceable to different child-rearing practices that reinforce these dispositions. They observed both Taiwanese and American parents interact with their children in constructing a story about the child's past behavior. Quite striking cultural differences were evident in the interpretation that parents gave to this behavior, particularly when the stories concerned misdeeds.

For example, Taiwanese parents encouraged their children to make their misbehavior a central part of the story they constructed and to relate this behavior to other past transgressions. Thus, the stories that emerged from these parent–child co-narrations were likely to be self-critical and to focus on the child's responsibility for the misdeed. Furthermore, by relating the child's current misdeed to earlier ones, the stories encouraged a more general conceptualization of the child's undesirable behavior that had implications for his or her moral character. At the same time, the mothers' stories about themselves and others typically provided examples of admirable behavior that set a standard for the child to use in evaluating his or her own actions.

In contrast, the stories that emerged from American parent–child interactions focused much less frequently on a child's past transgressions, and when they did, these transgressions were treated humorously, portraying the child in a positive light despite his or her misdeeds. Thus, for example, one story concerned a child who had written on the wall and lied about it. Although the mother acknowledged the seriousness of the child's negative act, she made light of it when helping the child to communicate about the act to others. As another example:

> "Tommy and his older brother remembered being punished for some misdeed committed a few days earlier, but none of the participants—Tommy's brother or mother—could remember what they had done wrong, a baffling if not inconceivable state of affairs from a Taiwanese perspective. This practice of downplaying transgressions... seemed to be part of a wider set of practices that [European American] caregivers used to protect their children's self-esteem."
>
> (MILLER ET AL., 2001, p. 168)

Furthermore, European American mothers' stories about themselves typically conveyed their own misdeeds, telling "hell raising" stories about times in their youth in which they had behaved in irresponsible ways. Thus, their stories conveyed that they were also not perfect and that to err is human.

In summary, the different socialization practices identified by Miller and her colleagues could give rise to three different dispositions.

1. Chinese parents' encouragement of their children to use others' behavior as standards of excellence is likely to dispose their children to evaluate themselves in relation to others. In contrast, Western parents' tendency to acknowledge their own imperfections and to convey that to err is human may encourage their children to consider themselves as having value independently of others.

2. Asian parents' encouragement of their children to evaluate their behavior with reference to others may induce them to think of themselves as part of a group and to feel responsible for the group's well-being. In contrast, Western parents encourage their children to think about themselves as independent of others.

3. European American parents encourage children to tell stories about themselves that preserved their self-esteem while treating misdeeds as an inevitable and relatively unimportant part of growing up. Thus, they encourage a general "promotion focus" (Higgins, 1997), that is, a focus on positive behavioral outcomes rather than negative ones. However, Chinese parents treat the child's misdeeds as subject to others' disapproval and as something to be avoided. This latter orientation is likely to lead to a more general "prevention" focus (Higgins, 1997), that is, a disposition to avoid negative consequences of their behavior independently of the positive consequences that might result from it.

Implications for goal-directed processing

The socialization practices suggested by Miller's research appear to have endur-ing effects. Triandis and Gelfand (1998) performed separate factor analyses of the Individualism–Collectivism scale (Singelis, Triandis, Bhawuk, & Gelfand, 1995) on North Americans and Koreans. Four varimax-rotated factors emerged in each analysis that they interpreted as defining the poles of two bipolar dimen-sions (individualism–collectivism and horizontal–vertical). However, this interpretation may be somewhat misleading, as the rotational procedure they employed identifies factors that are orthogonal to one another.

In fact, Briley and Wyer (2001), in a factor analysis of responses by both Hong Kong Chinese and Americans, extracted *five* independent factors, which they interpreted as reflecting the values attached to (a) individuality (being unique and different); (b) emotional connectedness; (c) self-sacrifice; (d) not being outperformed by others; and (e) winning. The last four factors all imply a dis-position to think of oneself in relation to others, albeit in quite different ways. Furthermore, cross-cultural comparisons indicated that Americans attached significantly higher value to individuality than Chinese did, whereas Chinese attached higher value to emotional connectedness, self-sacrifice, and not being outperformed.

These data reinforce Markus and Kitayama's (1991) conception of differences in Asians' and North Americans' self-construals. Furthermore, the greater value that Asians attached to not being outperformed is consistent with evidence that these individuals are relatively more prevention focused (i.e., they attach more importance than North Americans to the avoidance of negative outcomes. That is, these individuals are not necessarily motivated to do better than others, but simply are motivated to avoid doing worse.

Finally, North Americans are apparently socialized to view positive consequences of their behavior as indicative of their self-worth but to perceive negative consequences as irrelevant to their value as individuals. Consequently, they may be likely to accept responsibility for success while attributing failure to external factors that do not reflect on themselves (Anderson, 1999; D. T. Miller, 1976). Asians, who have been socialized to perceive negative consequences of their behavior as a character deficiency, are more likely to take responsibility for failure but attribute positive outcomes to external factors (Anderson, 1999; Yamauchi, 1988). Consistent with implications of Anderson's and Miller's findings, Americans' attributions appear to be guided by a self-enhancement motive, whereas Asians' attributions are not (Heine, Lehman, Markus, & Kitayama, 1999).[1]

These cultural differences in self-construals and the factors that give rise to them do not bear directly on consumer behavior. If these construals give rise to different processing strategies, however, and if these strategies generalize over domains of experience, they should have an indirect impact on the processing of consumer information and the judgments and decision that result from this processing. The remainder of this chapter examines this possibility.

GLOBAL INFORMATION PROCESSING

To reiterate, chronic cultural differences are likely to exist in the disposition to think of oneself as a member of a collective rather than as a unique individual. Several studies (e.g., Markus, Mullally, & Kitayama, 1997; Rhee, Uleman, Lee, & Roman, 1995) provide evidence of these differences. Markus et al. (1997), for example, found that 50% of Japanese participants' spontaneous self-descriptions referred to a group to which they belonged, whereas only 24% of Americans' self-descriptions did so.

---

1. These differences in self-construals can have more general implications for individuals' perceptions of themselves and their future outlook. Oishi, Wyer and Colcombe (2000) found that European Americans were more likely to use their current life satisfaction to predict the future if they had been thinking about a positive life experience (for which they took responsibility) than if they had been thinking about a negative one. In contrast, Asian Americans were more likely to do so if they had been thinking about a negative past experience (for which these individuals took responsibility). Thus, the particular type of experience that participants happened to be thinking about not only affected their estimates of their current life satisfaction but also influenced the extent to which they considered their present life satisfaction to be a reliable predictor of the future.

This difference may be reflected in a failure to distinguish between one's personal interests and those of the group to which one belongs, and a disposition to accept the norms and values of the group as one's own. To the extent that this disposition reflects a more general processing strategy, however, it could also be manifested in a tendency to respond to stimuli as a whole rather than construing the implications of its individual components. Furthermore, it could lead to a focus on more global characteristics of a stimulus rather than specific attributes. This difference could occur regardless of the nature of the stimuli being judged.

Motivational influences of group- and individual-based processing

People's disposition to think of themselves as a member of a group rather than as an individual might be reflected in their conformity to group-defined norms and values. However, it could also reflect a tendency to think of themselves in relation to others, as discussed in a later section of this chapter. A clearer indication of this disposition is provided by Iyengar and Lepper (1999). European American fifth-graders played a "Star Wars" game in which either (a) they could personally choose the name of their spaceship or (b) the name of the ship had been chosen by their classmates. The European American children persevered longer in the games in the first condition, but Asian American children persevered longer in the second.

One area of consumer behavior in which group identification comes into play concerns the effect of a product's country of origin on judgments. This effect is more complex than it might appear, as it can be influenced by processes at several stages of cognitive functioning (attention, comprehension, etc.) (Hong & Wyer, 1989, 1990). Motivational factors can contribute to these effects as well. Klein, Ettenson, and Morris (1998), for example, identified two different factors, ethnocentrism and animosity, that underlie individuals' reactions to information that a product is manufactured in their own country as opposed to other countries. Cultural differences in the effect of ethnocentrism may be partly a function of in-group versus out-group distinctiveness. To this extent, it is likely to exert more influence on Asians' reactions to a product than on Westerners' reactions. In fact, the tendency to evaluate products from their own country more favorably than products from foreign countries is more common among Japanese than among Westerners (Gürhan-Canli & Maheswaran, 2000).

Unlike ethnocentrism, the effect of animosity may be country-specific, resulting from the past history of the countries involved. Klein et al., 1998, for example, found that residents of Nanjing, who were victims of an atrocity by the Japanese during World War II, were particularly unwilling to purchase Japanese products. This reaction is unlikely to be universal. On the other hand, the reaction could also depend on both (a) situational factors that make the reaction salient and (b) the type of product being considered. A provocative study by Hong and Kang (2006) demonstrates these contingencies. South Korean participants were first primed with concepts associated with either industriousness or hostility as part of an ostensibly unrelated task. Later, they evaluated a series of products, some of which were manufactured in either Germany or Japan and others of which were not. Priming industriousness-related concepts increased the effect of country of origin on evaluations of the products that were manufactured in these countries. However, priming hostility-related concepts was assumed to remind participants of the countries' actions in World War II and, therefore, to decrease their willingness to purchase products from these countries. In fact, however, this was only true if the products were of little importance and their purchase would not entail a financial risk. In contrast, associating automobiles and electronic products with these countries increased participants' willingness to purchase them regardless of whether hostility or industriousness was primed. Thus, quality considerations overrode morality considerations when the use of the latter criteria was likely to require a sacrifice of cost and quality.

General effects of holistic processing

As research cited in the previous section indicates, the chronic disposition to process information holistically and to focus on broad, categorical criteria for judgment may be motivated by conscious desires to be individualistic or, alternatively, to conform to the norms and expectations of one's social or cultural group. However, these dispositions, once socially learned, may generalize to the processing of information in domains to which these social motives are irrelevant.

A study by Norenzayan, Smith, Kim, and Nisbett (2002) provides an example. European Americans and East Asians were asked to make similarity judgments that could be completed by applying either a deterministic rule to the stimuli's attributes or a more general "family resemblance" criterion that did not depend on the specific attributes that the stimuli had in common. European Americans were more inclined to use the first criterion, whereas East Asians were more likely to use the second.

More direct indications of this processing difference could be constructed. In a task constructed by Navon (1977), for example, participants are shown a large letter that is formed from small letters of a different type (e.g., an "F" formed from a number of "o's"), and are asked to identify either the small letter or the large one. Differences in the time required to make these responses can be used as an index of the tendency to focus on global versus local features of the stimuli and, therefore, as an indication of the disposition to employ either a holistic or a detailed processing strategy. (For an extensive review of the use of this measure, see Förster & Dannenberg, 2010.) In fact, Kühnen and Oyserman (2002) showed that participants identified the large letter more quickly, and the small letters more slowly, if they had been induced to use "we" in a prior sentence-construction task than if they had been primed to use "I," suggesting that individuals who are disposed to think of themselves as part of a collective are indeed more likely to employ a holistic processing strategy. To this extent, Asians and North Americans should differ in a similar way. This possibility remains to be determined, however.

The possibility that Asians typically use more global criteria for judgment than Westerners do is of particular relevance in considering consumers' reactions to brand extensions. The impact of an extension's similarity to the parent brand on evaluations of the extension is well established (Aaker, 2002; Aaker & Keller, 1990). Thus, if Asians typically employ broader criteria in comprehending information than Westerners do, they may be correspondingly more inclined to perceive a brand extension as similar to its parent and, therefore, evaluate it more favorably. In fact, brand extension similarity has more impact on Asian consumers' judgments of brand extensions than on Western consumers' judgments (Ahluwalia, 2008; Monga & Roedder-John, 2007). (Of course, it could also reflect the greater tendency for Asian consumers to process information relationally, as indicated in the next section of this chapter.)

The chronic tendency for Asians to think more holistically than European Americans could have further implications. Research conducted within the framework of construal level theory (Liberman, Trope, & Stephan, 2007; Trope, Liberman, & Wakslak, 2007) shows that individuals typically form more general representations of stimuli that they perceive to be psychologically (i.e., temporally, physically, or socially) distant than of those they perceive to be proximal. In the course of evaluating this general hypothesis, numerous effects of global versus concrete information processing have been detected. These effects are reflected in the relative focus on central versus peripheral features of a product (Trope & Liberman, 2003), in the relative impact of desirability versus feasibility considerations in making purchase decisions (Liberman & Trope, 1998; see also Kim, Park, & Wyer, 2009), in the relative emphasis on supportive rather than opposing aspects of a persuasive message (Eyal, Liberman, Trope, & Walther, 2004), and in the influence of nonalignable product attributes (i.e., attributes that one product has that others do not) on decisions rather than alignable attributes (those that vary along a common set of dimensions; Malkoc, Zauberman, & Ulu, 2005) To the extent that these differences reflect more general dispositions to engage in holistic versus piecemeal processing strategies, they might be more common in East Asians than in European Americans. However, these possibilities remain to be evaluated.

RELATIONAL INFORMATION PROCESSING

Westerners are inclined to view themselves independently, whereas Asians typically think of themselves in relation to others (Markus & Kitayama, 1991). If these dispositions reflect more general information processing strategies, they have implications for a variety of consumer phenomena. Differences may exist in the desire to think of oneself in relation to other individuals and to take others' opinions into account in making decisions. However, once the processes become well learned and chronically accessible, they may be applied to information in nonsocial situations as well.

Motivational differences

To the extent that individuals think of themselves in relation to others, their judgments are likely to be guided by their perceptions of what others consider to be desirable. As noted earlier, this tendency may result in part from the disposition to think of oneself as part of a group in which certain norms and values predominate. However, the tendency could also reflect a disposition to think about others' opinions in relation to one's own and, therefore, to take them into account in arriving at judgments and decisions.

General cultural differences in the disposition to think relationally were identified in conformity research. Bond and Smith (1996), for example, found that Asians were more likely than North Americans to accept the judgments of others in the Asch (1956) conformity paradigm. In a more subtle indication of this difference, Kim and Markus (1999) found that when participants were given an opportunity to choose a pen as a reward for participating in an experiment, Asian Americans typically chose a pen of a color that was common to the majority of those available (i.e., the color that was likely to be selected by most other participants) whereas European Americans typically chose a pen of the minority color.

Studies by Maheswaran (Maheswaran & Chaiken, 1991; Aaker & Maheswaran, 1997) also exemplify cultural differences in the motivation to think of oneself in relation to others. Maheswaran and Chaiken (1991) found that when Western college students are given both attribute information about an object and information about others' opinions, they only use the latter, consensus information as a heuristic when they are unmotivated to think carefully about the product they are judging. That is, they base their judgments on specific attribute information when making an accurate evaluation is important. In contrast, Aaker and Maheswaran (1997) found in a parallel study that Hong Kong Chinese participants relied upon consensus information regardless of their motivation to make accurate judgments, and that increasing the importance of the judgments *decreased* their reliance on specific attribute information rather than increasing it.

There are other indications of Asians' disposition to be influenced by persuasive appeals that stimulate relational thinking. Han and Shavitt (1994), for example, found that Korean advertisements are more likely than Western advertisements to employ appeals that emphasize harmony, family interactions, and in-group benefits. Furthermore, Koreans found advertisements with this emphasis to be more persuasive, particularly when the products being promoted are typically used with other persons. Aaker and Williams (1998) also found that Chinese participants were more persuaded by advertisements that employ other-focused emotions (e.g., empathy), whereas American participants found ego-focused emotional appeals (e.g., pride) to be more persuasive.

There may be qualifications on this conclusion. Zhang and Shavitt (2003) found that advertisements in China often emphasize *individualism*-related values, and that this was particularly true when the advertisements appeared in magazines that were targeted at young, educated, high income individuals. This tendency is more pronounced when the advertised products are likely to be purchased for personal use rather than for use in a group context. Thus, although Chinese are typically disposed to think relationally, situational factors that increase individuality can also have an impact on younger members of the culture.

In this regard, both relational and individuating processing strategies may be used by Asian and Western cultural representatives, depending on their relative accessibility. In bicultural societies (e.g., Hong Kong), both strategies may be fairly common. In a study by Lau-Gesk (2003), bicultural Chinese read advertising appeals that endorsed either individualism alone, interpersonal relations alone, or both values in combination. Participants were equally influenced by appeals that emphasized individualism and appeals that emphasized interpersonal values when each set of values was endorsed in isolation. (When an appeal endorsed *both* sets of values, however, bicultural participants with a disposition to integrate the two orientations were positively influenced, whereas bicultural participants with a tendency to compartmentalize the two opposing cultural orientations were negatively influenced.)

Relational Processing in the Exchange of Gifts and Favors

A second manifestation of relational processing that is likely to have motivational underpinnings surrounds the exchange of gifts and favors. As Fong (2006; Watkins, Scheer, Ovnicek, & Kolts, 2006) point out, a gift can stimulate both feelings of appreciation and feelings of indebtedness. However, the effects of these reactions can differ. That is, appreciation may be a reflection of the positive affect that is elicited spontaneously by perceptions of the gift's intrinsic desirability. Indebtedness, on the other hand, is a negative affective reaction that results from the perception that one is expected to reciprocate the gift or favor one receives. Both feelings of appreciation and feelings of indebtedness can motivate individuals to reciprocate a gift. However, the effects of appreciation are mediated by liking for the gift-giver and a general desire to benefit him or her, whereas the effects of indebtedness are motivated by the desire to eliminate the negative affect that results from the obligation to respond in kind.

To this extent, Asians, who are disposed to evaluate themselves in relation to others, are more likely to be influenced by feelings of indebtedness, whereas Americans are more likely to experience appreciation without feeling an obligation to respond. Shen, Wan, and Wyer (2011) confirmed these differences in research on the role of reciprocity norms in the acceptance of gifts. In two behavioral studies using both Hong Kong Chinese and Canadians as participants, participants agreed to complete either a long or a short questionnaire. Later, they were given an opportunity to take candy that happened to be available. The number of candies that Hong Kong participants accepted from the experimenter increased with the length of time they expected to spend completing the questionnaire. This was true even though the experimenter was ostensibly unaware of both their decision to complete the questionnaire and the number of candies they took. In contrast, the amount of candy that Canadians took under comparable conditions was unrelated to the length of the questionnaire they had agreed to complete.

In two other scenario studies, participants were asked to imagine that a casual acquaintance they happened to meet at the airport offered to buy them a cup of coffee while they waited for a flight. Canadians, whose decision was based on feelings of appreciation, were inclined to accept the offer. Asians, however, were inclined to refuse, presumably in order to avoid the feelings of indebtedness that would result if they accepted. (This difference was eliminated when the person offering the gift was a close friend and the need to reciprocate immediately was less pronounced.)

THE IMPACT OF RELATIONAL THINKING ON ANTICIPATED EMOTIONAL REACTIONS

The disposition to engage in relational thinking may not only influence the extent to which individuals use others' opinions as a basis for their decisions but also as a basis for self-evaluation. For example, when people anticipate having strong emotional responses to an event, they may use others' reactions to the event as a basis for evaluating the appropriateness of their own. This tendency was established many years ago by Schachter (1959) and others (Gerard & Rabbie, 1961). To the extent that Asians are more inclined than Westerners to think about themselves in relation to others, their tendency to use others as a basis for self-evaluation may be correspondingly more pronounced.

Fong and Wyer (2003) obtained indirect support for this hypothesis. Chinese and North American participants imagined they were preparing for an important examination and had to decide whether to study a particular topic. Studying the topic would yield a high grade if it turned out to be on the examination but a low grade if it was not. Ignoring the topic and devoting time to other topics was likely to result in an average grade regardless of whether the special topic appeared on the examination. Participants reported both the positive feelings they would experience if they made a correct decision and the negative feelings that they would have if they made a wrong one. These anticipated feelings had an impact on both the Asians' and Americans' decisions. However, the negative feelings that the Asian participants anticipated having as a result of a bad decision was significantly decreased when they were told that others had also made this decision, whereas the feelings that Americans' anticipated having were unaffected by others' behavior. In other words, Asians evaluated their feelings in relation to others and expected to feel better when others experienced the same negative outcome that they experienced, whereas Americans evaluated their reactions independently of whether others' decision was the same as their own.

Relational thinking in nonsocial contexts

Once the disposition to think about oneself either independently or in relation to others has been acquired, however, it may give rise to a chronic processing style that generalizes over content domains and that influences judgments and decisions in situations that are unrelated to those in which the disposition was acquired. Evidence of this generalizeability has been identified both in psychology (Kühmen & Oyserman, 2002) and consumer judgment (Kim & Meyers-Levy, 2007; for reviews, see Oyserman & Sorensen, 2009; Wyer & Xu, 2010; Wyer, Shen, & Xu, 2014). Kühmen and Oyserman (2002), for example, stimulated individuals to think about themselves either individually or in relation to others by priming the use of "I" or "we" in a sentence-construction task. Later, individuals were asked to study an array of objects that were randomly positioned on a page and then, after doing so, to recall the objects by writing the objects' names in the positions they had been located. The number of objects recalled did not differ in the two conditions. However, participants who had been primed to think of themselves in relation to others were significantly more accurate in positioning the objects in relation to one another. Although these differences in processing strategies were situationally induced, chronic differences in the disposition to employ the strategies should have similar effects

Thus, if European Americans and Asians are socialized to think about themselves independently or interdependently, they may acquire chronic dispositions to consider information items independently or in relation to one another that affect processing in domains to which their self-construals are irrelevant. Evidence of these chronic differences has been obtained in numerous studies by Nisbett. Norenzayan and their colleagues (for reviews, see Nisbett, 2003; Norenzayan, Choi, & Peng, 2007; Nisbett, Peng, Choi, & Norenzayan, 2001). These differences are both perceptual and conceptual. In the first regard, Ji, Peng, and Nisbett (2000) showed participants a line that was surrounded by a tilted rectangular frame and asked them to position it vertically. Asians were more influenced by the frame than Americans were and thus positioned the line less accurately. Kitayama, Duffy, Kawamura, and Larson (2003) showed participants a line that was enclosed in a large frame and asked them to draw a line within a smaller frame that was either (a) the same length as the one in the large frame or (b) was the same length relative to the size of the frame. European Americans were more accurate than Asians in performing the first task but were less accurate than Asians in performing the second.

Conceptual differences have been identified at three stages of processing: comprehension, recall, and inference. In the first regard, Ji, Zhang, and Nisbett (2004) gave participants sets of three stimuli (e.g., monkey, panda, banana) and asked them to identify the two which belonged together. Whereas Americans were more likely to employ categorical criteria (grouping the monkey and panda together), Asians employed thematic relatedness (grouping the monkey with the banana).

Differences on memory were demonstrated in a particularly provocative study by Park, Nisbett, and Hedden (1999). Asian and American participants were asked to learn a series of words, each of which was presented on a separate card. In some conditions, only the word was presented on each card. In other conditions, the word was surrounded by pictures of people and objects that were irrelevant to the word's meaning. Later, participants were asked to recall the words they had read. One might expect the irrelevant context stimuli to be distracting and to decrease participants' attention to the words. In fact, however, Asians' recall of the words was actually *greater* when the contextual stimuli were presented. This was not true of the Americans.

Asians' sensitivity to contextual features is also evident at the inference stage of processing. Norenzayan and et al. (2002), for example, found that Asians were more likely than North Americans to base their estimates of the validity of syllogisms on their real world experience rather than their logical consistency. (For example, they were more likely than North Americans to judge "Cigarettes are good for the health" to be an invalid conclusion based on the premises "All things made from plants are good for the health; Cigarettes are made from plants.")

CONTEXTUAL INFLUENCES ON CONSUMER INFORMATION PROCESSING

Given the pervasiveness of cultural differences in relational thinking at different stages of information processing, it seems inevitable that these differences play a role in consumer judgment and decision making. In fact, surprisingly little research has examined this possibility. Several predictions seem obvious. Television commercials and magazine advertisements often present product information in the context of stimuli that are largely irrelevant to the attributes of the product being presented. Asian consumers may be more influenced by these contextual features than Western consumers are. Moreover, to the extent Park et al.'s (1999) findings generalize to the product domain, they suggest that these product-irrelevant features of an advertisement may actually *increase* Asians' memory for the more central product-related information (i.e., brand name and specific attributes) on which the advertisement is focused.

Cultural differences in the sensitivity to contextual features of information could also have implications for the criteria that are used as bases for judgment. Asians' disposition to think relationally could contribute to their relatively greater tendency to base their judgments of brand extensions on characteristics of the parent brand category than the attributes of the extension itself, and to be relatively more influenced by a product's country of origin. The disposition to engage in relational processing could also contribute to the effect of celebrity endorsers on advertising effectiveness. In considering the latter effects, it is necessary to distinguish between the different types of endorsers and the role they are likely to play. The use of endorsers is pervasive in both Asian and Western countries. How they are used may depend on the processing style that is dominant in these countries. For example, consumers with an individualistic processing style may be influenced to a greater extent by endorsers that are identified as individuals, whereas consumers who think of themselves in relation to others may be more influenced by endorsers who are presented in terms of their relationships. Consistent with this conjecture, Choi, Lee, and Kim (2005) found that in advertisements appearing in the United States, celebrity endorsers were typically identified by name or profession and their individual status was emphasized. In Korea, however, endorsers were less often identified by name and played roles that emphasized interpersonal relations (friendship, belongingness, etc.). In other words, the endorsers were characterized in ways that were consistent with the processing style that was dominant in the culture at hand.

The role of celebrity endorsers in Chinese and American advertisements deserves further consideration. As Kelman (1961) pointed out many years ago, the source of a communication can be influential because: (a) the source represents a group that has control over the recipient's well-being; (b) the source's opinion provides an indication of views that are socially desirable; or (c) the source is particularly knowledgeable in the domain in which the communication is relevant. The effects of different types of celebrity endorsers and when these effects occur are likely to depend on the type of product being advertised as well as the values of the recipient. However, these questions have rarely if ever been examined in consumer research in general, and their implications for the impact of advertising appeals in China and other countries in East Asia are particularly unclear.

METAPHORICAL AND ANALOGICAL REASONING

Relational processing also comes into play in comprehending metaphors. The use of metaphors in advertising is widespread. Unless a metaphor is very well established, however, consumers may not spontaneously recognize the similarity between one concrete situation and another, and thus may not appreciate the metaphor that is employed. This is true even when the similarity seems obvious. For example, suppose individuals are given a problem of destroying a tumor that requires substantial radiation without destroying the health tissue that surrounds it. The problem can be solved by irradiating the tumor with small doses from multiple directions simultaneously, converging on the tumor with sufficient intensity to destroy it. However, individuals are no more likely to identify this solution if they have read about a general who attacks a fortress by having his army converge on it from multiple directions simultaneously than if they have not (Gick & Holyoak, 1980, 1983; see also Colcombe & Wyer, 2002). Rather, several instances of the same general principle are required before the principle is identified and applied (Colcombe & Wyer, 2002).

However, to the extent that East Asians are more disposed than North Americans to think relationally, they may be relatively more inclined to identify such analogies. More generally, they may be more inclined than Westerners to understand the metaphors that are used in advertising (e.g., portraying a kangaroo with a baby in is pouch in the context of an advertisement promoting automobile safety).

PROMOTION AND PREVENTION
PROCESSING STRATEGIES

The socialization practices that dispose Asians to evaluate themselves in relation to others may lead them to be particularly concerned with avoiding behavior that will elicit disapproval and reflect negatively on themselves. Moreover, the disposition to think of themselves as members of a group may stimulate them to feel responsibility for others (Hong, Ip, Chiu, Morris, & Menon, 2001) and, therefore, induce them to avoid taking risks that might be to their detriment. These factors may combine to produce a general disposition to avoid negative behavioral consequences that generalizes over situations. Correspondingly, Westerners' socialization leads them to treat negative consequences of their behavior as relatively unimportant and thus to seek positive behavioral consequences without considering the negative consequences that might also result. These dispositions may give rise to a prevention or promotion focus (Higgins, 1997, 1998) that generalizes over situations and influences decisions in situations that are independent of the social motives that initially led to their creation.

Cultural differences in promotion and prevention focus and their implications for a behavior in many areas are reviewed by Rao (this volume). Several studies provide evidence that focusing individuals' attention on their membership in a group increases their concern with negative behavioral consequences. Aaker and Lee (2001), for example, asked participants to imagine themselves as a protagonist in an advertisement for tennis racquets. In the scenario, they were playing either singles or doubles. Furthermore, the advertisement focused on either the desirability of winning or the negative consequences of losing. Individuals who imagined themselves playing singles recalled more features of the advertisement, and evaluated the tennis racquet more favorably, if the advertisement emphasized winning. However, participants who imagined themselves playing doubles recalled more features and made more favorable product evaluations when the advertisement focused on the undesirability of losing.

Briley and Wyer (2002) provided further demonstrations of this difference. In one series of studies, participants initially performed a task as either individuals or as part of a group. In a different series of studies, both Hong Kong Chinese and North American participants were made aware of their cultural group membership by exposing them to cultural icons representative of either their own country or another. Both manipulations were expected to activate concepts associated with their membership in a collective and thus to induce a prevention orientation. Multiple dependent measures over the two series of studies confirmed these expectations. Individuals whose group identity was primed, for example, were more likely to choose equality in a resource allocation task, thereby minimizing the negative reactions that might result if one person obtained more than the other. More relevant to the concerns of this chapter, participants in some conditions performed a product choice task that involved sets of three options (A, B, and C) that varied along two dimensions in a manner similar to the following:

	Option A	Option B	Option C
Dimension 1	+3	−3	+1
Dimension 2	−3	+3	−1

Thus, individuals who focus on the positive consequences of their decision are likely to choose either A or B, whereas those who are motivated to minimize the negative consequences of their decision are likely to choose C. In fact, participants in Briley and Wyer's studies were more likely to choose the latter option if their cultural group identity was made salient to them than if it was not. This was true regardless of whether the participants were Chinese (and were primed with Chinese icons) or Americans (and were primed with American icons).

When individuals' cultural identity is not called to their attention, Asian and Westerners' choice behavior in the aforementioned situation may be influenced by their chronic disposition to focus on positive or negative decision outcomes. This disposition may only be evident when situational conditions call attention to culture-related norms and values. A series of studies by Briley, Morris, and Simonson (2000, 2005) provide evidence of this contingency. Briley et al. (2000), for example, found that cultural differences in the disposition to avoid negative outcomes occurred only when participants were asked to give a reason for their choice, thus leading them to retrieve and use culture-related concepts as a basis for judgment.

In later studies, Briley et al. (2005) used Hong Kong bicultural students as subjects and activated cultural norms and values by administering the experiment in different languages. Participants were more inclined to choose the option that minimized the negative consequences of their decision when the experiment was conducted in Chinese than when it was conducted in English. Subsequent studies, however, suggested that this difference did not reflect the automatic activation of prevention or promotion dispositions, but rather, resulted largely from their motivation to respond in a way that was consistent with implicit social expectations. To distinguish between these possibilities, Briley et al. (2005) asked participants to perform the decision task while trying to remember an 8-digit number. If the language in which participants were communicating spontaneously activated culture-related decision criteria, putting them under processing load should increase their likelihood of using these criteria rather than other, less accessible criteria. Consequently, it should increase the effects of language differences. If, however, the language influenced the criteria that participants *deliberately* apply in order to comply with implicit social expectations, processing load should decrease their ability to engage in this cognitive deliberation and should decrease the influence of language. In fact, the latter was the case. A third study confirmed the conclusions drawn from this experiment, showing that participants' decisions were influenced by the nationality of the individuals who were ostensibly conducting the study independently of the language in which the study was conducted.

Briley et al.'s (2005) findings have implications for the comprehension of advertisements that are presented in a bicultural context. In Hong Kong, for example, television commercials and billboards can convey information in Chinese, in English, or in both. Consumers' attitudes toward the advertised products are influenced by their perceptions of the desirability of owning or using the product in a particular social context. In such conditions, the language in which the advertisement is conveyed could activate normative standards of social desirability that influence recipients' acceptance of the ad's implications. This suggests that an advertisement's effectiveness can depend on whether the context in which the advertised product is considered desirable is consistent with the context implied by the language in which the product is promoted.

There are several other indications that these dispositions can be situationally induced. Chen, Ng, and Rao (2005), for example, found that exposing Singaporean bicultural participants to visual images associated with Asian culture activated a prevention orientation, increasing their willingness to pay for the expedited delivery of a product when a promotion appeal emphasized the avoidance of negative consequences (i.e., a delay). In contrast, exposing them to Western cultural images increased their willingness to pay for the service when positive consequences (i.e., early enjoyment of the product) was emphasized. Similarly, Aaker and Lee (2001) found that leading individuals to think of themselves as interdependent increased the influence of appeals that emphasized safety and security rather than positive features of the choice alternatives.

Other implications of Briley et al.'s (2005) findings should be noted. The evidence that cultural differences in prevention orientation are not evident when participants are unable to think carefully about their decision is particularly noteworthy in the context of Lee and Semin's (2009) observation that these differences are also eliminated when participants deliberate *extensively* about the decisions they make (Briley & Aaker, 2006). Perhaps when Chinese individuals are asked to make a decision in which they have little interest, they may do so with little thought and thus without considering culture-related norms, beliefs, and values. When they think extensively about their decision, on the other hand, they may access decision-relevant knowledge in addition to culture-related criteria, and so the latter criteria have little effect in these conditions as well. Thus, cultural norms may have their greatest impact on participants whose motivation to make a decision falls between these extremes.

A second qualification on the conclusion that Chinese avoid negative outcomes is suggested by research on risk taking. Hsee and Weber (1999) found that although Chinese participants were less likely than North Americans to make "safe" choices in a risk-taking situation in which financial concerns were not involved, they were relatively more likely than Westerners to take financial risks. Although this contingency seems surprising on first consideration, it may indicate that whereas Chinese persons perceive themselves as responsible for others in social situations (and consequently desire to avoid negative decision outcomes), they also perceive themselves as able to depend *on* others (e.g., family) in financial situations and therefore feel relatively comfortable about taking a risk. (See Mandel, 2003, for evidence of similar effects of priming self-construals.)

The disproportionate emphasis that Chinese appear to place on negative consequences of their decisions is likely to be reflected in their impulsiveness. As Zhang and Shrum (2009) found, individuals with interdependent self-construals, who presumably are prevention focused, are more likely to suppress impulsive consumption than others are. To this extent, Chinese individuals should be less inclined toward impulsive buying and consumption than representatives of other cultures. Indeed, a multi-country survey of consumers in Australia, United States, Hong Kong, Singapore, and Malaysia (Kacen & Lee, 2002) confirms this speculation.

CONCLUDING REMARKS

This chapter provides a general framework for conceptualizing differences in the procedures that members of different cultures bring to bear on the processing of consumer information. In doing so, it distinguishes between procedures that are applied automatically and often without awareness and those that are employed in the course of conscious goal-directed activity. In each case, the procedures, although socially learned, become autonomous of the conditions that gave rise to their acquisition and are used in unrelated situations without consciousness of the reason for their selection.

In considering cultural differences in goal-directed information processing, I distinguished between: (a) the disposition to process information holistically rather than construing individual pieces of information separately; (b) the disposition to consider entities in relation to one another rather than separately; and (c) the disposition to attach differential weight to positive versus negative features of choice alternatives. These different processing dispositions may all be manifestations of socialization practices that are employed at an early stage of development. Once acquired, however, they become functionally autonomous, consequently influencing behavior and decisions in both social and nonsocial situations. The effects of these different dispositions, like their antecedents, are not as clearly separable as one might like. Several differences between Asians and Westerners could be a reflection of more than one procedural disposition. A clear understanding of these effects will ultimately require a more precise articulation of both (a) the processes that underlie responses to information of the sort that consumers encounter in the situations of concern to them and (b) the strategies that cultural representatives are likely to apply. If the enormous progress that has been made over the past ten years of research is any indication, however, the attainment of this goal may be just around the corner.

REFERENCES

Aaker, D. A. (2002). *Building strong brands*. London, UK: Simon & Schuster.

Aaker, D. A., & Keller, K. L. (1990). Consumer evaluations of brand extensions. *Journal of Marketing, 54*, 27–41.

Aaker, J. L., & Lee, A. Y. (2001). "I" seek pleasures and "we" avoid pains: The role of self-regulatory goals in information processing and persuasion. *Journal of Consumer Research, 28*, 33–49.

Aaker, J. L., & Maheswaran, D. (1997). The effect of cultural orientation on persuasion. *Journal of Consumer Research, 24*, 315–328.

Aaker, J. L., & Williams, P. (1998). Empathy vs. pride: The influence of emotional appeals across cultures. *Journal of Consumer Research, 25*, 241–261.

Ahluwalia, R. (2008). How far can a brand stretch? Understanding the role of self-construal. *Journal of Marketing Research, 45*, 337–350.

Ambady, N., Krabbenhoft, M.A., & Hogan, D. (2006). The 30-sec sale: Using thin-slice judgments to evaluate sales effectiveness. *Journal of Consumer Psychology, 16*, 4–13.

Anderson, C. A. (1999). Attributional style, depression and loneliness: A cross-cultural comparison of American and Chinese students. *Personality and Social Psychology Bulletin, 25*, 482–499.

Anderson, J. R. (1982). Acquisition of cognitive skill. *Psychological Review, 89*, 369–406.

Anderson, J. R. (1983). *The architecture of cognition*. Cambridge, MA: Harvard University Press.

Asch, S. E. (1956). Studies of independence and conformity: I. A minority of one against a unanimous majority. *Psychological Monographs, 70*, 1–70.

Bargh, J. A. (1997). The automaticity of everyday life. In R. S. Wyer (Ed.), *Advances in social cognition* (Vol. 10, pp. 1–62). Mahwah, NJ: Erlbaum.

Bargh, J. A., Bond, R. N., Lombardi, W. J., & Tota, M. E. (1986), The additive nature of chronic and temporary sources of construct accessibility, *Journal of Personality and Social Psychology, 50*, 869–878.

Bargh, J. A., Chen, M., & Burrows, L. (1996). Automaticity of social behavior: Direct effects of trait construct and stereotype activation on action. *Journal of Personality and Social Psychology, 71*, 230–244.

Bond, M. H. (1993). Emotions and their expression in Chinese culture. *Journal of Nonverbal Behavior, 17*, 245–262.

Bond, M. H., Zegarac, V., & Spencer-Oatley (2000). Culture as an explanatory variable: Problems and possibilities. In H. Spencer-Oatley (Ed.), *Culturally speaking: Managing relations in talk across cultures* (pp. 47–71). London: Cassell.

Bond, R., & Smith, P. B. (1996). Culture and conformity: A meta-analysis of studies using Asch's (1952b, 1956) line judgment task. *Psychological Bulletin, 119*, 111–137.

Briley, D. A., & Aaker, J. L. (2006). When does culture matter? Effects of personal knowledge on the correction of culture-based judgments. *Journal of Marketing Research, 43*, 395–408.

Briley, D. A., Morris, M. W., & Simonson, I. (2000). Reasons as carriers of culture: Dynamic versus dispositional models of cultural influence on decision making. *Journal of Consumer Research, 27*, 157–178.

Briley, D. A., Morris, M. W., & Simonson, I. (2005). Cultural chameleons: Biculturals, conformity motives and decision making. *Journal of Consumer Psychology, 15,* 351–362.

Briley, D. A., & Wyer, R. S. (2001). Transitory determinants of values and decisions: The utility (or nonutility) of individualism and collectivism in understanding cultural differences. *Social Cognition, 19,* 198–229.

Briley, D. A., & Wyer, R. S. (2002). The effect of group membership salience on the avoidance of negative outcomes: Implications for social and consumer decisions. *Journal of Consumer Research, 29,* 400–416.

Carlston, D. E. (1980). Events, inferences and impression formation. In R. Hastie, T. Ostrom, E. Ebbesen, R. Wyer, D. Hamilton, & D. Carlston (Eds.), *Person memory: The cognitive basis of social perception* (pp. 89–119). Hillsdale, NJ: Erlbaum.

Chen, H., Ng., S., & Rao, A. R. (2005). Cultural differences in consumer impatience. *Journal of Marketing Research, 42,* 291–301.

Childers, T. L., Houston, M. J., & Heckler, S. E. (1985). Measurement of individual differences in visual versus verbal information processing. *Journal of Consumer Research, 12,* 125–134.

Chiu, C-y., & Hong, Y-y. (2007). *Social psychology of culture.* New York: Psychology Press.

Choi, S. M., Lee, W.-n., & Kim, H.-J. (2005). Lessons from the rich and famous: A cross-cultural comparison of celebrity endorsement in advertising. *Journal of Advertising, 34,* 85–98.

Colcombe, S. J., & Wyer, R. S. (2002). The role of prototypes in the mental representation of temporally-related events. *Cognitive Psychology, 44,* 67–103.

DePaulo, B. M., & Friedman, H. S. (1998). Nonverbal communication. In D. T. Gilbert, S. T. Fiske, & G. Lindzey (Eds.), *Handbook of social psychology* (4th ed., Vo. 2, pp. 3–40). New York: McGraw-Hill.

Diamond, J. (1997). *Guns, germs, and steel.* New York: W. W. Norton

Dijksterhuis, A., & Bargh, J. A. (2001). The perception-behavior expressway: Automatic effects of social perception on social behavior. In M. P. Zanna (Ed.), *Advances in Experimental Social Psychology* (Vol. 33, pp.1–40). San Diego: Academic Press.

Elfenbein, H. A., & Ambady, N. (2002). Is there an in-group advantage in emotion recognition? *Psychological Bulletin, 128,* 243–249.

Eyal, T., Liberman, N., Trope, Y., & Walther, E. (2004). The pros and cons of temporally near and distant action. *Journal of Personality and Social Psychology, 86,* 781–795.

Förster, J., & Liberman, N. (2007). Knowledge activation. In A. Kruglanski & E. T. Higgins (Eds.), *Social psychology: Handbook of basic principles* (2nd ed., pp. 201–231). New York: Guilford.

Fong, C. P. S. (2006). *The impact of favor-elicited feelings on reciprocity behavior across time.* Unpublished doctoral dissertation, Hong Kong University of Science and Technology.

Fong, C. P. S., & Wyer, R. S. (2003). Cultural, social and emotional determinants of decisions under uncertainty. *Organizational Behavior and Human Decision Processes, 90,* 304–322.

Förster, J., & Dannenberg, L. (2010). GLOMO: A systems account of global versus local processing. *Psychological Inquiry, 21,* 175–197.

Förster, J., & Liberman, N. (2007). Knowledge activation. In A. Kruglanski & E. T. Higgins (Eds.), *Social psychology: Handbook of basic principles* (2nd ed., pp. 201–231). New York: Guilford.

Gerard, H. B., & Rabbie, J. H. (1961). Fear and social comparison. *Journal of Abnormal and Social Psychology, 62,* 586–592.

Gick, M. L., & Holyoak, K. J. (1980). Analogical problem solving. *Cognitive Psychology, 12,* 306–355.

Gick, M. L., & Holyoak, K. J. (1983). Chema induction and analogical transfer. *Cognitive Psychology, 14,* 1–38.

Gürhan-Canli, Z., & Maheswaran, D. (2000). Cultural variations in country of origin effects. *Journal of Marketing Research, 37,* 309–317.

Han, S.-P., & Shavitt, S. (1994). Persuasion and culture: advertising appeals in individualistic and collectivistic societies. *Journal of Experimental Social Psychology, 30,* 326–350.

Heine, S. J., Lehman, D. E., Markus, H., & Kitayama, S. (1999). Is there a universal need for positive regard? *Psychological Review, 106,* 766–794.

Higgins, E. T. (1996). Knowledge activation: Accessibility, applicability, and salience. In E. T. Higgins & A. Kruglanski (Eds.), *Social psychology: Handbook of basic principles* (pp. 133–168). New York: Guilford.

Higgins, E. T. (1997). Beyond pleasure and pain. *American Psychologist, 55,* 1217–1233.

Higgins, E. T. (1998). Promotion and prevention: Regulatory focus as a motivational principle. In M.P. Zanna (Ed.), *Advances in experimental social psychology* (Vol. 30, pp. 1–46). San Diego, CA: Academic Press.

Higgins, E. T., Bargh, J. A., & Lombardi, W. (1985). The nature of priming effects on categorization. *Journal of Experimental Psychology: Learning, Memory, and Cognition, 11,* 59–69.

Higgins, E. T & Lurie, L. (1983). Context, categorization and recall: The "change-of-standard" effect. *Cognitive Psychology, 15,* 525–547.

Hoffman, C., Lau, I., & Johnson, D. R. (1986). The linguistic relativity of person cognition: An English-Chinese comparison. *Journal of Personality and Social Psychology, 51,* 1097–1105.

Hofstede, G. H. (1980). *Culture's consequences: International differences I work-related values.* Beverley Hills, CA: Sage.

Hofstede, G. H. (2001). *Culture's consequences: Comparing values, behaviors, institutions and organizations across nations.* Thousand Oaks, CA: Sage.

Hong, S.-t., & Kang, D. K. (2006). Country-of-origin influences on product evaluations: The impact of animosity and perceptions of industriousness and brutality on judgments of typical and atypical products. *Journal of Consumer Psychology, 16,* 232–240.

Hong, S.-t., & Wyer, R. S. (1989). Effects of country-of-origin and product-attribute information on product evaluation: An information processing perspective. *Journal of Consumer Research, 16,* 175–187.

Hong, S.-t, & Wyer, R. S. (1990). Country of origin, attributes, and product evaluations: The effects of time delay between information and judgments. *Journal of Consumer Research, 17,* 277–288.

Hong, Y.-y., Ip, G., Chiu, C.-y., Morris, M. W., & Menon, T. (2001). Cultural identity and dynamic construction of the self: Collective duties and individual rights in Chinese and American cultures. *Social Cognition, 19,* 251–269.

Hsee, C. K., & Weber, E. U. (1999). Cross-national differences in risk preference and lay predictions. *Journal of Behavioral Decision Making, 12*, 165–179.

Hunt, E., & Agnoli, F. (1991). The Whorfian hypothesis: A cognitive psychology perspective. *Psychological Review, 98*, 377–389.

Iyengar, S. S., & Lepper, M. R. (1999). Rethinking the value of choice: A cultural perspective on intrinsic motivation. *Journal of Personality and Social Psychology, 76*, 349–366.

Ji, L., Peng, K., & Nisbett, R. E. (2000). Culture, control, and perception of relationships in the environment. *Journal of Personality and Social Psychology, 78*, 943–955.

Ji, L., Zhang, Z., & Nisbett, R. E. (2004). Is it culture or is it language? Examination of language effects in cross-cultural research on categorization. *Journal of Personality and Social Psychology, 87*, 57–65.

Jiang, Y., Steinhart, Y., & Wyer, R. S. (2008). *The role of visual and semantic processing strategies in consumer information processing.* Unpublished manuscript, Hong Kong University of Science and Technology.

Jiang, Y., & Wyer, R. S. (2009). The role of visual perspective in information processing. *Journal of Experimental Psychology, 45*, 486–495.

Kacen, J. J, & Lee, J. A. (2002). The influence of culture on consumer impulsive buying behavior. *Journal of Consumer Psychology, 12*, 163–176.

Kelman, H. C. (1961). Processes of opinion change. *Public Opinion Quarterly, 25*, 57–78.

Kim, H. S., & Markus, H. R. (1999). Deviance or uniqueness, harmony or conformity? A cultural analysis. *Journal of Personality and Social Psychology, 77*, 785–800.

Kim, K., & Meyers-Levy, J. (2007). Context effects in diverse-category brand environments: The influence of target product positioning and consumers' processing mindset. *Journal of Consumer Research, 34*, 882–896.

Kim, Y.-j., Park, J. W., & Wyer, R. S. (2009). The effects of temporal distance and memory on consumer judgments. *Journal of Consumer Research, 36*, 634–645.

Kitayama, S., Duffy, S., Kawamura, T., & Larson, J. T. (2003). Perceiving an object and its context in different cultures: A cultural look at newlook. *Psychological Science, 14*, 201–206.

Klein, J. G., Ettenson, R., & Morris, M. D. (1998). The animosity model of foreign product purchase: An empirical test in the People's Republic of China. *Journal of Marketing, 62*, 89–100.

Kühnen, U., & Oyserman, D. (2002). Thinking about the self influences thinking in general: Cognitive consequences of salient self-concept. *Journal of Experimental Social Psychology, 38*, 492–499.

Lau-Gesk, L. G. (2003). Activating culture through persuasion appeals: An examination of the bicultural consumer. *Journal of Consumer Psychology, 13*, 301–315.

Lee, A. Y., & Semin, G. R. (2009). Culture through the lens of self-regulatory orientations. In R. S. Wyer, C.-y. Chiu, & Y.-y. Hong (Eds.), *Understanding culture: Theory, research and application* (pp. 299–310). New York: Psychology Press.

Liberman, N., & Trope, Y. (1998). The role of feasibility and desirability considerations in near and distant future decisions: A test of temporal construal theory. *Journal of Personality and Social Psychology, 75*, 5–18.

Liberman, N., Trope, Y., & Stephan, E. (2007). Psychological distance, In A. W. Kruglanski & E. T. Higgins (eds.)., *Social psychology: Handbook of basic principles* (2nd ed., pp. 353–383) New York: Guilford Press.

Maheswaran, D., & Chaiken, S. (1991). Promoting systematic processing in low-motivation settings: Effect of incongruent information on processing and judgment. *Journal of Personality and Social Psychology, 61*, 13–25.

Malkoc, S. A., Zauberman, G., & Ulu, C. (2005). Consuming now or later: The interactive effect of timing and attribute align ability. *Psychological Science, 16*, 411–417.

Mandel, N. (2003). Shifting selves and decision making: The effects of self-construal priming on consumers' risk taking. *Journal of Consumer Research, 30*, 30–40.

Markus, H. R., & Kitayama, S. (1991). Culture and the self: Implications for cognition, emotion and motivation. *Psychological Review, 98*, 224–253.

Markus, H. R., Mullally, P. R., & Kitayama, S. (1997). Selfways: Diversity in modes of cultural participation. In U. Neisser & D. A. Jopling (Eds.), *The conceptual self in context: Culture, experience, self-understanding* (pp. 13–61). New York: Cambridge University Press.

Marsh, A. A., Elfenbein, H. A., & Ambady, N. (2007). Separated by a common language: Nonverbal accents and cultural stereotypes about Americans and Australians. *Journal of Cross-Cultural Psychology, 38*, 284–300.

Matsumoto, D., Yoo, S. H., Fontaine, J., Anguas-Wong, A. M., Ariola, M., Ataca, B., et al. (2008). Mapping expressive differences around the world: The relationship between emotion display rules and individualism versus collectivism. *Journal of Cross-Cultural Psychology, 39*, 55–74.

Miller, D. T. (1976). Ego involvement and attribution for success and failure. *Journal of Personality and Social Psychology, 34*, 213–225.

Miller, P. J. (1995). Personal storytelling in everyday life: Social and cultural perspectives. In R. S. Wyer (Ed.), *Advances in social cognition: Knowledge and memory* (Vol. 8, pp. 177–184). Mahwah, NJ: Lawrence Erlbaum Associates.

Miller, P. J., Fung, H., & Koven, M. (2007). Narrative reverberations: How participation in narrative practices co-creates persons and cultures. In S. Kitayama & D. Cohen (Eds.), *Handbook of cultural psychology* (pp. 595–614). New York: Guilford Press.

Miller, P. J., Fung, H., & Mintz, J. (1996). Self-construction through narrative practices: A Chinese and American comparison of early socialization. *Ethos, 24*, 237–280.

Miller, P. J, Sandel, T. L, Liang, C-h., & Fung, H. (2001). Narrating transgressions in Longwood: The discourses, meanings, and paradoxes of an American socializing practice. *Ethos, 29*, 159–186.

Miller, P. J., Wiley, A. R., Fung, H., & Liang, C. H. (1997). Personal storytelling as a medium of socialization in Chinese and American families. *Child Development, 68*, 557–568.

Monga, A. B., & Roedder-John, D. (2007). Cultural differences in brand extension evaluation: The influence of analytic versus holistic thinking. *Journal of Consumer Research, 33*, 529–536.

Navon, D. (1977). Forest before trees: The precedence of global features in visual perception. *Cognitive Psychology, 9*, 353–383.

Nisbett, R. E. (2003). *The geography of thought: How Asians and westerners think differently.* New York: Free Press.

Nisbett, R. E., Peng, K., Choi, I., & Norenzayan, A. (2001). Culture and systems of thought: Holistic vs. analytic cognition. *Psychological Review, 108*, 291–310.

Norenzayan, A., Choi, I., & Peng, K. (2007). Perception and cognition. In S. Kitayama & D. Cohen (Eds.), *Handbook of cultural psychology* (pp. 569–594). New York: Guilford Press.

Norenzayan, A., Smith, E. E., Kim, B. J., & Nisbett, R. E. (2002). Cultural preferences for formal versus intuitive reasoning. *Cognitive Science, 26*, 653–684.

Oishi, S., Wyer, R. S., & Colcombe, S. (2000). Cultural variation in the use of current life satisfaction to predict the future. *Journal of Personality and Social Psychology, 78*, 434–445.

Oyserman, D., & Sorensen, N. (2009). Understanding cultural syndrome effects on what and how we think: A situated cognition model. In R. S. Wyer, C.-y. Chiu, & Y.-y. Hong (Eds.), *Understanding culture: Theory, research and application* (pp. 25–52). New York: Psychology Press.

Pan, Y., & Schmitt, B. (1996). Language and brand attitudes: The impact of script and sound matching in Chinese and English. *Journal of Consumer Psychology, 5*, 263–278.

Park, D. C., Nisbett, R. E., & Hedden, T. (1999). Culture, cognition, and aging. *Journal of Gerontology, 54B*, 75–84.

Patterson, M. L. (1966). An arousal model of interpersonal intimacy. *Psychological Review, 83*, 235–245.

Rhee, E., Uleman, J., & Lee, H. K. (1996). Variations in collectivism and individualism by in-group and culture: confirmatory factor analysis. *Journal of Personality and Social Psychology, 71*, 1037–1054.

Rhee, E., Uleman, J. S., Lee, H. K., & Roman, R. J. (1995). Spontaneous self-descriptions and ethnic identities in individualistic and collectivistic cultures. *Journal of Personality and Social Psychology, 69*, 142–152.

Schachter, S. (1959). *The psychology of affiliation*. Stanford, CA: Stanford University Press.

Schmitt, B. H., Pan, Y., & Tavassoli, N. T. (1994). Language and consumer memory: The impact of linguistic differences between Chinese and English. *Journal of Consumer Research, 21*, 419–431,

Schmitt, B. H., & Zhang, S. (1998). Language structure and categorization: A study of classifiers in consumer cognition, judgment and choice. *Journal of Consumer Research, 25*, 108–122.

Schwartz, S. H. (2009). Culture matters: National value cultures, sources and consequences. In R. S. Wyer, C.-y. Chiu, & Y.-y. Hong (Eds.), *Understanding culture: Theory, research and application* (pp. 127–150). New York: Psychology Press.

Shavitt, S., Lee, A. Y., & Torelli, C. J. (2009). Cross-cultural issues in consumer behavior. In M. Wänke (Ed.), *Social psychology of consumer behavior* (pp.227–250). New York: Psychology Press.

Shen, H., Wan, F., & Wyer, R. S. (2011). Cross cultural differences in the refusal to accept a small gift: The differential influence of reciprocity norms on Asians and North Americans. *Journal of Personality and Social Psychology, 100*, 271–281.

Shen, H., & Wyer, R. S. (2008). Procedural priming and consumer judgments: Effects on the impact of positively and negatively valenced information. *Journal of Consumer Research, 34*, 727–737.

Shen, H., & Wyer, R. S. (2010). The effect of past behavior on variety seeking: Automatic and deliberative influences. *Journal of Consumer Psychology, 20*, 33–42.

Shen, H., Wyer, R. S., & Cai, F. (2012). The generalization of deliberative and automatic behavior: The role of procedural knowledge and affective reactions. *Journal of Experimental Social Psychology, 48*, 819–828.

Sherif, M. (1966). *Group conflict and cooperation: Their social psychology.* London: Routledge, Kaen Paul.

Sherman, S. J., Ahlm, K., Berman, L., & Lynn, S. (1978). Contrast effects and the relationship to subsequent behavior. *Journal of Experimental Social Psychology, 14*, 340–350.

Singelis, T. M., Triandis, H. C., Bhawuk, D., & Gelfand, M. J. (1995). Horizontal and vertical dimensions of individualism and collectivism: A theoretical and measurement refinement. *Cross-Cultural Research: The Journal of Comparative Social Science, 29*, 240–275.

Smith, P. B., Bond, M. H., & Kagitcibasi, C. (2006). *Understanding social psychology across cultures.* London: Sage.

Srull, T. K., & Wyer, R. S. (1979). The role of category accessibility in the interpretation of information about persons: Some determinants and implications. *Journal of Personality and Social Psychology, 37*, 1660–1672.

Srull, T. K., & Wyer, R. S. (1980). Category accessibility and social perception: Some implications for the study of person memory and interpersonal judgments. *Journal of Personality and Social Psychology, 38*, 841–856.

Srull, T. K., & Wyer, R. S. (1983). The role of control processes and structural constraints in models of memory and social judgment. *Journal of Experimental Social Psychology, 19*, 497–521.

Jiang, Y., Steinhart, Y., & Wyer, R. S. (2010). Imagery and consumer information processing: The role of visual and verbal processing strategies in comprehension and information integration. Unpublished manuscript, Hong Kong University of Science and Technology.

Tavassoli, N. T., & Lee, Y. H. (2003). The differential interaction of auditory and visual advertising elements with Chinese and English. *Journal of Marketing Research, 40*, 468–480.

Triandis, H. C. (1995). *Individualism and collectivism.* Boulder, CO: Westview.

Triandis, H. C., & Gelfand, M. J. (1998). Converging measurement of horizontal and vertical individualism and collectivism. *Journal of Personality and Social Psychology, 74*, 118–128.

Whorf, B. L. (1956). *Language, thought and reality: Selected writings of Benjamin Lee Whorf.* New York: Wiley.

Trope, Y., & Liberman, N. (2003). Temporal construal," *Psychological Review, 110*, 403–421.

Trope, Y., Liberman, N., & Wakslak, C. (2007). Construal levels and psychological distance: Effects on representation, prediction, evaluation, and behavior, *Journal of Consumer Psychology, 17*, 83–95.

Watkins, P., Scheer, J., Ovnicek, M., & Kolts, R. (2006). The debt of gratitude: Dissociating gratitude and indebtedness. *Cognition & Emotion, 20*, 217–241.

Wyer, R. S. (2008). The role of knowledge accessibility in cognition and behavior: Implications for consumer information processing. In C. P. Haugtvedg, P. M. Herr, & F. R. Kardes (Eds.), *Handbook of consumer psychology* (pp.31–76). Mahwah, NJ: Erlbaum.

Wyer, R. S., Adaval, R., & Colcombe, S. J. (2002). Narrative-based representations of social knowledge: Their construction and use in comprehension, memory and judgment. In M. P. Zanna (Ed.), *Advances in experimental social psychology* (Vol. 34, pp.131–197). San Diego, CA: Academic Press.

Wyer, R. S., & Hong, J. (2010). Chinese consumer behavior: The effects of content, process and language. In M. H. Bond (Ed.), *The Oxford handbook of Chinese psychology* (2nd ed.). New York: Oxford University Press.

Wyer, R. S., Hung, I. W., & Jiang, Y. (2008). Visual and verbal processing strategies in comprehension and judgment. *Journal of Consumer Psychology, 18,* 244–257.

Wyer, R. S., Shen, H., & Xu, A. J. (2014). The role of procedural knowledge in the generalization of social behavior. In D. Carlston (ed.), *Handbook of social cognition* (3rd ed.); Oxford University Press.

Wyer, R. S., & Xu, A. J. (2010). The role of behavioral mind-sets in goal-directed activity: Conceptual underpinnings and empirical evidence. *Journal of Consumer Psychology, 20,* 107–125.

Xu, A. J. (2010) On behavioral mind-sets: The influence of procedure accessibility on consumer decision making, effectiveness of persuasion and acquisition dispositions. Unpublished Ph.D. dissertation, University of Illinois at Urbana-Champaign.

Xu, A. J., & Wyer, R. S. (2007). The effect of mindsets on consumer decision strategies. *Journal of Consumer Research, 34,* 556–566.

Xu, A. J., & Wyer, R. S. (2008). The comparative mindset: From animal comparisons to increased purchase intentions. *Psychological Science, 19,* 859–864.

Yamauchi, H. (1988). Effects of actor's and observer's roles on causal attributions by Japanese subjects for success and failure in competitive situations. *Psychological Reports, 63,* 619–626.

Zhang, J., & Shavitt, S. (2003). Cultural values in advertisements to the Chinese X-generation. *Journal of Advertising, 32,* 23–33.

Zhang, Y., & Shrum, L. J. (2009). The influence of self-construal on impulsive consumption. *Journal of Consumer Research, 35,* 838–850.

4

Consumer Behavior, Culture, and Emotion

JEANNE L. TSAI, LOUISE CHIM, AND TAMARA SIMS ■

INTRODUCTION

Imagine that you are seeking a tutoring service to help you prepare for your college entrance examinations, and you come across an advertisement for the Sylvan Learning Center that shows a family standing next to each other and facing the camera. The family members all have broad, toothy smiles. Above the family is the caption, "Less stress, more success!" Are you drawn to this advertisement? Is it convincing? Would you use these services?

We presented this scenario to a group of college students from Stanford University, USA, and another group of college students from the Chinese University of Hong Kong, China. The differences in their responses to the advertisement were striking. Whereas the Stanford students were drawn to the advertisement, found it convincing, and seriously considered using the Sylvan Learning Center, the Hong Kong Chinese students strongly disliked the advertisement and had a difficult time taking it seriously. Whereas the Stanford students appreciated the simplicity of the advertisement, were drawn to its smiling faces ("Everyone looks happy!"), and endorsed the goal of "less stress, more success," the Hong Kong Chinese students found the advertisement to be uninformative ("What is their success rate?" "Why isn't there a picture of a teacher and student?" "What kind of services do they actually offer?"), and found the idea of "less stress, more success" during college entrance examination preparation to be silly and unrealistic ("How could studying for college entrance exams be 'less stressful'?").

Examples like these suggest that culture plays a significant role in shaping how we respond to advertisements, which products we develop attachments to, and which appeals we find persuasive. But why do these differences exist? In this chapter, we argue that because many of these consumer behaviors are affective (i.e., involve emotions and other feeling states), they reflect cultural beliefs, values, and ideals regarding affect and emotion. In the above example, Stanford students may have liked the slogan "less stress and more success" because it is consistent with the American ideal of feeling good and not feeling bad. In contrast, Chinese University of Hong Kong students may have disliked the slogan because it goes against the Chinese ideal of emotional moderation, or maintaining a balance between feeling good and feeling bad.

Many studies have demonstrated that culture shapes consumer behavior (e.g., evaluation of products, product preference) and that affect shapes consumer behavior. Surprisingly few studies have considered how culture and affect *jointly* shape consumer behavior. For instance, research consistently shows that when consumers feel good, they evaluate products more favorably. The conditions under which consumers feel good, however, largely depend on their cultural contexts. Therefore, in this chapter, we will review existing research on affect and consumer behavior, present our work on ideal affect (how people ideally want to feel) and consumer behavior, and finally, discuss how understanding a culture's ideal affect can help us understand the relations among culture, affect, and consumer behavior. First, we define our key terms.

DEFINITIONS

Affect: actual and ideal

By "affect," we refer to neurophysiological states that are experienced as emotions, moods, and other feelings, and that can be categorized along the dimensions of arousal and valence. The valence dimension corresponds to the feeling of environmental gain (positive valence; e.g., "happy"', "satisfied") or losses (negative valence; e.g., "sad", "unhappy"), and the arousal dimension corresponds to the feeling that one's environment requires energy and mobilization (high arousal, e.g., "aroused") or allows rest and recuperation (low arousal; e.g., "inactive") (Barrett & Russell, 1999; Russell, 2003). Studies of self-reported mood, emotional facial expressions, and emotion lexicons suggest that different feeling states can be categorized in terms of at least these two dimensions (Kuppens, Ceulemans, Timmerman, Diener, & Kim-Prieto, 2006; Russell, Lewicka, & Niit, 1989; Yik & Russell, 2003). For instance, excitement, enthusiasm, and elation are high-arousal positive (HAP) states, whereas calm, peacefulness, and serenity are low-arousal positive (LAP) states (see Figure 4.1).

Most research on affect and consumer behavior has focused on how people actually feel, or what we refer to as their "actual affect." However, in this chapter we argue that *how people ideally want to feel*, what we refer to as their "ideal affect," may matter as much as (and sometimes even more than) their actual affect in shaping consumer behavior. How are actual affect and ideal affect different? Whereas actual affect is a response to an event or an outcome (e.g., *actually* feeling anxious on a Ferris wheel), ideal affect is a goal or a desired state (e.g., *wanting* to feel calm on a Ferris wheel). Although both ideal affect and

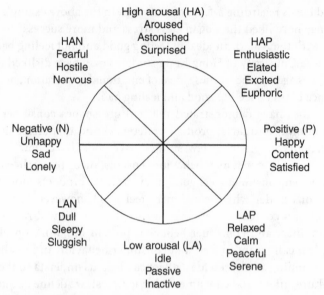

Figure 4.1 Two-Dimensional Map of Affective States.
Adapted from Barrett & Russell (1999); Larsen & Diener (1992); Watson & Tellegen (1985).

actual affect are critically important to emotional life, they serve different functions: whereas actual affect represents how someone is feeling ("I feel good"), ideal affect serves as a yardstick against which one can interpret that state ("Is this feeling good?" "Does this feel right?"). Because ideal affect is primarily culturally shaped, one source of cultural differences in consumer behavior may be cultural differences in ideal affect. While actual affect shapes consumer behavior, these relationships may depend at least in part on ideal affect. We discuss our work on ideal affect in greater detail following our review of the literature on actual affect and consumer behavior.

Consumer behavior

We use the term "consumer behavior" to refer to the "behavior of the consumer or decision making in the marketplace of products and services" (American Marketing Association, 2012). We focus particularly on how consumers respond to and evaluate different products, providers, and services, and the options they prefer.

ACTUAL AFFECT AND CONSUMER BEHAVIOR: A REVIEW OF EXISTING FINDINGS

In this section, we review existing findings regarding the role of affect on consumer behavior. This review is not intended to be comprehensive, but instead to reflect the most consistent patterns in the empirical literature to date. As mentioned above, most of this research has focused on how consumers' actual affect shapes their behavior.

The role of actual affect versus reason in consumer decision making

Historically, dominant models of decision making, derived primarily from economic theory, assumed that individuals behave rationally (i.e., select options that provide the greatest benefit and lowest cost). Because reason and affect are often pitted against each other, these models largely ignored the role of affect in decision making. As demonstrated by the recent global economic crisis, however, individuals often behave in ways that cannot be predicted by these models alone. Prospect theory argues that these "anomalies" occur when individuals cannot make rational decisions, and instead must rely on heuristics that are often sensitive to affective processes (Tversky & Kahneman, 1983). Thus, affect was initially used to explain irrational decisions, or those not accounted for by the rational actor model. Indeed, in the consumer decision-making literature, most research assumes a "dual processing" approach, in which cognitive processes are described as high level, deliberate, utilitarian, rational, systematic, and often conscious, whereas affective processes are described as low level, automatic, gut-like, hedonic, and usually unconscious (Damasio, 2005; Edell & Burke, 1987; Epstein, 1994; Forgas, 1995; Holbrook & Hirschman, 1982; Kahneman & Frederick, 2002; Pham, 2004; Schwarz & Clore, 1996; Sloman, 1996; Slovic, Finucane, Peters, & MacGregor, 2007).

For instance, in Shiv and Fedorikhin (1999) American undergraduates were randomly assigned to either a high or low cognitive load condition. In the high cognitive load condition, participants were required to remember a seven-digit number that they had to report to a researcher down the hall. In the low cognitive load condition, participants only had to remember and report a two-digit number. Participants were then told to choose an item from a food cart in the hall and to tell the researcher which item they wanted after they reported their number. The food cart contained a piece of chocolate cake (presumably the more affectively pleasant but less rational option) and a fruit salad (presumably the less affectively pleasant but more rational option). Participants in the high cognitive load condition were more likely to choose the chocolate cake than those in the low cognitive load condition. Consistent with prospect theory, the authors concluded that when individuals' cognitive abilities are impaired, affective processes lead people to make more impulsive and less rational choices (i.e., to select the chocolate cake).

Work by Zajonc and colleagues (Zajonc, 1980; Zajonc & Markus, 1982) was among the first to suggest that affect, independent of cognition, functions as an influential guide in consumer preferences and decision making.

Based on this work, significant research has since treated affect as a valid source of information that can even facilitate optimal choices and decisions (Damasio, 2005; Loewenstein & Lerner, 2003; Loewenstein, Weber, Hsee, & Welch, 2001; Pham, 2004; Schwarz & Clore, 1983, 1996; Slovic, Finucane, Peters, & MacGregor, 2002; Slovic et al., 2007). Indeed, recent studies have observed that compared to normal control subjects, brain-damaged patients with impaired emotional functioning (e.g., difficulties processing emotional stimuli, difficulties anticipating how they would feel in the future) made lower quality decisions and were slower at learning to select favorable (versus unfavorable) options (for reviews, see Bechara, 2004; Damasio, 2005). Thus, rather than prevent optimal decision making, increasing research suggests that affective processes can promote optimal decision making. For example, American and Canadian older adults, who have more emotion-focused goals than younger adults, made better decisions (e.g., engaged in more healthy eating behaviors) when they focused on the affective (versus informational) properties of health care information (Löckenhoff & Carstensen, 2007; Mikels, Löckenhoff, Maglio, Carstensen, Goldstein, & Garber 2010; Zhang, Fung, & Ching, 2009). As a result, researchers have begun to examine more directly *how* affect shapes consumer behavior, in particular people's evaluation of and preferences for specific consumer products, services, and service providers.

Actual affect: anticipated, online, and recalled

Prior to consumption (i.e., trying a product or service or engaging with a service provider), consumers may have expectations about how they will feel during consumption ("anticipated" actual affect). During consumption, they may experience feelings ("online" actual affect) that may or may not be related to the product, service, or service provider. Sometime afterwards, consumers may remember how they felt during consumption ("recalled" actual affect). For example, as illustrated in Figure 4.2, prior to riding a Ferris wheel, an individual might think about how she will feel on the Ferris wheel (anticipated actual affect). While she is riding the Ferris wheel, she may feel relaxed ("integral" online actual affect; i.e., affect that is related to the product or service), even though an insect flying around her ear may annoy her ("incidental" online actual affect; i.e., affect that is unrelated to the product or service). After the ride is over, she may think about how she felt on the Ferris wheel (recalled actual affect).

The bulk of existing research suggests that these three types of actual affect—anticipated, online, and recalled—have similar implications for consumer evaluation and preference. We first describe this research, and then review our work on culture and ideal affect, which—as shown in Figure 4.2—we believe influences the links between the types of actual affect and consumer behavior described below.

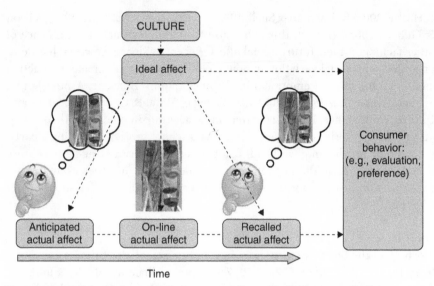

Figure 4.2 Model of proposed links between culture, ideal affect, actual affect (anticipated, on-line, and recalled), and consumer behavior.

ANTICIPATED ACTUAL AFFECT

It is well documented that people base their decisions on how they expect they will feel after making a choice or decision (Bagozzi, Baumgartner, Pieters, & Zeelenberg, 2000; Bell, 1985; Chaudhuri, 2002; Loewenstein & Lerner, 2003; Mellers Schwartz, & Ritov, 1999; Richard, van der Pligt, & de Vries, 1996). For instance, using bipolar scales (i.e., good–bad, nice–awful, pleasant–unpleasant), Dutch college students rated how they felt toward various behaviors (e.g., taking drugs, drinking alcohol, studying hard), how much they intended to engage in each behavior, and how they expected to feel after engaging in each behavior (i.e., anticipated affect) (Richard et al., 1996). Students' anticipated actual affect predicted their intentions to engage in each behavior more than did their feelings toward each behavior. Similarly, several studies find that anticipated actual negative affect, such as regret, loss, and disappointment, is a motivator of choice (e.g., Bar-Hillel & Neter, 1996; Bell, 1985; Connolly, Ordóñez, & Coughlan, 1997; Loomes & Sugden, 1982; Simonson, 1992; Zeelenberg, 1999; Zeelenberg, van Dijk, Manstead, & vanr de Pligt, 2000). For example, employees at Rutgers University in the United States were more likely to get the influenza vaccine the more they anticipated regretting not getting the vaccine and worrying about getting influenza. Furthermore, among people who did not get vaccinated, those who anticipated more regret and worry were more likely to get vaccinated one year later (Chapman & Coups, 2006).

Ironically, although people base their decisions on their anticipated actual affect, a significant body of research suggests that people are generally bad at forecasting or predicting how they will feel after a particular outcome (e.g., Hsee

& Hastie, 2006; Kahneman & Snell, 1992; Loewenstein & Schkade, 1999; Wilson & Gilbert, 2003). In part, this is because they underestimate the influence of other factors on their future actual affect. Recent evidence, however, has demonstrated substantial variation in how accurately people anticipate their actual affect as a function of emotional intelligence (Dunn, Brackett, Ashton-James, Schneiderman, & Salovey, 2007), age (Scheibe, Mata, & Carstensen, 2011), and culture. For instance, East Asians were more accurate in predicting their actual affect during positive events (e.g., finishing a school project, attending a party, going home for the long weekend) compared to European Canadians because they tended to view the positive event in the context of other events rather than focus on just the positive event itself (Lam, Buehler, McFarland, Ross, & Cheung, 2005).

ONLINE ACTUAL AFFECT

The bulk of the literature focuses on how online actual affect shapes consumer behavior (e.g., Andrade & Cohen, 2007; Finucane, Alhakami, Slovic, & Johnson, 2000; see Gardner, 1985; Schwarz, 2000 for reviews), both incidental and integral (Peters, 2006). For instance, in a study of incidental online actual affect, American college students were assigned to either a positive or a neutral mood condition (by showing them humorous or non-humorous commercials, respectively) (Lee & Sternthal, 1999). Afterwards, participants were shown twenty-five brand names not shown in the commercials and given a surprise recall test ten minutes later. Participants in the positive mood condition recalled more brand names than did those in the neutral mood condition. Effects of incidental mood have also been found for favorability toward a brand. For example, the more positively American consumers felt, the more favorably they rated BMW advertisements, particularly when the advertisement was difficult to process (Bakamitsos & Siomkos, 2004).

Similar effects are observed when a particular product makes people feel positively (integral online actual affect). A meta-analysis of fifty-five studies (Brown, Homer, & Inman, 1998) revealed a strong association between actual positive affect elicited by an advertisement and positive evaluation of the advertisement, and between actual negative affect elicited by an advertisement and negative evaluation of the advertisement.

Some studies suggest that affective responses are especially relevant when evaluating service providers (i.e., people) compared to products (Abelson, Kinder, Peters, & Fiske, 1982; Alford & Sherrell, 1996; Jayanti, 1995). An observational study of a US metropolitan hospital (Locke, 1996) demonstrated that American patients' positive feelings toward their pediatricians predicted subsequent satisfaction, cooperation, and perceived quality of care.

Other studies have attempted to examine whether anticipated and online actual affect interact to influence consumer behavior. Here the results seem to vary as a function of whether the online affect is integral or incidental. For example, on the one hand, American undergraduates were more likely to try a product (i.e., chocolate or coconut water) when they were in a positive (versus negative) mood (unrelated to the product) (Andrade, 2005). However, when people expected that a product would make them feel good, those in a negative mood were as likely to try the product as those in a positive mood. When people were led to expect that they would feel bad if they tried a product (i.e., they would have to fill out a long survey), those in a positive mood were as likely *not* to try a product as those in a negative mood. These findings suggest that when determining whether or not to try a product, anticipated actual affect matters more than incidental online actual affect.

On the other hand, consumer satisfaction can also depend on the *discrepancy* between how people anticipated a product would make them feel and what they actually experienced while consuming the product, above and beyond the individual effects of anticipated and online actual affect (Phillips & Baumgartner, 2002). American college students rated how they thought they would feel when drinking orange juice. Right after drinking the orange juice, they rated how they felt (online actual affect), how much this differed from how they thought they would feel (discrepancy), and how satisfied they were with the juice. The smaller the discrepancy between how negative participants expected the orange juice to be and how negative it actually was, the more satisfied they were with the orange juice. The discrepancy in negative affect predicted satisfaction above and beyond the individual effects of how they actually felt and how they expected to feel when drinking the juice. Thus, whereas anticipated actual affect seems to matter more than incidental online actual affect, anticipated actual affect seems to interact with integral online actual affect to influence consumer behavior.

RECALLED ACTUAL AFFECT

How people remember feeling about a particular product, provider, or service also has a significant impact on consumer decision making. For example, American car buyers were more satisfied with their purchases if they recalled feeling pleasant more often since buying the car (Westbrook & Oliver, 1991). In a seminal study, male students from an American university experienced 60-seconds of steady pain (by immersing their hand in 14 °C water), and then the same 60-seconds of steady pain (by immersing their other hand in 14 °C water) followed by 30-seconds of lesser pain (keeping their hand in the water as the temperature was increased to 15 °C). Participants recalled feeling more positively in the latter condition, and therefore, were more likely to prefer it, even though it was 30 seconds longer than the former condition (Kahneman, Fredrickson, Schreiber, & Redelmeier, 1993). In a related study, colonoscopy patients' recalled pain was most strongly predicted by the most painful and most recent parts of the procedure (Redelmeier & Kahneman, 1996). In a follow-up study, patients were randomly assigned to a "shorter" colonoscopy or an "extended" one, which was longer but did not involve any additional pain or discomfort than the shorter procedure. Those who had the extended procedure were more likely to return for a colonoscopy a few years later than were those who had the shorter procedure (Redelmeier, Katz, & Kahneman, 2003). These findings suggest that recalled actual affect can influence preferences, at times even more than online actual affect.

Other studies also show that recalled actual affect has a greater impact on consumer preferences than online actual affect (Abelson et al., 1982; Dubé & Menon, 2000; Morewedge, Gilbert, & Wilson, 2005). For instance, American college students reported how they felt while they were on vacation, and then four weeks later, how they recalled feeling while they were on vacation. Participants were then asked to indicate what they would like to do for their next vacation. Participants recalled feeling more extremely (positive and negative) than they actually felt, and they based their vacation preferences on their recalled more than their online actual affect (Wirtz, Kruger, Scollon, & Diener, 2003). However, it is possible that online actual affect may have more strongly predicted vacation preferences if those preferences were assessed during or immediately after the vacation. Future work comparing the relative effects of online and recalled affect on immediate and longer-term preferences may provide a better understanding of these processes.

How do anticipated and online actual affect shape recalled actual affect? A study of vacation and film preferences (Klaaren, Hodges, & Wilson, 1994) attempted to answer this question. American undergraduates were asked to rate how positively they expected to feel on their upcoming vacation. When they returned, in an "unrelated" study, they were asked to rate their specific experiences on vacation (e.g., whether they got to do everything they wanted, whether their travel went smoothly) and to recall how positive their experience was. Participants' anticipated actual affect predicted their recalled actual affect almost twice as much as their online actual affect.

In a follow-up study (Klaaren et al., 1994), American undergraduates were either told that they were going to "watch a really neat movie that everyone likes a lot," or were not given any affective information about the film. Half of the participants were assigned to either a comfortable or uncomfortable (i.e., poor lighting, hard chair) viewing environment. A few weeks later, participants reported how much they were willing to participate in the same study again. Participants who expected to watch the positive film were more willing to participate again and recalled a more enjoyable experience than did those who were not given any affective information about the film, regardless of whether they had a comfortable or uncomfortable experience. Thus, how people expect to feel strongly influences what they recall feeling.

In summary, the studies reviewed above demonstrate that anticipated, online, and recalled actual affect shape consumer experience and behavior. In general, the more positively people expect to feel, feel in the moment, and recall feeling, the more positive their consumer experience and preference for that option. Moreover, a series of studies have examined the interaction among these different types of affect, and suggest that anticipated and recalled affect may be more important than online affect.

One main limitation of this work, however, is its focus on Western samples. As a result, it is unclear what role culture plays in this process. We refer to Kroeber and Kluckhohn's definition of "culture" as historically derived and socially transmitted ideas that are instantiated through cultural rituals (e.g., birthday celebrations, weddings), practices (e.g., greetings), products and artifacts (e.g., magazines, advertisements), and institutions (e.g., companies and corporations). Kroeber and Kluckhohn (1952) described culture as what humans create as well as the "conditioning elements" (i.e., creators) of future human action. Does anticipated, online, and recalled actual positive affect shape consumer behavior in other cultural contexts? Does culture shape how consumers respond to specific products, providers, and services, and what preferences they have?

Previous work demonstrates that cultural contexts shape the relationship between preferences and consumer choices. For instance, in Indian cultural contexts, individuals were less likely to make choices based on their own preferences compared to those in American cultural contexts (Savani, Markus, & Conner, 2008). The authors suggest that this reflects different models of agency: in American contexts, people's choices should reflect their own personal preferences, whereas in Indian contexts, people's choices must also consider the preferences and needs of others. Although cultural ideas and practices likely influence consumer behavior in a multitude of ways, here we focus on only one.

Specifically, we argue that in order to examine how affect shapes preferences and consumer behavior, researchers have to consider not only people's actual affect, but also their *culturally shaped ideal affect*. As illustrated in Figure 4.2, cultural factors shape ideal affect, and ideal affect may shape consumer behavior directly, or may shape consumer behavior through anticipated, online, and recalled actual affect. In the next section, we discuss what ideal affect is and how it varies across cultures.

The importance of ideal affect: Affect Valuation Theory

Whereas the bulk of research in psychology has focused on actual affect, significantly less research has examined people's *ideal affect*. In part, this may be because most researchers of emotion and consumer behavior are from Western cultural contexts, and therefore, assume that everyone wants to feel a similar way. In reality, however, although most people want to feel good, people differ in the specific good feelings they ideally want to feel, and this varies both within and between cultures. Affect Valuation Theory (AVT) is a theoretical framework that attempts to incorporate ideal affect into existing models of actual affect by: (a) distinguishing between actual and ideal affect; (b) identifying how culture and temperament shape actual and ideal affect; and (c) describing the behavioral consequences of ideal affect (Tsai, 2007). We describe these three premises of AVT next.

Ideal affect differs from actual affect

The first premise of AVT is that ideal affect differs from actual affect. When we first started this work, there were no existing measures of "ideal affect," and therefore, we developed a measure of ideal affect based on existing measures of actual affect (Barrett, 1996; Larsen & Diener, 1992; Watson & Tellegen, 1985). Thus, in addition to asking people how much they actually feel various states (see Figure 4.1 for specific states) either "on average," "over the course of a typical week," or "right now," using a 5-point rating scale (ranging from 1 = not at all to 5 = all the time), we asked them to rate how much they would *ideally like to feel* those same states, using the same scale. We have administered this measure (the Affect Valuation Index [AVI]) to a variety of college student and community samples and found that as predicted, people report wanting to feel significantly different from how they actually feel. Perhaps not surprisingly, people from a variety of cultures report wanting to feel more positively and less negatively than they actually feel. Moreover, actual affect and ideal affect are weakly to moderately correlated with each other (approximately 0.30 on average) (Tsai, Knutson, & Fung, 2006). Using structural equation modeling, we have found that across diverse cultural contexts, models that treat ideal and actual affect as separate factors fit the data better than those that treat them as a single factor. These findings hold whether we compare global or momentary ratings of actual and ideal affect (using experience sampling methods) (Koopmann-Holm & Tsai, 2014; Tsai et al., 2006).

More recently, we have collected data suggesting that ideal and actual affect are associated with distinct neural correlates (Chim, Sims, Samanez Larkin, Tsai, & Knutson, unpublished data). In this study, American participants saw cues indicating that they would either gain or lose money if they pressed a button within an allotted period of time (Monetary Incentive Delay Task; Knutson, Adams, Fong, & Hommer, 2001). During anticipation of monetary gain, participants' actual high-arousal positive affect was correlated with activity in the nucleus accumbens (a brain region associated with reward); however, participants' ideal high-arousal positive affect was correlated with activity in the ventral medial prefrontal cortex (a brain region typically associated with valuation). Together, these studies suggest that ideal affect differs from actual affect.

Culture shapes ideal affect more than actual affect; temperament shapes actual affect more than ideal affect

The second premise of AVT is that actual affect and ideal affect also differ in the degree to which they are shaped by cultural and temperamental factors. Shweder (2003) and Rozin (2003) argue that cultural factors shape what people view as good, moral, and virtuous. Similarly, AVT predicts that cultural factors should shape what affective states people view as good, moral, and virtuous (i.e., their ideal affect). Much of this socialization may occur through interaction with parents, peers, and teachers, through exposure to popular media, and through engagement in various rituals and practices.

Indeed, in a series of studies (Tsai, 2007; Tsai et al., 2006; Tsai, Louie, Chen, & Uchida, 2007; Tsai, Miao, Seppala, Fung, & Yeung, 2007), we have demonstrated that American culture values excitement, elation, and other HAP states more than Chinese culture does. Chinese culture, in contrast, values calm, peacefulness, and other LAP states more than American culture does (Figure 4.3). Other research teams have replicated these results; for example, European Canadians valued HAP more and LAP less than did Hong Kong Chinese (Ruby, Falk, Heine, Villa, & Silberstein, 2012, Study 1). Although most of our studies have compared American and Chinese cultures, we have also administered our measure of actual and ideal affect to members of various Western (United States, England, France, Germany) and East Asian (Beijing China, Japan, South Korea) cultures and found that overall, Western cultures value HAP more and LAP less than East Asian cultures, although there is considerable variation among individual Western and East Asian cultures (Tsai et al., unpublished data).

These cultural differences in ideal affect are reflected in popular and widely distributed cultural products. For example, in a comparison of best-selling children's storybooks in the United States and Taiwan, characters in the American storybooks had more excited (versus calm) smiles, and they engaged in more physically rigorous activities than did characters in the Taiwanese storybooks (Tsai, Louie, et al., 2007). Similarly, American advertisements had more excited (versus calm) smiles than did Chinese advertisements, and European American Facebook profile photos had more excited smiles than did Hong Kong Chinese Facebook profile photos, with Asian American Facebook profile photos falling in between the two groups (Moon, Chim, Tsai, Ho, & Fung, 2011). These latter findings are consistent with other findings that American college students had

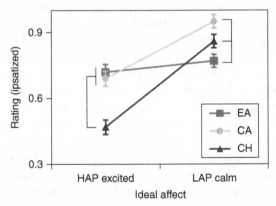

Figure 4.3 Cultural differences in ideal affect. CA= Chinese Americans; CH= Hong Kong Chinese; EA = European Americans.
Reprinted from Tsai, Knutson, & Fung (2006).

more intense smiles than did East Asian college students in their Facebook profiles (Huang & Park, 2012).

Why does American culture value excitement states more and calm states less than Chinese culture? We predicted that between and within-culture differences in interpersonal goals (i.e., influencing versus adjusting to others) result in differences in the value placed on excitement and calm states, respectively. Previous studies show that North American contexts value influence more and adjustment less than East Asian contexts (Morling, Kitayama, & Miyamoto, 2002). We predicted that because influencing others initially involves acting or doing something (e.g., expressing an opinion, explicitly asking someone to do something), and action involves increases in physiological arousal, when people *aim* to influence others, as they do in American culture, they *desire* or want to feel excitement and other high-arousal positive states. Conversely, because adjusting to others initially involves suspending action (e.g., waiting for others to speak first, allowing others to make plans or decisions), and suspending action involves decreases in arousal, when people *aim* to adjust to others, as they do in Chinese culture, they *desire* or want to feel calm and other low-arousal positive states.

To test this hypothesis, we administered survey measures of influence and adjustment goals (Locke, 2000) and the AVI (Tsai et al., 2006) to European American, Asian American, and Hong Kong Chinese college students. As in previous work, European Americans valued excitement states more and calm states less than Hong Kong Chinese, and Asian Americans valued excitement states more than Hong Kong Chinese and calm states more than European Americans. As predicted, influence goals fully mediated group differences in the value placed on excitement states. Adjustment goals partially mediated the difference in the value placed on calm states between European Americans and Hong Kong Chinese (Tsai, Miao, et al., 2007).

To assess experimentally whether having influence versus adjustment goals altered the degree to which people wanted to feel HAP (versus LAP) states, we conducted a series of studies in which participants were randomly assigned to either the (a) Value Influence condition, in which participants' task was to arrange cards in a personally meaningful order (or to build an object of their choice out of Lego pieces) and then to describe the cards (or object) to their partners, or the (b) Value Adjustment condition, in which participants' task was to listen carefully to the instructions of their partner and try to put their cards in the same order (or build the same object) as their partners. Across cultures, participants in the Value Influence condition reported valuing HAP states more and LAP states less than participants in the Value Adjustment condition (Tsai, Miao, et al., 2007).

In another experimental study, we used a behavioral rather than a self-report measure of ideal affect, the choice of listening to exciting (versus calming) music. Participants were ostensibly waiting for their partners to arrive, and were given the opportunity to listen to music that "has been shown to be good for increasing your performance" in the experimental task. As in the other studies, half of the participants were preparing to either influence or adjust to their partners.

Participants were then asked to choose between listening to an exciting or calm CD. The exciting CD was "Soundsplash:" its front cover depicted a man surfing, and its back cover contained fictitious reviews such as "High energy, lively jives." The calm CD was "Windchants:" its front cover depicted a man meditating on a rock, and its back cover contained reviews such as "Relaxing tunes." Across cultural groups (European Americans, Asian Americans, and Hong Kong Chinese), participants in the Value Influence condition were significantly more likely to choose the exciting (versus calm) CD than those in the Value Adjustment condition. Furthermore, across conditions, European Americans were significantly more likely to choose the exciting (versus calm) CD than Asian Americans or Hong Kong Chinese. Together, these studies suggest that cultural differences in ideal affect are at least partly due to cultural differences in interpersonal goals, and that increasing the value of these goals alters consumer preferences.

What about temperament? Although cultural factors also shape what affective states people actually feel, decades of empirical research suggest that across cultures, actual affect is largely shaped by people's temperament. For example, the more extroverted individuals are, the more likely they are to experience high-arousal positive affective states (e.g., Costa & McCrae, 1980; Emmons & Diener, 1986; Rusting & Larsen, 1997), and the more neurotic individuals are, the more likely they are to experience high-arousal negative affective states (e.g., hostility, nervousness) (e.g., Costa & McCrae, 1980; Gross, Sutton, & Ketelaar, 1998). Other factors that may influence people's actual affect include their ability to regulate their emotions and their immediate life circumstances (e.g., number of life stressors) (e.g., Gross & John, 2003; Watson, 1988).

Thus, AVT predicts that although cultural and temperamental factors likely influence both ideal and actual affect, cultural factors shape ideal affect more than actual affect, and temperamental factors shape actual more than ideal affect. Consistent with this prediction, in the samples of European Americans, Chinese Americans, and Hong Kong Chinese described above, cultural variables such as influence and adjustment goals predicted a greater percentage of variance in ideal affect than in actual affect, whereas temperamental variables such as extraversion and neuroticism predicted a greater percentage of variance in actual affect than in ideal affect (Tsai, 2007). AVT is one of the few theories that specify how culture and temperament shape affective life.

Ideal affect predicts mood-producing behavior

What are the consequences of these cultural and individual differences in ideal affect? The third premise of AVT is that ideal affect predicts what people do— consciously or not—to feel good or to stop feeling bad. Although most theories of emotion include behavior, they tend to focus on immediate response behaviors. AVT is unique in its inclusion of more proactive behaviors such as preference-based decision making. Because some activities are more effective at inducing specific affective states than others, when people feel bad and want to do something to feel better, they may engage in activities that most effectively elicit their ideal state. Indeed, this may explain why some people reduce their stress by running, whereas others reduce their stress by practicing yoga. People may also regularly engage in these specific activities to prevent negative feelings and to promote the specific positive feelings that they desire. Finally, people's everyday behavioral choices may also reflect their ideal affect. People may prefer "stimulating" versus "soothing" lotions and shampoos because they promise to elicit their ideal affective state. They may even choose friends and romantic partners who express the affective states that they value and ideally want to feel.

For example, in our previous studies, the more people valued excitement states, the more they preferred exciting vacations (e.g., partying versus. reading), leisure activities (e.g., running versus. walking), music (e.g., exciting versus calming), and drugs (e.g., frequency of stimulant use). Ideal affect also accounted for cultural differences in these mood-producing behaviors, even after controlling for actual affect (Tsai, 2007). Consistent with these findings, the more people want to feel happy and angry, the more they prefer happy and angry music and activities, respectively (Tamir & Ford, 2012).

To examine the links between ideal affect and product choice experimentally, we randomly assigned European American, Asian American, Hong Kong Chinese, and Beijing Chinese college students to one of three conditions: (a) Value Excitement; (b) Value Calm; and (c) Control (Tsai et al., unpublished data). All participants were told that they would be engaging in a puzzle task with a partner who had not yet arrived to the laboratory. Participants were then shown two videos of "past participants" (of the participant's culture). One "past participant" engaged in the task in an excited way (with a high pitched voice, excited smiles); the other engaged in the task in a calm way (with a low pitched voice, calm smiles). In the Value Excitement condition, participants were told that the excited past participant did well in the study, whereas the calm past participant did not (we did not use exciting and calm descriptors). In the Value Calm condition, participants were told the reverse. In the Control condition, participants were not told anything about the performance of the past participants in the videos. Participants were then told to begin the second part of the study until their partners arrived. They were presented with pairs of exciting versus calm consumer products (e.g., CDs of exciting versus calm music) as well as pairs of filler items, and asked to choose the product that they preferred from each pair. As predicted, participants in the Value Excitement condition chose more exciting products than did those in the Control and Value Calm conditions. Moreover, consistent with cultural differences in ideal affect, European Americans also chose more exciting products than Beijing Chinese; Asian Americans and Hong Kong Chinese fell in between the other two groups. Thus, although there are stable cultural differences in ideal affect, we can also manipulate how much people want to feel excitement and calm in the moment, and this alters their product preferences.

In a recent series of studies using survey and experimental methods, the more people valued HAP states, the more likely they were to select a physician that promoted excitement (versus calm) states (Sims, Tsai, Koopmann-Holm, Thomas, & Goldstein, 2014). Why? The more people valued HAP, the more trustworthy they found the excited (versus calm) physician, which increased their likelihood of selecting the excited physician. These findings were consistent across European Americans and Chinese Americans ranging in age from 20 to 80 years old. Interestingly, how often people actually felt HAP states was not related to their health care preferences, suggesting that ideal affect may be more influential than actual affect in shaping physician preferences among health care consumers. Ideal affect also predicts adherence to physicians' recommendations. In another study, participants were randomly assigned to either a HAP-focused or LAP-focused physician. The more participants valued HAP, the more they adhered to the HAP-focused physicians' recommendations over the course of a week. Similarly, the more participants valued LAP, the more they adhered to the LAP-focused physicians' recommendations (Sims & Tsai, 2014). Again, these findings held after controlling for actual HAP and actual LAP.

Thus, findings from our studies and others suggest that how people ideally want to feel: (a) is different from how people actually feel; (b) is shaped by culture; and (c) has consequences for a variety of behaviors. In the next section, we discuss the specific implications of ideal affect for existing research on affect and consumer behavior.

IMPLICATIONS OF CULTURAL VARIATION IN IDEAL AFFECT FOR CONSUMER BEHAVIOR

As described above, much of our research suggests that ideal affect may predict preference-based choices above and beyond actual affect. However, AVT has a number of other implications for research on consumer behavior, especially consumer behavior in other cultural contexts.

Ideal affect predicts variation in responses to and evaluation of consumer products and services

What determines whether people respond positively or negatively to a particular product, provider, or service? As illustrated in Figure 4.3, we predict that ideal affect shapes people's responses to various products, providers, and services. Specifically, we predict that people will feel more positively toward products, providers, and services that match their ideal affect. To test this hypothesis, we exposed participants to exciting and calm amusement park rides or treadmill exercises. Participants completed measures of ideal affect prior to the rides or exercises, and were asked immediately after these activities to rate how enjoyable they found the rides or exercises. For both American and Hong Kong Chinese samples, the more individuals valued LAP, the more they enjoyed the calm (but not the exciting) rides and exercises (Chim, 2013). Similar results emerged for anticipated and recalled actual affect, suggesting that ideal affect may also shape these types of actual affect. In addition, as described above, the more individuals value HAP, the more likely they are to choose exciting (versus calm) physicians because they evaluate them more positively (i.e., view them as more trustworthy) (Sims et al., 2014). Similarly, calm states increase the monetary value of products (i.e., how much a product is worth) in East Asian contexts (Pham, Hung, & Gorn, 2011). Thus, individual and cultural differences in ideal affect may influence how people perceive and respond to different products, providers, and services, which should then impact people's preferences and choices.

Previous findings that cultures vary in their responses to consumer products may also be due to ideal affect. For example, when participants received an unexpected gift, East Asians reported feeling less pleasure than did Westerners (Valenzuela, Mellers, & Strebel, 2010). This may be because unexpected gifts elicit high levels of arousal, which are valued less in East Asian than Western cultural contexts.

Ideal affect predicts variation in consumer preferences

Variation in consumer preferences may also be due to ideal affect. For example, the more Chinese participants had "high uncertainty avoidance," the more they preferred advertisements that had complete (versus incomplete) endings (e.g., a person in danger clearly reaches safety at the end versus a person in danger may or may not reach safety at the end) (Lee & Lim, 2008). "High uncertainty avoidance" is similar to anxiety avoidance, and anxiety is the opposite of calm; therefore, it is possible that uncertainty avoidance is a proxy for valuing calm. Thus, Chinese participants who had high uncertainty avoidance (or who valued calm more) may have preferred the complete endings because they elicited less arousal than the incomplete endings. In another study, East Asian cultural groups (i.e., Chinese, Asian American) showed more favorable attitudes toward and were more persuaded by advertisements conveying both positive and negative emotions compared to European Americans, who preferred advertisements conveying positive emotion only (Hong & Lee, 2010; Williams & Aaker, 2002). This may be because East Asian cultural groups (i.e., Chinese American, Hong Kong Chinese, Beijing Chinese) value positive affect less and negative affect more than European Americans (Sims, Tsai, Jiang, Wang, Fung, & Zhang, unpublished data).

Similarly, in our own work (Sims & Tsai, unpublished data), cultural differences in physician preference were mediated by cultural differences in ideal affect. Middle-aged and older European American adults preferred a physician who promoted excitement states (versus a physician who promoted calm states) more than did middle-aged and older Chinese Americans in a hypothetical scenario; these differences were mediated by the degree to which individuals valued HAP. We observed similar variation in real world contexts in which European Americans evaluated an exciting vs. calming physician more positively than East

Asian Americans. Moreover, European American community college students remembered more health recommendations presented in a brief video clip by an exciting vs. calm physician relative to Asian American students.

Ideal affect influences assumptions about affect in consumer behavior literature

In the same way that consumers are shaped by their ideal affect, researchers are influenced by their ideal affect as well. In the consumer behavior literature, there are two ways in which researchers' ideal affect may influence how they conduct their research. First, ideal affect may shape how they assess positive and negative affect. In most studies of affect and consumer behavior, positive affect and negative affect are typically measured on a unidimensional scale, with "extremely positive" at one end and "extremely negative" at the other (e.g., Connolly et al., 1997; Klaaren et al., 1994; Lee & Sternthal, 1999; Mazaheri, Richard, & Laroche, 2011; Mellers et al., 1999; Morewedge et al., 2005; Murray, Sujan, Hirt, & Sujan, 1990; Richard et al., 1996). Although people across cultures classify emotions along a bipolar continuum of positive and negative valence (Russell & Carroll, 1999; Tellegen, Watson, & Clark, 1999), the bipolarity of positive and negative states (i.e., the degree to which the two are negatively correlated) is greater in Western than Eastern cultures (Bagozzi, Wong, & Yi, 1999; Kitayama, Markus, & Kurokawa, 2000; Perunovic, Heller, & Rafaeli, 2007; Schimmack, Oishi, & Diener, 2002; Scollon, Diener, Oishi, & Biswas-Diener, 2005; Shiota, Campos, Gonzaga, Keltner, & Peng, 2010). Although these differences have been attributed to the greater emphasis on dialecticism (i.e., the notion that two seemingly opposite statements can be simultaneously true) in East Asian versus Western cultures (Schimmack et al., 2002), we find that cultural differences in the bipolarity of negative and positive affect are also due to different affective ideals. Whereas in American culture, people want to maximize positive feelings and minimize negative ones, in Chinese culture, people want to moderate positive and negative feelings. In two experience sampling studies, Americans' momentary reports of positive and negative actual affect were *more* bipolar than those of Chinese, and these differences were mediated by how much individuals ideally wanted to feel positive (ideal positive affect) and how little they wanted to feel negative affect (ideal negative affect) (Sims, Tsai, Jiang, et al., unpublished data). When experimentally manipulating ideal affect, American and Chinese participants who wanted to maximize feeling positive and minimize feeling negative showed more bipolarity of positive and negative affect while watching a pleasant television clip than who did not. These findings suggest that for cultural groups that have different affective ideals than American culture, positive and negative affect should be measured independently.

Indeed, European American and Asian American college students recalled the amount of positive (pleasant, sociable, calm, happy, joyful) and negative affect (unpleasant, irritated, guilty, sad, worried) they experienced during their spring break trip (positive and negative affect were assessed separately) (Wirtz, Chiu, Diener, & Oishi, 2009). For European Americans only, recalled positive actual affect predicted vacation preference: the more positively they recalled feeling, the more willing they were to go on that vacation again. However, for Asian Americans, both recalled positive and negative actual affect predicted willingness to go on the vacation again: the more positively they recalled feeling and the less negatively they recalled feeling, the more willing they were to go on that vacation again.

The second way in which researchers' ideal affect may shape research on affect and consumer behavior is through their definitions of "emotion." Because most researchers are from Western cultural contexts that value high-arousal positive states, it should not be surprising that "emotions" are defined as high-arousal states (e.g., Zevon & Tellegen, 1982). The assumption that affective processes work against rather than with reason may also be specific to Western contexts. Because high-arousal states narrow attention more than do low-arousal states (Gable & Harmon-Jones, 2008; Gable & Harmon-Jones, 2010), integrating cognitive and affect processes may be more difficult for high- versus low-arousal states. In contexts that value low-arousal states, however, consumers may be less torn between affective impulses and rational thought.

To illustrate, in a study of food preferences, affective (taste, associated memories) and informational (nutritional content) judgments were negatively correlated (i.e., the more nutritious a food, the less tasty they found it) for French participants, whereas for Chinese participants, affective and informational judgments were positively correlated (i.e., the more nutritious a food, the tastier they found it) (Dubé, Cervellon, & Jingyuan, 2003). This suggests that compared to French participants, the Chinese participants are better able to integrate affective and informational attributes of a product and therefore experience less duality between cognition and emotion. Thus, the validity of dual processing models may vary as a function of cultural differences in ideal affect.

CURRENT AND FUTURE DIRECTIONS

In our current and future research, we plan to follow up on some of the hypotheses presented in this chapter. In addition, future research should include other contexts, other affective states, and other types of consumer behavior.

Other contexts

Most of the research described in this chapter has focused on Western and East Asian comparisons. However, it would be important to examine other cultural contexts as well. For example, even though they live in a collectivistic culture, Mexican participants value HAP more than LAP (Ruby et al., 2012). Consistent with these findings, the combination of peacefulness and passion (intellectual autonomy, enjoyment and exploration of affective life) is a personality trait unique to Spanish brands compared to American brands (Aaker, Benet-Martínez, & Garolera, 2001). These findings suggest that cultural factors other than individualism-collectivism also shape ideal affect.

In addition to culture, age differences in ideal affect may explain variation in consumer behavior. Emotional goals are particularly salient among older adult consumers (e.g., Fung & Carstensen, 2003; Löckenhoff & Carstensen, 2007). Further, studies show significant variation by age in ideal affect (Scheibe et al., 2011; Sims, Tsai, Thomas, et al., 2012), which may lead to age differences in consumer behavior. For instance, in the health care domain, European Americans and Chinese American older adults prefer a physician who promotes a stimulating lifestyle significantly less than do younger adults (Sims & Tsai, unpublished data). Similarly, in an American sample, older adults associate happiness with calm more than excitement (Mogilner, Kamvar, & Aaker, 2011). Moreover, when reporting their next planned purchase and a recent purchase that made them feel happy, older adults are more likely to report calming and are less likely to report exciting purchases than younger adults. Thus, while European Americans may show a greater preference for HAP consumer products, services, and experiences, this preference may attenuate as people age. Increasingly preferring LAP vs. HAP products and providers with age may be because older adults are more aware of the finitude of life. As such, their preferences shift to calm states that facilitate savoring and reflecting on existing relationships rather than excitement states that facilitate influencing others and expanding networks (Jiang, Fung, Sims, Tsai, & Zhang, unpublished data).

Other affective states and types of affect

Most studies focus on actual positive and negative affect. Although many studies include different positive and negative states, few studies actually differentiate among them, and when they do, they tend to differentiate among negative (e.g., anger, fear, regret) rather than positive states.

Of the few studies that distinguish among positive states, including our own, most differentiate between positive states that are high and low in arousal, such as cheerfulness versus quiescence (Bosmans & Baumgartner, 2005), excitement versus calm (Kim, Park, & Schwarz, 2010; Mogilner, Aaker, & Kamvar, 2011; Tsai, 2007), joy versus interest (Oliver, 1993), or upbeat versus warm emotions (Burke & Edell, 1989). For example, American participants rated an adventurous (high-arousal positive) vacation advertisement as more positive when they felt excited (versus calm), and they rated a serene vacation advertisement as more positive when they felt calm (versus excited) (Kim et al., 2010). Thus, future research should examine further how the effects of positive and negative affect on consumer behavior vary as a function of arousal.

Affective states, however, also vary along an interpersonal dimension, which may exert an independent influence on consumer behavior. For example,

American participants who felt more pride reported more satisfaction with a hypothetical computer purchase (Louro, Pieters, & Zeelenberg, 2005). However, the effect of pride on consumer satisfaction may be specific to contexts that value pride. Kitayama et al. (2000) examined daily reports of emotions and found that pride was more strongly associated with general positive emotional experience for Americans than for Japanese. Conversely, socially engaging emotions (e.g., close, friendly feelings) were more strongly associated with general positive emotional experience for Japanese than for Americans. Thus, pride may be associated with different consumer outcomes for Japanese than Americans (e.g., see Aaker & Williams, 1998). Future studies are needed to examine the effects of more interpersonal affective states (e.g., compassion, shame) on consumer behavior across cultures.

In this chapter, we have primarily focused on actual and ideal affect, but other work in our laboratory has focused on "avoided affect," or the affective states that people want to avoid feeling. In this work, we find that Americans want to avoid negative states more than Germans, and that these differences are reflected in the content of sympathy cards in the US and Germany (Koopmann-Holm, et al., 2014). Specifically, American sympathy cards contain more positive (vs. negative) words and more living (vs. dying) images than German sympathy cards. These findings suggest that for certain products, avoided affect may predict product evaluation and preference even more than actual or ideal affect. Future work should examine the role that avoided affect plays in consumer behavior.

Other consumer behaviors

Finally, future research should examine the effects of ideal and actual affect on other types of "consumer behaviors" such as risk taking and social preferences.

FINANCIAL RISK TAKING
Perhaps surprisingly, many studies show that Chinese participants are generally more risk seeking than Americans in the domain of financial decision making (Hsee & Weber, 1999; Wang & Fischbeck, 2004; for reviews, see Weber & Hsee, 2000; Weber & Morris, 2010). These differences have been attributed to how socioeconomic (e.g., how technological a society is [Whitcomb, Önkal, Curley, & George Benson, 1995; Yates, Zhu, Ronis, Wang, Shinotsuka, & Toda, 1989], how experienced a society is with financial markets [Fan & Xiao, 2005]), as well as sociocultural (e.g., social networks: Hsee & Weber, 1999; views of self: Mandel, 2003) factors.

Based on our findings that European Americans want to maximize positive and minimize negative affect more than East Asians, we predict that East Asians may be more risk seeking because they are more willing to accept the negative feelings associated with a financial loss. Conversely, European Americans may be more risk averse because the losses associated with risk taking conflict with their goal to maximize positive affect. Indeed, Westerners (American and Dutch participants) base their perceptions of risk for different lotteries more on the probability of positive outcomes than do Chinese (Taiwan and Hong Kong participants) (Bontempo, Bottom, & Weber, 1997). Thus, future research should examine how cultural variation in ideal affect leads to cultural differences in financial risk taking.

SOCIAL PREFERENCES

Earlier in this chapter, we described studies related to consumers' evaluation of their physicians. However, we also expect that ideal affect shapes consumer evaluations of social partners and even political leaders. In a study of preferences for politicians (Abelson et al., 1982), the more actual positive affect and the lower actual negative affect (e.g., happy, hopeful, sad, angry) participants felt toward a politician, the more favorable the candidate was rated and the higher was his ranking. Moreover, actual affect predicted favorability ratings and ranking order of the candidates more than did ratings of candidates' characteristics (e.g., weak, power hungry, inspiring). According to AVT, feelings toward the candidate should depend on whether the candidates' characteristics appeal to voters' ideal affect. Consistent with previous results, the more people value HAP, the friendlier they perceive an excited (versus calm) leader, and the more likely they are to rate them as a better leader (Tsai et al., unpublished data). Findings from others studies are consistent with this work. For example, although the strength of a political candidate's smile is correlated with the percentage of the vote he received in Japan and Australia, the smile is a much stronger predictor in Australia than in Japan (Horiuchi, Komatsu, & Nakaya, 2012). Similarly, whereas smile intensity was positively correlated with trustworthiness for Americans, it was negatively correlated with trustworthiness for Japanese (Ozono, Watabe, Yoshikawa, Nakashima, Rule, Ambady, & Adams Jr., 2010). Thus, ideal affect may predict not only what consumer products, service providers, or recreational experiences people choose, but also behaviors that reveal their social preferences.

CONCLUSION

Increasingly, researchers are examining how affect shapes various consumer behaviors. While feeling good or bad indisputably matters for consumer behavior, researchers should consider how culture shapes what constitutes a good or bad feeling. To date, most research has focused on Western samples and has been conducted by Western researchers. As a result, many of the assumptions about emotion and affect in these studies reflect Western beliefs, norms, and ideals regarding emotion, in particular, the Western emphasis on excitement and other high-arousal positive states. In today's global economy, understanding how culture shapes these processes is critical. In this chapter, we have argued that one way of understanding cultural differences in consumer behavior is through cultural differences in ideal affect, or how people ideally want to feel.

REFERENCES

Aaker, J. L., Benet-Martínez, V., & Garolera, J. (2001). Consumption symbols as carriers of culture: A study of Japanese and Spanish brand personality constructs. *Journal of Personality and Social Psychology, 81*(3), 492–508. doi: 10.1037/0022-3514.81.3.492

Aaker, J. L., & Williams, P. (1998). Empathy versus Pride: The influence of emotional appeals across cultures. *Journal of Consumer Research, 25*(3), 241–261.

Abelson, R. P., Kinder, D. R., Peters, M. D., & Fiske, S. T. (1982). Affective and semantic components in political person perception. *Journal of Personality and Social Psychology, 42*(4), 619–630. doi: 10.1037/0022-3514.42.4.619

Alford, B. L., & Sherrell, D. L. (1996). The role of affect in consumer satisfaction judgments of credence-based services. *Journal of Business Research, 37*(1), 71–84. doi: 10.1016/0148-2963(96)00030-6

American Marketing Association. (2012). Retrieved October 30, 2012, from http://www.marketingpower.com/_layouts/Dictionary.aspx?dLetter=C#consumer+behavior

Andrade, E. B. (2005). Behavioral consequences of affect: combining evaluative and regulatory mechanisms. *Journal of Consumer Research, 32*(3), 355–362.

Andrade, E. B., & Cohen, J. B. (2007). On the consumption of negative feelings. *Journal of Consumer Research, 34*(3), 283–300.

Bagozzi, R. P., Baumgartner, H., Pieters, R., & Zeelenberg, M. (2000).The role of emotions in goal-directed behavior. In S. Ratneshwar, D. G. Mick, & C. Huffman (Eds.), *The Why of consumption: Contemporary perspectives on consumer motives, goals and desires* (pp. 36–58). New York: Routledge.

Bagozzi, R. P., Wong, N., & Yi, Y. (1999). The role of culture and gender in the relationship between positive and negative affect. *Cognition & Emotion, 13*(6), 641–672. doi: 10.1080/026999399379023

Bakamitsos, G. A., & Siomkos, G. J. (2004). Context effects in marketing practice: the case of mood. *Journal of Consumer Behaviour, 3*(4), 304–314. doi: 10.1002/cb.144

Bar-Hillel, M., & Neter, E. (1996). Why are people reluctant to exchange lottery tickets? *Journal of Personality and Social Psychology, 70*(1), 17–27. doi: 10.1037/0022-3514.70.1.17

Barrett, L. F. (1996). Hedonic tone, perceived arousal, and item desirability: Three components of self-reported mood. *Cognition & Emotion, 10*(1), 47–68. doi: 10.1080/026999396380385

Barrett, L. F., & Russell, J. A. (1999). The structure of current affect: controversies and emerging consensus. *Current Directions in Psychological Science, 8*(1), 10–14. doi: 10.1111/1467-8721.00003

Bechara, A. (2004). The role of emotion in decision-making: Evidence from neurological patients with orbitofrontal damage. *Brain and Cognition, 55*(1), 30–40. doi: 10.1016/j.bandc.2003.04.001

Bell, D. E. (1985). Putting a premium on regret: Reply. *Management Science, 31*(1), 117–120.

Bontempo, R. N., Bottom, W. P., & Weber, E. U. (1997). Cross-cultural differences in risk perception: A model-based approach. *Risk Analysis, 17*(4), 479–488. doi: 10.1111/j.1539-6924.1997.tb00888.x

Bosmans, A., & Baumgartner, H. (2005). Goal-relevant emotional information: When extraneous affect leads to persuasion and when it does not. *Journal of Consumer Research, 32*(3), 424–434.

Brown, S. P., Homer, P. M., & Inman, J. J. (1998). A meta-analysis of relationships between ad-evoked feelings and advertising responses. *Journal of Marketing Research, 35*(1), 114–126.

Burke, M. C., & Edell, J. A. (1989). The impact of feelings on ad-based affect and cognition. *Journal of Marketing Research, 26*(1), 69–83. doi: 10.2307/3172670

Chapman, G. B., & Coups, E. J. (2006). Emotions and preventive health behavior: Worry, regret, and influenza vaccination. *Health Psychology, 25*(1), 82–90. doi: 10.1037/0278-6133.25.1.82

Chaudhuri, A. (2002). A study of emotion and reason in products and services. *Journal of Consumer Behaviour, 1*(3), 267–279. doi: 10.1002/cb.72

Chim, L. (2013). *The relationship between wanting and actually feeling happy depends on the activities you engage in and how you ideally want to feel.* Unpublished doctoral dissertation. Stanford University.

Connolly, T., Ordóñez, L. D., & Coughlan, R. (1997). Regret and Responsibility in the evaluation of decision outcomes. *Organizational Behavior and Human Decision Processes, 70*(1), 73–85. doi: 10.1006/obhd.1997.2695

Costa, P. T., & McCrae, R. R. (1980). Influence of extraversion and neuroticism on subjective well-being: Happy and unhappy people. *Journal of Personality and Social Psychology, 38*(4), 668–678. doi: 10.1037/0022-3514.38.4.668

Damasio, A. (2005). *Descartes' Error: Emotion, Reason, and the Human Brain*: Penguin (Non-Classics).

Dubé, L., Cervellon, M.-C., & Jingyuan, H. (2003). Should consumer attitudes be reduced to their affective and cognitive bases? Validation of a hierarchical model. *International Journal of Research in Marketing, 20*(3), 259–272. doi: 10.1016/s0167-8116(03)00036-3

Dubé, L., & Menon, K. (2000). Multiple roles of consumption emotions in post-purchase satisfaction with extended service transactions. *International Journal of Service Industry Management, 11*(3), 287–304. doi: 10.1108/09564230010340788

Dunn, E. W., Brackett, M. A., Ashton-James, C., Schneiderman, E., & Salovey, P. (2007). On emotionally intelligent time travel: Individual differences in affective forecasting ability. *Personality and Social Psychology Bulletin, 33*(1), 85–93. doi: 10.1177/0146167206294201

Edell, J. A., & Burke, M. C. (1987). The power of feelings in understanding advertising effects. *Journal of Consumer Research, 14*(3), 421–433.

Emmons, R. A., & Diener, E. (1986). Influence of impulsivity and sociability on subjective well-being. *Journal of Personality and Social Psychology, 50*(6), 1211–1215. doi: 10.1037/0022-3514.50.6.1211

Epstein, S. (1994). Integration of the cognitive and the psychodynamic unconscious. *American Psychologist, 49*(8), 709–724. doi: 10.1037/0003-066x.49.8.709

Fan, J., & Xiao, J. J. (2005). A cross-cultural study in risk tolerance: Comparing Chinese and Americans. *Available at SSRN 939438.*

Finucane, M. L., Alhakami, A., Slovic, P., & Johnson, S. M. (2000). The affect heuristic in judgments of risks and benefits. *Journal of Behavioral Decision Making, 13*(1), 1–17. doi: 10.1002/(sici)1099-0771(200001/03)13:1<1::aid-bdm333>3.0.co;2-s

Forgas, J. P. (1995). Mood and judgment: The affect infusion model (AIM). *Psychological Bulletin, 117*(1), 39–66. doi: 10.1037/0033-2909.117.1.39

Fung, H. H., & Carstensen, L. L. (2003). Sending memorable messages to the old: Age differences in preferences and memory for advertisements. *Journal of Personality and Social Psychology, 85*(1), 163–178. doi: 10.1037/0022-3514.85.1.163

Gable, P., & Harmon-Jones, E. (2010). The blues broaden, but the nasty narrows attentional consequences of negative affects low and high in motivational intensity. *Psychological Science, 21*(2), 211–215. doi: 10.1177/0956797609359622

Gable, P. A., & Harmon-Jones, E. (2008). Approach-motivated positive affect reduces breadth of attention. *Psychological Science, 19*(5), 476–482. doi: 10.1111/j.1467-9280 .2008.02112.x

Gardner, M. P. (1985). Mood states and consumer behavior: A critical review. *Journal of Consumer Research, 12*(3), 281–300.

Gross, J. J., & John, O. P. (2003). Individual differences in two emotion regulation processes: Implications for affect, relationships, and well-being. *Journal of Personality and Social Psychology, 85*(2), 348–362. doi: 10.1037/0022-3514.85.2.348

Gross, J. J., Sutton, S. K., & Ketelaar, T. (1998). Relations between affect and personality: Support for the affect-level and affective reactivity views. *Personality and Social Psychology Bulletin, 24*(3), 279–288. doi: 10.1177/0146167298243005

Holbrook, M. B., & Hirschman, E. C. (1982). The experiential aspects of consumption: consumer fantasies, feelings, and fun. *Journal of Consumer Research, 9*(2), 132–140.

Hong, J., & Lee, A. Y. (2010). Feeling mixed but not torn: The moderating role of construal level in mixed emotions appeals. *Journal of Consumer Research, 37*(3), 456–472.

Horiuchi, Y., Komatsu, T., & Nakaya, F. (2012). Should candidates smile to win elections? An application of automated face recognition technology. *Political Psychology, 33*(6), 925–933. doi: 10.1111/j.1467-9221.2012.00917.x

Hsee, C. K., & Hastie, R. (2006). Decision and experience: why don't we choose what makes us happy? *Trends in Cognitive Sciences, 10*(1), 31–37. doi: 10.1016/j. tics.2005.11.007

Hsee, C. K., & Weber, E. U. (1999). Cross-national differences in risk preference and lay predictions. *Journal of Behavioral Decision Making, 12*(2), 165–179. doi: 10.1002/(sic i)1099-0771(199906)12:2<165::aid-bdm316>3.0.co;2-n

Huang, C.-M., & Park, D. (2012). Cultural influences on Facebook photographs. *International journal of psychology: Journal international de psychologie.* doi: 10.108 0/00207594.2011.649285

Jayanti, R. K. (1995). The impact of affective responses on physician evaluations. *Health Marketing Quarterly, 12*(3), 49–62. doi: 10.1300/J026v12n03_0610.1300/ J026v12n03_06</p>

Kahneman, D., & Frederick, S. (2002). Representativeness revisited: Attribute substitution in intuitive judgment. In T. Gilovich, D. Griffin & D. Kahneman (Eds.), *Heuristics and biases: The psychology of intuitive judgment* (pp. 49–81). New York, NY, USA: Cambridge University Press.

Kahneman, D., Fredrickson, B. L., Schreiber, C. A., & Redelmeier, D. A. (1993). When more pain is preferred to less: Adding a better end. *Psychological Science, 4*(6), 401–405.

Kahneman, D., & Snell, J. (1992). Predicting a changing taste: Do people know what they will like? *Journal of Behavioral Decision Making, 5*(3), 187–200. doi: 10.1002/bdm.3960050304

Kim, H., Park, K., & Schwarz, N. (2010). Will this trip really be exciting? The role of incidental emotions in product evaluation. *Journal of Consumer Research, 36*(6), 983–991.

Kitayama, S., Markus, H. R., & Kurokawa, M. (2000). Culture, emotion, and well-being: Good feelings in Japan and the United States. *Cognition & Emotion, 14*(1), 93–124. doi: 10.1080/026999300379003

Klaaren, K. J., Hodges, S. D., & Wilson, T. D. (1994). The role of affective expectations in subjective experience and decision-making. *Social Cognition, 12*(2), 77–101. doi: 10.1521/soco.1994.12.2.77

Knutson, B., Adams, C. M., Fong, G. W., & Hommer, D. (2001). Anticipation of increasing monetary reward selectively recruits nucleus accumbens. *Journal of Neuroscience, 21*(16), RC159.

Koopmann-Holm, B., & Tsai, J. L. (2014). Focusing on the negative: Cultural differences in expressions of sympathy. *Journal of Personality and Social Psychology, 107*. http://dx.doi.org/10.1037/a0037684

Kroeber, A. L., & Kluckhohn, C. (1952). Culture: a critical review of concepts and definitions. *Papers. Peabody Museum of Archaeology & Ethnology, Harvard University, 47*(1), viii,-223.

Kuppens, P., Ceulemans, E., Timmerman, M. E., Diener, E., & Kim-Prieto, C. (2006). Universal intracultural and intercultural dimensions of the recalled frequency of emotional experience. *Journal of Cross-Cultural Psychology, 37*(5), 491–515. doi: 10.1177/0022022106290474

Lam, K. C. H., Buehler, R., McFarland, C., Ross, M., & Cheung, I. (2005). Cultural differences in affective forecasting: The role of focalism. *Personality and Social Psychology Bulletin, 31*(9), 1296–1309. doi: 10.1177/0146167205274691

Larsen, R. J., & Diener, E. (1992). Promises and problems with the circumplex model of emotion. *Emotion* (pp. 25–59). Thousand Oaks, CA, USA: Sage Publications, Inc.

Lee, A. Y., & Sternthal, B. (1999). The effects of positive mood on memory. *Journal of Consumer Research, 26*(2), 115–127.

Lee, Y. H., & Lim, E. A. C. (2008). What's funny and what's not: The moderating role of cultural orientation in ad humor. *Journal of Advertising, 37*(2), 71–84. doi: 10.2753/joa0091-3367370206

Locke, K. (1996). A funny thing happened! The management of consumer emotions in service encounters. *Organization Science, 7*(1), 40–59. doi: 10.1287/orsc.7.1.40

Locke, K. D. (2000). Circumplex scales of interpersonal values: Reliability, validity, and applicability to interpersonal problems and personality disorders. *Journal of Personality Assessment, 75*(2), 249–267. doi: 10.1207/s15327752jpa7502_6

Löckenhoff, C. E., & Carstensen, L. L. (2007). Aging, emotion, and health-related decision strategies: Motivational manipulations can reduce age differences. *Psychology and Aging, 22*(1), 134–146. doi: 10.1037/0882-7974.22.1.134

Loewenstein, G., & Lerner, J. S. (2003). The role of affect in decision making. In R. J. Davidson, K. R. Scherer & H. H. Goldsmith (Eds.), *Handbook of affective sciences* (pp. 619–642). New York, NY, USA: Oxford University Press.

Loewenstein, G., & Schkade, D. (1999). Wouldn't it be nice? Predicting future feelings. In D. Kahneman, E. Diener & N. Schwarz (Eds.), *Well-being: The foundations of hedonic psychology* (pp. 85–105). New York, NY, USA: Russell Sage Foundation.

Loewenstein, G., Weber, E. U., Hsee, C. K., & Welch, N. (2001). Risk as feelings. *Psychological Bulletin, 127*(2), 267–286. doi: 10.1037/0033-2909.127.2.267

Loomes, G., & Sugden, R. (1982). Regret Theory: An alternative theory of rational choice under uncertainty. *The Economic Journal, 92*(368), 805–824.

Louro, M. J., Pieters, R., & Zeelenberg, M. (2005). Negative returns on positive emotions: The influence of pride and self-regulatory goals on repurchase decisions. *Journal of Consumer Research, 31*(4), 833–840.

Mandel, N. (2003). Shifting Selves and decision making: The effects of self-construal priming on consumer risk-taking. *Journal of Consumer Research, 30*(1), 30–40.

Mazaheri, E., Richard, M.-O., & Laroche, M. (2011). Online consumer behavior: Comparing Canadian and Chinese website visitors. *Journal of Business Research, 64*(9), 958–965. doi: 10.1016/j.jbusres.2010.11.018

Mellers, B., Schwartz, A., & Ritov, I. (1999). Emotion-based choice. *Journal of Experimental Psychology: General, 128*(3), 332–345. doi: 10.1037/0096-3445.128.3.332

Mikels, J. A., Löckenhoff, C. E., Maglio, S. J., Carstensen, L. L., Goldstein, M. K., & Garber, A. (2010). Following your heart or your head: Focusing on emotions versus information differentially influences the decisions of younger and older adults. *Journal of Experimental Psychology: Applied, 16*(1), 87–95. doi: 10.1037/a0018500

Mogilner, C., Aaker, J. L., & Kamvar, S. D. (2011). *How happiness impacts choice.* Stanford, CA: Graduate School of Business, Stanford University.

Mogilner, C., Kamvar, S. D., & Aaker, J. (2011). The shifting meaning of happiness. *Social Psychological and Personality Science, 2*(4), 395–402. doi: 10.1177/1948550610393987

Moon, A., Chim, L., Tsai, J. L., Ho, Y., & Fung, H. H. (2011). The influence of cultural differences in ideal affect on self-presentation and other-perception of Facebook profiles. *Poster presented at the 12th Annual Meeting of the Society of Personality and Social Psychology, San Antonio, TX, USA.*

Morewedge, C. K., Gilbert, D. T., & Wilson, T. D. (2005). The least likely of times how remembering the past biases forecasts of the future. *Psychological Science, 16*(8), 626–630. doi: 10.1111/j.1467-9280.2005.01585.x

Morling, B., Kitayama, S., & Miyamoto, Y. (2002). Cultural practices emphasize influence in the United States and adjustment in Japan. *Personality and Social Psychology Bulletin, 28*(3), 311–323. doi: 10.1177/0146167202286003

Murray, N., Sujan, H., Hirt, E. R., & Sujan, M. (1990). The influence of mood on categorization: A cognitive flexibility interpretation. *Journal of Personality and Social Psychology, 59*(3), 411–425. doi: 10.1037/0022-3514.59.3.411

Oliver, R. L. (1993). Cognitive, affective, and attribute bases of the satisfaction response. *Journal of Consumer Research, 20*(3), 418–430.

Ozono, H., Watabe, M., Yoshikawa, S., Nakashima, S., Rule, N. O., Ambady, N., & Adams R. B. Jr (2010). What's in a smile? Cultural differences in the effects of smiling on judgments of trustworthiness.

Perunovic, W. Q. E., Heller, D., & Rafaeli, E. (2007). Within-person changes in the structure of emotion: The role of cultural identification and language. *Psychological Science, 18*(7), 607–613. doi: 10.1111/j.1467-9280.2007.01947.x

Peters, E. (2006). The functions of affect in the construction of preferences. *The construction of preference*, 454–463.

Pham, M. T. (2004). The logic of feeling. *Journal of Consumer Psychology, 14*(4), 360–369. doi: 10.1207/s15327663jcp1404_5

Pham, M. T., Hung, I. W., & Gorn, G. J. (2011). Relaxation increases monetary valuations. *Journal of Marketing Research, 48*(5), 814–826. doi: 10.1509/jmkr.48.5.814

Phillips, D. M., & Baumgartner, H. (2002). The role of consumption emotions in the satisfaction response. *Journal of Consumer Psychology, 12*(3), 243–252. doi: 10.1207/s15327663jcp1203_06

Redelmeier, D. A., & Kahneman, D. (1996). Patients' memories of painful medical treatments: real-time and retrospective evaluations of two minimally invasive procedures. *Pain, 66*(1), 3–8. doi: 10.1016/0304-3959(96)02994-6

Redelmeier, D. A., Katz, J., & Kahneman, D. (2003). Memories of colonoscopy: a randomized trial. *Pain, 104*(1–2), 187–194. doi: 10.1016/s0304-3959(03)00003-4

Richard, R., van der Pligt, J., & de Vries, N. (1996). Anticipated affect and behavioral choice. *Basic and Applied Social Psychology, 18*(2), 111–129. doi: 10.1207/s15324834basp1802_1

Rozin, P. (2003). Five potential principles for understanding cultural differences in relation to individual differences. *Journal of Research in Personality, 37*(4), 273–283. doi: 10.1016/s0092-6566(02)00566-4

Ruby, M. B., Falk, C. F., Heine, S. J., Villa, C., & Silberstein, O. (2012). Not all collectivisms are equal: opposing preferences for ideal affect between East Asians and Mexicans. *Emotion*, No-Pagination Specified. doi: 10.1037/a0029118

Russell, J. A. (2003). Core affect and the psychological construction of emotion. *Psychological Review, 110*(1), 145–172. doi: 10.1037/0033-295x.110.1.145

Russell, J. A., & Carroll, J. M. (1999). On the bipolarity of positive and negative affect. *Psychological Bulletin, 125*(1), 3–30. doi: 10.1037/0033-2909.125.1.3

Russell, J. A., Lewicka, M., & Niit, T. (1989). A cross-cultural study of a circumplex model of affect. *Journal of Personality and Social Psychology, 57*(5), 848–856. doi: 10.1037/0022-3514.57.5.848

Rusting, C. L., & Larsen, R. J. (1997). Extraversion, neuroticism, and susceptibility to positive and negative affect: A test of two theoretical models. *Personality and Individual Differences, 22*(5), 607–612. doi: 10.1016/s0191-8869(96)00246-2

Savani, K., Markus, H. R., & Conner, A. L. (2008). Let your preference be your guide? Preferences and choices are more tightly linked for North Americans than for Indians. *Journal of Perspectives on Social Psychology, 95*(4), 861–876. doi: 10.1037/a0011618

Scheibe, S., Mata, R., & Carstensen, L. L. (2011). Age differences in affective forecasting and experienced emotion surrounding the 2008 US presidential election. *Cognition & Emotion, 25*(6), 1029–1044. doi: 10.1080/02699931.2010.545543

Schimmack, U., Oishi, S., & Diener, E. (2002). Cultural influences on the relation between pleasant emotions and unpleasant emotions: Asian dialectic philosophies or individualism-collectivism? *Cognition & Emotion, 16*(6), 705–719. doi: 10.1080/02699930143000590

Schwarz, N. (2000). Emotion, cognition, and decision making. *Cognition & Emotion, 14*(4), 433–440. doi: 10.1080/026999300402745 10.1080/026999300402745

Schwarz, N., & Clore, G. L. (1983). Mood, misattribution, and judgments of well-being: Informative and directive functions of affective states. *Journal of Personality and Social Psychology, 45*(3), 513–523. doi: 10.1037/0022-3514.45.3.513

Schwarz, N., & Clore, G. L. (1996). Feelings and phenomenal experiences. In E. T. Higgings & A. W. Kruglanski (Eds.), *Social psychology: Handbook of basic principles* (pp. 433–465). New York, NY, USA: Guilford Press.

Scollon, C. N., Diener, E., Oishi, S., & Biswas-Diener, R. (2005). An experience sampling and cross-cultural investigation of the relation between pleasant and unpleasant affect. *Cognition & Emotion, 19*(1), 27–52. doi: 10.1080/02699930441000076

Shiota, M. N., Campos, B., Gonzaga, G. C., Keltner, D., & Peng, K. (2010). I love you but. . .: Cultural differences in complexity of emotional experience during interaction with a romantic partner. *Cognition & Emotion, 24*(5), 786–799. doi: 10.1080/02699930902990480

Shiv, B., & Fedorikhin, A. (1999). Heart and mind in conflict: The interplay of affect and cognition in consumer decision making. *Journal of Consumer Research, 26*(3), 278–292. doi 10.1086/209563

Shweder, R. (2003). *Why do men barbecue?: Recipes for cultural psychology.* Cambridge, MA, USA: Harvard University Press.

Simonson, I. (1992). The influence of anticipating regret and responsibility on purchase decisions. *Journal of Consumer Research, 19*(1), 105–118.

Sims, T., & Tsai, J.L (2014). Patients respond more positively to physicians who focus on their ideal affect. *Emotion.* http://dx.doi.org/10.1037/emo0000026

Sims, T., Tsai, J. L., Koopmann-Holm, B., Thomas, E., & Goldstein, M. (2014). Choosing a physician depends on how you want to feel: The role of ideal affect in health related decision-making. *Emotion, 14,* 187–192.

Sims, T., Tsai, J. L., Thomas, E., Park, C., Hong, J., & Fung, H. H. (2012). You're as young as you want to feel: Cultural variation in ideal affect across the life span. *Paper presented at International Society for the Study of Behavioural Development, Alberta, Canada.*

Sims, T., Tsai, J. L., Jiang, D., Wang, I., Fung, H. H., & Zhang, X. (2014). Wanting to maximize the positive and minimize the negative: Implications for mixed affective experience in American and Chinese contexts. *Paper presented at Society for Personality and Social Psychology, San Diego, CA.*

Sloman, S. A. (1996). The empirical case for two systems of reasoning. *Psychological Bulletin, 119*(1), 3–22. doi: 10.1037/0033-2909.119.1.3

Slovic, P., Finucane, M., Peters, E., & MacGregor, D. G. (2002). Rational actors or rational fools: implications of the affect heuristic for behavioral economics. *The Journal of Socio-Economics, 31*(4), 329–342. doi: 10.1016/s1053-5357(02)00174-9

Slovic, P., Finucane, M. L., Peters, E., & MacGregor, D. G. (2007). The affect heuristic. *European Journal of Operational Research, 177*(3), 1333–1352. doi: 10.1016/j.ejor.2005.04.006

Tamir, M., & Ford, B. Q. (2012). Should people pursue feelings that feel good or feelings that do good? Emotional preferences and well-being. *Emotion, 12*(5), 1061–1070. doi: 10.1037/a0027223

Tellegen, A., Watson, D., & Clark, L. A. (1999). On the Dimensional and Hierarchical Structure of Affect. *Psychological Science, 10*(4), 297–303. doi: 10.1111/1467-9280.00157

Tsai, J. L. (2007). Ideal affect: Cultural causes and behavioral consequences. *Perspectives on Psychological Science, 2*(3), 242–259. doi: 10.1111/j.1745-6916.2007.00043.x

Tsai, J. L., Knutson, B., & Fung, H. H. (2006). Cultural variation in affect valuation. *Journal of Personality and Social Psychology, 90*(2), 288–307. doi: 10.1037/0022-3514.90.2.288

Tsai, J. L., Louie, J. Y., Chen, E. E., & Uchida, Y. (2007). Learning What Feelings to Desire: Socialization of Ideal Affect Through Children's Storybooks. *Personality and Social Psychology Bulletin, 33*(1), 17–30. doi: 10.1177/0146167206292749

Tsai, J. L., Miao, F. F., Seppala, E., Fung, H. H., & Yeung, D. Y. (2007). Influence and adjustment goals: Sources of cultural differences in ideal affect. *Journal of Personality and Social Psychology, 92*(6), 1102–1117. doi: 10.1037/0022-3514.92.6.1102

Tversky, A., & Kahneman, D. (1983). Extensional versus intuitive reasoning: The conjunction fallacy in probability judgment. *Psychological Review, 90*(4), 293–315. doi: 10.1037/0033-295x.90.4.293

Valenzuela, A., Mellers, B., & Strebel, J. (2010). Pleasurable Surprises: A cross-cultural study of consumer responses to unexpected incentives. *Journal of Consumer Research, 36*(5), 792–805.

Wang, M., & Fischbeck, P. S. (2004). Incorporating framing into prospect theory modeling: A mixture-model approach. *Journal of Risk and Uncertainty, 29*(2), 181–197. doi: 10.1023/b:risk.0000038943.63610.16

Watson, D. (1988). Intraindividual and interindividual analyses of positive and negative affect: Their relation to health complaints, perceived stress, and daily activities. *Journal of Personality and Social Psychology, 54*(6), 1020–1030. doi: 10.1037/0022-3514.54.6.1020

Watson, D., & Tellegen, A. (1985). Toward a consensual structure of mood. *Psychological Bulletin, 98*(2), 219–235. doi: 10.1037/0033-2909.98.2.219

Weber, E., & Hsee, C. (2000). Culture and individual judgment and decision making. *Applied Psychology, 49*(1), 32–61. doi: 10.1111/1464-0597.00005

Weber, E. U., & Morris, M. W. (2010). Culture and judgment and decision making: The constructivist turn. *Perspectives on Psychological Science, 5*(4), 410–419. doi: 10.1177/1745691610375556

Westbrook, R. A., & Oliver, R. L. (1991). The dimensionality of consumption emotion patterns and consumer satisfaction. *Journal of Consumer Research, 18*(1), 84–91.

Whitcomb, K. M., Önkal, D., Curley, S. P., & George Benson, P. (1995). Probability judgment accuracy for general knowledge. Cross-national differences and assessment methods. *Journal of Behavioral Decision Making, 8*(1), 51–67. doi: 10.1002/bdm.3960080105

Williams, P., & Aaker, Jennifer L. (2002). Can mixed emotions peacefully coexist? *Journal of Consumer Research, 28*(4), 636–649.

Wilson, T. D., & Gilbert, D. T. (2003). Affective forecasting. *Advances in Experimental Social Psychology* (Vol. Volume 35, pp. 345–411): Academic Press.

Wirtz, D., Chiu, C.-y., Diener, E., & Oishi, S. (2009). What constitutes a good life? Cultural differences in the role of positive and negative affect in subjective well-being. *Journal of Personality, 77*(4), 1167–1196. doi: 10.1111/j.1467-6494.2009.00578.x

Wirtz, D., Kruger, J., Scollon, C. N., & Diener, E. (2003). What to do on spring break? The role of predicted, on-line, and remembered experience in future choice. *Psychological Science, 14*(5), 520–524. doi: 10.1111/1467-9280.03455

Yates, J. F., Zhu, Y., Ronis, D. L., Wang, D.-F., Shinotsuka, H., & Toda, M. (1989). Probability judgment accuracy: China, Japan, and the United States. *Organizational Behavior and Human Decision Processes, 43*(2), 145–171. doi: 10.1016/0749-5978(89)90048-4

Yik, M. S. M., & Russell, J. A. (2003). Chinese affect circumplex: I. Structure of recalled momentary affect. *Asian Journal of Social Psychology, 6*(3), 185–200. doi: 10.1046/j.1467-839X.2003.00120.x

Zajonc, R. B. (1980). Feeling and thinking: Preferences need no inferences. *American Psychologist, 35*(2), 151–175. doi: 10.1037/0003-066x.35.2.151

Zajonc, R. B., & Markus, H. (1982). Affective and cognitive factors in preferences. *Journal of Consumer Research, 9*(2), 123–131. doi: 10.2307/2489121

Zeelenberg, M. (1999). Anticipated regret, expected feedback and behavioral decision making. *Journal of Behavioral Decision Making, 12*(2), 93–106. doi: 10.1002/(sici)1099-0771(199906)12:2<93::aid-bdm311>3.0.co;2-s

Zeelenberg, M., van Dijk, W. W., Manstead, A. S. R., & vanr de Pligt, J. (2000). On bad decisions and disconfirmed expectancies: The psychology of regret and disappointment. *Cognition & Emotion, 14*(4), 521–541. doi: 10.1080/026999300402781 10.1080/026999300402781</p>

Zevon, M. A., & Tellegen, A. (1982). The structure of mood change: An idiographic/nomothetic analysis. *Journal of Personality and Social Psychology; Journal of Personality and Social Psychology, 43*(1), 111.

Zhang, X., Fung, H., & Ching, B. H.-h. (2009). Age differences in goals: Implications for health promotion. *Aging and Mental Health, 13*(3), 336–348. doi: 10.1080/13607860802459815

5

Categories of Cultural Variations

SHARON SHAVITT AND MINKYUNG KOO ■

A global marketer is preparing to launch a marketing communications campaign across numerous countries. Should they run the same campaign across culturally or ethnically distinct customer segments, or capitalize on economies of scale by running the same campaign globally? The question at the heart of this business decision is "Do consumers who have different cultural values respond to advertising messages in similar ways?". In the last several years, culture has emerged as a central focus of research in consumer behavior. A large body of social psychological research on culture has provided a robust theoretical foundation for this work. Thus, we now have extensive research to help marketers to resolve the globalization versus localization debate and make informed decisions about attitudes and persuasion across cultures.

OUR SCOPE

Research in consumer behavior and social psychology has addressed the role of culture in multiple ways—across nations, across ethnic groups within nations, across individuals within nations (focusing on cultural orientation), and across situations through the priming of cultural values. These studies have established that regardless of how culture is studied, cultural distinctions have important implications for advertising content, persuasiveness of appeals, consumer motivation, and consumer judgment processes. The findings often emerge in parallel across these cultural operationalizations. Thus, our coverage will address national or ethnic/subcultural group differences, as well as individual differences in cultural values or intraindividual processes such as salient self-construal.

The constructs of individualism and collectivism, or independent and interdependent self-construal have in recent years received significant research attention. Along with this focus, research on thinking styles, specifically cultural differences in analytic versus holistic thinking tendencies, has also taken center stage. Our chapter reviews the implications of these cultural differences for consumer attitudes, information processing, and persuasion. Our review is necessarily selective, giving greater attention to findings in the consumer domain rather than providing a general review of cultural differences (for an excellent general review, see Wyer, Chiu & Hong, 2009). Although we do not cover some major topics relevant to cross-cultural consumer persuasion such as self-regulation and risk-taking, detailed reviews of these subjects are available elsewhere (e.g., Shavitt, Lee, & Torelli, 2009)

CATEGORIES OF CULTURAL VARIATION

There are numerous ways to conceptualize and classify cultures (Triandis & Suh, 2002). Our coverage of cross-cultural differences in message persuasiveness is informed by the growing literature on East Asian versus Western cultural contexts. Most of what we know about non-Western societies is based on research conducted in Eastern and Southern Asia (e.g., China, Korea, Japan, and India). Yet, other less explored sociocultural contexts (other geographic regions and socioeconomic contexts; e.g., nonmiddle class, see Henrich, Heine, & Norenzayan, 2010) may share similar features with non-Western and nonmiddle class social contexts. Thus, although we mainly build upon East–West comparisons, our coverage may apply to other sociocultural contexts as well.

The primary variations between cultures can be grouped into two categories: differences in values and differences in thinking styles. Differences between cultures in *individualism* versus *collectivism* values have been the primary focus of cross-cultural research (Hofstede, 1980; Triandis, 1989). This research is covered in the next section, and differences in thinking styles are addressed in a subsequent section.

National cultures that celebrate the values of independence (primarily Western societies such as the United States, Canada, Germany, and Denmark) are typically categorized as individualistic societies in which an independent self-construal is common. In these cultures, people tend to value fulfilling their personal goals and desires, and tend to subordinate the goals of their in-groups to their own goals. Most East Asian societies are generally characterized as collectivistic. In these societies, in which an interdependent self-construal is common, people value their social groups and relationships, and thus tend to subordinate their personal goals to those of their in-groups (Hofstede, 1980; Triandis, 1995).

East Asians and Westerners also differ in their thinking styles, that is, in the way they perceive, understand, and explain their social and physical environments. Westerners tend to endorse an *analytic* view that emphasizes the independence of objects (Nisbett, Peng, Choi, & Norenzayan, 2001). In contrast, Easterners tend to endorse a *holistic* view, emphasizing that the world is composed of inter-related elements. The difference in emphasis between analytic and holistic thinking means that the thought processes of Easterners and Westerners differ in a number of important respects, including: attentional processes, attributional processes, and (dis)comfort with contradictions. Next, we consider in detail the implications of these cultural differences for attitudes and persuasion.

INDIVIDUALISM VERSUS COLLECTIVISM

The fundamental differences in the values of collectivists and individualists have implications for the importance placed on social norms (Triandis, 1989), the value placed on (dis)similarity to others (Kim & Markus, 1999), and the value of choice (Savani, Markus, & Conner, 2008). The key distinction involves the extent to which one defines the self in relation to others. In individualistic cultural contexts, people tend to have an independent self-construal whereby the self is defined as autonomous and unique. In collectivistic cultural contexts, by contrast, people tend to have an interdependent self-construal whereby the self is seen as inextricably and fundamentally embedded within a larger social network of roles and relationships (Markus & Kitayama, 1991).

A large body of research in psychology has demonstrated the many implications of individualism/collectivism and independent/interdependent self-construals for social perception and social behavior (see Markus & Kitayama, 1991; Triandis, 1995). These findings indicate consistently that individualists and people with an independent self-construal are oriented toward products and experiences that promote achievement and autonomy, offer personal benefits, and enable expression of one's distinctive qualities. On the other hand, collectivists and people with an interdependent self-construal are oriented toward products and experiences that allow one to avoid negative outcomes, maintain harmony and strong social connections with others, and dutifully fulfill social roles. Advertising messages (such as magazine advertisements and TV commercials) from Western cultures are in general more individualistic and less collectivistic than advertising from Asian cultures (Han & Shavitt, 1994; Morling & Lamoreaux, 2008), and consumers from Western cultures are more likely to be persuaded by individualistic advertisements whereas those from East Asian cultures are more likely to be persuaded by collectivistic advertisements (Han & Shavitt, 1994).

Although a given self-construal can be more chronically accessible in a particular culture, cultures generally provide sufficient experiences with independent and interdependent views of the self to allow either self-construal to be primed (see Oyserman & Lee, 2007; Oyserman, Coon, & Kemmelmeier, 2002). Numerous studies have established that these activated self-views impact judgments in ways that parallel cross-national differences (see Shavitt, Lee, & Torelli, 2009, for a review), for instance, by activating distinct self-goals (Lalwani & Shavitt, 2009).

People can generally switch between independent and interdependent cultural frames in response to their contexts. This is especially the case for bicultural people (Fu, Chiu, Morris, & Young, 2007), who can switch back and forth very readily. Thus, Lau-Gesk (2003) found that independent (interdependent) self-construals were temporarily activated when bicultural consumers were exposed to individually-focused (interpersonally-focused) appeals.

Refined individualism versus collectivism

The conceptualizations of individualism and collectivism, and independence/ interdependence, have been construed in broad and multidimensional ways, summarizing a host of differences in self-definitions, motivations, and emotional connections to in-groups, as well as belief systems and behavioral patterns (see Hofstede, 1980; Oyserman et al., 2002). Thus, there have recently been calls for more nuanced cultural distinctions, together with work that has offered useful refinements to these broader cultural categories (e.g., Brewer & Chen, 2007). Although the breadth of the individualism–collectivism constructs lends integrative strengths, further refinements of these categories can enhance the prediction of consumer behavior.

THE HORIZONTAL/VERTICAL DISTINCTION

Within the individualism–collectivism framework, Triandis and his colleagues (e.g., Triandis, 1995; Triandis & Gelfand, 1998) have recently introduced a further distinction between societies that are *horizontal* (valuing equality) and those that are *vertical* (emphasizing hierarchy), and a scale to measure these orientations at the individual level. The horizontal/vertical distinction emerges from the observation that American or British individualism differs from, say, Norwegian or Danish individualism in much the same way that Japanese or Korean collectivism differs from the collectivism of the Israeli kibbutz.

In vertical individualist (VI) societies (e.g., United States, Great Britain, France), people tend to be concerned with improving their individual status and with distinguishing themselves from others via competition. In contrast, in horizontal individualist (HI) societies (e.g., Sweden, Denmark, Australia), people tend to view themselves as equal to others in status, and the focus is on expressing one's uniqueness and self-reliance. In vertical collectivist (VC) societies (e.g., East Asia, India, Eastern Europe), people focus on complying with authorities and on enhancing the cohesion and status of their in-groups, even when that entails sacrificing their own personal goals. In horizontal collectivist (HC) societies (exemplified historically by the Israeli kibbutz), the focus is on sociability and interdependence with others in an egalitarian context.

Thus, although individualist societies all share a focus on self-reliance, independence, and hedonism, Scandinavians and Australians (HI) show aversion to conspicuously successful persons and to braggarts, emphasizing instead the virtues of modesty (e.g., Askgaard, 1992; Daun, 1991; Daun, 1992; Feather, 1994; Nelson & Shavitt, 2002; Triandis & Gelfand, 1998). In contrast, people in the United States (VI) have been shown to aspire to distinction, achievement, success, and being or having "the best" (e.g., Markus & Kitayama, 1991;

Triandis & Gelfand, 1998; Weldon, 1984). In fact, in the United States, "success is communicated, shared and displayed because it is natural to show off" (de Mooij, 1998, p. 195)

Similarly, although collectivists share an interdependent worldview, Koreans and other East Asians (VC) emphasize deference to authority, filial piety, and preservation of harmony in the context of hierarchical relations with others. Indeed, the status of one's family or other in-groups establishes one's individual social standing in VC cultures. In contrast, in the Israeli kibbutz (HC), the emphasis is neither on harmony nor status. Instead, honesty, directness, and cooperation are valued, within a framework of assumed equality (Gannon, 2001; Triandis & Gelfand, 1998).

However, the modal comparisons in studies of persuasion and consumer behavior are between the United States (VI) and one or more East Asian countries (VC). This means that much of what is known about consumer behavior in individualistic and collectivistic societies reflects vertical forms of these syndromes and may not generalize, for example, to comparisons between Sweden (HI) and Israel (HC) or other sets of relatively horizontal cultures. As an example, the emphasis on conformity in advertising messages, as examined by Kim and Markus (1999), may be a tendency specific to VC cultures, in which deference to authority and to in-group wishes is stressed. Much less emphasis on conformity may be observed in HC cultures, which emphasize sociability but not deference (Triandis & Gelfand, 1998). Thus, differences in advertising appeals observed between Korea (VC) and the United States (VI) may not generalize to comparisons of HC versus HI cultural contexts.

Several recent studies of this horizontal/vertical cultural distinction have provided evidence for its value as a predictor of new consumer psychology phenomena and as a basis for refining the understanding of known phenomena (for reviews, see Shavitt, Lalwani, Zhang, & Torelli, 2006; Shavitt, Torelli, & Wong, 2009). For instance, Lalwani, Shavitt, and Johnson (2006) showed that differences in the self-presentational responses observed for individualists and collectivists are mediated at the individual level by the horizontal but not the vertical versions of these cultural orientations. Overall, people in individualistic contexts (e.g., the United States) compared to collectivistic contexts (e.g., Singapore) engage in more self-deceptive enhancement, and engage less in impression management (Paulhus, 1991). Moreover, these links between self-presentational efforts and cultural context are observed at the ethnic group level, as well (e.g., comparing European Americans and Asian Americans).

However, these broad relationships are mediated specifically by HI and HC orientations, respectively. This suggests that culturally linked self-presentational efforts reflect distinct goals of being seen as self-reliant and capable (valued in HI contexts) versus sociable and benevolent (valued in HC contexts).

Further evidence for the value of the horizontal–vertical distinction comes from a study of country-of-origin effects. Gürhan-Canli and Maheswaran (2000) demonstrated that the tendency to favor products from one's own country over foreign products emerged more strongly in Japan (a VC culture) than in the United States (a VI culture). Mediation analyses using individual consumers' self-rated cultural values further indicated that only the vertical aspect of individualism and collectivism accounted for the country-of-origin effects in Japan. In other words, the collectivistic tendency to favor one's own country's products appeared to be driven by cultural values that stress hierarchy, competition, and deference to in-group wishes, not by values that stress interdependence more generally.

In line with this, research suggests that mental representations of power in terms of status and competition (personalized power) versus benevolence and helpfulness (socialized power) differ reliably between vertical and horizontal cultural backgrounds and orientations. Torelli and Shavitt (2010) showed that this cultural patterning of power concepts can be observed both at the individual and at cultural group levels. For instance, a VI orientation predicted liking for brands that symbolize personalized power values of status and prestige, whereas an HC orientation predicted liking for brands that embody concerns for the welfare of others. Moreover, these relations emerged across cultural groups. Brazilians, who scored relatively highly on an HC orientation (compared to European Americans, Canadians, East Asians, Norwegians, and Turks), liked brands that symbolize prosocial values better than did the other cultural groups. Norwegians, who scored relatively low in VI orientation, liked brands that symbolize personalized power values less than did all the other groups. A multilevel analysis further indicated that people's VI and HC cultural orientations partially mediated group-level differences in liking for such brands (Torelli & Shavitt, 2010, Study 3). In short, a growing body of work highlights the notion that drawing finer distinctions within individualistic and collectivistic value categories can significantly enhance the understanding of consumer attitudes and behavior. Next, we examine a fundamental cultural distinction in styles of thinking.

CULTURE AND ANALYTIC VERSUS HOLISTIC THINKING STYLES

In comparison to work addressing differences in individualism–collectivism, relatively little research has been done on cross-cultural differences in consumers' thinking orientations. This section provides a general review of cultural differences in thinking styles in addition to the findings of relevant studies of consumer behavior and advertising effects.

Broadly speaking, Westerners tend to adopt an analytic thinking style that emphasizes the independence of individual objects, whereas East Asians tend to adopt a holistic view emphasizing that the world is composed of interrelated elements (Nisbett et al., 2001). The analytic style of Westerners and the holistic style of East Asians have been demonstrated in various cognitive domains such as attention, causal reasoning, perception of change, tolerance of contradiction, and categorization.

The analytic style of attention is field independent—mainly oriented toward an object itself. In contrast, the holistic style of attention is field dependent—focused on the relationship between objects and/or the field in which they are embedded (see Nisbett et al., 2001, for a review).

Holistic thinking implies that objects cannot be understood apart from their whole, which makes it difficult to evaluate them independent of their context. Research shows that Westerners tend to "separate and distinguish" among objects or between objects and their contexts (Oyserman & Lee, 2007). In contrast, East Asians' holistic style of attention is more context-oriented (Ji, Peng, & Nisbett, 2000) and they tend to "integrate and connect" objects in their environment (Oyserman & Lee, 2007). For example, when asked to recall a visual scene, the memory of East Asians for focal objects in that scene was impacted by changes in the background. In contrast, the memory of Westerners for focal objects was independent of the background (Masuda & Nisbett, 2001).

This difference in the orientation of attention is also seen in the way East Asians and Westerners perceive and explain social events. East Asians tend to assume that each element in the world is somehow intertwined with others, and thus an event or object can be understood only in the context of the whole set of relevant factors. By contrast, Westerners tend to explain events in terms of direct causal links, thereby considering fewer reasons than East Asians, who tend to consider a broader set of reasons, regardless of their relevance to the event (Choi, Dalal, Chu Kim-Prieto, & Park, 2003).

Furthermore, in explaining causality of a social event, analytic thinkers tend to focus on the internal dispositions of an actor whereas holistic thinkers tend to consider a broader set of reasons (including both dispositional and contextual information) and are therefore less likely to attribute an outcome to an actor's internal characteristics (see Nisbett et al., 2001, for a review). This has implications for the effect of messages on brand judgments, as well. Monga and John (2008) found that negative publicity influences analytic (versus holistic) thinkers more heavily and thus changes their beliefs about a brand to a greater degree because analytic thinkers are less likely to consider contextual information, and thus are more likely to attribute negative product information to the brand.

Westerners are more accustomed to formulating rules that govern internal properties of objects and tend to categorize things by applying those rules. In contrast, East Asians organize objects on the basis of their relationship to other objects or to the field (see Nisbett, 2003, for a review), and therefore they tend to categorize objects according to their overall similarities. Thus, when presented with pictures of a cow, a chicken, and grass, East Asians tend to categorize the cow and grass together based on the relationship between the two (the cow eats the grass) whereas Westerners tend to categorize the cow and the chicken into one group based on the traits that characterize them (Ji, Zhang, & Nisbett, 2004).

These cultural differences in the way people categorize objects (rule/trait based versus similarity/relationship based) have implications for the way they organize and store brand information. For example, Ng and Houston (2006) showed that Americans are less likely to retrieve brand exemplars (i.e., specific

products or subcategories) than brand beliefs (i.e., general descriptive or evaluative thoughts), whereas the reverse was the case for Singaporeans. These results
emerged from an analytic tendency to focus on "global beliefs" abstracted from
prior product experiences and a holistic tendency to focus on contextual and
incidental details about the product.

This suggests that East Asians' brand evaluations should be more dependent
on contextual inputs. Their attitudes toward products, for example, may be
formed not only on the basis of attributes, but also based on salient contexts (e.g.,
where the product comes from, where it can be used). In line with this, research
shows that cultural orientation influences the extent to which contextual factors
impact judgments. For example, Jain, Desai, and Mao (2007, study 3), showed
that participants with an interdependent self-construal judged the fat content of
snacks differently when they were placed in a taxonomic versus goal-driven setting; those with an independent self-construal judged the fat content similarly
regardless of the snacks' placement. Consistent with this, Gürhan-Canli and
Maheswaran (2000) showed that the country of origin of a brand affected East
Asians' versus Westerners' brand preferences to a greater degree.

Furthermore, differences between East Asians and Westerners in holistic versus analytic thinking suggest that they are likely not only to evaluate objects
differently but also to perceive targets differently. Westerners tend to perceive
objects as separate from the context. East Asians tend to perceive objects as
embedded in a context—in other words, the objects themselves change with
the context. In line with this notion, Zhu and Meyers-Levy (2009) showed that
holistic thinkers are more likely to view a product and the table on which it is
displayed as continuous parts of a larger whole, whereas analytic thinkers view
the product and display table as separate pieces of data. Thus, as compared to
Westerners, East Asians may be less likely to evaluate objects in a decontextualized manner and to maintain attitudes that apply across contexts. A product
itself may be perceived differently when displayed on different tables.

Related to this point, Monga and John (2007) found that, compared to
Americans, Indians tend to perceive a higher degree of fit between a parent brand
(e.g., Kodak) and its brand extension (e.g., Kodak filing cabinet, Kodak greeting
cards), and to evaluate the brand extension more positively. This result reflects
Indians' holistic tendency to base their judgments more heavily on the relationships between brand extensions and parent brands than do their American
counterparts. Because holistic (versus analytic) thinkers are better able to think
of alternative ways to relate the extension to the parent brand (see Ahluwalia,
2008), they perceive them to fit better and, hence, evaluate them more favorably.
However, this difference was not found for prestige brands (e.g., Rolex), which
have abstract and elastic brand concepts that may facilitate a broader set of associations for both holistic and analytic thinkers (Monga & John, 2010).

A core finding in the marketing literature is the robust tendency to judge
quality based on price (Rao & Monroe, 1988; Rao & Monroe, 1989). However,
because holistic versus analytic thinking styles are associated with differences
in the ability to identify relationships, Lalwani and Shavitt (2013) reasoned that

thinking styles may also predict the strength of the perceived price-quality relation. Indeed, their findings demonstrated that a cultural self-construal of interdependence (versus independence) is associated with a greater tendency to use
price to judge quality and, importantly, that this effect is mediated by holistic
thinking. Differences in a variety of price–quality judgments emerged between
national groups (United States and Indian consumers), ethnic groups (European
Americans compared to East Asians and Hispanics, both of whom tend to think
holistically), and people primed with either independent or interdependent
self-construals.

However, this thinking-style effect was moderated by the breadth of associations that tend to come to mind in the context. When a broader set of associations
was brought to mind, such as when judging symbolic and prestige products that
foster abstract associations and multiple connections with quality (e.g., Schlosser
and Shavitt, 2002; Shavitt, 1990, 1992), both analytic and holistic thinkers made
strong price–quality judgments.

From the analytic perspective, because objects exist independently, the
essence of objects is stable over time. This assumption promotes a linear perception of change in which no drastic deviation is expected in the pattern of
stability or change of a phenomenon (see Nisbett, 2003, for a review). By contrast, as described earlier, the holistic view of the world assumes that objects
are interrelated. Therefore, it is less likely that a phenomenon will remain stable
over time. This perspective results in a cyclic perception in which people tend to
predict fluctuating trends for an event. For example, in predicting future stock
market trends and making investment decisions, Canadians are more likely to
make judgments based on recent trends than are Chinese people; thus, when
compared to the Chinese, Canadians are more willing to buy stocks when they
are in an increasing trend and less willing to buy when stock prices are decreas-
ing (Ji, Zhang, & Guo, 2008).

The cyclic perception of change and expectation of instability prevalent among
East Asians renders a Yin–Yang belief that a characteristic of an object can
potentially transform into its opposite. Consequently, East Asians tend to hold
a dialectical perception in which apparently opposing concepts can simultaneously be true and can peacefully coexist (see Nisbett et al., 2001, for a review).
When confronted with opposing propositions, East Asians tend to resolve contradictions by choosing a middle ground, whereas Westerners to rely on formal
logic in resolving contradictions by choosing one of the opposing propositions.
For example, US consumers tend to resolve incongruities with an attenuation
strategy in which one piece of information is favored over another, inconsistent
piece of information. In contrast, Hong Kong Chinese consumers tend to follow
an additive strategy in which both pieces of information are combined to influence judgments (Aaker & Sengupta, 2000).

East Asians and Westerners also perceive conflicting emotions in different ways. For example, Bagozzi, Wong, and Yi (1999) showed that Chinese
tend to hold a dialectical perception that pleasant and unpleasant emotions
can be experienced at the same time. Thus, their frequency judgment for

pleasant emotions is positively correlated with their frequency judgment for unpleasant emotions. By contrast, this study found that for Americans, the perceived frequency of pleasant emotions is inversely correlated with the perceived frequency of unpleasant emotions. Schimmack, Oishi, and Diener (2002) analyzed thirty-eight nationalities and demonstrated that this cultural difference results from dialectical thinking, not from a difference in individualistic–collectivistic values. Moreover, Williams and Aaker (2002) demonstrated that opposing emotions (e.g., both happiness and sadness) in persuasion appeals elicit more positive attitudes among Asian Americans than among European Americans.

A variety of methods and techniques have been developed to measure cultural differences in thinking styles (e.g., Choi, Koo, & Choi, 2007; Ji et al., 2004; Monga & John, 2008), including responses to cognitive tasks, scenarios and questions, physiological measures, a scale, and analyses of various cultural products. Furthermore, priming an independent versus interdependent view of self has also been found to promote analytic and holistic modes of thinking, respectively. For example, people primed with an independent self-view were more likely to focus on a focal object and thus were better at finding an embedded figure by separating a figure from its background than were those primed with an interdependent self-view (see Oyserman & Lee, 2007, for a review).

As noted earlier, research is only beginning to address the implications of thinking styles for product attitudes, yet the data so far suggest that thinking styles have fundamental implications for understanding some of the most important phenomena in marketing, such as price–quality perceptions (Lalwani and & Shavitt, 2013) and evaluations of brand extensions (Monga & John, 2007; Monga & John, 2010).

CULTURE AND THE CONTENT AND PERSUASIVENESS OF APPEALS

Most research on cultural influences on judgment and persuasion has examined the implications of individualism/collectivism or independent/interdependent self-construals. In general, the findings suggest that the prevalence or the persuasiveness of a given type of appeal matches the cultural value orientation of the society. For instance, appeals to individuality, personal benefits, and achievement are usually more prevalent and persuasive in individualistic compared to collectivistic cultures, whereas appeals to group benefits, harmony, and conformity are usually more prevalent and persuasive in collectivistic compared to individualistic cultures. Such evidence for "cultural matching" in the nature of appeals has been followed by studies examining the distinct psychological processes driving persuasion across cultures. These studies suggest that culture can affect how people process and interpret product-related information. It can determine the type of information that is weighed more heavily for making judgments (e.g., product attributes versus other consumers' opinions). However, brand and product characteristics can constrain the role of cultural variables in information processing and persuasion, with some brands and products serving as stronger carriers of cultural values (see Shavitt, Lee, & Torelli, 2009, for a review).

CULTURAL DIFFERENCES IN THE CONTENT OF MESSAGE APPEALS

Cross-cultural content analyses of advertisements can reflect and yield evidence about cultural value profiles. For instance, American advertisers and consumer researchers often assume that consumer learning about the brand precedes other marketing effects, such as liking and buying the brand. Thus, advertisements that attempt to teach the consumer about the brand are typical in the United States, although other types of advertisements are also used.

In contrast, as Miracle (1987) suggested, the typical goal of advertisements in Japan appears very different. There, advertisements tend to focus on "making friends" with the audience and showing that the company understands their feelings. The assumption is that consumers will buy once they feel familiar with and have a sense of trust in the company. Because Japan, Korea, and other Pacific Rim countries are collectivist cultures that tend toward implicit and indirect communication practices (Triandis, 1995), Miracle suggested that the mood and tone of commercials in these countries will be particularly important in establishing good feelings about the advertiser. Several studies have supported these notions, showing that advertisements in Japan and Korea, compared to those in the United States, rely more on symbolism, mood, and aesthetics and less on direct approaches such as brand comparisons. The advertisements may be equally informative about the brand across cultures. It is the type of appeal that will vary.

For instance, a content analysis of magazine advertisements revealed that in Korea, compared to the United States, advertisements are more focused on family well-being, interdependence, group goals, and harmony, whereas they are less focused on self-improvement, ambition, personal goals, independence, and individuality (Han & Shavitt, 1994). However, as one might expect, the nature of the advertised product moderated these effects. Cultural differences emerged strongly only for products that tend to be purchased and used along with other persons (e.g., groceries, cars). Products that do not tend to be shared (e.g., health and beauty aids, clothing) are promoted more in terms of personal, individualistic benefits in both countries.

A content analysis by Kim and Markus (1999) reviewed earlier indicated that Korean advertisements, compared to United States advertisements, were characterized by more conformity themes (e.g., respect for collective values and beliefs) and fewer uniqueness themes (e.g., rebelling against collective values and beliefs). Website content in Eastern and Western countries also appears to differ in the emphasis on individual versus collective activities (see Shavitt, Lee, & Torelli, 2009, for a review).

Differences in advertising content have also been observed as a function of the horizontal or vertical cultural orientation of a country. Specifically, a large-scale content analyses of magazine advertisements in five countries suggested that the degree of emphasis on status in advertising appeals—including depictions of luxury, or references to prestige, impressing others, prominence, membership in high status groups (e.g., ivy league graduates), endorsements by high status persons (e.g., celebrities), or other distinctions (e.g., "award-winning")—corresponded to the cultural profile of the society (Shavitt et al., 2011). Advertisements in three societies presumed to have a primarily VC cultural profile (Korea, Russia, and Poland) and one society presumed to have a primarily VI cultural profile (the United States) evidenced a greater emphasis on status benefits than did advertisements in a society presumed to have a primarily HI cultural profile (Denmark). These advertising differences were observed regardless of the type of magazine examined, comprising major business, women's, news, and entertainment titles in each country. Indeed, status appeared to be a dominant advertising theme in all of the vertical societies examined (relative to appeals that emphasized pleasure, uniqueness, or relationships). In contrast, pleasure appeals dominated in the HI society.

Also as expected, Shavitt et al. (2011) reported that the emphasis on uniqueness in advertising appeals—including depictions of differentiation, self-expression, self-reliance, and novelty—was greater in HI versus VI (and VC) cultures. These types of appeals frame the product as a form of self-expression, appropriate in cultural contexts that emphasize being distinct and self-reliant (rather than better than others). Thus, although the United States and Denmark are both considered individualistic societies, their analyzed advertisements differed significantly in the emphasis on uniqueness and on status in ways that were consistent with their vertical versus horizontal cultural values. These patterns would not have been anticipated by analyses based on the broader individualism–collectivism classification.

A consideration of vertical and horizontal cultural values also offers refinements to predictions about the kinds of appeals that distinguish individualistic and collectivistic cultures. For instance, Kim and Markus's (1999) research, reviewed earlier, suggests that United States appeals are more focused on being unique than are Korean appeals. However, uniqueness was defined broadly in that research, incorporating themes of choice and freedom. In contrast, Shavitt et al.'s (2011) analysis suggested that appeals that more specifically emphasize uniqueness and self-expression (e.g., being different, not better than others) may be especially relevant to an HI cultural context. Indeed, advertisements in VI versus VC societies did not differ in their focus on those specific uniqueness themes.

Finally, one caveat worth noting is that, in countries experiencing rapid economic growth, advertising content does not necessarily reflect existing cultural values. Instead, advertisements in such societies sometimes promote new, aspirational values such as individuality and modernity. For example, Westernized advertising appeals have become increasingly common in China in recent years. Appeals to youth/modernity, individuality/independence, and technology are especially salient in Chinese advertisements that target the younger generation living and working in urban multicultural environments (Zhang & Shavitt, 2003), even though advertisements pitched to the broader society may reflect more traditional values. Similarly, during a period of rapid transition in South Korea's economy (1968–1998), content analysis of advertisements in that country revealed substantial shifts toward individualistic, modernity-oriented appeals (Han & Shavitt, 2005).

CULTURAL DIFFERENCES IN JUDGMENT AND PERSUASION

Research suggests that the persuasiveness of appeals may mirror the cultural differences in their prevalence. An experiment by Han and Shavitt (1994) showed that appeals to individualistic values (e.g., "Solo cleans with a softness that you will love") were more persuasive in the United States and appeals to collectivistic values (e.g., "Solo cleans with a softness that your family will love") were more persuasive in Korea. Again, however, this effect was much more evident for products that are shared (laundry detergent, clothes iron) than for those that are not (chewing gum, running shoes).

Zhang and Gelb (1996) found a similar pattern in the persuasiveness of individualistic versus collectivistic appeals in an experiment conducted in the United States and China. Moreover, this effect appeared to be moderated by whether the advertised product is socially visible (camera) versus privately used (toothbrush). Finally, Wang and Mowen (1997) showed in a United States sample that individual differences in separateness/connectedness self-schema (i.e., the degree to which one views the self as independent of or interconnected with important others) predicts attitudes toward individualistic versus collectivistic advertising appeals for a credit card. Thus, cultural orientation as well as national culture has implications for the effectiveness of appeals. However, such cultural differences would only be anticipated for those products or uses that are relevant to both personal and group goals.

Cultural differences in persuasion are also revealed in the diagnosticity of certain types of information. For instance, the importance of social norms and similarity to others in East Asian contexts suggests that norms and others' preferences are heavily weighted in their attitude formation. Furthermore, for Easterners these factors are considered central, and as such are used in attitude formation under high motivation conditions (as opposed to only under low-motivation conditions in Westerners). Indeed, consensus information influences Easterners' brand evaluations regardless of their motivation (Aaker & Maheswaran, 1997), as opposed to Westerners, who consider consensus information primarily under low-motivation conditions (Maheswaran & Chaiken, 1991). Specifically, Aaker and Maheswaran (1997) showed that consensus information regarding other consumers' opinions is not treated as a heuristic cue by Hong Kong Chinese (as it is in the United States) but is instead perceived and processed as diagnostic information. Thus, collectivists resolve incongruity between these types of inputs in favor of consensus information, not brand attributes. This would be expected in a culture that stresses conformity and responsiveness to others' views. On the other hand, cues whose (low) diagnosticity is not expected to vary cross-culturally (e.g., number of attributes presented) elicited similar heuristic processing in the United States and Hong Kong.

Finally, as noted earlier, cognitive representations of power vary with horizontal and vertical cultural orientations and with ethnicity (Torelli & Shavitt, 2010) and it appears that these distinctions link to differences in information processing and persuasion. Torelli and Shavitt (2011) showed that cueing with power leads people of different cultural orientations to activate distinct mindsets when processing brand stimuli, even when those stimuli are not power-relevant. When personalized power is primed, people whose cultural orientation predisposes a status-oriented view of power (i.e., high VI people) activate cognitive processes that facilitate defending their power, such as reasserting control by confirming prior stereotypes about a brand (Fiske, 1993). Thus, these consumers focused more on brand information congruent with their expectations. For instance, they were better able to recall information congruent with their existing view of McDonald's. In contrast, when socialized power was primed, people whose cultural orientation predisposes a benevolence-oriented view of power (high HC people) activate cognitive processes that facilitate helping others, such as by forming accurate, careful impressions of brands (Goodwin, Gubin, Fiske, & Yzerbyt, 2000). Thus, these consumers showed improved recall of information incongruent with their expectations of McDonald's. These findings signal that the information processing consequences of powerful feelings depend on culturally specific power concepts.

CONCLUSIONS

As marketing efforts are increasingly globalized, understanding cross-cultural consumer behavior has become a key focus of consumer research. In recent years, research in consumer behavior has enhanced understanding of the relations between culture and consumer motivations, thinking styles, and persuasion. Research has also begun to address the psychological mechanisms underlying cross-cultural differences in consumer judgments, and the products and contexts for which these differences are most likely to be observed. These efforts are crucial for effective global marketing and advertising, and for identifying situations for which globalized versus localized communications efforts are required. In future research, it will be important to further distinguish cultural similarities and differences in consumer judgments, identify within-culture or subgroup differences that parallel between-culture differences, and explore their rich implications in consumer behavior.

ACKNOWLEDGMENTS

Preparation of this chapter was supported by Grant #1R01HD053636-01A1 from the National Institutes of Health, Grant #0648539 from the National Science Foundation, Grant #63842 from the Robert Wood Johnson Foundation, and Grant #2009456 from the United States–Israel Binational Science Foundation to Sharon Shavitt.

REFERENCES

Aaker, J. L., & Maheswaran, D. (1997). The effect of cultural orientation on persuasion. *Journal of Consumer Research*, *24*(3), 315–328.

Aaker, J. L., & Sengupta, J. (2000). Additivity versus attenuation: The role of culture in the resolution of information incongruity. *Journal of Consumer Psychology (Lawrence Erlbaum Associates)*, *9*(2), 67–82.

Ahluwalia, R. (2008). How far can a brand stretch? Understanding the role of self-construal. *Journal of Marketing Research*, *45*(3), 337–350.

Askgaard, H. (1992). As Denmark sees herself and is seen by others. *Discover Denmark--On Denmark and the Danes: Past, present and future* (P. Himmelstrup, K. Hegelund; H. Askgaard ed., pp. 7–26). Herning, Denmark: Danish Cultural Institute, Copenhagen and Systime Publishers.

Bagozzi, R. P., Wong, N., & Yi, Y. (1999). The role of culture and gender in the relationship between positive and negative Affect. *Cognition & Emotion*, *13*(6), 641–672.

Brewer, M. B., & Chen, Y. (2007). Where (Who) are collectives in collectivism? Toward conceptual clarification of individualism and collectivism. *Psychological Review*, *114*(1), 133–151.

Choi, I., Dalal, R., Chu Kim-Prieto, & Park, H. (2003). Culture and judgment of causal relevance. *Journal of Personality & Social Psychology*, *84*(1), 46–59.

Choi, I., Koo, M., & Choi, J. A. (2007). Individual differences in analytic Versus holistic thinking. *Personality and Social Psychology Bulletin*, *33*(5), 691–705.

Daun, A. (1991). Individualism and collectivity among Swedes. *Ethnos*, *56*(3-4), 165–172.

Daun, A. (1992). Modern and modest: Mentality and self-stereotypes among Swedes. *Culture and management* (Sjoegren, A.; Janson, L. ed., pp. 101–111). Stockholm, Sweden: Institution for International Business.

de Mooij, M. K. (1998). *Global marketing and advertising: Understanding cultural paradoxes*. CA, USA: Sage Publications, Inc.

Feather, N. T. (1994). Attitudes toward high achievers and reaction to their fall: Theory and research concerning tall poppies. *Advances in experimental social psychology, Vol. 26* (pp. 1–73). San Diego, CA, USA: Academic Press, San Diego, CA.

Fiske, S. T. (1993). Controlling other people: The impact of power on stereotyping. *American Psychologist, 48*(6), 621–628.

Fu, J. H., Chiu, C., Morris, M. W., & Young, M. J. (2007). Spontaneous inferences from cultural cues: Varying responses of cultural insiders and outsiders. *Journal of Cross-Cultural Psychology, 38*(1), 58–75.

Gannon, M. J. (2001). *Understanding global cultures: Metaphorical journeys through 23 nations* (Second ed.). Thousand Oaks, CA: Sage Publications.

Goodwin, S. A., Gubin, A., Fiske, S. T., & Yzerbyt, V. Y. (2000). Power can bias impression processes: Stereotyping subordinates by default and by design. *Group Processes & Intergroup Relations, 3*(3), 227–256.

Gürhan-Canli, Z., & Maheswaran, D. (2000). Cultural variations in country of origin effects. *Journal of Marketing Research, 37*(3), 309–317.

Han, S., & Shavitt, S. (2005). Westernization of cultural values in Korean advertising: A longitudinal content analysis of magazine ads from 1968-1998. *Advances in Consumer Research, 32*(1), 249–250.

Han, S., & Shavitt, S. (1994). Persuasion and culture: advertising appeals in individualistic and collectivistic societies. *Journal of Experimental Social Psychology, 30*(4), 326–350.

Henrich, J., Heine, S. J., & Norenzayan, A. (2010). The weirdest people in the world? *Behavioral and Brain Sciences, 33*(2-3), 61–135.

Hofstede, G. H. (1980). *Culture's consequences, international differences in work-related values.* Sage Publications.

Jain, S. P., Desai, K. K., & Mao, H. (2007). The influence of chronic and situational self-construal on categorization. *Journal of Consumer Research, 34*(1), 66–76.

Ji, L. J., Zhang, Z., & Guo, T. (2008). To buy or to sell: cultural differences in stock market decisions based on price trends. *Journal of Behavioral Decision Making, 21*(4), 399–413.

Ji, L. J., Zhang, Z., & Nisbett, R. E. (2004). Is it culture or is it language? Examination of language effects in cross-cultural research on categorization. *Journal of Personality & Social Psychology, 87*(1), 57–65.

Ji, L. J., Peng, K., & Nisbett, R. E. (2000). Culture, control, and perception of relationships in the environment. *Journal of Personality and Social Psychology, 78*(5), 943–955.

Kim, H., & Markus, H. R. (1999). Deviance or uniqueness, harmony or conformity? A cultural analysis. *Journal of Personality & Social Psychology, 77*(4), 785–800.

Lalwani, A. K., & Shavitt, S. (2009). The "me" I claim to be: Cultural self-construal elicits self-presentational goal pursuit. *Journal of Personality & Social Psychology, 97*(1), 88–102.

Lalwani, A. K., & Shavitt, S. (2013). You get what you pay for?: Self-construal influences price-quality judgments, *Journal of Consumer Research, 40*(2), 255–267.

Lalwani, A. K., Shavitt, S., & Johnson, T. (2006). What is the relation between cultural orientation and socially desirable responding? *Journal of Personality & Social Psychology, 90*(1), 165–178.

Lau-Gesk, L. (2003). Activating culture through persuasion appeals: An examination of the bicultural consumer. *Journal of Consumer Psychology, 13*(3), 301.

Maheswaran, D., & Chaiken, S. (1991). Promoting systematic processing in low-motivation settings: Effect of incongruent information on processing and judgment. *Journal of Personality and Social Psychology, 61*(1), 13–25.

Markus, H. R., & Kitayama, S. (1991). Culture and the self: Implications for cognition, emotion, and motivation. *Psychological Review, 98*(2), 224–253.

Masuda, T., & Nisbett, R. E. (2001). Attending holistically versus analytically: Comparing the context sensitivity of Japanese and Americans. *Journal of Personality and Social Psychology, 81*(5), 922–934.

Miracle, G. E. (1987). Feel-Do-Learn: An alternative sequence underlying Japanese consumer response to television commercials. *Proceedings of the L.A. Conference of the American Academy of Advertising* (F. G. Feasley ed.). Columbia, S.C.: The University of South Carolina.

Monga, A. B., & John, D. R. (2008). When does negative brand publicity hurt? The moderating influence of analytic versus holistic thinking. *Journal of Consumer Psychology, 18*(4), 320–332.

Monga, A. B., & John, D. R. (2007). Cultural differences in brand extension evaluation: The influence of analytic versus holistic thinking. *Journal of Consumer Research, 33*(4), 529–536.

Monga, A. B., & John, D. R. (2010). What makes brands elastic? The influence of brand concept and styles of thinking on brand extension evaluation. *Journal of Marketing, 74*(3), 80–92.

Morling, B., & Lamoreaux, M. (2008). Measuring culture outside the head: A meta-analysis of individualism-collectivism in cultural products. *Personality & Social Psychology Review (Sage Publications Inc.), 12*(3), 199–221.

Nelson, M. R., & Shavitt, S. (2002). Horizontal and vertical individualism and achievement values: A multi-method examination of Denmark and the U.S. *Journal of Cross-Cultural Psychology, 33*(5), 439–458.

Ng, S., & Houston, M. J. (2006). Exemplars or beliefs? The impact of self-view on the nature and relative influence of brand associations. *Journal of Consumer Research, 32*(4), 519–529.

Nisbett, R. E. (2003). *The geography of thought: How Asians and Westerners think differently. . . and why.* New York, NY, USA: Free Press, New York, NY.

Nisbett, R. E., Peng, K., Choi, I., & Norenzayan, A. (2001). Culture and systems of thought: Holistic versus analytic cognition. *Psychological Review, 108*(2), 291–310.

Oyserman, D., Coon, H. M., & Kemmelmeier, M. (2002). Rethinking individualism and collectivism: Evaluation of theoretical assumptions and meta-analyses. *Psychological Bulletin, 128*(1), 3–72.

Oyserman, D., & Lee, S. W. S. (2007). Priming 'culture': Culture as situated cognition. *Handbook of cultural psychology* (Kitayama, Shinob; Cohen, Dov ed., pp. 255–282). New York: Guilford Press.

Paulhus, D. L. (1991). Measurement and Control of Response Bias. *Measures of personality and social psychological attitudes* (Robinson, John P.; Shaver, Phillip R.; Wrightsman, Lawrence S. ed., pp. 17–59). San Diego, CA: Academic Press.

Rao, A. R., & Monroe, K. B. (1988). The moderating effect of prior knowledge on cue utilization in product evaluations. *Journal of Consumer Research, 15*(2), 253–264.

Rao, A. R., & Monroe, K. B. (1989). The effect of price, brand name, and store name on buyers' perceptions of product quality: An integrative review. *Journal of Marketing Research*, 26(3), 351–357.

Savani, K., Markus, H. R., & Conner, A. L. (2008). Let Your Preference be your guide? Preferences and choices are more tightly linked for North Americans than for Indians. *Journal of Personality & Social Psychology*, 95(4), 861–876.

Schimmack, U., Oishi, S., & Diener, E. (2002). Cultural influences on the relation between pleasant emotions and unpleasant emotions: Asian dialectic philosophies or individualism-collectivism? *Cognition and Emotion*, 16(6), 705–719.

Schlosser, A. E., & Shavitt, S. (2002). Anticipating discussion about a product: Rehearsing what to say can affect your judgments. *Journal of Consumer Research*, 29(1), 101–115.

Shavitt, S. (1990). The role of attitude objects in attitude functions. *Journal of Experimental Social Psychology*, 26(2), 124–148.

Shavitt, S. (1992), "Evidence for predicting the effectiveness of value-expressive versus utilitarian appeals: A reply to Johar and Sirgy", *Journal of Advertising*, 21(2), 47–51.

Shavitt, S., Johnson, T. P., & Zhang, J. (2011). Horizontal and vertical cultural differences in the content of advertising appeals. *Journal of International Consumer Marketing*, 23(3-4), 297–310.

Shavitt, S., Lalwani, A. K., Zhang, J., & Torelli, C. J. (2006). The Horizontal/Vertical distinction in cross-cultural consumer research. *Journal of Consumer Psychology*, 16(4), 325–342.

Shavitt, S., Lee, A., & Torelli, C. (2009). New directions in cross-cultural consumer psychology. *The Social Psychology of Consumer Behavior* (M. Wänke ed., pp. 227–250). New York: Psychology Press.

Shavitt, S., Torelli, C. J., & Wong, J. (2009). Identity-based motivation: Constraints and opportunities in consumer research. *Journal of Consumer Psychology*, 19(3), 261–266.

Torelli, C. J., & Shavitt, S. (2010). Culture and concepts of power. *Journal of Personality & Social Psychology*, 99(4), 703–723.

Torelli, C. J., & Shavitt, S. (2011). The impact of power on information processing depends on cultural orientation. *Journal of Experimental Social Psychology*, 47(5), 959–967.

Triandis, H. C. (1989). The self and social behavior in differing cultural contexts. *Psychological Review*, 96(3), 506–520

Triandis, H. C., & Gelfand, M. J. (1998). Converging measurement of horizontal and vertical individualism and collectivism. *Journal of Personality & Social Psychology*, 74(1), 118–128.

Triandis, H. C., & Suh, E. M. (2002). Cultural influences on personality. *Annual Review of Psychology*, 53, 133–160.

Triandis, H. C. (1995). *Individualism & collectivism*. Boulder, CO, USA: Westview Press, Boulder, CO.

Wang, C. L., & Mowen, J. C. (1997). The Separateness-connectedness self-schema: Scale development and application to message construction. *Psychology & Marketing*, 14(2), 185–207.

Weldon, E. (1984). Deindividualization, interpersonal affect and productivity in laboratory task groups. *Journal of Applied Social Psychology*, 14(5), 469–485.

Williams, P., & Aaker, J. L. (2002). Can mixed emotions peacefully coexist? *Journal of Consumer Research, 28*(4), 636–649.

Wyer, R. S., Chiu, C. Y., & Hong, Y. Y. (2009). *Understanding culture: Theory, research and application.* New York: Psychology Press.

Zhang, J., & Shavitt, S. (2003). Cultural values in advertisements to the Chinese X-Generation. *Journal of Advertising, 32*(1), 23–33.

Zhang, Y., & Gelb, B. D. (1996). Matching advertising appeals to culture: The influence of products' use conditions. *Journal of Advertising, 25*(3), 29–46.

Zhu, R., & Meyers-Levy, J. (2009). The influence of self-view on context effects: How display fixtures can affect product evaluations. *Journal of Marketing Research, 46*(1), 37–45.

PART II

Attitudes, Persuasion and Response Biases

6

Culture and Persuasion

NIDHI AGRAWAL ■

India! Picture yourself as a fly on the wall of a dining room in suburban Mumbai where a girl named Rima is having lunch with her "joint" family. The family constitutes the entire family tree of four generations living under the same roof. Everyone is engrossed in conversation at the same time and yet there is a method in this madness. People who are otherwise chattering away, stop and listen when the elders speak. Every child's demands are given heed by the women around the room. The men and women play out their roles. Rima speaks to the uncles in a tone and language that indicates deep respect. She plays aunt to her nephews with ease. She accepts her grand-mother's opinions the Alphonso variety of mangoes has the most luscious taste despite her quite vote for the Kesar variety. She and her cousin dis-cuss a recent Bollywood potboiler and passionately disagree about the acting prowess of Katrina Kaif. This Indian family setting represents values deeply rooted in Indian or more generally Eastern cultures: collectivism, hierarchy, gender roles, and harmony. Rima's behaviors at lunch seamlessly fit in with these values.

Now imagine Rima in her work environment. She earned her undergradu-ate and master's degrees at universities in the United States of America. She now works for a multinational corporation in a Westernized corporate setting. She is at a conference promoting her product as superior to other products, is ambitious and determined to stand out, and considers herself better or at par with her colleagues regardless of age or gender. Rima's behaviors or attitudes in her professional context are more consistent with our perceptions of Western rather than Eastern or Asian cultures and are triggered by the context of her professional environment.

As one observes Rima, one may ask what determines her behaviors in the two big domains of her life—her home and her work. Rima's upbringing and living in India allows her to naturally embrace Eastern cultural values and practices. However, her professional context of a multinational company, pushes her to fit in with an environment where Western values are appreciated. When does Rima behave in ways that are consistent with her Eastern cultural roots and when does Rima act in a manner consistent with the Western values represented in her professional context?

Embedded in these two daily life scenarios are several questions relating to what is culture and how culture and context shape who we are and how we act. To study how culture shapes behavior, we must tackle the question of how do we begin to dissect something as rich and complex as culture? Approaching culture as a set of "isolatable" and chronic constructs can help us define culture in ways that allows us to systematically investigate it in an experimental setting. Having defined culture, when do culture and context diverge? Which one dominates? What are determinants of which one influences persuasion? Viewing culture and context through the lenses of accessibility theories can help us get started in answering this second set of questions. Third, what are the effects of when culture and context converge? Does convergence add to persuasion? Finally, while studying something as complex as culture, what can we learn that would illuminate the study of the consumer's mind? Studying a complex construct like culture from an accessibility perspective allows us to enrich current theories of accessibility and information processing. The chapter will elaborate on each of these themes while drawing on the literature on culture and persuasion in consumer research. Figure 6.1 lays out the framework I will develop in this chapter to lay out the dynamics between the effects of culture versus context on persuasion.

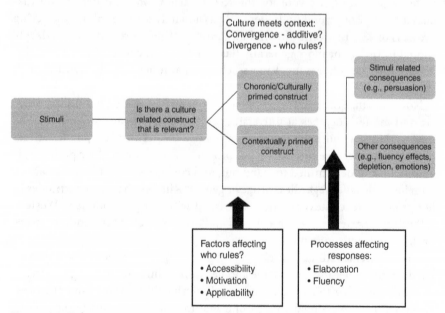

Figure 6.1 Culture versus context: a framework.

THE VALUE OF VIEWING CULTURE AS A CHRONICALLY ACCESSIBLE CONSTRUCT

Culture is multidimensional and shaped over time and history

In the example of Indian culture offered at the beginning of this chapter, Indian culture maybe examined from many different aspects or dimensions. If we think about studying "culture" as a whole, we can only use "ethnicity," nationality, or cultural background as ways of getting to culture. However, it would be difficult to then examine the psychology underlying the effects of culture and outline what aspect of a particular culture leads to a specific effect. Hence, to be able to examine and make with greater precision about which aspect of culture drives our effects, it is valuable to think of culture as a multidimensional construct and study any one construct at a time. This also allows for greater control and the ability to study culture within an experimental paradigm. We can study hierarchy, collectivism, gender dynamics, power distance, or many other broad or narrow aspects of what constitutes Indian culture. These various aspects of culture as can be termed cultural constructs. One of the more frequently studied aspects of culture or cultural constructs is that of individualism–collectivism. In this chapter, I will use the research related to individualism–collectivism as an illustrative domain for the culture versus context analyses. The insights about the theoretical architecture of this analysis should generalize to most other cultural constructs related to culture (e.g., hierarchy, holistic-analytical processing, power distance, masculinity, etc.)

The traditional view of culture has been to see culture as a static variable. In research following this tradition, countries represent cultures based on broad surveys characterizing countries along different dimensions or cultural constructs. For example, comparing individualism–collectivism measures across countries, researchers choose two countries that vary significantly across the cultural construct of individualism–collectivism measure and then compare responses to stimuli in these two countries/cultures to make an inference about how individualism–collectivism affects culture. This view sees culture as something that is more like a personality trait, as something that is cultivated as a function of social environment, as something that is endorsed by the individuals of the society and developed as a function of the history of the society.

Culture as a set of chronically accessible Constructs within an individual

Recognizing this origin of "culture" as something that is constantly endorsed by living in a particular social environment, leads us to view culture as a set of beliefs, attitudes, mindsets, preferences, psychological processes, decision-rules, emotional states, etc. that are *chronically* activated and

applied. This allows us to apply accessibility theories to the domain of culture research. Now, we can take constructs in the broader social psychology
and consumer research literatures and see how they conceptually map onto
constructs frequently examined in culture research. For example, research
that views culture as a "chronically accessible" construct and examines the
individualism–collectivism dimension of culture has benefitted from the literature on self-construal. Self-construal is a construct that deals with how
individuals perceive themselves. It identifies the extent to which individuals see of themselves as distinct from or as part of a group—one may have
an independent or interdependent self-construal. Those with an independent
self-construal view themselves as distinct from groups and other individuals
and define themselves in terms of their traits, qualities, and achievements.
Those with an interdependent self-construal often define themselves based on
their relationships, group memberships, and roles in relation to other people.
This literature is rooted in social psychology and argues that both types of
self-construal are present (or available) within any individual. Depending
on the situation, one self-construal may be more accessible than the other
and may affect judgments and decision making. Given the definitions, we can
note that independent and interdependent self-construals map onto individualism and collectivism, respectively. This mapping may enable us to tap into
the individualistic or collectivistic sides of individuals, as well as document
situations, boundaries, and the extent of variation in those constructs across
and within cultures as well as within cultures and individuals over time and
situations. Seeing culture as a chronic source of accessibility helps us implicate the self-construal literature. People from collectivistic cultures may be
seen as having a chronically accessible interdependent self-construal. Those
from individualistic cultures may be seen as having a chronically accessible
independent self-construal. Consistent with the ideas underlying individualism–collectivism, individuals with an independent self-construal consider
themselves as unique and value the characteristics that distinguish them from
other members of the group. In contrast, individuals with an interdependent
self-construal see themselves as part of a group and define themselves with
respect to other group members. Western cultures (e.g., United States) reward
independence and frequently endorse the independent self-construal, making the independent self-construal chronically accessible. In contrast, Asian
cultures tend to reward interdependence and frequently endorse the interdependent self-construal making it chronically accessible.

Relevance to situation determines which cultural constructs will affect responses

Similar to the mapping of self-construal onto cultural differences, we can
also map other psychological constructs into cultural constructs or differences (e.g., relationship styles, processing styles, construal level, regulatory

focus, emotions, etc.). Drawing from the principle of applicability or relevance in the literature on accessibility and on persuasion, one can say that of all the various constructs that constitute culture (i.e., cultural constructs), the one(s) most relevant to the situation or decision at hand will be ones that are most likely to influence consumer responses (Chaiken & Maheswaran, 1994; Higgins & King, 1981). For example, in Agrawal and Maheswaran (2005a), the target message varied by way of presenting the same product in a collectivistic frame that talked about benefits related to the family or friends or an individualistic frame that talked about the benefits of features exclusively related to the individual. Given these appeals, it is likely that cultural constructs related to individualism–collectivism or self-construal would be relevant rather than say the cultural constructs of power distance or hierarchy.

Viewing culture as chronic highlights its interaction with context

The key benefit of this "chronic" self perspective of the culture is that it recognizes that there may be other sides to the individual that may not be chronic or culturally endorsed but may still influence the individual's behavior. In the context of self-construal it allows us to recognize that the other less frequently activated self-construal also exists within every individual and can be made temporarily accessible by referencing tasks, priming, or in situational contexts (Aaker & Williams, 1998; Aaker & Lee, 2001). For ease of exposition, in this chapter, we will refer to the temporarily (versus chronically) accessible self as the latent self. For an American person, who most likely has a chronically accessible independent self-construal, the interdependent self-construal can be made temporarily accessible by asking him to think about family obligations. Similarly, in our Indian example, most of the time, Rima behaves in accordance with her chronic interdependent self endorsed by the collectivistic culture nurtured in India. But, when she is moved to a setting that primes or activates her latent independent self, she is more likely to behave like people in an individualistic culture. Contexts can activate the latent self, which may be different from the chronic self.

EFFECTS OF CULTURE AND CONTEXT ON PERSUASION

Some research has shown that culture or the chronic self influences attitudes (Aaker & Maheswaran, 1997; Agrawal & Maheswaran, 2005a; Gurhan-Canli & Maheswaran, 2000; Han & Shavitt, 1994). For example, Han and Shavitt (1994) suggest that individualist appeals (i.e., messages emphasizing individual benefits) would be more effective than collective appeals for people with an independent self-construal. Collectivistic appeals (i.e., messages emphasizing group benefits, family expectations, and in-group relationships) would be more persuasive with people who have an interdependent self-construal. On a similar note, Aaker and Maheswaran (1997) and Gurhan-Canli and Maheswaran (2001) showed that appeals consistent with cultural traits were more persuasive. In contrast to these studies, Aaker and Williams (1998) found messages that are counter to the culture (e.g., Americans exposed to collectivist rather than individualist messages) may sometimes be more per-suasive. They argue that messages that are inconsistent with one's culture may appeal due to their novelty. These studies conceptualize culture as endur-ing constructs that are made chronically accessible as a function of cultural orientation and are often quite stable over time and contexts (Oishi, Wyer, & Colcombe, 2000). They use country or nationality as a proxy for culture and in some cases employ manipulation checks to confirm that the culturally endorsed or the chronic self was indeed the activated self at the time of the studies.

Other research has shown that the chronic and latent selves may coexist within every individual, in any culture (Aaker & Lee, 2001). Aaker and Lee (2001), in a series of four experiments, used a situational context to prime self-construals. When the primed self-construal was the same as the chronic self-construal, appeals that were compatible (or consistent) with the chronicself-construal were more favorably evaluated than appeals that were compatible with the latent self-construal. When primed self-construal was different from the chronic self-construal, appeals that were consistent with the primed self-construal were more persuasive than appeals that were consistent with the chronically acces-sible self-construal. It appears that appeals that are consistent with the prime are more persuasive than appeals that are consistent with the chronic self.

In sum, viewing culture as a chronically accessible self allows us to recog-nize that an alternate latent self may be present that may be made accessible through contexts and priming. This chronic versus latent self framework then raises the issue of how do culture and context interact?

If there is a stimuli-relevant cultural trait or chronic self as well as an alternate or similar primed self that is available, then we can use models of accessibility and persuasion to predict how culture versus context will affect responses. Two key situations arise from the interaction of culture and context and their impact on persuasion will be discussed in the follow-ing sections: (a) when context diverges from culture; and (b) when context converges with culture. Both culture and context can affect persuasion, and understanding which one will guide persuasion in a given consumer setting will enable us to design better messages. I will now describe my framework for understanding how such convergence or divergence shapes thoughts, message processing, and persuasion (Figure 6.1). On the particular question of divergence, we will review and develop determinants of whether culture overrides context or vice versa. On the particular question of convergence, we will discuss the consequences of when culture and prime both endorse the same type of self.

DIVERGENCE: WHEN WILL CULTURE OVERRIDE CONTEXT?

The first condition is the situation when culture and prime activate different selves. What happens when culture asserts the accessibility of the chronic self (e.g., independence in North America) while the contextual primes makes the latent self (e.g., interdependence) accessible? Which one is more likely to affect persuasion and what factors determine that? Factors that boost the accessibility of or offer motivation to rely on the chronic or primed self will determine which one will affect persuasion.

Which self is more accessible?

Being in particular context or situation might prime participants with a particular self. For example, in the scenario offered at the beginning of the chapter, the professional context of working for a multinational corporation makes Rima's independent self temporarily highly accessible. Given that her chronic self is interdependent (given her Asian background), we would expect her interdependent self to be constantly accessible. However, when the situation or context is associated or consistent with an independent self, the independent self becomes temporarily accessible. If the context primes a particular self, it becomes temporarily accessible and is likely to influence decision making. However, there might be conditions when despite the context, the chronic self might remain more accessible or more influential in decision making. To contrast the nature of culture with the nature of contextual influences (e.g., primes, situations), the literature on accessibility of information puts forth factors that lead to reliance on chronically accessible versus contextual or temporarily accessible information (e.g., Higgins & King, 1981; Bargh, Lombardi, & Higgins, 1988). The aim is to identify the determinants of when chronic accessibility overrides temporary accessibility. One such determinant is time. Bargh et al. (1988) show that contextually primed effects dissipate after a delay leading to weaker effects of prime on responses, but chronically activated constructs continue have effects after a delay. Similar analyses might apply to culture as a source of chronic primes.

Another set of determinants might be factors that boost the accessibility of either the chronic or latent self. For example, Agrawal and Maheswaran (2005a) show that in contexts where consumers tend to think deeply about who they are and what values truly represent them, they rely on the chronic self in forming attitudes. They identify brand commitment as a factor that enhances the accessibility of the chronic self even in the presence of an alternative self by encouraging consumers to reflect on the values that connected them to the brand in the first place. As a result, when people are committed to a brand, message frames that are compatible with the chronic rather than primed self are more persuasive. When people are familiar with but not committed to the brand, message frames compatible with the primed self are more persuasive. In terms of process, Agrawal and Maheswaran (2005a) argued that the process underlying their effects was that brand commitment brought forth greater favorable elaboration when the message was consistent with the chronic versus the primed self. When brand commitment was absent, the primed self led to more favorable thoughts about the prime-consistent message. This suggests that accessibility of the chronic versus primed self affects persuasion via thoughtful elaboration. These findings about an elaboration process are also supported by Aaker and Lee (2001).

What role does motivation play?

Motivation to process information (e.g., motives that govern depth of processing or selective nature of processing) might play a role in multiple ways. One role that motivation might play is to help us identify the various psychological processes by which culture/chronic self and latent self affect persuasion. It might be that the chronic self and the latent self affect persuasion by different processes. For example, motivation might help us answer questions such as whether and when is influence of the chronic or latent self deliberate versus automatic. Since we constantly rely on the chronic self and it has been frequently activated due to culture, could its influence be more habitual or automatic? Since contextual situations are frequently judged by their relevance, could the effect of the latent self on persuasion be more deliberative? In the service of this process question, we may look at an analysis of opportunity or motivation to process information presented by Briley and Aaker (2006). They found that culture was more likely to affect responses in immediate automatic responses but its effects weakened and were corrected for when more thoughtful and deliberate responses were sought. When participants were primed through a sentence formation task to give immediate (versus deliberate) responses, when they were under high (versus low) cognitive load or time pressure, the effects of culture were observed—appeals consistent with the chronic rather than latent self were more persuasive. In their studies, the alternate latent self was not primed and an inference about that cannot be made. It is likely that a prime might have greater effect when people are provided the opportunity to deliberate on it. Although, note that a delay after priming without a nudge to deliberate might lead to culture effects (Higgins & King, 1981).

These studies suggested that processes by which culture/chronic self and latent self affect persuasion might be different. Culture might affect responses via an automatic path and allow for the processing of messages consistent with the chronic self because relying on the chronic self is frequent and almost habitual. We might also speculate that, in contrast to this automatic process driven by culture, the prime or latent self might work in a more deliberate rather than automatic way where the role of the relevance of the latent self to the decision at hand is put under more stringent scrutiny. Thus, when people are motivated to make quick decisions, they tend to rely on culture. But, when they have the opportunity and motivation to deliberate on various aspects of the self and the situation, the latent self may have more of a chance to influence persuasion.

As discussed above, while the literature offers evidence that the chronic self may exert its influence in a more automated fashion, more research is needed to generally understand how the chronic versus latent selves influence persuasion and more specifically to study whether and when the latent self affects decisions in a more deliberate rather than automatic way.

Another set of motivation-related analyses is to think about matches between culture and primes with certain motivations. Persuasion theories have discussed that consumers might approach processing information with various goals in mind (accuracy, defense, impression; Agrawal & Maheswaran, 2005b; Chen, Shechter, & Chaiken, 1996). Accuracy-motivated consumers are driven to be objective and look thoughtfully through information to form an accurate opinion. Defense-motivated consumers are driven to be selective and process information to reach a preferred conclusion. The Agrawal and Maheswaran (2005a) study described previously can also be seen in the light of accuracy and defense motivations. One explanation that may emerge from the Agrawal and Maheswaran (2005a) study is that when people are motivated by defense motives (as they were when reading about a product to which they are committed), they are likely to rely on the chronic rather than the primed self. It might be the case that when we commit to something and it is a central or well-networked part of our self, it is likely to be associated with the chronic self. When such an attitude is presented in a way consistent with the latent self, it may be either seen as inconsistent with the chronic self and its related attitudes and values (despite being consistent with the context), or may be seen as a threat to the chronic self. In such contexts, it might be better to approach persuasion using the chronic self rather than the latent self. When consumers are motivated by accuracy motives (as they were when reading about a product to which they were not committed in a high-involvement environment), they were more likely to rely on the primed self. Accuracy-driven consumers are not invested in reaching a particular conclusion or protecting a particular attitude or aspect of the self. Hence, they may be more flexible with adapting to the context and judging the message in the light of the current context. This analysis of the Agrawal and Maheswaran (2005a) study suggests that the motivations described in the persuasion literature may have systematic effects on use of culture or the primed self in persuasion.

The area of how motivation determines the influence of culture or context in persuasion could benefit greatly from future research. Researchers might examine how various motivations might influence the role of chronic versus latent self. For example, would need to impress someone lead people to agree with an attitude even though it might be inconsistent with the accessible self? Similarly, would motivations like the need to cope with the existential anxiety generated from mortality salience lead people to adopt or reject their chronic selves (Maheswaran & Agrawal, 2004).

Which self is more applicable?

Whether the chronic self or the primed self will affect responses should also depend on which of these two selves is more relevant to evaluating the stimuli. A nice example of this is found in Han and Shavitt (1994) within the culture condition since they did not manipulate primes. These authors asked Korean and American consumers to evaluate individualistic or collectivistic advertisements for products that are used in public or those that are used in private. They found that cultural differences emerge more for products that were usually shared (e.g., detergent, clothes iron) and were weaker or absent for products that are used individually (e.g., running shoes). This effect held in both cultures. This suggests that cultural effects are more likely to emerge for public products than private products. Research should examine whether latent self is more likely to emerge for private product or that people are indifferent between the latent and chronic self when it comes to private products.

What processes shape responses to divergence?

So far we have discussed factors that determine whether culture or context affect persuasion via specific changes in accessibility, motivation, and applicability. Several processes that might lead to persuasion emerged—namely elaboration, correction, novelty, and fluency.

In addition to having direct effects on persuasion, the fit between the chronic self and appeals might have effects above and beyond persuasion. In some cases it might lead to a systematic set of emotional experiences related to the self that is activated (Lee, Aaker, & Gardner, 2000; Agrawal, Menon, & Aaker, 2007). For example, Agrawal et al. (2007) exposed consumers with an independent or interdependent self to an emotionally aversive health message framed in an individualistic or a collectivistic way (e.g., about the consequences of getting a disease for themselves versus their family). As we might expect, messages consistent with their self were more effective. More interestingly, consumers' emotional responses to the "effective message" were closely associated with the self that was primed. Independent consumers exposed to an individualistic message experienced changes in individualist emotions—decrease in happiness and increase in sadness. Their collectivist emotions of peace and anxiety did not show any change. Interdependent consumers exposed to a collectivist message experienced changes in collectivist emotions, namely a decrease in calmness and an increase in anxiety, but did not show any movement in individualistic emotions. These studies suggest that the emotional processes that may underlie responses to stimuli might be systematically different based on whether the self is independent or interdependent. The role of emotions and culture in persuasion is another area of research where more research is warranted.

Another process possibility is that fluency comes from an antecedent of engagement that has been shown to happen when a fit between the message frame and viewer orientation occurs (Camacho, Higgins, & Luger, 2003; Higgins, 2002). This literature referred to frequently as the domain of "fit" effects shows that the processes resulting from a match between a message and the orientation (in this case, cultural or primed self) results in some psychological processes (e.g., fluency) which are carried forward to subsequent tasks. Fluency and engagement might have effects above and beyond the relevant stimuli. They might get carried over to the next task that may be unrelated to the stimuli such as evaluations of subsequent products, likelihood of exerting self-control, etc. These effects have not yet been shown in a culture domain and offer lucrative avenues of research. When culture and context diverge, researchers may ask whether and when value from fit with culture (i.e., chronic self) will be higher or lower than the value of fit with the context.

We may also speculate that another process that might be driven by divergence is the feeling of novelty or inconsistency or suspicion that might lead to greater elaboration (Aaker & Williams, 1998). When the primed self diverges from the chronic self, the following stimuli or situation may feel new leading to greater elaboration and engagement.

Finally, recent research in the area of chronic versus primed motivational orientations (not necessarily culture) has shown that priming latent tendencies may be effective but it leads to depletion because the chronic tendency is suppressed by the latent one (Lisjak, Molden, & Lee, 2012). Some of these processes have not been tested in culture research and provide opportunities for future research.

CONVERGENCE: HOW WILL CULTURE AND CONTEXT COMBINE?

To understand how culture will combine with context, we go to the literature in information processing and persuasion to identify how two convergent versus divergent cues influence information processing and persuasion. Models of elaboration and those of fluency have been used to describe the consequences of convergence. For example, elaboration models endeavor to see whether there is an additive effect of convergence. Convergence of inputs in the elaboration literature frequently leads to stronger and more extreme attitudes (Chen & Chaiken, 1999). Agrawal and Maheswaran (2005a, study 2) found mixed evidence on additive effects of culture and prime. They did not find a reliable additive effect of being persuaded by an appeal that matched culture and the primed self both of which were convergent (e.g., when individualist appeal was presented to North American consumers primed with independent self-construal). However, on thoughts related to chronic self, an additive effect of convergence was found. The lack of effects on attitude might be attributable to the ceiling effects on attitudes in their study as attitudes were overall high enough not allowing for the additive effect to emerge. Future research could specifically design studies to investigate the additive effects.

Fluency from convergence has been shown to have beneficial effects on subsequent valuation tasks (Camacho et al., 2003; Lee, Keller, & Sternthal, 2010). The effects of convergence are not well documented partly because it is difficult to find convergence effects due to calibration issues and ceiling effects. Most of the research that has looked at convergence takes the perspective of "fit" effects where the convergence studied is usually between the message and the chronic self or between the message and the primed self. Very few studies have examined the interactive effects of the chronic self and the prime self leading to little understanding of the additive effects or convergence between the chronic and primed selves. However, clever paradigms based on the studies described previously (e.g., Higgins, 2002; Lisjak et al., 2012) could be employed to better investigate the convergence effects. Future research that systematically establishes the value of converging context with culture will be valuable to understanding the dynamic role of the self in persuasion.

SUMMARY

My goal with the chapter is to start a discussion about the richness of processes and phenomena underlying the effects of culture on persuasion. By examining how culture interacts with context, we can illuminate directions and unanswered questions about how culture may influence information processing. This question about how culture and context interact is uniquely valuable for multiple reasons: (a) it allows us to examine how models of accessibility and information processing can provide a unique insight into culture; (b) it allows us to showcase how culture can help us understand the nature of accessibility and information processing in a broader context; and finally (c) it allows us to document the variety of ways in which culture interacts with the consumer context to mould consumers' processing of information and its consequent effect on judgments and decisions.

I hope that this chapter gets readers to approach culture research with an accessibility-driven framework that encompasses various constructs which constitute the complex multidimensional nature of culture. When we speak of examining how culture and context combine, it is important to consider what constitutes culture. As discussed in the beginning of this chapter, culture is a term that embraces many complex constructs. Narrowing culture down to one construct in any given study (e.g., self-construal in Agrawal & Maheswaran, 2005a) allows us to understand the broader processes (e.g., accessibility in Agrawal & Maheswaran, 2005a) underlying culture via the depth of process that can be studied via the use of more controlled tools offered by self-construal research. The most optimal outcome for culture research would be if scholars tested out the accessibility and other frameworks or models by tapping on other constructs involved with culture such as holistic/analytic processing, regulatory focus, construal level, emotions, relationship styles, etc.

The influence of chronically and temporarily accessible constructs is not only of interest from a theoretical standpoint, but also has several implications for the practitioner. Marketers are often faced with a choice of various advertising appeals that will maximize consumer favorability toward the brand. Should they choose to use appeals that cater to the local culture, or should they choose appeals that are more consistent with a brand's global position but might be in conflict with the local culture. Understanding factors that aid in making both sets of appeals effective or ineffective would be helpful to managers in designing brand communications and consumer environments.

Having a broader and systematic model that allows us to study culture within an experimental paradigm should encourage scholars to explore the breadth and diversity of potential constructs relevant to culture. My hope is also that scholars will see the scope of culture research as a tool in advancing our understanding of information processing and persuasion.

REFERENCES

Aaker, J. L., & Lee, A. Y. (2001). 'I' seek pleasures and 'we' avoid pains: The role of self-regulatory goals in information processing and persuasion. *Journal of Consumer Research, 28* (June), 33–49.

Aaker, J. L., & Maheswaran, D. (1997). The effects of cultural orientation on persuasion. *Journal of Consumer Research, 24* (December), 315–328.

Aaker, J. L., & Williams, P. (1998). Empathy versus pride: The influence of emotional appeals across cultures. *Journal of Consumer Research, 25* (December), 241–261.

Agrawal, N., & Maheswaran, D. (2005a). The effects of self-construal and commitment on persuasion. *Journal of Consumer Research, 31* (March), 841–849.

Agrawal, N., & Maheswaran, D. (2005b). Motivated reasoning in outcome-bias effects. *Journal of Consumer Research, 31* (March), 798–805.

Agrawal, N., Menon G., & Aaker, J. L. (2007). Getting emotional about health. *Journal of Marketing Research, 44* (February), 100–113.

Bargh, J. A., Lombardi, W. J., & Higgins, E. T. (1988). Automaticity of chronically accessible constructs in person × situation effects on person perception: It's just a matter of time. *Journal of Personality and Social Psychology, 55*(4), 599–605.

Briley, D. A.& Aaker, J. L. (2006). When does culture matter? Effects of personal knowledge on the correction of culture-based judgments. *Journal of Marketing Research, 43* (August), 395–408.

Camacho, C. J., Higgins, E. T., & Luger, L. (2003). Moral value transfer from regulatory fit: What feels right *is* right and what feels wrong *is* wrong. *Journal of Personality and Social Psychology, 84*(3), 498–510.

Chaiken, S., & Maheswaran, D. (1994). Heuristic processing can bias systematic processing: Effects of source credibility, argument ambiguity, and task importance on attitude judgment. *Journal of Personality and Social Psychology, 66*(3), 460–473.

Chen, S., Shechter, D., & Chaiken, S. (1996). Getting at the truth or getting along: Accuracy- versus impression motivated heuristic and systematic processing. *Journal of Personality and Social Psychology, 71*(2), 262–275.

Chen, S., & Chaiken, S. (1999). The heuristic-systematic model in its broader context. In S. Chaiken & Y. Trope (Eds.), *Dual-process Theories in Social Psychology* (pp. 73–96). New York, NY, USA: Guilford.

Gurhan-Canli, Z., & Maheswaran, D. (2000). Cultural variations in country of origin effects. *Journal of Marketing Research, 37* (3), 309–317.

Han, S. -p., & Shavitt, S. (1994). Persuasion and culture: Advertising appeals in individualistic and collectivistic societies. *Journal of Experimental Social Psychology, 30* (July), 326–350.

Higgins, E. T. (2002). Lawrence Erlbaum Associates. *Journal of Consumer Psychology, 12*(3), 177–191.

Higgins, E. T., & King, G. A. (1981). Accessibility of social constructs: information-processing consequences of individual and contextual variability. In N. Cantor & J. F. Kihlstrom (Eds.), *Personality, Cognition, and Social Interaction*. Hillsdale, NJ, USA: Erlbaum.

Lee, A. Y., Aaker, J. L., & Gardner, W. L. (2000). The pleasures and pains of distinct self-construals: The role of interdependence in regulatory focus. *Journal of Personality and Social Psychology, 78* (June), 1122–1134.

Lee, A., Keller, P. A., & Sternthal, B. (2010). Value from regulatory construal fit: The persuasive impact of fit between consumer goals and message concreteness. *Journal of Consumer Research, 36* (February), 735–747.

Lisjak, M., Molden, D. C., & Lee, A. Y. (2012). Primed interference: The cognitive and behavioral costs of an incongruity between chronic and primed motivational orientations. *Journal of Personality and Social Psychology, 102*(5), 889–909.

Maheswaran D., & Agrawal, N (2004). Motivational and cultural variations in mortality salience effects: Contemplations on terror management theory and consumer behavior. *Journal of Consumer Psychology, 14*(3), 213–218.

Oishi, S., Wyer, R. S., & Colcombe, S. (2000). Cultural variation in the use of current life satisfaction to predict the future. *Journal of Personality and Social Psychology, 78*(3), 434–445.

7

The Effects of Self-Construal Fit on Motivation, Attitudes, and Charitable Giving

ANGELA Y. LEE AND TONYA WILLIAMS BRADFORD ■

Stores commonly advertise their sales by putting signs in the shop windows to beckon consumers to go into the store. In some Asian cities, often one would see sale signs in English as well as in Chinese. What is interesting about the signs is that they differ not just in the language used, but also in the literal meaning of the words in the signs. The sign in English typically advertises how much of the original price consumers would save (e.g., "40% off—Big Sale"), the parallel sign in Chinese indicates how much of that original price consumers would have to pay ("六 折 大 减 价" literally translates into "Pay 60%—Big Sale").

This seemingly minor twist in the message conveyed in the sale signs reflects one of the fundamental differences between an individualist and a collectivist culture: whereas members from an individualist culture who are more likely to have an independent self-construal tend to focus their attention on the presence and absence of positive outcomes (hence the sale sign emphasizing savings), those from a collectivist culture who are more likely to have an interdependent self-construal tend to focus their attention on the absence and presence of negative outcomes (hence the sign emphasizing payment). This difference in sensitivity to positive and negative outcomes is one of the differences that reflect the psychological processes and motivational orientations associated with the two distinct ways that people from an individualist versus a collectivist culture view the self (Lee, Aaker, & Gardner, 2000).

The objective of this chapter is to provide insights into the key construct underlying one of the major cultural divides—individualism–collectivism— that maps onto an independent versus interdependent self-construal and discuss how the way that people view the self may influence decision making by way of their regulatory orientations, their temporal perspectives, and their empathic concerns for others.

Members of individualist cultures tend to have a more accessible independent self-construal, whereas members of collectivist cultures tend to have a more accessible interdependent self-construal. Individuals with a more accessible independent self-construal place high values on self-reliance and autonomy. They strive toward growth and accomplishments and adopt a competitive mindset when relating to others—they value being unique and different from others. Of key importance to the independents is the "inner core" of the self that is invariant over time and across contexts. In contrast, individuals with a more accessible interdependent self-construal value social connectedness and relationship harmony (Kwan, Bond, & Singelis, 1997). They view the self as part of a larger collective and strive toward fulfilling one's obligations and responsibilities over personal wishes or desires—they hold group goals over personal goals (Markus & Kitayama, 1991; Triandis, 1989).

While the independent and interdependent self-construals were first conceptualized as distinct self-schemas across two different cultures (Markus & Kitayama, 1991), subsequent research shows that both ways of viewing the self coexist within an individual, regardless of their cultural background (Gardner, Gabriel, & Lee, 1999; Hong, Morris, Chiu, & Benet-Martinez, 2000; Singelis, 1994), and that the difference in how people view the self across cultures or across individuals within each culture reflects which of the two self-schemas is more accessible in memory. The implication is that situational primes and contextual factors can make one or the other self-construal temporarily more salient, irrespective of people's chronically salient self-construal, and in turn influence subsequent cognitive, emotional, and motivational processes (Hong et al., 2000; Lee et al., 2000; Briley & Wyer, 2002).

This chapter discusses three psychological processes related to people's self-construal that have important implications for consumer behavior. First, people's self-construal has been shown to be associated with distinct self-regulatory orientation (Higgins, 1997). In particular, those with an independent self-construal tend to have a promotion regulatory orientation, whereas those with an interdependent self-construal tend to have a prevention regulatory orientation (Higgins, 1997; Lee et al., 2000). The different self-construals have also been shown to be associated with different temporal perspectives, such that those with an independent self-construal tend to adopt a temporally distal view of future events, whereas those with an interdependent self-construal have a temporally proximal view (Spassova & Lee, 2013; Lee, Lee, & Kern, 2011). Finally, people's self-construal has also been found to influence their empathic responses toward others in need, such that those with an independent self-construal are more empathic toward those in need of tangible aids, whereas those with an interdependent self-construal are more empathic toward those in need of relationship support (Bradford & Lee, 2013).

In this chapter, we first describe the relationship between self-construal (Markus & Kitayama, 1991) and self-regulatory orientation (Higgins, 1997), then we discuss how this relationship may influence consumer decision making. Similar discussions relating to temporal perspective (Lee et al., 2011) and empathy (Bradford & Lee, 2013) ensue. Common across these three different domains are findings illustrative of a matching effect between the information that people encounter and their self-construal. The general finding is that people's motivation, perception, and attention are heightened when there is a match (versus mismatch) with their self-construal, and that they are more persuaded by appeals that match (versus mismatch) with their self-construal.

SELF-CONTRUAL AND REGULATORY ORIENTATION

According to self-regulatory focus theory (Higgins, 1997), people are motivated to fulfill two fundamental needs: the need for growth and nurturance, and the need for safety and security. Although both needs are critical to survival, the strategies that individuals employ to satisfy these needs often take them in different directions such that at any one time, they may only be able to attend to just one set of needs and not both. Those who orient their attention, attitudes, and behaviors toward servicing their needs for growth and nurturance are promotion oriented, whereas those who orient themselves toward servicing their needs for safety and security are prevention oriented. People with a promotion orientation strive to fulfill their ideals and aspirations and are motivated to approach gains and avoid nongains. In contrast, those with a prevention orientation strive toward fulfilling their duties and responsibilities and are motivated to approach nonlosses and avoid losses.

As discussed earlier, while the goal of the independent self is to distinguish the self from others, the goal of the interdependent self is to maintain relationship harmony among others (Heine, Lehman, Markus, & Kitayama, 1999). It is in the service of these different goals that distinct self-regulatory strategies emerge. The independent goal of being positively distinct, with its emphasis on achievement and autonomy, is consistent with a promotion orientation that focuses on fulfilling ideals and aspirations, approaching gains, and avoiding nongains. In contrast, the interdependent goal of harmoniously fitting in with others, with its emphasis on fulfilling social responsibilities and maintaining harmony when interacting with others, is more consistent with a prevention orientation that focuses on fulfilling duties and obligations, approaching nonlosses, and avoiding losses.

The notion that independents are promotion oriented is consistent with prior cultural studies showing that independents are more likely to focus on the positive features of the self as well as potential gains in situations in order to positively distinguish themselves from others (Holmberg, Markus, Herzog, & Franks, 1997). People from an individualist culture (e.g., Americans) are more likely to praise those who compliment them while derogating those who criticize them; they have also been found to more readily accept and elaborate on positive feedback, while critically review or ignore negative feedback (Frey & Stahlberg,

1986). On the other hand, interdependents' attention to negative aspects of the self or situations in an attempt to avoid social mishaps and foster relationship harmony (Heine & Lehman, 1999) is consistent with a prevention orientation. Studies showing Japanese to be more likely than Americans to take steps to improve on their deficits to help them become a more unified part of the relevant social unit are in line with this view (Kitayama, Markus, Matsumoto, & Norasakkunkit, 1997).

The greater emphasis by members from collectivist cultures on negative information may have a genetic underpinning. In particular, Chiao and Blizinsky (2010) document a positive correlation ($r = .70$) between different nations' collectivism score and the frequencies of the short allele serotonin transporter gene (5-HTTLPR) that has been shown to be associated with heightened anxiety, harm avoidance, fear conditioning, as well as an attentional bias to negative information. An interesting observation is that while Southeast Asians are more likely (relative to North Americans) to carry the short allele serotonin transporter gene, lower incidences of mood disorders and anxiety are reported in Southeast Asia than in North America. The authors suggest that societies with a genetic composition that make them more vulnerable to heightened anxiety, harm avoidance, and fear conditioning may over time develop social norms and values to help their members deal with negative emotions. Subsequent findings of similar correlation between the collectivism score and frequencies of the short allele gene in societies within the United States provide further support for the cultural gene coevolution hypothesis. Thus, it is plausible that while cultural norms and collectivistic values serve as a buffer for heightened anxiety and mood disorders, the attentional bias toward negative information associated with the short allele version of the gene remains; hence members from Eastern cultures tend to be more prevention oriented.

More direct evidence demonstrating the relationship between self-construal and regulatory orientation is reported by Lee and her colleagues (Lee et al., 2000). Across a series of studies where independent and interdependent self-construals were operationalized using individual difference measures (Singelis, 1994), situational prime (individual events versus team events), and cultural orientations (Americans versus Chinese), independents were shown to weigh gain-framed information more heavily than loss-framed information, whereas interdependents exhibited the opposite pattern. In particular, independents view decisions to take home what they have won from a game show to be more important than decisions to leave what they have lost (Study 1). They also place more importance on a tennis match that determines whether or not they will win the tournament than one that determines whether or not they will lose the tournament (Study 2-4). The reverse is true of interdependents. Finally, Americans reported experiencing more intense promotion-focused emotions (cheerfulness when they have won and dejection when they have lost), whereas Chinese reported experiencing more intense prevention-focused emotions (peacefulness when they have won and anxiety when they have lost), as consistent with regulatory focus theory (Study 5).

The self-construal regulatory fit effect

The observation that members from individualist and collectivist cultures are associated with different self-regulatory orientations has important implications for consumer decision making. The fact that members of individualist cultures are more likely to focus on positive information, whereas members of collectivist cultures are more likely to focus on negative information leads to obvious divergence in how they allocate cognitive resources. However, despite these differences, people from both cultures exhibit very similar patterns in terms of their attitudes and behaviors when their goal pursuit strategies are consistent with their regulatory orientation.

According to regulatory fit theory (Higgins, 2000, 2005), people experience regulatory fit (nonfit) when they process information or make decisions in a manner that matches (mismatches) their regulatory orientation (for a review, see Lee & Higgins, 2009). When people experience regulatory fit, they become more motivated; they perceive fit (versus nonfit) information to be easier to process (Labroo & Lee, 2006; Lee & Aaker, 2004; Lee et al., 2010); and the decisions they make under fit (versus nonfit) conditions feel more "right" (Camacho, Higgins, & Luger, 2003). This feeling "right" experience in turn intensifies their reactions such that positive reactions become more positive and negative reactions become more negative. For the independents who tend to be promotion oriented, they are more persuaded by appeals that emphasize promotion benefits (e.g., energizing and flavorful, fun to drink) than appeals that emphasize prevention benefits (e.g., reduces risks of cancer and promotes cardiovascular functioning, healthy to drink); and the reverse is true among the interdependents who tend to be prevention oriented (Aaker & Lee, 2001, Study 1). Independents have also been shown to be more discerning between strong and weak gain-framed information and have better memory for it. In contrast, interdependents are more discerning between strong and weak loss-framed information and have better memory for it (Aaker & Lee, 2001, Studies 2 and 3).

However, it is important to note that fit appeals are not always more persuasive. First, because regulatory fit intensifies reactions, fit messages are less persuasive than nonfit messages when the argument quality is weak. Under these circumstances, independents may find prevention appeals more persuasive than promotion appeals, and vice versa for interdependents (Aaker & Lee, 2001, Study 3). Further, fit messages may lose their advantage over nonfit messages when people are motivated to process information. Under high-involvement conditions, people are less likely to rely on processing fluency or "feeling right" as the basis of their judgment (Wang & Lee, 2006). When involved consumers encounter nonfit information, their experience of "feeling wrong" may even prompt them to pay more attention to and engage in more elaborate processing of the nonfit (versus fit) message, and in turn be more persuaded by nonfit (versus fit) appeals when arguments are strong (Harding, Lisjak, & Lee, 2011).

Taken together, these findings seem to suggest that people rely on different metacognitive experiences arising from the correspondence (or the lack thereof) between their self-construal and the goal pursuit strategies they employ depending on whether or not they are involved with the decision task. When people are not particularly involved, they tend to focus on the regulatory fit experience of feeling right as the basis of their decision such that appeals that fit with their regulatory orientation are more persuasive. However, when they are involved, their decisions are more influenced by their regulatory nonfit experience of feeling wrong, which prompts them to elaborate more on the information, resulting in nonfit appeals being more persuasive. Thus, under low-involvement conditions, to the extent that the appeals contain strong arguments, those with an independent self-construal are more persuaded by promotion (versus prevention) appeals that emphasize growth and accomplishments, whereas those with an interdependent self-construal are more persuaded by prevention (versus promotion) appeals that emphasize safety and security. The reverse is likely to hold under high-involvement conditions such that independents are more persuaded by prevention (versus promotion) appeals whereas interdependents are more persuaded by promotion (versus prevention) appeals.

SELF-CONSTRUAL AND CONSTRUAL LEVEL

Not only are the two distinct self-construals associated with different motivational orientations, the way that people view the self has also been shown to be associated with different levels of construal and psychological distances. For the independents who are concerned about growth and accomplishments, they likely hold a more distal view of the future to allow for maximal growth opportunities. In contrast, for the interdependents who are concerned about social connectedness and interpersonal relationships, it is important that they pay close attention to the immediate environment to ensure that relationship harmony is attained and preserved. This attention to the proximal environment inevitably prompts them to focus on the "here" and "now," which likely prompts a low-level construal and the corresponding proximal temporal construal.

From this perspective, it is not surprising that one's self-construal, whether culturally or situationally determined, has consequences for how people may construe information in memory as well as future events and activities. Indeed, it has been demonstrated that individuals with an independent self-construal are likely to represent the self and others in more general and decontextualized terms, using abstract attributes such as internal traits. In contrast, individuals with an interdependent self-construal are likely to represent the self and others with reference to social situations, using more concrete social or contextual information such as membership, relationship roles, or various temporal and spatial markers (Cousins, 1989; English & Chen, 2007; Markus & Kitayama, 1991; Kinagawa, Cross, & Markus, 2001; Rhee, Uleman, Lee, & Roman, 1995). To illustrate, North Americans are more likely to describe themselves in terms of abstract personality traits (e.g., "I am tall"), whereas East Asians are more likely to describe themselves in terms of specific contexts or social relations (e.g., "I am the youngest in my family"). Similarly, when asked to describe acquaintances and their behavior, South Indian participants are more likely to provide the specific situational or interpersonal context (e.g., "He behaves properly with guests but feels sorry if money is spent on them"), whereas American participants are more likely to focus on general, context-free personality traits (e.g., "He is selfish;" Shweder & Bourne, 1984). Members of Western cultures are also more likely to attribute people's behaviors to abstract traits or general dispositions (e.g., "He is lazy") and make predictions of others' behaviors based on dispositional information (Norenzayan, Choi, & Nisbett, 2002), whereas members of Eastern cultures are more likely to attribute behaviors to situational factors (e.g., "He missed class because he was sick;" Morris & Peng, 1994; Lee, Hallahan, & Herzog, 1996) and make predictions about future behaviors based on contextual information (Norenzayan et al., 2002).

To the extent that trait inferences and dispositional attributions constitute high-level construals of behavior (Nussbaum, Trope, & Liberman, 2003), these findings are consistent with the notion that independents represent information in memory more abstractly, whereas interdependents represent information more concretely. Indeed, recent research shows that those primed with an independent self-construal are more likely to construe actions in abstract terms that focus on why the actions are performed, whereas those primed with an interdependent self-construal are more likely to construe actions in concrete terms that focus on how the actions are performed. Independents also use fewer categories to classify objects relative to interdependents (Spassova & Lee, 2013; Study 1a and Study 1b). These findings lend further credence to the relationship between self-construal and level of construal.

Given the close correspondence between construal level and psychological distance, it follows that the two self-construals are associated with different temporal perspectives, such that those with an independent self-construal would be more likely to construe future events or behaviors not only in more abstract terms, but also as taking place in the more distant future; and those with an interdependent self-construal would be more likely to construe future events or behaviors as taking place in the more proximal future. The notion that people with distinct self-construals differ in their temporal construal is consistent with other findings reported in the literature. In particular, people have more promotion concerns when thinking about events in the distant future, but more prevention concerns when thinking about events in the near future (Pennington & Roese, 2003). Further, positive information has been found to be more salient in the distant future, whereas negative information is more salient in the more proximal future (Eyal, Liberman, Trope, & Walther, 2004). To the extent that independents are promotion oriented, and interdependents are prevention oriented, these findings provide further corroboration for the view that independents are likely to adopt a distal temporal perspective, whereas interdependents are likely to adopt a proximal temporal perspective.

That interdependents would construe future events closer to the present than independents may appear at first glance to contradict the commonly held view that members of collectivist cultures who are more mindful of the interrelatedness between objects, persons, and events have a longer-term orientation than members of individualist cultures (Hofstede & Bond, 1988; Triandis, 1989). For example, Maddux and Yuki (2006) show that Japanese perceive events as having more far-reaching consequences than Americans. This apparent paradox may be resolved when one takes into account the distinction between time perspective in terms of when a future event is perceived to occur (i.e., temporal distance to the event), and how long the consequences of an event are perceived to last (i.e., temporal consequences of the event). While temporal distance is conceptualized as the distance between a future event and the here and now (Liberman & Förster, 2009), long-term orientation is about the long-term consequences of certain actions. The inclination of interdependents relative to independents to pay close attention to the interrelationships between people, objects, and situations is what accounts for their low-level construal and proximal temporal perspective on one hand and for their long-term orientation and far-reaching perspective on the other. Indeed, when research participants were asked to think about when a future event was going to take place and how long the enthusiasm for that event would last, European Americans indicated that the event was taking place at a more distal future, but that people's enthusiasm for the event was perceived to be more short-lived relative to Asian Americans and Koreans (Lee et al., 2011, Study 2).

The self-construal temporal fit effect

An important implication of the relationship between self-construal and temporal construal is that people would experience regulatory fit when they construe future events at a temporal distance that matches with their self-construal. Regulatory fit theory (Higgins, 2000, 2005) posits that people become more motivated when they experience regulatory fit. Indeed, independents (interdependents) indicated they would be more motivated to work on a task that is scheduled in the distant (near) future, but only if the task is pleasant and engaging (Lee et al., 2011, Study 3). Consistent with the notion that regulatory fit intensifies reactions, independents and interdependents reported being less motivated when the task that matches their self-construal is unpleasant (Lee et al., 2011, Study 4).

A similar self-construal temporal fit effect also has been observed for persuasion. In particular, Spassova and Lee (2013) show that those with a chronic independent self-construal evaluated an advertisement for holiday destinations more favorably when they were thinking about taking a vacation next year versus next month, and the reverse was true for those with a chronic interdependent self-construal. In another study, they primed participants with either an independent or interdependent self-construal and then presented them with an advertisement for a brand of prepackaged meals that emphasizes either immediate benefits, or benefits to be realized in the more distant future. They find that fit appeals (i.e., appeals advocating future benefits for independents and immediate benefits for interdependents) lead to more favorable attitudes when the arguments are strong, but to less favorable attitudes when the arguments are weak, as compared to nonfit appeals (i.e., appeals advocating immediate benefits for independents and future benefits for interdependents). That is, the self-construal temporal fit effect on persuasion exhibits very similar pattern of results as the self-construal regulatory fit effect.

SELF-CONSTRUAL AND EMPATHY

So far, the two types of self-construal fit discussed are closely related to consumer decisions that benefit the self. But effects of a self-construal fit also have been found to apply to decision making that concerns benefiting others. The helping literature cites altruism as the key motive driving helping behaviors (Batson, Dyck, Brandt, Batson, Powell, McMaster, & Griffitt, 1988), and the empathy–altruism model suggests that people who experience greater empathic concerns for others are more likely to help (Batson et al., 1988; Schroeder, Matthews, Sibicky, Dovidio, & Allen, 1988). According to Batson and his colleagues, when people recognize others' needs and value their welfare, they are likely to spontaneously adopt their perspective, leading to greater empathic concerns and greater inclination to help (Batson, Eklund, Chermok, Hoyt, & Ortiz, 2007). Consistent with this notion that people's empathic concern for others grows out of understanding their needs, feeling their pain, and valuing their welfare, it follows that people with distinct self-construals who value different things in life would be more empathic toward those whose needs match what they value.

For the independents who strive toward personal accomplishments and value personal goals over group goals, success in life is often gauged by social status and ownership of tangible assets. For the interdependents who strive toward relationship harmony and value group goals over personal goals, success in life may be more readily assessed by interpersonal relationships and well-being of their in-group (Markus & Kitayama, 1991; Triandis, 1989). Indeed, in a study where research participants were presented with photographs of people smiling and looking happy, the more accessible is their chronic independent self-construal, the more likely they thought the people in the photographs possess tangible assets such as a home, luxury cars and investments; and the more accessible is their chronic interdependent self-construal, the more likely they thought the people in the photographs have supportive family and friends who care about them (Bradford & Lee, 2013, Study 1). In another study, individuals primed with either an independent or an interdependent self-construal were asked to imagine living a lifestyle that either boasts financial success (e.g., comfortable home in the most sought-after neighborhood, designer wardrobe, income from investments) or one that is enriched with meaningful relationships (e.g., wonderful relationship with parents and family, friends who care, participating in the community). Independents reported being happier with the financially successful lifestyle, whereas interdependents were happier with the relationship enriched lifestyle (Bradford & Lee, 2013, Study 1).

To the extent that people are more empathic when the need states of others match what they value, the implication of these findings is that independents should be more empathic and generous toward those who lack tangible assets and material possessions, whereas interdependents should be more empathetic and generous toward those who are socially isolated.

The self-construal empathy-altruism fit effect

According to the empathy–altruism model of helping (Batson et al., 1988), the greater people's empathic concern toward others, the more likely they are to help; hence independents should be more generous toward those who lack tangible assets, whereas interdependents should be more generous toward those who need nurturing relationships. Consistent with these views, it has been shown that when individuals were given the opportunity to donate money to support education at a homeless shelter, while independents and interdependents did not differ in the amount of money they gave, independents were more likely to designate their donation dollars toward the purchase of books and supplies, whereas interdependents were more likely to designate their donation dollars to support mentors for the children (Bradford & Lee, 2013, Study 2). In another study (Bradford & Lee, 2013, Study 3), those with an independent (versus interdependent) self-construal reported greater empathic concerns and willingness to help when they read about a first-grader who "spends time on the computer, and his eyes shine when he is handed a new book." In contrast, those with an interdependent (versus independent) self-construal expressed greater empathic concerns and willingness to help when they read about the first-grader who "spends time interacting with new friends, and his eyes shine when he is encouraged to answer a question." Participants' greater willingness to help when others' need state matches what they value as a function of their self-construal was found to be mediated by their heightened empathic concerns under the self-construal fit conditions.

The self-construal empathy–altruism fit effect has implications not just for *how much* people help, but also for *how* they help—whether to donate money or to volunteer time. Because tangible assets can be more readily acquired with money, and relationships can be more easily nurtured by spending time, those with a more accessible independent versus interdependent self-construal were found to place differential values on charitable gifts of money versus time (Bradford & Lee, 2013, Study 4). In two studies where individuals were presented with an appeal to support the Make-A-Wish Foundation, independents were more likely to donate money whereas interdependents were more likely to volunteer time (Bradford & Lee, 2013, Studies 5 & 6).

This self-construal fit effect on the type of prosocial behavior people prefer likely emerges from their perception that their support could really make a difference. To the independents who value tangible assets, donating money is more conducive to providing material aids; whereas to the interdependents who value social connectedness, volunteering time is more conducive to helping nurture relationships.

These findings suggest that when people engage in prosocial behaviors, they are inclined to provide what they believe to be of the greatest assistance to address the needs of others and to enhance their welfare, irrespective of their self-construal. Thus, charities seeking support are well advised to make salient the interdependent self-construal of their prospective donors when recruiting volunteers or when soliciting support to enhance social connectedness; but they should make salient prospective donors' independent self-construal when soliciting monetary donations to acquire tangible assets.

CONCLUSION

This chapter discusses how people from an individualist versus collectivist culture may differ as a function of their self-construals. The two self-construals have been found to be associated with different regulatory orientations, different construal levels and temporal perspectives, as well as different sources of happiness and metrics of success in life that in turn arouse different degrees of empathic concerns depending on others' need state. These various orientations, perspectives, and perceived sources of happiness and success associated with the two self-construals lead to differences in perception, motivation, processing style, judgment, and choice. For those with an independent self-construal who view the self as an autonomous individual, success is represented by personal growth and accomplishment that can be readily assessed by one's accumulation of worldly possessions, and their temporal attention is focused on the distal future to maximize growth opportunities. In contrast, for those with an interdependent self-construal who view the self as part of a larger social collective, success is often gauged by harmony within the group, and their attention is more on the here and now to prevent mishaps.

But beyond these differences between the two self-construals is the interesting phenomenon that people respond in a similar fashion to the match and mismatch between their self-construal and the different orientations and perspectives related to goal pursuits, regardless of whether they have an independent or interdependent self-construal. In particular, the correspondence (or lack thereof) between individuals' self-construal and their regulatory focus means of goal pursuit, their temporal perspective, and their altruistic means has been shown to result in heightened motivation, selective attention, enhanced persuasion, more intense empathic concerns, and greater depth of charitable gifting. Our view is that these self-construal fit effects are automatic and likely operate at a nonconscious level such that the effects are stronger when people are not particularly involved in the decision task, and may dissipate or even reverse when people are motivated to process information (Harding et al., 2011; Hong & Lee, 2010; Wang & Lee, 2006).

The individualism–collectivism cultural differences discussed in this chapter are viewed from the perspective of two distinct self-construals, each with its corresponding goals and regulatory orientations. In particular, the promotion and prevention orientations represent two complex motivational systems that engage and reflect different cognitive and affective processes (for a review, see Lee & Higgins, 2009). The promotion system is known to be associated with abstract, global processing, distant temporal construal, affect-based decision making, and additive counterfactuals; whereas the prevention system is known to reflect concrete, local processing, proximal temporal construal, reason-based processing, and subtractive counterfactuals. It is conceivable that other characteristics of the promotion and prevention systems not discussed here may be carried over to the two self-construals and to the two cultures. At the same time, it is important to bear in mind that the distinction between the two self-construals goes beyond the two motivational systems, and that the East–West difference is more complex than just the distinction between the two self-construals. For example, while the regulatory focus literature suggests that those with a promotion orientation tend to think more globally whereas those with a prevention orientation tend to think more locally (Lee et al., 2010), the culture literature shows that Westerners are more likely to have an analytical thinking style whereas Easterners are more likely to have a holistic thinking style (Nisbett, Peng, Choi, & Norenzayan, 2001). Future research should examine how different thinking styles stemming from different social systems may interact with different construal levels associated with distinct regulatory orientations to influence attitudes and behaviors.

Finally, with increased globalization and the rapid modernization of emergent markets, many consumers are multi-nationals who live in or travel to multiple countries and speak multiple languages. Finer distinctions have also been made within the individualist and collectivist cultures (Shavitt, Lalwani, Zhang, & Torelli, 2006). It would be of particular importance and interest to researchers and practitioners to examine how these global consumers may view the self, and how they may experience self-construal fit.

REFERENCES

Aaker, J. L., & Lee, A. Y. (2001). "I" seek pleasures and "we" avoid pains: The role of self-regulatory goals in information processing and persuasion. *Journal of Consumer Research*, 28(1), 33–49.

Batson, C. D., Dyck, J. L., Brandt, J. R., Batson, J. G., Powell, A. L., McMaster, M. R., & Griffitt, C. (1988). Five studies testing two new egoistic alternatives to the empathy-altruism hypothesis. *Journal of Personality and Social Psychology*, 55(1), 52–77.

Batson, C. D., Eklund, J. H., Chermok, V. L., Hoyt, J. L., & Ortiz, B. G. (2007). An additional antecedent of empathic concern: Valuing the welfare of the person in need. *Journal of Personality and Social Psychology, 93*, 65–74.

Bradford, T. W., & Lee, A. Y. (2013). Tangible assets versus social connectedness: A self-construal empathy-altruism fit model of charitable giving. Working paper, Kellogg School of Management, Northwestern University.

Briley, D. A., & Wyer, R. S. (2002). The effects of group membership on the avoidance of negative outcomes: Implications for social and consumer decisions. *Journal of Consumer Research, 29*(3), 400–415.

Camacho, C. J., Higgins, E. T., & Luger, L. (2003). Moral value transfer from regulatory fit: What feels right is right and what feels wrong is wrong. *Journal of Personality and Social Psychology, 84*(3), 498–510.

Chiao, J. Y., & Blizinsky, K. D. (2010). Culture-gene coevolution of individualism-collectivism and the serotonin transporter gene. *Proceedings of the Royal Society B-Biological Sciences, 277*(1681), 529–537.

Cousins, S. D. (1989). Culture and self-perception in Japan and the United States. *Journal of Personality and Social Psychology, 56*(1), 124.

English, T., & Chen, S. (2007). Culture and self-concept stability: Consistency across and within contexts among Asian Americans and European Americans. *Journal of Personality and Social Psychology, 93*(3), 478–490.

Eyal, T., Liberman, N., Trope, Y., & Walther, E. (2004). The pros and cons of temporally near and distant action. *Journal of Personality and Social Psychology, 86*(6), 781–795.

Frey, D., & Stahlberg, D. (1986). Selection of information after receiving more or less reliable self-threatening information. *Personality and Social Psychology Bulletin, 12*(4), 434–441.

Gardner, W. L., Gabriel, S., & Lee, A. Y. (1999). "I" value freedom, but "we" value relationships: Self-construal priming mirrors cultural differences in judgment. *Psychological Science, 10*, 321–326.

Harding, L., Lisjak, M., & Lee, A. Y. (2011). The persuasive power of regulatory nonfit. Working paper, Kellogg School of Management, Northwestern University.

Heine, S. J., & Lehman, D. R. (1999). Culture, self-discrepancies, and self-satisfaction. *Personality and Social Psychology Bulletin, 25*(8), 915–925.

Heine, S. J., Lehman, D. R., Markus, H. R., & Kitayama, S. (1999). Is there a universal need for positive self-regard? *Psychological Review, 106*(4), 766–794.

Higgins, E. T. (1997). Beyond pleasure and pain. *American Psychologist, 52*(12), 1280–1300.

Higgins, E. T. (2000). Making a good decision: Value from fit. *American Psychologist, 55*(11), 1217–1230.

Higgins, E. T. (2005). Value from regulatory fit. *Current Directions in Psychological Science, 14*(4), 209–213.

Hofstede, G., & Bond, M. H. (1988). The Confucius connection--from cultural roots to economic growth. *Organizational Dynamics, 16*(4), 5–21.

Holmberg, D., Markus, H., Herzog, A. R., & Franks, M. (1997). American selves: As independent as we thought? [Meeting Abstract]. *International Journal of Psychology, 31*(3-4), 3697–3697.

Hong, J., & Lee, A. Y. (2010). Feeling mixed but not torn: The moderating role of construal level in mixed emotions appeals. *Journal of Consumer Research, 37*(3), 456–472.

Hong, Y., Morris, M. W., Chiu, C., & Benet-Martinez, V. (2000). Multicultural minds: A dynamic constructivist approach to culture and cognition. *American Psychologist, 55,* 709–720.

Kanagawa, C., Cross, S. E., & Markus, H. R. (2001). 'Who am I?' The cultural psychology of the conceptual self. *Personality and Social Psychology Bulletin, 27* (January), 90–103.

Kitayama, S., Markus, H. R., Matsumoto, H., & Norasakkunkit, V. (1997). Individual and collective processes in the construction of the self: Self-enhancement in the United States and self-criticism in Japan. *Journal of Personality and Social Psychology, 72*(6), 1245–1267.

Kwan, V. S. Y., Bond, M. H., & Singelis, T. M. (1997). Pancultural explanations for life satisfaction: Adding relationship harmony to self-esteem. *Journal of Personality and Social Psychology, 73*(5), 1038–1051.

Labroo, A., & Lee, A. Y. (2006). Between two brands: A goal fluency account of brand evaluation. *Journal of Marketing Research, 18,* 374–385.

Lee, A. Y., & Aaker, J. L. (2004). Bringing the frame into focus: The influence of regulatory fit on processing fluency and persuasion. *Journal of Personality and Social Psychology, 86*(2), 205–218.

Lee, A. Y., Aaker, J. L., & Gardner, W. L. (2000). The pleasures and pains of distinct self-construals: The role of interdependnce in regulatory focus. *Journal of Personality and Social Psychology, 78*(6), 1122–1134.

Lee, A. Y., & Higgins, E. T. (2009). The persuasive power of regulatory fit. In A. Y. Lee & E. T. Higgins (Eds.), *Social Psychology of Consumer Behavior* (pp. 319–333). New York, NY, USA: Psychology Press, New York, NY.

Lee, A. Y., Keller, P. A., & Sternthal, B. (2010). Value from regulatory construal fit: The persuasive impact of fit between consumer goals and message concreteness. *Journal of Consumer Research, 36*(5), 735–747.

Lee, F., Hallahan, M., & Herzog, T. (1996). Explaining real-life events: How culture and domain shape attributions. *Personality and Social Psychology Bulletin, 22*(7), 732–741.

Lee, S., Lee, A. Y., & Kern, M. (2011). Viewing time through the lens of the self: The fit effect of self-construal and temporal distance on task perception. *European Journal of Social Psychology, 41,*191–200.

Liberman, N., & Förster, J. (2009). Distancing from experienced self: How global-versus-local perception affects estimation of psychological distance. *Journal of Personality and Social Psychology, 97*(2), 203–216.

Maddux, W. W., & Yuki, M. (2006). The "Ripple Effect": Cultural differences in perceptions of the consequences of events. *Personality and Social Psychology Bulletin, 32*(5), 669–683.

Markus, H. R., & Kitayama, S. (1991). Culture and the self: Implications for cognition, emotion, and motivation. *Psychological Review, 98*(2), 224–253.

Morris, M. W., & Peng, K. (1994). Culture and cause: American and Chinese attributions for social and physical events. *Journal of Personality and Social psychology, 67*(6), 949.

Nisbett, R. E., Peng, K., Choi, I., & Norenzayan, A. (2001). Culture and systems of thought: Holistic vs. analytic cognition. *Psychological Review*, *108*(April), 291–310.

Norenzayan, A., Choi, I., & Nisbett, R. E. (2002). Cultural similarities and differences in social inference: Evidence from behavioral predictions and lay theories of behavior. *Personality and Social Psychology Bulletin*, *28*(1), 109–120.

Nussbaum, S., Trope, Y., & Liberman, N. (2003). Creeping dispositionism: the temporal dynamics of behavior prediction. *Journal of Personality and Social Psychology*, *84*(3), 485–497.

Pennington, G. L., & Roese, N. J. (2003). Regulatory focus and temporal distance. *Journal of Experimental Social Psychology*, 39 (6), 563–576.

Rhee, E., Uleman, J. S., Lee, H. K., & Roman, R. J. (1995). Spontaneous self-descriptions and ethnic identities in individualistic and collectivistic cultures. *Journal of Personality and Social Psychology*, *69*,142–152.

Schroeder, D. A., Matthews, L. L., Sibicky, M. E., Dovidio, J. F., & Allen, J. L. (1988). Empathic concern and helping behaviour: egoism or altruism? *Journal of Experimental Social Psychology*, *24*, 333–353.

Shavitt, S., Lalwani, A. K., Zhang, J., & Torelli, C. J. (2006). The horizontal / vertical distinction in cross-cultural consumer research. *Journal of Consumer Psychology*, *16*(4), 325–342.

Shweder, R. A., & Bourne, E. J. (1984). *Does the concept of the person vary cross-culturally?* In R. A. Shweder & R. A. LeVine (Eds.), *Culture Theory: Essays on Mind, Self, and Emotion* (pp. 158–199). New York: Cambridge University Press.

Singelis, T. M. (1994). The measurement of independent and interdependent self-construals. *Personality and Social Psychology Bulletin*, *20*(5), 580–591.

Spassova, G., & Lee, A. Y. (2013). Looking into the future: A match between self-view and temporal distance. *Journal of Consumer Research*, *40*(1), 159–171.

Triandis, H. C. (1989). The self and social behavior in differing cultural contexts. *Psychological Review*, *96*(3), 506–520.

Wang, J., & Lee, A. Y. (2006). The role of regulatory focus in preference construction. *Journal of Marketing Research*, *43*(1), 28–38.

8

Response Biases in Cross-Cultural Measurement

HANS BAUMGARTNER AND BERT WEIJTERS ■

A frequent goal of cross-cultural research is to compare mean values on constructs or the strength of relationships between constructs across cultures. If these comparisons are to be meaningful, it is necessary that the data collected from respondents in different cultures validly assess the focal constructs and that certain requirements of measurement equivalence be satisfied (Steenkamp & Baumgartner, 1998). Unfortunately, it has been known for a long time that people's responses to survey questions do not only measure the intended content that the items in questionnaires are trying to tap, but may also reflect content-irrelevant influences (Cronbach, 1946, 1950; Lentz, 1938). In particular, substantial evidence has accumulated which shows that various systematic sources of error can contaminate cross-cultural data and invalidate simple comparisons across cultures. The purpose of this chapter is to review the most common response biases and to provide guidelines for cross-cultural researchers about how to deal with them (see also Church, 2010; Hui & Triandis, 1985; Leung, 2008).

Three categories of measurement bias will be considered. First, there are systematic response tendencies that are more or less independent of the content that the survey questions are trying to assess. In other words, the respondent ignores the substantive content of the questions and responds on some basis other than what the questions were designed to measure. Such tendencies are usually referred to as response styles (Baumgartner & Steenkamp, 2001; Weijters, 2006), particularly if they are assumed to be stable characteristics of respondents. The best-known response styles are those that assume that respondents have a preference for certain response options on the rating scale, such as acquiescence (a preference for the response categories reflecting agreement or, more generally, the positive side of the rating scale), disacquiescence (a preference for the response categories reflecting disagreement), extreme response style (a preference for the extremes of the response scale), and midpoint response style (a preference for the middle or neutral response category).

Second, there are systematic response tendencies where respondents do not ignore the content of the questions, but the answers provided are not an accurate reflection of their personalities, beliefs, attitudes, or whatever else is being measured. This is sometimes referred to as a response set, in contrast to a response style (see Rorer, 1965; Weijters, 2006), although the terms response style and response set are also used to distinguish between stable and transient response biases (e.g., Paulhus, 1991). The differentiation between response styles and response sets in terms of dependence on item content is somewhat controversial, because even response styles seem to depend on item content to some extent (e.g., acquiescence has been found to be stronger for ambiguous items and items that are neutral in desirability; cf. Messick, 1991), but item content is a much more important determinant of response sets than response styles. The best-known response set is social desirability, which refers to a tendency to present an overly favorable image of oneself (Steenkamp, de Jong, & Baumgartner, 2010). Other response sets such as deviant responding (e.g., a desire not to follow the modal response) have been identified, but they are not covered here.

Both response styles and response sets (in the sense used here) have been considered from either a situational perspective (as a characteristic of items, such as the ambiguity of the question, or more general contextual factors, such as the ethnicity of the interviewer or time pressure present during the survey administration) or a dispositional perspective (e.g., acquiescence as an aspect of personality). Here we focus on the latter view, although in practice biased responding is probably an interactive function of both (e.g., a respondent may be predisposed to socially desirable responding, but a survey about sensitive topics administered in a setting in which there is little guarantee of anonymity may heighten the concern with projecting a favorable image; see Baumgartner & Steenkamp, 2001).

For both response styles and response sets, we will begin with a discussion of the conceptualization and measurement of each response bias, then review the cross-cultural research relevant to each bias, and finally describe the consequences of these various biases and methods to cope with them. One important issue with regard to the post-hoc control of response biases is whether the measures used to assess the extent to which answers to questionnaires are contaminated by nonsubstantive responding actually capture response biases rather than substantive content; this is known as the substance versus style controversy in the literature. For example, even though researchers often assume that social desirability scales only measure biased responding, this is not necessarily the case because at least some of the variance in social desirability scales may reflect substantive content. We will raise this issue in several places in this chapter and recommend valid measurement methods and appropriate correction procedures for different response biases.

Third, there are several other response biases that may threaten cross-cultural comparisons, such as effects due to differences in question order, anchor effects, differential problems with reverse-worded items, and reference-group effects. In contrast to response styles and response sets, these response biases are an undifferentiated collection of situational influences on survey responses that have not been studied as systematically as response styles and response sets. However, because of their relevance, they will be discussed briefly at the end of this chapter.

RESPONSE STYLES IN CROSS-CULTURAL RESEARCH

Conceptualization and measurement

CONCEPTUALIZATION

The response styles that are of primary interest in this chapter are respondents' tendencies to select specific subsets of response options disproportionately. Specifically, respondents may make disproportionate use of the response categories on the positive side (acquiescence response style or ARS) or the negative side (disacquiescence response style or DARS), the extremes (extreme response style or ERS), or the middle of the scale (midpoint response style or MRS) (e.g., Weijters, Geuens, & Schillewaert, 2010b). Although, intuitively, ARS and DARS should be negatively correlated, they need not be (Bachman & O'Malley, 1984). Similarly, ERS and MRS need not be opposite tendencies, as some respondents may use both the midpoint and the endpoints disproportionately (cf. Figure 1 in Weijters et al., 2010b).

With regard to *(dis)acquiescence*, some authors have discussed a variety of situational factors that may encourage (dis)acquiescent responding (see Baumgartner & Steenkamp, 2006). For example, ARS is expected to be higher when items are ambiguous, vague, or neutral in desirability, or when a respondent is uncertain about an issue. In addition, peripheral (heuristic) processing conditions should favor acquiescent responding. Here, we will focus on dispositional determinants of (D)ARS. Messick (1991) distinguished two dimensions of acquiescence, which he called impulsive acceptance and uncritical agreement. Consistent with the former, ARS has been found to characterize stimulation-seeking extroverts who impulsively accept statements. In contrast, DARS has been argued to be characteristic of controlled and reflective introverts (see Couch & Keniston, 1960). Consistent with the latter perspective, some researchers argue that acquiescence reflects uncritical agreement with statements by respondents low in cognitive abilities. This explanation is closely related to the proposition in the survey research literature that acquiescence may be due to deference shown by lower-status respondents to higher-status interviewers, or as an attempt to avoid confrontation (see Baumgartner & Steenkamp, 2006).

In the cross-cultural literature, the deference or conformity reflected in acquiescent responding has been hypothesized to be positively related to Hofstede's (1980, 1991) dimensions of power distance, collectivism, and femininity (Harzing, 2006; Johnson, Kulesa, Cho, & Shavitt, 2005). Power distance refers to the extent to which members of a culture consider human inequality as normal, collectivism (versus individualism) refers to the extent to which group goals take precedence over individual goals, and femininity (versus masculinity) refers to a culture's emphasis on warm interpersonal relationships as opposed to assertiveness. Harzing (2006) argues that uncertainty avoidance (the degree to which a culture prefers structured over unstructured situations) should also be positively associated with ARS, but Johnson et al. (2005) believe the relationship is not clear.

Extreme response style has been related to respondents' desire to express decisiveness, intolerance of ambiguity, and a lack of differentiated cognitive structures, whereas *midpoint response style* has been conceptualized as being reflective of modesty and caution, evasiveness, indecision, or indifference (Baumgartner & Steenkamp, 2006). There is general agreement that individualism should be positively related to ERS (because decisiveness is a virtue in individualistic cultures) and negatively related to MRS (because collectivist cultures value modesty; e.g., Johnson et al., 2005). In particular, the dialectical thinking characteristic of East Asian (collectivist) cultures encourages tolerance for contradictions, compromise, and moderation (pursuit of the "middle way"; Peng & Nisbett, 1999), all of which suggest a positive (negative) relationship between collectivism and MRS (ERS). In addition, since intolerance of ambiguity corresponds to uncertainty avoidance at the cultural level, ERS is more likely in cultures that are high in uncertainty avoidance; the reverse holds for MRS. ERS may also be positively related to masculinity through its link to assertiveness (de Jong, Steenkamp, Fox, & Baumgartner, 2008). Finally, Johnson et al. (2005) hypothesized a positive relation between power distance and ERS, because high power distance relates to decisiveness in communications by superiors. But, as pointed out by de Jong et al. (2008), this implies that the effect depends on a person's position in the social hierarchy, such that a null effect is likely in general. Apparently, researchers have not considered explicit hypotheses about the relationship between MRS and masculinity or power distance.

MEASUREMENT

Response styles are typically measured by examining respondents' use of particular response categories (e.g., the midpoint for MRS) across a range of items. To obtain valid measures of response styles, these items should be highly heterogeneous in content (Baumgartner & Steenkamp, 2001). The reason is that otherwise it is not clear whether systematic response tendencies are due to content or style (Rorer, 1965; Greenleaf, 1992b). For example, if respondents tend to be extremely positive in response to ten items that all measure satisfaction and all items are keyed in the same direction (i.e., there are no reversed items), it is impossible to disentangle the effect of content (respondents are very satisfied) and style (respondents tend to respond positively regardless of content). Unfortunately, when studying secondary data, item heterogeneity may be limited because items in the same questionnaire typically are related to some extent.

Once a set of items has been selected as the basis for response style measurement, response style measures can be constructed based on the frequencies with which certain response categories are used. Unweighted counts (or proportions) of agreement responses and disagreement responses can be used to measure ARS and DARS (i.e., ARS is the number of items a respondent agrees with; DARS is the number of items a respondent disagrees with). Alternatively, weights can be assigned to different response categories to reflect that some responses convey a stronger sense of agreement or disagreement than others. For example, for a five-point agreement scale with the categories defined as strongly disagree, disagree, neutral, agree, and strongly agree, an ARS score can be computed by assigning a weight of 2 to strongly agree responses, a weight of 1 to agree responses, and 0 to all other responses, and then summing the recoded variables across items. Similarly, a DARS score can be obtained by counting strongly disagree responses as 2 and disagree responses as 1, and then summing across items. It is quite common to subtract DARS from ARS to obtain an overall score for net acquiescence response style (NARS). NARS corresponds to the expected bias away from the midpoint (positive or negative).

ARS has also been operationalized as the tendency to agree with both an item and its reversal (Winkler, Kanouse, & Ware, 1982). To create such an ARS measure, multiple pairs of regular and reversed items are needed. For example, respondents who agree with the item "I like brand A" and also agree with the item "I dislike brand A" get one point, others get a zero. By summing such scores across multiple pairs of regular and reversed items, researchers obtain an overall score that presumably measures ARS. A similar approach can be used by counting double disagreements with regular and reversed item pairs to obtain a DARS measure. If desired, one can also weight the strength of simultaneous agreement or disagreement (i.e., strong agreement with an item and its reversal is scored as 3, strong agreement with one item and agreement with the other is scored as 2, and mere agreement with both items is scored as 1). Conceptually, this approach can be called into question based on recent research showing that ARS and misresponse to reversed items are distinct response biases (Swain, Weathers, & Niedrich, 2008). For this reason it may be more appropriate to use the ARS and DARS operationalizations based on heterogeneous items, provided the collection of items is truly heterogeneous (i.e., the items do not share common substantive content).

ERS can be measured as the number or proportion of items on which the respondent chooses the most extreme scale categories (either positive or negative) across a heterogeneous collection of items. It has also been operationalized as the standard deviation of respondents' scores across a series of heterogeneous items, but strictly speaking this is a measure of response range (RR; Baumgartner & Steenkamp, 2001). RR and ERS tend to be correlated quite highly, but they are not the same. Whereas RR may indicate meaningful differentiation of responses across items, ERS can be an attempt on the part of the respondent to minimize cognitive effort, especially since it is common for researchers to only label the endpoints in rating scales (Weijters, Cabooter, & Schillewaert, 2010). This results in a special status of the endpoints of rating scales as anchor points that are relatively more salient to respondents and less demanding in terms of interpretation (Arce-Ferrer, 2006; Hui & Triandis, 1989; Weijters, Geuens, & Schillewaert,

2010a). In sum, ERS clearly conforms to the definition of a response style, while the nature of RR is somewhat more ambiguous.

ERS has been found to be relatively consistent over the course of a single questionnaire (Weijters et al., 2010a). On the other hand, some research suggests that not all items are equally biased by ERS. It may therefore be necessary to differentially weight each ERS indicator (i.e., the binary variables that indicate whether or not an extreme response was given to a particular item). De Jong et al. (2008) propose an item response theory (IRT)-based measure which does exactly that.

To obtain a measure of MRS, researchers usually compute the number or proportion of midpoint responses across a set of heterogeneous items. Of course this is only possible if a researcher uses an odd number of scale categories with an explicit neutral option.

Typical measures of response styles yield individual scores for each respondent in terms of each response style. Indirect ways of testing for the presence of response styles at the aggregate level by means of measurement invariance testing have been proposed as well (Cheung & Rensvold, 2000; Greenleaf, 1992a). The rationale underlying this approach is that ARS (DARS) leads to an increase (decrease) in item intercepts, whereas ERS (MRS) leads to higher (lower) factor loadings (in addition to differences in intercepts). Unfortunately, this approach has a fundamental limitation. The reason is that response styles by definition affect all items in a scale (Weijters et al., 2010a). Even if the bias varies across items, some component will likely be uniform. To the extent that the bias is uniform across items, it will consistently inflate all item intercepts and/or loadings. Such bias cannot be detected by means of measurement invariance testing, as invariance testing only detects item-specific biases (Little, 1997, 2000; Weijters, Schillewaert, & Geuens 2008). For example, if all items in a brand-liking scale are inflated by ARS in country A as compared to country B, this is likely to result in a significant latent mean difference rather than a significant difference for particular item intercepts. A difference in item intercepts could be detected, on the other hand, if only one item were biased upwards in country A, for example due to translation problems. So, although response styles do threaten the equivalence of scores and measurement parameters across cultures, measurement invariance tests cannot always detect nonequivalence. Therefore, the safest way to measure response styles is to construct response style measures based on heterogeneous items (i.e., items that share minimal common content).

Evidence of cross-cultural response style differences

Ross and Miroswsky (1984) studied acquiescence for Anglo and Mexican American respondents in Texas and Mexican respondents in Mexico. Their acquiescence measure was based on "agree" or "strongly agree" responses to a twenty-item locus of control scale in which all items are keyed in the same direction and ten items each assess internal and external locus of control, respectively. Mexicans provided the most and Anglos the least acquiescent responses.

Acquiescence was unrelated to self-reported psychological distress, and acquiescence did not moderate the strength of the relationships between various sociocultural variables and distress.

Some researchers have compared response styles across subcultures within the same nationality. Bachman and O'Malley (1984) compared ARS, DARS, and ERS across black and white high school seniors within the United States over three subsequent data collections. They measured ARS as the proportion of "agree" responses, DARS as the proportion of "disagree" responses, and ERS as the proportion of endpoint responses across 404 diverse items (some were measured on a four-point rating scale so MRS could not be assessed for all items). They found higher ARS, DARS, and ERS among black respondents, with the net effect that black respondents had higher agreement scores and higher variance in their scores. They also note that ARS and DARS tend to be positively correlated. Furthermore, the response styles, especially ERS, are shown to be stable over time. Bachman and O'Malley suggest subcultural differences in language usage as the most likely explanation of these response style differences.

Hui and Triandis (1989) compared Hispanic and non-Hispanic US respondents in terms of ERS (frequency of use of the endpoints). They found that Hispanics tended to have higher ERS for a five-point scale. The difference was mitigated when a ten-point scale was used. In this case, both Hispanics and non-Hispanics showed a response pattern where the majority of responses fell into the middle and extreme categories.

Marín, Gamba, and Marín (1992) compared Hispanic and non-Hispanic whites in terms of acquiescence (whether or not a respondent agreed with questions) and extreme response style (use of the endpoints). Across four data sets, Hispanics were generally both more acquiescent and more extreme in their responses. An interesting aspect of the study was that acculturation moderated this finding, such that increasing acculturation lessened both ARS and ERS.

Many studies have reported comparisons of stylistic responding between two countries (see Table 1 in Harzing, 2006, for a review). Although the findings of these studies have been fairly consistent, the results are largely descriptive, and while they make the general point that response style differences are a threat to the comparability of scores across countries, the findings are not very revealing (unless one is particularly interested in the specific countries studied) and the generalizability of the conclusions is limited. In the following discussion, we will focus on studies that have considered a larger set of countries, particularly those in which the authors explicitly related cross-country differences to more basic dimensions of cultural variation.

Stening and Everett (1984) studied the incidence of ERS and MRS in judgments of managerial stereotypes by managers from nine countries (mostly in Asia plus Great Britain and the United States). There were significant cross-country differences in the use of the endpoints and the midpoint of the response scale across 54 items, but it is difficult to draw generalizable conclusions from the study and it is not entirely clear whether the differences in scale usage really reflect stylistic responding.

Chen, Lee, and Stevenson (1995) compared high school students from Japan, Taiwan, Canada, and the United States in terms of ERS and MRS (across 57 items covering many different topics). They found that Asian respondents were more likely to use the midpoint of the scale than North American respondents, and that US respondents had higher ERS than respondents from the three other countries. An ad hoc measure of individualism–collectivism with poor reliability (available for Japan, Taiwan, and the United States) showed that US respondents on average were more individualistic than Asian respondents. Furthermore, individual-level correlations between MRS (ERS) and individualism were negative (positive) in each country. Finally, converting the original seven-point scale into three-point and two-point scales (which has been proposed as a control for differences in stylistic responding) had little effect on mean comparisons between countries. Based on their results, Chen et al. (1995) suggest that the "difference in response style between North Americans and East Asians was in line with the distinction often made between individualist and collectivist cultures" (p. 174).

Watkins and Cheung (1995) studied response biases in a self-esteem instrument, the so-called Self-Description Questionnaire (SDQ). The SDQ includes six control scales that assess various response biases. Of particular interest is the fifth control scale, which can be interpreted as a measure of NARS because it assesses simultaneous agreement or disagreement with regular and reversed item pairs. Watkins and Cheung conducted their study with children from Australia, China, Nepal, Nigeria, and the Philippines, and found significant main effects of country and significant interactions of country with gender for all six response biases studied, including net acquiescence. However, it is not very obvious what these differences mean theoretically.

In a study of response styles in eleven European countries, Baumgartner and Steenkamp (2001) investigated the influence of five response styles (including ARS, DARS, ERS, and MRS) on scale scores and relationships between scales. Although they did not report explicit cross-cultural comparisons, they do mention that in Greece and Portugal stylistic responding had a strong biasing effect on estimated correlations between several commonly used scales (e.g., ethnocentrism, environmental consciousness).

Smith (2004) computed country-level acquiescence scores from several large-scale cross-cultural surveys, which are essentially indices of NARS (e.g., the mean endorsement of all fifty-six values included in the Schwartz Values Survey), and correlated them with various dimensions of cultural variation, including the Hofstede dimensions. He found that individualism and power distance had consistently negative and positive correlations, respectively, with acquiescence scores. Acquiescence was not associated with Hofstede's uncertainty avoidance, but did have a highly consistent positive relationship with the "should be" uncertainty avoidance index based on the GLOBE project (see Smith, 2004, for details).

Van Herk, Poortinga, and Verhallen (2004) analyzed data from three separate surveys dealing with attitudes toward cooking, doing laundry, and shaving conducted in different countries of the European Union. The authors' interest was in acquiescence and extreme responding, although the acquiescence measure is really a measure of NARS. The authors found consistent differences in acquiescence and extreme responding across countries, and Greek respondents had the highest NARS and ERS scores. More generally, Mediterranean countries tended to have higher NARS and ERS scores than northwestern European countries, which would be consistent with the notion that individualism is negatively related to acquiescence and extreme responding, but the authors are reluctant to interpret their findings in this way. Because the items were not heterogeneous in content and no reversed items were used, it is difficult to clearly interpret the authors' measures as indicators of stylistic responding. However, the authors did correlate the attitudinal data with measures of "actual" behavior (e.g., sales of detergents and razors) across countries, and the lack of significant positive relationships suggests that the self-reports may suffer from response bias. Van Herk et al. (2004) also make the valid point that if the scores for the cultural dimensions were obtained by means of self-reports, they may themselves be biased by response styles (and/or other response effects).

Johnson et al. (2005) studied ARS and ERS differences across ten (8079 respondents) and nineteen countries (18,307 respondents), respectively (the countries used in the ARS analyses were a subset of the full set of countries available for the ERS analyses), and related these response styles to power distance, masculinity, individualism, and uncertainty avoidance (as well as gross national product per capita). The ARS measure was based on simultaneous agreement with nine pairs of regular and reverse-keyed items. Based on a multilevel model in which several sociodemographic variables were included at the individual level, they found that, as hypothesized, ARS was negatively related to individualism and masculinity. ARS also had negative relationships with uncertainty avoidance and power distance; the negative effect of power distance was contrary to the authors' prediction, while no a priori prediction was stated for uncertainty avoidance. They also found a positive relation between ERS and the dimensions of power distance and masculinity, as predicted. However, the hypothesized positive relationships with individualism and uncertainty avoidance were not obtained. Additionally, ARS was negatively correlated with gross national product.

Harzing (2006) compared final-year university students (in business) from twenty-six countries in terms of NARS, MRS, and ERS (separately for positive and negative extreme responding). The response styles were related to three of Hofstede's (2001) dimensions (power distance, individualism–collectivism, uncertainty avoidance) as well as extraversion. In an analysis based on country-level averages, NARS and (positive) ERS were found to have a negative correlation with individualism and a positive correlation with power distance. In a regression analysis including the three Hofstede dimensions and extraversion, power distance and extraversion were positively and individualism was negatively related to NARS, but only extraversion was positively related to (positive) ERS. MRS was negatively correlated with both power distance and uncertainty avoidance, and in a simultaneous regression analysis power distance, individualism, and uncertainty avoidance had significant negative effects. Harzing also investigated (at the individual level) whether completing the questionnaire in one's native language or in English influenced stylistic responding and whether English language competence had an impact. She found that the English questionnaire led to lower ERS and higher MRS than the native language questionnaire, and that for the English questionnaire self-rated ability to understand written English was positively related to ERS and negatively related to MRS. Apparently, language competence makes respondents more willing to respond more extremely.

De Jong, et al. (2008) proposed a sophisticated method based on item response theory to measure ERS, which takes into account that the items used to measure ERS may not be equally good indicators of ERS and may be correlated for substantive reasons. The model is also applicable to multilevel data structures in which both individual level and cultural variables influence ERS. In a study with representative samples of consumers from twenty-six countries on four continents, they found that ERS was positively related to national-cultural individualism, uncertainty avoidance, and masculinity. The effect of power distance was not significant.

Van Rosmalen, van Herk, and Groenen (2010) identified response style segments across five European countries, but did not specifically report the cross-country incidence rates of these response style segments. Their graphical report suggests, however, that the extreme positive response category is most commonly used in Italy and Spain and least commonly in Germany, with France and the UK situated in between.

Summary

Table 8.1 summarizes the results of previous studies concerning the relationships between response styles and Hofstede's dimensions of cultural variation. The findings are most consistent for individualism–collectivism: individualism is negatively associated with (N)ARS and MRS, and tends to have a positive relationship with ERS. There is less consistency across studies for the other dimensions.

Effects of response styles

If data collected in different cultures are contaminated by response styles to varying degrees, the comparability of the data is compromised (Baumgartner & Steenkamp, 2001). In essence, response styles influence the response frequency distributions of the variables, irrespective of the distribution of the underlying latent construct. That is, even if two samples have identical latent distributions, their observed response distributions may be different as a consequence of response style differences. As a result, there may be artificial differences in central tendency (means), dispersion (variance), and higher-order moments of the distribution (skewness and kurtosis), although the latter have received little

Table 8.1. RELATIONSHIP BETWEEN RESPONSE STYLES AND DIMENSIONS
OF CULTURAL VARIATION

	Power distance	Uncertainty avoidance	Individualism (versus collectivism)	Masculinity (versus femininity)	Other cultural variables studied
ACQUIESCENCE RESPONSE STYLE					
Johnson et al. (2005)	–	–	–	–	GNP (–)
NET ACQUIESCENCE RESPONSE STYLE					
Smith (2004)	+	0	–	0	GLOBE uncertainty avoidance (+)
Harzing (2006)	+	0	–	n.a.	Extraversion (+)
EXTREME RESPONSE STYLE					
Chen et al. (1995)	n.a.	n.a.	+	n.a.	
Johnson et al. (2005)	+	0	0	+	GNP (0)
Harzing (2006)	0	0	0	n.a.	Extraversion (+)
De Jong et al. (2008)	0	+	+	+	
MIDPOINT RESPONSE STYLE					
Chen et al. (1995)	n.a.	n.a.	–	n.a.	
Harzing (2006)	–	–	–	n.a.	

NOTE: Table entries of +, – or 0 refer to a significantly positive or negative effect or a nonsignificant effect; n.a. means no effect was reported. The negative effect of power distance on acquiescence response style (ARS) in Johnson et al. (2005) was opposite to predictions, and no hypothesis was stated for the relationship between uncertainty avoidance and ARS, although a negative effect was obtained. The positive effect of extraversion on ERS in Harzing (2006) was for positive extreme responding. GNP refers to gross national product.

attention in the literature. Moreover, because response styles typically exert a biasing effect throughout the course of a questionnaire (Weijters et al., 2010a), response styles may result in common variance that is not due to content (i.e., method variance). The amount of common variance may differ across cultures, resulting in nonequivalent factor structures or artifactual differences (or lack of differences) in relationships between constructs.

Baumgartner and Steenkamp (2001) identified the specific biasing effects that ARS, DARS, ERS, and MRS have on means and variances across cultures. Specifically, higher ARS results in artificially higher observed means if there are no or few reverse-scored items. DARS has the opposite effect, so the two may offset each other to some extent (although DARS is less common). Moreover, higher variance in ARS and/or DARS contributes to increased method variance. The effect of ERS and MRS on observed means depends on the scale average. For scales with average scores above the midpoint, ERS biases observed scores upwards, whereas MRS biases observed scores downwards. The reverse holds for scales with average scores below the midpoint. In terms of dispersion, higher ERS typically results in artificially higher observed variances because extreme positive responding tends to be positively correlated with extreme negative responding. MRS has the opposite effect.

Correction procedures

The goal of correction is to analyze observed data in such a way that the findings are not biased by response styles. Depending on the assumed measurement level of rating scale data (i.e., interval, ordinal, or nominal), different correction procedures have been proposed.

CORRECTION FOR INTERVAL MEASUREMENT

For a given individual and a given item, the confirmatory factor analysis (CFA) model can be mathematically described as follows:

$$X = \tau + \lambda\,\xi + \delta \tag{1}$$

where X is the observed response to a specific item, τ is the intercept for the item, λ is the factor loading, ξ is the score on the latent construct, and δ is the residual term. As is apparent from equation (1), the CFA model assumes linearity of the regression function of the response on the construct. An example of a regression plot of an observed item/indicator on its latent construct is given in Figure 8.1. In the example, the graph indicates that a respondent with a ξ level of zero has an expected item score of 4, the midpoint.

Response styles affect the item-construct relation. Cheung and Rensvold (2000) discuss the effect in a CFA context (see also Greenleaf, 1992a). In this linear model, two parameters, representing the slope and the intercept, are needed

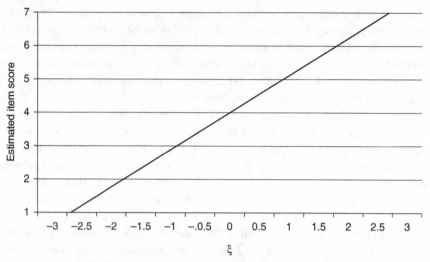

Figure 8.1 Example of confirmatory factor analysis item regression plot between construct and item.

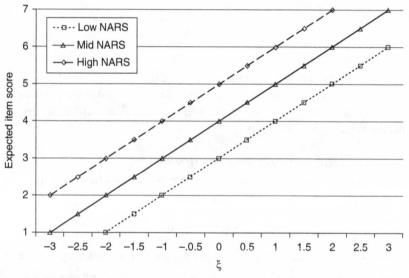

Figure 8.2 Net acquiescence response style effects on the confirmatory factor analysis measurement model.

to capture the expected relation between item and construct. The impact of ARS and DARS reduces to the effect of NARS (Baumgartner & Steenkamp, 2001) on the intercept. In particular, respondents with high (low) NARS have a higher (lower) intercept (Cheung & Rensvold, 2000), as illustrated in Figure 8.2. As a consequence, for equal levels of a latent construct, high (low) NARS respondents have higher (lower) observed scores.

The effect of ERS is rather subtle. Essentially, it can be viewed as an amplification factor in the mapping function of internal states/latent variables to reported responses (Van der Kloot, Kroonenberg, & Bakker, 1985). On measures for which the mean is not equal to the scale's midpoint, this may result in directional bias of observed scores (Baumgartner & Steenkamp, 2001). In the more general case, ERS will lead to differences in the relation between latent variables and observed variables (Cheung & Rensvold, 2000). Respondents with high (low) ERS levels will show a steeper (shallower) slope of the item-construct function line. This is illustrated in Figure 8.3. Hence, for latent scores above (below) the intercept, ERS has an inflating (deflating) effect on observed scores.

When performing an exploratory or confirmatory factor analysis, researchers typically model rating scale data under the assumption that the item scores are interval scaled and are linearly related to the underlying latent construct (the factor). In addition, the variables are commonly assumed to be normally distributed. This implies that the distribution of a variable is fully described by its mean and variance. In this view, response styles can affect the mean and variance of individual items, as well as the covariance between items and other items or factors (the latter through the systematic effect on means and variances).

A straightforward solution is therefore to use within-subject standardization. That is, compute the mean and standard deviation for each respondent across items in a questionnaire and transform the raw scores into z-scores by subtracting the mean and dividing the result by the standard deviation. This approach is common in cross-cultural research, and Fischer (2004) provides an overview of variations of the method. Standardization has some severe shortcomings,

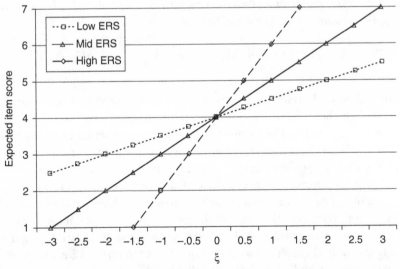

Figure 8.3 Extreme response style effects on the confirmatory factor analysis measurement model.

however. Most importantly, if the items across which scores are standardized are related, the mean and standard deviation are driven by content as well as style, and the correction procedure may also eliminate content-related information. For this reason it is better to construct response style measures for all response styles that may be relevant, based on heterogeneous items other than the items being corrected.

In particular, Baumgartner and Steenkamp (2001) suggest taking the following steps. First, construct response style measures based on a series of heterogeneous items. Second, regress each observed item of interest on all response style measures. Finally, save the residuals of these regressions and use these residualized variables in further analyses. This approach is also endorsed by de Jong et al. (2008). A limitation of this approach is that measurement error in the response style indicators is passed on to the corrected (residualized) scores. A possible solution is to specify response styles as latent constructs with multiple indicators each (based on different subsets of items taken from the total item set used to measure response styles; see Weijters et al., 2008). Unfortunately, in order to be able to measure response styles a large number of heterogeneous items is necessary (Greenleaf, 1992b). This increases data collection costs and may induce respondent fatigue.

CORRECTION FOR ORDINAL MEASUREMENT

Although interval based models are elegant and parsimonious, rating scales result in ordinal data, or at least data that are likely non-normally distributed and discrete. For this reason, viable alternative ways of analyzing rating scale data have been based on IRT. In IRT, the likelihood that a respondent selects a given response category is estimated for each response category conditional on the latent construct level. For rating scale data (such as Likert items), the graded response model (Samejima, 1969) is generally appropriate (Maydeu-Olivares, 2005). The fundamental equation of this model is

$$P\left(X = k \mid \xi\right) = 1 / \left[1 + \exp\left(-a\left(\xi - b_{k-1}\right)\right)\right] - 1 / \left[1 + \exp\left(-a\left(\xi - b_{k}\right)\right)\right] \qquad (2)$$

where $P\left(X = k \mid \xi\right)$ refers to the probability of an individual responding in category k of the ordered categorical variable X, conditional on the level of the latent construct ξ. The response categories are assumed to be separated by thresholds on the underlying ξ dimension corresponding to the b parameters. For each response category, an item characteristic curve (ICC) is estimated which captures the probability of a specific category response as a function of ξ. The parameter a is the item discrimination parameter, and its value is proportional to the slope of the item response function. An example of an ICC for a five-point scale is given in Figure 8.4. To illustrate the interpretation, the ICC graph shows that individuals who have a ξ score between approximately –1 and +1 will most probably select response category 3, the mid-response.

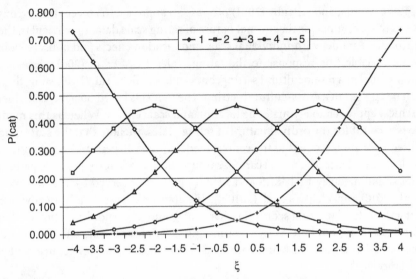

Figure 8.4 Example of item response theory item characteristic curve.

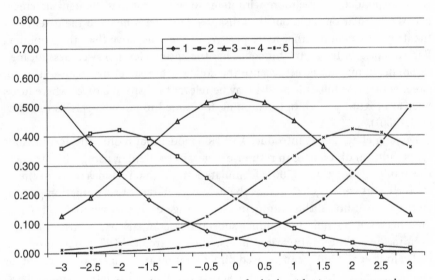

Figure 8.5 Example of item characteristic curve for high midpoint response style respondents.

Cross-cultural differences in response styles can be captured by differences in the discrimination and threshold parameters (de Jong, Steenkamp, and Fox, 2007; Johnson, 2003). For example, respondents with higher NARS levels have lower threshold parameters overall. Respondents with high MRS levels are more likely to select the midpoint, which translates into an item characteristic function like the one shown in Figure 8.5.

Rossi, Gilula, and Allenby (2001) propose an approach to correct for response styles that accounts for the ordinal nature of rating scale data. In particular, they introduce a model with individual scale and location effects and a discrete outcome variable (the response to the rating scale). Rossi et al. (2001) developed their model in a monocultural setting, but van Rosmalen et al. (2010) show that it can be applied in a cross-cultural setting. The model is based on a Bayesian hierarchical approach to estimate the location and scale effects. Whereas this model does account for the ordinal nature of rating scales, we note that the scale usage differences are restricted to the central tendency and dispersion in respondents' scale usage. Hence, the model cannot capture more subtle response style patterns like simultaneously high ERS and MRS (a pattern observed by van Rosmalen et al. (2010) and Weijters et al. (2010b)). The approach is essentially an advanced version of standardizing scores (Fischer, 2004), and the major limitation of standardization applies here as well: estimating location and scale effects based on the same items that are being corrected is very risky as it may reduce content variance.

Javaras and Ripley (2007) propose a variant of the Rossi et al. (2001) model that treats Likert data from an unfolding perspective. In the unfolding framework, respondents agree more with items to the extent that the item statement is closer to their opinion, but they disagree more with items to the extent that the item statement is either more positive or more negative than their opinion. For example, for the item "this coffee has the optimal level of sweetness for me," respondents may disagree because the coffee is too sweet or because it is not sweet enough. While this model may be relevant for specific cases where items refer to proximity to an optimal point, the same limitations apply as for Rossi et al. (2001).

De Jong et al. (2007) introduced an IRT model that more fully accounts for cross-cultural differences in response styles. In particular, using a hierarchical IRT model, de Jong et al. (2007) formulate a model that includes random effects for the latent construct as well as the item parameters (discrimination parameters and thresholds, thus capturing scale usage differences across countries). This makes it possible to conduct substantive comparisons across countries even in the absence of invariant items. The hierarchical IRT model proposed by De Jong et al. (2007) can be used directly for mean comparisons, but not for comparing structural relationships across countries. The latter issue is tackled in a more recently proposed model by de Jong and Steenkamp (2010). In this finite mixture multilevel IRT model, multiple constructs can be modeled simultaneously. Additional benefits of this recent development are that model fit can be evaluated and that the use of finite mixtures increases the flexibility to accommodate situations where different groups of countries have different measurement operations, while countries within these groups are still allowed to be heterogeneous. This model offers a lot of potential for cross-cultural researchers who work with data from a large number of countries. For now, an obstacle to implementation may be the lack of availability of the algorithm in standard statistical packages.

An important caveat is that the models proposed by de Jong et al. (2007) and de Jong and Steenkamp (2010) work under the assumption that the response style bias is nonuniform, that is, items are differentially affected by response styles. De Jong et al. (2008) provide evidence in support of the nonuniformity assumption for ERS, but the results by Weijters et al. (2010a, 2010b) are in line with the uniformity assumption, and Javaras and Ripley (2007) assume uniformity of response style bias by definition. In sum, this seems to be a question that deserves further research. An additional interesting route for future research would be to integrate IRT-based models incorporating measurement parameters that vary across cultures with approaches that explicitly measure and model response styles. For example, it may be feasible to model measurement parameters (e.g., thresholds) as latent variables that have their own indicators, the latter being based on the response frequencies observed across a range of heterogeneous items in the questionnaire.

CORRECTION FOR NOMINAL MEASUREMENT

As rating scales typically result in ordinal measurement, nominal level models are less common to analyze such data. However, if a response category is offered for which the ordinal position vis-à-vis other categories is undetermined, like a "don't know" or "not applicable" option and/or missing data, nominal models may be useful (Javaras & Ripley, 2007; van Rosmalen et al., 2010). Latent class analysis makes use of nominal observed variables, the probability distribution of which is conditional on a nominal latent variable (the latent classes). This probability relation is typically modeled as a multinomial model. Van Rosmalen et al. (2010) propose a model that simultaneously classifies respondents into latent classes that capture content and latent classes that capture response style differences. Both latent class variables can then be related to antecedent variables, including nationality. Van Rosmalen et al. (2010) identify eleven response style segments, including segments that are characterized by high ARS, moderate ARS, low ARS, high ERS, and high MRS. The content-driven segmentation can be used as a corrected latent variable. An obvious limitation is the nominal nature of this latent variable, but of course this is no limitation if segmentation is the main goal of the study. As mentioned, a major strength of this approach is that it can account for "don't know" categories and/or missing values. In the short term, the major obstacle to implementation will be the lack of availability of the algorithm in standard statistical packages.

RESPONSE SETS IN CROSS-CULTURAL RESEARCH

Conceptualization and measurement

Similar to response styles, a response set leads to a deviation between observed and true scores, but respondents do not ignore the content that the question is trying to assess. The best-known example is socially desirable responding (SDR), which refers to a tendency to provide answers that make the respondent look good (Steenkamp et al., 2010). Since perceptions of what looks good depend on prevailing cultural norms, it follows that cross-cultural differences in SDR are likely to exist.

The conceptualization of SDR has evolved over the years (Paulhus, 2002; Paulhus & Trapnell, 2008). At first, unidimensional formulations were prevalent, in which social desirability was regarded as a general concern with responding in a culturally approved way (e.g., Crowne & Marlowe, 1960). Low intercorrelations among different SDR scales led to multidimensional conceptualizations, and the latest thinking views SDR as varying on two underlying dimensions: (a) domain of content (whether respondents make themselves look good in agency contexts, which are related to achievement, dominance, uniqueness, and independence, or communion contexts, which deal with affiliation, nurturance, conformity, and approval); and (b) degree of awareness (whether respondents unconsciously describe themselves in an overly positive way or deliberately present themselves in a self-favoring manner). Thus, Paulhus and John (1998) argue that SDR can lead to either an egoistic or a moralistic bias in self-perception, depending on the context, and the bias can be either honestly held or strategically projected. The latter clearly constitutes a threat to the validity of self-report data, but opinions diverge as to whether unconscious self-favoring bias should be treated as a substantive aspect of personality or as a stylistic component of response variance that needs correction.

Social desirability has been regarded as both a characteristic of items (i.e., a behavior described in an item on a questionnaire may be more or less susceptible to SDR) and as a characteristic of respondents. With regard to the latter, several scales have been proposed to assess individual differences in SDR (see Paulhus, 1991, for a review). By far the most commonly used instrument has been the Marlowe-Crowne social desirability scale (SDS; Crowne & Marlowe, 1960). It consists of thirty-three items and social desirability is indexed by the endorsement of culturally approved behaviors (e.g., "Before voting, I thoroughly investigate the qualifications of all the candidates") and the disavowal of culturally disapproved behaviors (e.g., "I like to gossip at times"). Several short forms are available as well (see Barger, 2002, for a review). A problem with this scale is that it does not reflect the more recent multidimensional conceptualizations of SDR and that, in fact, it confounds the multiple dimensions of SDR.

Paulhus (see Paulhus, 1991, for a description) developed a scale called the Balanced Inventory of Desirable Responding (BIDR), which consists of two twenty-item subscales (self-deceptive enhancement or SDE and impression management or IM). Example items are "I never regret my decisions" (SDE) and "I always obey laws, even if I am unlikely to get caught" (IM). The BIDR was originally thought to differentiate unconscious from deliberate self-presentation, but more recently the scale has been used to assess agentic/egoistic (SDE) and communion-oriented/moralistic (IM) response tendencies.

Paulhus (2002; see also Paulhus & Trapnell, 2008) argues that SDE more specifically taps unconscious agency concerns and IM reflects deliberate communion motivation (communion management); additional scales are available to assess unconscious moralistic response tendencies and deliberate agency management. However, while there is good evidence that SDE and IM measure egoistic and moralistic response tendencies, respectively, it remains to be seen whether unconscious and deliberate forms of SDR can be validly assessed using existing verbal response scales (see Steenkamp et al., 2010).

Evidence on cross-cultural differences in socially desirable responding

Although much research has studied the social desirability phenomenon in general, the literature on social desirability in cross-cultural perspective is thin (Johnson & Van De Vijver, 2003). Here we will review the studies that have investigated cross-cultural influences on SDR.

Ross and Mirowsky (1984) reported one of the first cross-cultural studies and argued that SDR was an attempt to answer questions in a normatively appropriate way, that it was motivated by efforts to conform and to present a good face to out-group members, and that it was particularly likely to occur in groups that were relatively powerless and respondents for whom image was important. In a study with Anglo, Mexican American, and Mexican adults, based on a shortened version of the Marlowe-Crowne SDS, the authors showed that Anglos were less likely and Mexican Americans (who are a minority group in the United States) were more likely than Mexicans (in Mexico) to engage in SDR, controlling for gender, age, and socioeconomic status. Also as expected, socioeconomic status was negatively related to SDR. Furthermore, SDR had a negative effect on self-reported symptoms of psychological distress, and controlling for SDR increased (decreased) the negative effect of socioeconomic status (age) on psychological distress, although it had no influence on the effect of ethnicity.

Heine and Lehman (1995) collected data for SDE and IM from small samples of Canadian and Japanese students (studying at a Canadian university) and found no significant mean differences on either scale.

Warnecke, Johnson, Chávez, Sudman, O'Rourke, Lacey, & Horm (1997) conducted a study in the Chicago metropolitan area with four groups of respondents differing in ethnicity: non-Hispanic whites, African Americans, Mexican Americans, and Puerto Ricans. Based on the Marlowe-Crowne scale, both African Americans and Mexican Americans had higher SDR scores than white Americans, controlling for gender, age, education, and income. No differences were found for Puerto Ricans.

Keillor, Owens, and Pettijohn (2001) reported a comparison of SDR scores (based on the Marlowe-Crowne scale) across the United States, France, and Malaysia. Malaysia was significantly higher in SDR than France and the United States, which did not differ from each other. The authors attributed the difference to the level of economic development.

Van Hemert, van de Vijver, Poortinga, and Georgas (2002) related the Lie scale of the Eysenck Personality Questionnaire, which can be regarded as a proxy for IM, to a wide variety of ecosocial, sociopolitical, value-related and psychological factors across up to thirty-eight countries. Many correlations were significant and sometimes substantial. Country-level Lie scores were positively correlated with temperature and humidity, high birth and death rates, low life expectancy, and bribery and corruption. Negative correlations were obtained for various indices of economic and human development (e.g., gross national product), education, communication infrastructure, factors related to human rights and democracy, and subjective well-being. Among the Hofstede dimensions, individualism had a significant positive and power distance a significant negative relation with Lie scores. In general, the findings reflect a strong negative relationship between Lie scores and affluence.

Bernardi (2006) investigated the association between IM and Hofstede's dimensions of cultural variation across twelve countries (North and South America, Europe, Asia, and Australia). He found significant positive correlations for uncertainty avoidance and power distance and significant negative correlations for individualism. The correlation for masculinity was positive but nonsignificant. In a simultaneous regression including all four dimensions as well as gender (based on ten countries), only uncertainty avoidance and individualism were significant because power distance had a strong negative association with individualism.

Lalwani, Shavitt, and Johnson (2006) investigated the relationship between SDE and IM on the one hand and national culture/ethnicity and cultural orientation on the other hand. Cultural orientation refers to a respondent's degree of individualism or collectivism, measured at the individual level using scales developed by Triandis and Gelfand (1998), which additionally distinguish between horizontal and vertical forms of individualism and collectivism. While individualism is generally characterized by a focus on personal goals, horizontal individualism (HI) stresses values of self-direction and independence, whereas vertical individualism (VI) emphasizes power and status. Similarly, although collectivism is generally characterized by a focus on in-group goals, horizontal collectivism stresses values of benevolence and loyalty, whereas vertical collectivism (VC) emphasizes values of dutifulness and order. The research undertaken by Lalwani et al. (2006) supports the following conclusions. First, US respondents, particularly those of European descent, are higher on SDE but lower on IM than Singaporeans and Asian Americans. Second, individualism is related to SDE, while collectivism is associated with IM. This is particularly the case for the horizontal forms of individualism and collectivism, because the relationships were strongest for (and sometimes restricted to) the link of HI with SDE and HC with IM. Third, national culture/ethnicity and cultural orientation independently influenced SDR, although the findings converged in the nature of the influence.

In follow-up research, Lalwani, Shrum, and Chiu (2009) supported the associations between individualism and SDE on the one hand and collectivism and IM on the other hand. In addition, they showed, using both group-level (European American versus Hong Kong Chinese students) and individual-level data, that a promotion focus mediated the individualism–SDE relationship, while a prevention focus mediated the collectivism–IM relationship. Furthermore, the promotion-focus mediation was more pronounced for respondents low in private self-consciousness, whereas the prevention-focus mediation was more pronounced for respondents high in public self-consciousness.

Steenkamp et al. (2010) reported a study involving twenty-six countries in Europe, Asia, and the Americas in which they investigated the relationship between SDE and IM on the one hand and the Big Five personality factors, the Schwartz Value Survey, and individualism/collectivism and masculinity/femininity on the other hand. Based on a multilevel model, the personality factors of openness to experience, conscientiousness, emotional stability, and extraversion, and the value dimensions of self-enhancement and openness to change were positively related to SDE at the individual level. Similarly, the personality factors of conscientiousness and agreeableness, and to a lesser extent emotional stability, and the value dimensions of self-transcendence and conservation had positive relationships with IM. Furthermore, extraversion, self-enhancement, and openness to change exhibited negative associations. At the cultural level, individualism (collectivism) was negatively (positively) related to both SDE and IM (the negative association with SDE was contrary to predictions), whereas masculinity (femininity) had a positive (negative) relationship with SDE and a negative (positive) relationship with IM.

SUMMARY

Previous research has consistently shown that SDR in general is less likely in cultures that are relatively affluent and high in economic development. More recent studies, which have considered SDE and IM as separate dimensions of SDR, indicate that IM is higher in collectivist cultures, and that the effect might be more pronounced in horizontal collectivist cultures. There is also limited evidence that uncertainty avoidance and femininity are positively associated with IM. The findings for SDE are sparse and the hypothesized positive relationship between SDE and individualism has not been consistently supported.

Effects of SDR and correction procedures

In contrast to response styles such as acquiescence, it is not at all clear whether SDR should always be regarded as a response bias that contaminates scale scores and requires corrective action. In the literature this is known as the substance versus style controversy. While early research tended to treat an association between a substantive scale and a social desirability scale as evidence of response distortion, some authors have argued that SDR may at times be a valid component of personality (e.g., McCrae & Costa, 1983). Three distinct cases can be distinguished (see Tourangeau & Yan, 2007). One the one hand, some respondents may actually engage in the seemingly socially desirable behaviors assessed with SDR scales. After all, some people will thoroughly investigate the qualifications of all the candidates before voting and refrain from gossiping behind others' back. If this is the case, then a high SDR score certainly does not indicate a biased response. On the other hand, if respondents deliberately distort their answers in order to project a certain image and an SDR scale is able to capture such response tendencies, the scale measures bias. The most ambiguous situation occurs when respondents describe themselves in an overly favorable light but the self-presentation is sincere. Although the resulting response is "objectively" distorted, a correction may not be warranted, particularly if SDR is part of the nexus of substantive relationships involving the construct of interest.

The consensus in the literature at this point seems to be that a high score on a social desirability scale should not automatically be interpreted as a proneness to biased responding on self-report measures and that an association between SDR and a measure of a substantive construct does not necessarily reflect a contamination of the substantive scale (see Steenkamp et al., 2010; Uziel, 2010). Steenkamp et al. (2010, Figure 1) provide country-level scores on SDE and IM for twenty-six countries, and their results clearly show that there are substantial differences in SDR across countries. Furthermore, they also report regressions between nine substantive marketing scales (e.g., material success, susceptibility to normative influence, ethnocentrism) and both SDE and IM for each of the twenty-six countries, and the findings show that the standardized regression coefficients vary widely across countries. However, although egoistic and moralistic response tendencies differ across cultures and differentially affect substantive constructs, it is not clear that these results signal a contamination of scale scores. Steenkamp et al. (2010) propose a procedure for distinguishing between substance and style, but at present no empirical evidence is available about the efficacy of the method. It appears that if there are real concerns that respondents may provide distorted self-reports (e.g., when they are asked about sensitive topics such as illicit drug use), there may be more effective methods of dealing with SD biases (e.g., the randomized response technique; see de Jong, Pieters, and Fox, 2010, for a recent application and extension) than administering an SDR scale and trying to control for potential confounds statistically.

OTHER RESPONSE BIASES IN CROSS-CULTURAL RESEARCH

In addition to response styles and response sets, there are several other response effects that may threaten cross-cultural comparisons, such as differences in question order effects, anchor effects, differential problems with reverse-worded items, and reference-group effects.

Two studies by Haberstroh, Oysterman, Schwarz, Kühnen, and Ji (2002; see also Schwarz, 2003) show that there might be cross-cultural differences in how the order in which questions are asked influences the results. Responding to questions can be thought of as a form of communication and thus follows certain rules of conversational logic. One of these rules is that answers to different questions should not be redundant. For example, if students are first asked to rate their satisfaction with life as a whole and then their satisfaction with their studies, they might assume that the second question asks for new information, which should lower the correlation between the two responses, compared to the order where the question about academic satisfaction is asked first, because in the latter case it is made salient to respondents that academic satisfaction is part of life satisfaction for a student and the motivation to avoid redundancy is less relevant. Haberstroh et al. (2002) argue that this prediction holds in cultures in which an independent self-construal is prevalent, whereas in a culture dominated by an interdependent view of the self, respondents should be particularly attuned to the norms of conversational conduct. This may suggest that a concern with avoiding redundancy is present even in the academic satisfaction first and life satisfaction second sequence.

In an experiment with respondents from Germany (a more individualistic culture) and China (a more collectivistic culture), the correlation between academic satisfaction (asked first) and life satisfaction (asked second) was indeed much higher in Germany than China, whereas the correlations were about the same in the reverse question order. In a second experiment, the authors document that the result is likely due to the different conceptions of the self in individualistic and collectivistic cultures, not unknown differences between Germany and China, because priming either an independent or interdependent self-construal in respondents from the same culture had similar effects. As pointed out by Haberstroh et al. (2002), if a researcher were not aware of cultures' differential sensitivity to conversational norms, the difference in results in the academic-life satisfaction question order could be misattributed to the greater contribution of academic satisfaction to life satisfaction for German students relative to Chinese students.

Recent research by De Langhe et al. (2011) shows that completing a questionnaire in one's native language or in a second language (e.g., English) may have a systematic effect on the results. Specifically, the authors demonstrate that respondents indicate more intense emotions when filling out a questionnaire in a nonnative language than in their native language. Presumably, this is due to the greater emotional intensity of verbal labels (particularly scale anchors) in one's native language (i.e., for a Dutch respondent, the Dutch word for love is emotionally stronger than the English word love and therefore less likely to be endorsed), so the authors call the effect the anchor contraction effect. The effect is shown to be restricted to emotional items and does not occur for more cognitive judgments such as product evaluations. Fortunately, the anchor contraction effect can be eliminated fairly easily by using emoticons (stylized facial expressions indicating emotions) or colors of varying intensity as additional response cues.

Although cross-cultural researchers have been cognizant of the adverse effects of response styles on the comparability of findings across cultures, differences in response distributions have traditionally been attributed to respondents' nationality and the influence of language has been neglected. Often, nationality and language are confounded, but there are nations in which multiple languages are officially recognized and respondents may share the same language with citizens of other countries but not their compatriots. The question then arises whether researchers should be more concerned about differences in nationality or differences in language. In a recent program of research, Weijters, Geuens, and Baumgartner (2013) show that stylistic responding (preferences for certain scale positions that are not driven by the content of the items) is more similar within language groups than countries (i.e., Dutch speakers in Belgium and the Netherlands are more similar in their response patterns than Dutch- and French-speaking Belgians) and they identify the mechanism leading to this result. The effect seems to be due to differences in the familiarity of the category labels used in the response scales in different languages, not differences in the intensity of the category labels or characteristics of the respondents such as their mother tongue. In other words, if a completely agree–completely disagree response scale is used in the United States and a fortement d'accord–fortement en désaccord response scale is used in France, and completely agree is more commonly used in everyday speech (and thus more familiar) than fortement d'accord, then the endpoints of the scale are more likely to be endorsed in the United States than in France. Cross-cultural researchers are usually quite concerned about the optimal translation of the specific items making up a measurement instrument, but it appears that less attention is often being paid to the scale categories used in the response scale, which are common across items and therefore more likely to constitute a systematic source of difference. In particular, the research conducted by Weijters et al. suggests that the scale categories used in different languages have to be equally familiar, not necessarily literally equivalent.

In order to avoid confounds due to acquiescence, researchers have sometimes suggested the use of balanced scales in which half of the items are keyed in a direction opposite to that of the remaining items. Since acquiescence presumably has opposite effects on regular-worded and reverse-worded items, ARS bias should cancel out after reverse-scoring the negatively-worded items. Unfortunately, research has shown that item reversal does not work well with East Asian respondents, because they have a tendency to agree with both the original items and their reversals (Wong, Rindfleisch, & Burroughs, 2003). Wong et al. attribute this tendency to East Asians' Confucian belief system, which encourages dialectical thinking and compromise (see also Hamamura, Heine, & Paulhus, 2008), and they show that an interrogative scale format (e.g., "How do you feel about people who own expensive homes, cars, and clothing?" rated on a scale from do not admire to greatly admire) controls the problems introduced by reverse-worded items at least to some extent (see Weijters and Baumgartner, 2012, for a more general review of reversed and negated items in surveys).

Cross-cultural comparisons on such constructs as individualism or collectivism have sometimes led to counterintuitive results, such as North Americans rating higher than East Asians on collectivism. Heine, Lehman, Peng, and

Greenholtz (2002) offer an explanation for these results, which they call the reference-group effect. The idea is that when respondents answer questions on subjective Likert scales, they compare themselves to members of their own cultural group and the standards used in the comparison therefore differ (i.e., North Americans rate their individualism relative to other North Americans, and Japanese assess their collectivism relative to other Japanese). In support of their argument Heine et al. (2002) show, for example, that when the reference group used in comparisons is explicitly manipulated (respondents were asked to evaluate themselves relative to North Americans or Japanese), responses to items measuring individualism were significantly affected (e.g., bicultural Canadians rated themselves as more independent and less interdependent than bicultural Japanese when they compared themselves to Japanese, but not when they used other Canadians as the standard). Heine et al. (2002) discuss several strategies that can be used to avoid the reference-group effect, such as using concrete, objective response options or behavioral measures referring to directly observable acts. Of course, these remedies are not always applicable.

CONCLUSION

It is not uncommon to read cross-cultural research reports in which the authors seem to have paid very little attention to the possibility that comparisons across cultures may be compromised by measurement biases. Although we acknowledge that response biases may not be of primary interest to researchers investigating substantive phenomena or theoretical issues, it is our hope that the present chapter will contribute to a greater appreciation of the difficulties involved in conducting valid cross-cultural comparisons.

REFERENCES

Arce-Ferrer, A. J. (2006). An investigation into the factors influencing extreme-response style. *Educational and Psychological Measurement*, 66(June), 374–392.

Bachman, J. G., & O'Malley, P. M. (1984). Yea-saying, nay-saying, and going to extremes: Black-white differences in response styles. *Public Opinion Quarterly*, 48, 491–509.

Barger, S. D. (2002). The Marlowe-Crowne affair: Short forms, psychometric structure, and social desirability. *Journal of Personality Assessment*, 79(2), 286–305.

Baumgartner, H., & Steenkamp, J. -B. E. M. (2001). Response styles in marketing research: A cross-national investigation. *Journal of Marketing Research*, 38(May), 143–156.

Baumgartner, H., & Steenkamp, J. -B. E. M. (2006). Response biases in marketing research. In: R. Grover & M. Vriens (Eds.), *The handbook of marketing research* (pp. 95–109). Thousand Oaks, CA, USA: SAGE Publications Inc.

Bernardi, R. A. (2006). Associations between Hofstede's cultural constructs and social desirability response bias. *Journal of Business Ethics, 65*, 43–53.

Chen, C., Lee, S-y., & Stevenson, H. W. (1995). Response style and cross-cultural comparisons of rating scales among East Asian and North American students. *Psychological Science, 6*(May), 170–175.

Cheung, G. W., & Rensvold, R. B.(2000). Assessing extreme and acquiescent response sets in cross-cultural research using structural equation modeling. *Journal of Cross-Cultural Psychology, 31*(2), 187–212.

Church, A. T. (2010). Measurement issues in cross-cultural research. In E. Tucker & G. Walford (Eds.), *The handbook of measurement: How social scientists generate, modify, and validate indicators and scales* (pp. 151–175). Thousand Oaks, CA, USA: Sage Publications Inc.

Couch, A., & Keniston, K. (1960). Yeasayers and naysayers: Agreeing response set as a personality variable. *Journal of Abnormal and Social Psychology, 60*(2), 151–172.

Cronbach, L. J. (1946). Response set and test validity. *Educational and Psychological Measurement, 6*, 475–494.

Cronbach, L. J. (1950). Further evidence on response sets and test design. *Educational and Psychological Measurement, 10*, 3–31.

Crowne, D. P., & Marlowe, D. (1960). A new scale of social desirability independent of psychopathology. *Journal of Consulting Psychology, 24*(4), 349–354.

De Jong, M. G., Pieters, R., & Fox, J. -P. (2010). Reducing social desirability bias through item randomized response: An application to measure underreported desires. *Journal of Marketing Research, 47*(February), 14–27.

De Jong, M. G., Steenkamp J.-B, E. M., & Fox, J. -P. (2007). Relaxing measurement invariance in cross-national consumer research using a hierarchical IRT model. *Journal of Consumer Research, 34*(22), 260–278.

De Jong, M. G., Steenkamp, J. -B. E. M., Fox, J. P., & Baumgartner, H. (2008). Using item response theory to measure extreme response style in marketing research: A global investigation. *Journal of Marketing Research, 45*(February), 104–115.

De Jong, M., & Steenkamp, J. -B. E. M. (2010). Finite mixture multilevel multidimensional ordinal IRT models for large scale cross-cultural research. *Psychometrika, 71*(1), 3–32.

de Langhe, B., Puntoni, S., Fernandes, D., & van Osselaer, S. M. J. (2011). The anchor contraction effect in international marketing research. *Journal of Marketing Research, 48*(2), 366–380.

Fischer, R. (2004). Standardization to account for cross-cultural response bias: A classification of score adjustment procedures and review of research in JCCP. *Journal of Cross-cultural Psychology, 35*(3), 263–282.

Greenleaf, E. A. (1992a). Improving rating scale measures by detecting and correcting bias components in some response styles. *Journal of Marketing Research, 29*(May), 176–188.

Greenleaf, E. A. (1992b). Measuring extreme response style. *Public Opinion Quarterly, 56*(Fall), 328–351.

Haberstroh, S., Oysterman, D., Schwarz, N., Kühnen, U., & Ji, L. -J. (2002). Is the interdependent self more sensitive to question content than the independent self? Self-construal and the observation of conversational norms. *Journal of Experimental Social Psychology, 38*, 323–329.

Hamamura, T., Heine, S. J., & Paulhus, D. L. (2008). Cultural differences in response styles: The role of dialectical thinking. *Personality and Individual Differences*, 44(March), 932–942.

Harzing, A.-W. (2006). Response styles in cross-national survey research. *International Journal of Cross Cultural Management*, 6(2), 243–266.

Heine, S. J.& Lehman, D. R. (1995). Social desirability among Canadian and Japanese students. *Journal of Social Psychology*, 135(December), 777–779.

Heine, S. J., Lehman, D. R., Peng, K., & Greenholtz, J. (2002). What's wrong with cross-cultural comparisons of subjective Likert scales?: The reference-group effect. *Journal of Personality and Social Psychology*, 82(6), 903–918.

Hofstede, G. (1980), *Culture's consequences: International differences in work-related values*. Beverly Hills, CA, USA: Sage Publications Inc.

Hofstede, G. (1991), *Cultures and organizations: Software of the mind*, London, UK: McGraw-Hill.

Hofstede, G. (2001), Culture's consequences: Comparing values, behaviors, institutions, and organizations across nations, 2nd edition, Thousand Oaks, CA, USA: Sage Publications Inc.

Hui, C. H., & Triandis, H. C. (1985). Measurement in cross-cultural psychology: A review and comparison of strategies. *Journal of Cross-Cultural Psychology*, 16(June), 131–152.

Hui, C. H., & Triandis, H. C. (1989). Effects of culture and response format on extreme response style. *Journal of Cross-Cultural Psychology*, 20(September), 296–309.

Javaras, K. N., & Ripley, B. D. (2007). An 'unfolding' latent variable model for Likert attitude data: Drawing inferences adjusted for response style. *Journal of the American Statistical Association*, 102(June), 454–463.

Johnson, T. R. (2003). On the use of heterogeneous thresholds ordinal regression models to account for individual differences in response style. *Psychometrika*, 68, 563–583.

Johnson, T., Kulesa, P., Cho, Y. I., & Shavitt, S. (2005). The relation between culture and response styles. *Journal of Cross-Cultural Psychology*, 36(2), 264–277.

Johnson, T. P., & Van de Vijver, F. J. R. (2003). Social desirability in cross-cultural research. In: J. A. Harkness, F. Van de Vijver, & P. P. H. Mohler (Eds.), *Cross-cultural survey methods* (pp. 195–204). Hoboken, NJ, USA: John Wiley & Sons.

Keillor, B., Owens, D., & Pettijohn, C. (2001). A cross-cultural/cross-national study of influencing factors and socially desirable response biases. *International Journal of Market Research*, 43, 63–84.

Lalwani, A. K., Shavitt, S., & Johnson, T. (2006). What is the relation between cultural orientation and socially desirable responding. *Journal of Personality and Social Psychology*, 90(1), 165–178.

Lalwani, A. K., Shrum, L. J., & Chiu, C-y. (2009). Motivated response styles: The role of cultural values, regulatory focus, and self-consciousness in socially desirable responding. *Journal of Personality and Social Psychology*, 96(April), 870–882.

Lentz, T. F. (1938). Acquiescence as a factor in the measurement of personality. *Psychological Bulletin*, 35, 659.

Leung, K. (2008). Methods and measurements in cross-cultural management. In: P. B. Smith, M. F. Peterson, & D. C. Thomas (Eds.), *The handbook of cross-cultural management research*. Thousand Oaks, CA, USA: Sage Publications, Inc.

Little, T. D. (1997). Mean and covariance structures (MACS) analyses of cross-cultural data: Practical and theoretical issues. *Multivariate Behavioral Research, 32*(1), 53–76.

Little, T. D. (2000). On the comparability of constructs in cross-cultural research: A critique of Cheung and Rensvold. *Journal of Cross-Cultural Psychology, 31*(March), 213–219.

Marín, G., Gamba, R. J., & Marín, B. V. (1992). Extreme response style and acquiescence among Hispanics. *Journal of Cross-Cultural Psychology, 23*(December), 498–509.

Maydeu-Olivares, A. (2005). Further empirical results on parametric vs. non-parametric IRT modeling of Likert-type personality data. *Multivariate Behavioral Research, 40*, 275–293.

McCrae, R. R., & Costa, P. T. Jr. (1983). Social desirability scales: More substance than style. *Journal of Personality and Social Psychology, 83*(December), 882–888.

Messick, S. (1991). Psychology and methodology of response styles. In: R. E. Snow & D. E. Wiley (Eds.), *Improving inquiry in social science: A volume in honor of Lee J. Cronbach* (pp. 161–200). Hillsdale, NJ, USA: Lawrence Erlbaum Associates.

Paulhus, D. L. (1991). Measurement and control of response bias. In J. P. Robinson, P. R. Shaver, & L. S. Wright (Eds.), *Measures of personality and social psychological attitude* (pp. 17–59). San Diego, CA, USA: Academic Press.

Paulhus, D. L. (2002). Socially desirable responding: The evolution of a construct. In H. I. Braun, D. N. Jackson, & D. E. Wiley (Eds.), *The role of constructs in psychological and educational measurement* (pp. 49–69). Mahwah, NJ, USA: Erlbaum.

Paulhus, D. L., & Trapnell, P. D. (2008). Self-presentation of personality: An agency-communion framework. In O. P. John, R. W. Robins, & L. A. Pervin (Eds.), *Handbook of personality psychology* (pp. 492–517), New York, NY, USA: Guilford.

Paulhus, D. L., & John, O. P. (1998). Egoistic and moralistic biases in self-perception: The interplay of self-deceptive styles with basic traits and motives. *Journal of Personality, 66*(December), 1025–1060.

Peng, K., & Nisbett, R. E. (1999). Culture, dialectics, and reasoning about contradiction. *American Psychologist, 54*(9), 741–754.

Rorer, L. G. (1965). The great response-style myth. *Psychological Bulletin, 63*, 129–156.

Ross, C. E., & Miroswsky, J. (1984). Socially-desirable response and acquiescence in a cross-cultural survey of mental health. *Journal of Health and Social Behavior, 25*(June), 189–197.

Rossi, P. E., Gilula, Z., & Allenby, G. M. (2001). Overcoming scale usage heterogeneity: A Bayesian hierarchical approach. *Journal of the American Statistical Association, 96*(March), 20–31.

Samejima, F. (1969). Estimation of latent ability using a response pattern of graded scores. *Psychometrika Monograph*, No. 17. Richmond, VA: Psychometric Society.

Schwarz, N. (2003). Self-Reports in consumer research: The challenge of comparing cohorts and cultures. *Journal of Consumer Research, 29*(March), 588–594.

Smith, P. B. (2004). Acquiescent response bias as an aspect of cultural communication style. *Journal of Cross-Cultural Psychology, 35*(1), 50–61.

Steenkamp, J. -B. E. M., & Baumgartner, H. (1998). Assessing measurement invariance in cross-national consumer research. *Journal of Consumer Research, 25*(June), 78–90.

Steenkamp, J. -B. E. M., de Jong, M. G., & Baumgartner, H. (2010). Socially desirable response tendencies in survey research. *Journal of Marketing Research*, 47(April), 199–214.

Stening, B. W., & Everett, J. E. (1984). Response styles in cross-cultural managerial study. *The Journal of Social Psychology*, 122, 151–156.

Swain, S. D., Weathers, D., & Niedrich, R. W. (2008). Assessing three sources of misresponse to reversed Likert items. *Journal of Marketing Research*, 45(February), 116–131.

Tourangeau, R., & Yan, T. (2007). Sensitive questions in surveys. *Psychological Bulletin*, 133(5), 859–883.

Triandis, H. C., & Gelfand, M. J. (1998). Converging measurement of horizontal and vertical individualism and collectivism. *Journal of Personality and Social Psychology*, 74, 118–128.

Uziel, L. (2010). Rethinking social desirability scales: From impression management to interpersonally oriented self-control. *Perspectives on Psychological Science*, 5(3), 243–262.

Van der Kloot, W. A., Kroonenberg, P. M., & Bakker, D. (1985). Implicit theories of personality: Further evidence of extreme response style. *Multivariate Behavioral Research*, 20, 369–387.

Van Hemert, D. A., van de Vijver, F. J. R., Poortinga, Y. H., & Georgas, J. (2002). Structural and functional equivalence of the Eysenck Personality Questionnaire within and between countries. *Personality and Individual Differences*, 33, 1229–1249.

Van Herk, H., Poortinga, Y. H., & Verhallen, T. M. M. (2004). Response styles in rating scales: Evidence of method bias in data from six EU countries. *Journal of Cross-Cultural Psychology*, 35(May), 346–360.

van Rosmalen, J., van Herk, H., & Groenen, P. J. F. (2010). Identifying response styles: A latent-class bilinear multinomial logit model. *Journal of Marketing Research*, 47(February), 157–172.

Warnecke, R. B., Johnson, T. P., Chávez, N., Sudman, S., O'Rourke, D. P., Lacey, L., & Horm, J. (1997). Improving question wording in surveys of culturally diverse populations. *Annals of Epidemiology*, 7(5), 334–342.

Watkins, D., & Cheung, S. (1995). Culture, gender, and response bias: An analysis of responses to the Self-Description Questionnaire. *Journal of Cross-Cultural Psychology*, 26(September), 490–504.

Weijters, B. (2006). *Response styles in consumer research*, Doctoral Dissertation, Faculty of Economics and Business Administration, Ghent University, Ghent, The Netherlands.

Weijters, B., & Baumgartner, H. (2012). Misresponse to reversed and negated items in surveys: A review. *Journal of Marketing Research*, 49(5), 737–747.

Weijters, B., Cabooter, E., & Schillewaert, N. (2010). The effect of rating scale format on response styles: The number of response categories and response category labels. *International Journal of Research in Marketing*, 27, 236–247.

Weijters, B., Geuens, M., & Baumgartner, H. (2013). The Effect of familiarity with the response category labels on item response to Likert scales. *Journal of Consumer Research*, 40, 368–381.

Weijters, B., Geuens, M., & Schillewaert, N. (2010a). The individual consistency of acquiescence and extreme response style in self-report questionnaires. *Applied Psychological Measurement, 34*(2), 105–121.

Weijters, B., Geuens, M., & Schillewaert, N. (2010b). The stability of individual response styles. *Psychological Methods, 15*(1), 96–110.

Weijters, B., Schillewaert, N., & Geuens, M. (2008). Assessing response styles across modes of data collection. *Journal of the Academy of Marketing Science, 36*(3), 409–422.

Winkler, J. D., Kanouse, D. E., & Ware, J. E Jr. (1982). Controlling for acquiescence response set in scale development. *Journal of Applied Psychology, 67*(October), 555–561.

Wong, N., Rindfleisch, A., & Burroughs, J. E. (2003). Do reverse-worded items confound measures in cross-cultural consumer research? The case of the material values scale. *Journal of Consumer Research, 3*(1), 72–91.

PART III

Branding and Brand Relationships

9

Culture, Emotions, and Nation Equity

CATHY YI CHEN, DURAIRAJ MAHESWARAN,
JIE WEI, AND PRASHANT SAXENA ■

INTRODUCTION

With the advent of globalization, the decrease of trade barriers, and the digitization of the world economy, consumers now have access to products from around the world. When the assortment of products is compared and evaluated, the country where products originate from will influence consumers' choice decisions with or without their conscious awareness. For example, a consumer who has invited an important guest for dinner at home may decide to pick up a bottle of wine from France and salmon from Norway. Similarly, because electronics from Japan have always enjoyed a premium image of superior quality, consumers may find it easier to justify a higher price for a product from Japan than comparable products from other countries. This has been referred to as the country-of-origin effect and has been studied extensively in consumer behavior and marketing literature.

In recent research, a new framework titled "nation equity" has been proposed to incorporate major extensions of the original country-of-origin effect and to integrate the various facets of country perceptions so as to systematically examine the effects of country of origin in the context of globalization (Maheswaran & Chen, 2006). Favorable or unfavorable country associations develop over time as a function of the superior or inferior performance history of products originating in that country. As the reputation of a country begins to evolve based on the quality of the existing products, these perceptions of superiority or inferiority will also be transferred to new products that originate in that country. This has been referred to as the traditional or classical country-of-origin effect. However, recent research provides evidence to suggest that country perceptions may go beyond inferences based on product performance alone. For example, despite a universally favorable belief toward the reliable performance of Japanese products, the historical animosity between Japan and some East Asian countries may affect the purchase of Japanese products in these countries. In accord, recent studies have shown that a product's country-of-origin effect has implications for the product's evaluations that extend beyond product attributes. Specifically, consumers may form positive or negative feelings toward a country based on cultural, political, historical, or economic factors. These feelings, though unrelated to the product performance, may influence consumers' evaluations and purchase intentions of the products originating in the target countries (Hong & Kang, 2006; Klein, Ettenson, & Morris, 1998; Maheswaran & Chen, 2006). Thus, research findings suggest that country of origin should be perceived as a multidimensional construct that incorporates perceptions based on both product performance-related and nonproduct-related aspects.

In the light of these findings, a concept of "nation equity" as the integrating framework is proposed to capture the traditional product-related country-of-origin effect and the effect of country-related emotions on consumer and business decision making. Nation equity is defined as "equity or goodwill associated with a country." These associations often go beyond company or product performance-related perceptions, and may be positive or negative as a function of culture, politics, economic development, religion, and other macro factors. Unlike brand or corporate equity that is primarily based on the company activities, nation equity associations can be induced by factors that are external to the company or the products, and yet have impact on the company and its products. For example, when a Danish newspaper, Jyllands-Posten, published cartoons that offended the religious sentiments of Islamic countries, it led to a boycott of the products from Denmark's largest dairy producer, Arla, in the Middle East, costing the company about US$ 50 million in 2006 (BBC News, 2006). Thus, a company and its products may be vulnerable to emotions arising from events that are beyond the immediate purview of a company. Similarly, when a few pro-Tibet protesters interrupted the Olympic torch relay and tried to snatch the torch from Paralympic fencer Jin Jing in Paris, Chinese consumers organized boycott toward French luxury brands Louis Vuitton and actively urged shoppers to stay away from French retailer Carrefour by circulating messages on the Internet and mobile phones.

These incidental emotions, though not directly related to the actions of the company, may affect its business because of the negative associations to the country of origin. Similarly, political events such as the Iraq conflict may evoke several types of emotional responses to the United States, and the extent that these emotions influence the perceptions of the United States are likely to have a corresponding effect on perceptions and acceptance of products from American companies. Research has shown that emotional responses in general could differ both in their valence (negative or positive) and in their focus on the decision criterion (e.g., country of origin or other product information) for evaluating the product (Lerner & Keltner, 2000; Maheswaran & Chen, 2006). Thus, the impact of incidental events such as military conflicts on the consumers will depend on the type of emotion (e.g., anger or sadness) invoked and whether the consumers focus on the country of origin in their decisions. For example, American Express, by virtue of its brand name association with the United States, may be unfavorably evaluated if the consumers in the Middle East have negative associations to United States and if they use the "country of origin" as a decision criterion. Alternately, if the United States is seen as a champion of democracy, it may induce positive emotions and the enhanced perceptions of United States would favor American Express.

The effect of nation equity can also be influenced by culture. For example, Gürhan-Canli and Maheswaran (2000a) demonstrated that cultural orientation influences the effect of country of origin on product evaluations. Japanese consumers evaluated the product originated in their home country more favorably than products from foreign countries, regardless of whether the product is indeed more superior or inferior to competition. American consumers, however, evaluated the product that originated in their home country more favorably only when the product is superior to competition. Investigating the effect of culture is important for us to understand when nation equity would have an impact, how nation equity can be developed, how to leverage positive nation equity, and how to overcome negative equity.

Thus, broadening the performance-based view of country-of-origin effects and viewing countries as having equity associated with them, would enable companies to gain a better understanding of the impact of country of origin on their operations as well as facilitate a more comprehensive study of country of origin in the academic domain. In this chapter, we first review past research on country-of-origin effects that focus on products, as well as recent research examining nonproduct-related emotional country-of-origin effects. Subsequently, we review the research on culture and emotion, and highlight the importance and future research directions in the area of nation equity. To be consistent with previous research, the term of "country-of-origin effects" would be used in this review to refer to the traditional product-related country-of-origin effects. Nation equity will refer to the generalized effects of country of origin that includes both traditional (product-related) and emotional (nonproduct-related) effects.

CURRENT RESEARCH FINDINGS

Halo effect

Country of origin can influence consumers' perceptions of a product's quality, performance, design, aesthetics, prestige, price, as well as consumers' product evaluations and purchase decisions. The impact of country of origin on product evaluations has been interpreted as a type of "halo effect" where consumers rely on their general impressions of a country to form some beliefs about a product's attributes or performance. Early research on the country-of-origin effect focused on its role as an information cue (see Bilkey & Nes, 1982, for a review).

For example, consumers may believe that there is a better trained and educated workforce as well as more stringent quality control system in countries that are economically more developed. Therefore, the products made in such countries tend to be perceived as having higher qualities and evaluated more favorably (Schooler, 1971).

Roth and Romeo (1992) investigated the relationship between consumer preferences for a country's products and perceptions of a country's economy. If there was a match between the perceived "strength" of a country and the skills that are needed to design and manufacture the product, the country of origin would have a positive effect on product evaluations. For example, France is associated with a positive image for design and fashion, which are important features for handbags (apparel, shoes) but not important for beer. In this situation, the country-of-origin information (i.e., made in France) should positively influence consumers' willingness to purchase handbags but not beer.

The general country-of-origin image may influence consumers' inference on other product attributes other than quality. For example, the image of France is related to hedonic characteristics that include aesthetic sensitivity, refined taste, and sensory pleasure (Peabody, 1985). As a result, French-sounding brand names make a product sound more "hedonic" (versus utilitarian), and thus have a positive impact on the evaluations of "hedonic" products like perfumes and wines (Leclerc, Schmitt, & Dubé, 1994).

Emotional country-of-origin effects

Country images also have strong emotional aspects that are formed in direct experiences, such as holidays or encounters with foreigners, or in indirect experiences with countries and their citizens through art, education, or mass media (Verlegh & Steenkamp, 1999). Relative to the extensive literature on traditional country-of-origin effects, the emotional effect of country of origin based on nonproduct- or nonperformance-related perceptions are not well understood. Three major types of emotional effects of the country of origin are summarized and reviewed below: foreignness effect, ethnocentrism effect, and animosity effect.

FOREIGNNESS EFFECT

A preference for foreign-made (or nonlocal) products has been documented in past research on country of origin. Specifically, a positive relationship between product evaluations and the degree of economic development is reported (Schooler, 1971), especially in many developing countries. It refers to a general preference for foreign products regardless of product category or performance.

To examine the underlying mechanism that guides the preferences for foreign products, Batra, Ramaswamy, Alden, Steenkamp, and Ramachander (2000) found that this effect is stronger for consumers who are highly susceptible to normative influences and for product categories that are high in social signaling value. Additionally, the effect of country of origin on brand attitudes is mediated by consumer's admiration of the lifestyles of economically developed countries. Foreignness effect is also observed in some developed countries like China and Singapore. For example, sending their children to international schools, summer camps abroad, and getting higher education in the West are highly valued. These observations suggest that in addition to economic factors, there might be other psychological reasons that lead to the foreignness effect (e.g., self-esteem). Consumers may achieve self-enhancement by using products from foreign countries, or signal their belonging to a certain élite group that is associated with desirable foreign products and thus acquire a collective reflected glory (Chen, Brockner, & Katz, 1998).

ETHNOCENTRISM EFFECT

In contrast to foreignness effect, past research has also documented a preference toward home country brands over foreign brands, referred to as ethnocentrism effect. The preferences for products made in their home countries are correlated with personality variables like level of dogmatism and conservatism (Bilkey & Nes, 1982). Several other related concepts like patriotism, internationalism, and nationalism may also stem from the consideration of domestic country origin of the product. An alternative manifestation of ethnocentrism is to reject foreign products based on their potential to harm domestic products or industry. It specifically describes consumers' attitudes toward foreign products and their beliefs about the appropriateness or even the morality of buying foreign-made products (Shimp & Sharma, 1987). A seventeen-item CETSCALE has been developed to measure consumers' ethnocentric tendencies (Shimp & Sharma, 1987).

ANIMOSITY EFFECT

Animosity is defined as the remnants of antipathy related to previous or ongoing military, political or economic events (Klein et al., 1998). It is different from consumer ethnocentrism in mainly two aspects. First, consumer ethnocentrism predicts consumers' purchasing behavior when the choice is between a domestic brand and a foreign brand, whereas animosity is more predictive when the choice is between two foreign brands, provided that consumers hold hostility toward one of the countries (Klein, 2002). Second, consumer ethnocentrism is correlated with quality judgment in the sense that those who score high in CETSCALE also believe that the products made in their own country have better quality. A consumer with animosity toward a certain country may refuse to buy the product originating from the target country without derogating the quality of the products. For example, Klein et al.'s (1998) survey in Nanjing demonstrates that Japanese products were viewed quite positively by Chinese consumers in terms of quality judgment. However, those consumers with high animosity toward Japan as a function of historical events were more reluctant to purchase Japanese products.

   While some animosity effects such as the Arla Foods and Freedom Fries have short-term implications for the purchase of products, others seem to have a continued impact on the conduct of business. The historical animosity between China and Japan provides an interesting case in point with an ongoing series of incidents that seem to go beyond the response warranted by the conflict situation. For example, in April 2005, Japan's Education Ministry approved textbooks that minimized the extreme nature of the country's wartime involvement in China. This resulted in a strong reaction of a series of boycotts of Japanese cars and electronics in major cities in China.

Animosity effect may also have a cultural basis and stem from perceived threat to the local culture. People have an intrinsic drive to protect the continuity of their culture (Chiu & Hong, 2006). When consumers perceive a foreign influence as harming their own culture or undermining the role of the central icons that they cherish, they may distance themselves from these alien values. For example, in 2007, Starbucks had to close its shop in the Forbidden City in China. Even though many Chinese consumers revealed that they do like Starbucks Coffee and it has been very popular in the Chinese market, the shop in the Forbidden City was perceived as detracting from the focus on Chinese culture and the harmony of the imperial museum.

Summary

The above review clearly identifies distinct effects that are associated with the use of country-of-origin information in product evaluations: halo effect, foreignness effect, ethnocentrism effect, and animosity effect. These effects stem from both product performance-related and unrelated factors. It is interesting to note that consumers have different sets of responses to foreign brands and local brands and these responses are both favorable and unfavorable. In addition to product-related evaluations, consumers also exhibit emotional responses that vary both in intensity and the content across situations. While extant research answers some questions, it identifies several areas that need further investigation. The diversity of effects also strongly underscores the need for an integrated framework to examine the multidimensional nation equity in multiple domains.

The traditional product-related nation equity and the nonproduct-related emotional nation equity can jointly influence the evaluations for products originating from the country of origin. In fact, the effect of nation equity on consumer's judgment and decision making may be the strongest when the traditional product-related equity and the emotion-related equity are consistent. For example, Centerbar, Clore, Schnall, and Garvin (2008) examined how the agreement between cognitive content made accessible by priming and the self-generated experiences of action, feelings, and expression influence the performance on a memory task. The cognitive concepts (happy or sad) were primed first, then embodied reactions were required as participants read the stimuli (e.g., arm flexion means approach, arm extension means avoidance; smiling or frown faces, happy or sad music). They found that coherence between the cognitive concepts and affective experience led to better recall of a story than did the incoherence.

In the context of nation equity, these findings suggest that the convergence between consumers' beliefs about the traditional product-related equity and the affective experiences consumers have toward the country that reflect the emotional equity will increase the propensity to recall and attend to more positive facts about the country's products. For example, one consumer may have positive perceptions about German products (e.g., high quality, advanced technology), but lack positive experience about Germany (e.g., only heard about it but never used any German products or traveled there). Thus, the effect of nation equity of Germany is likely to be limited at the time of judgment, which would undermine the favorable effects of positive, traditional product-based beliefs on the evaluations or purchase intentions toward products from Germany.

NATION EQUITY AND CULTURAL DIFFERENCES

The primary contribution of culture-based research in the domain of nation equity is to provide an understanding of how cultural differences systematically influence the various dimensions of nation equity. Even though there has only been limited research directly examining the effect of culture on nation equity, the findings so far provide strong evidence for the role of culture in the nation equity framework. Based on previous research, we discuss below how culture interacts with the dimensions of nation equity individually and collectively.

Foreignness effect

Cultural differences may exist in terms of how foreign products are viewed depending on how consumers process information. Recent literature suggests that power distance and equality are likely to be the underlying dimension that influences two types of processing styles: a global style that processes information by schema, stereotype or expectancy, and a local processing style that utilizes a more specific, detail-oriented approach (Fiske & Taylor, 1991). Power distance involves the extent to which a society (especially the lower members of the society) accepts and views as inevitable or functional human inequality in power, wealth, and prestige (Hofstede, 1980). Global processing is more likely to be in effect for those who have power in an unequal relationship, whereas local processing is effective for both of those in equality and for those who lack power in an unequal relationship (Oyserman, 2006). Thus, we can hypothesize that nation equity, as an overall schema, may have a stronger effect in a vertical hierarchical society than a horizontal society, and a stronger effect for those who have power than those who do not in a hierarchical society. This would be especially true for the foreignness effect that extends its effect through its impact on self-esteem.

Previous literature suggests that culture can moderate the underlying mechanism for the foreignness effect. For individualist consumers, their culture is organized around the view of the self as an independent and autonomous entity (Kitayama, Markus, Matsumoto, & Norasakkunkit, 1997). Creating and maintaining a positive sense of self involves feeling good about oneself and defining oneself in terms of differentiable attitudes, traits, and opinions (Oyserman, 2006). Thus, the self-esteem of individualist consumers can be enhanced by being unique, independent, and even exotic (Torelli, 2006). When promoting to these consumers, a product association with foreign origin can be described as unique and differentiated to elicit the foreignness effect. Collectivism, on the other hand, defines self-concept with group membership and the goals involve sacrifice for the common good and harmonious relationships with close others. For consumers from collectivist culture, self-esteem is enhanced by belonging to a social élite group. Thus, foreignness effect that is elicited to satisfy this goal can eventually enhance nation equity.

Ethnocentrism effects

Past research has shown that consumer ethnocentrism and its subsequent impact on preference for home country products can vary as a function of cultural orientation. As noted earlier, Gürhan-Canli and Maheswaran (2000a) found that home country products are not uniformly preferred across cultures (Japan versus United States).The vertical dimension of individualism and collectivism is found to explain the difference between the two countries. The preference for a superior product, regardless of its origin, is consistent with the characteristics of vertical individualism (United States), in which people are competitive and attempt to achieve individual goals at the expense of group goals, when there is a conflict. In contrast, consumer's preference for the home product regardless of its superiority is mediated by people's willingness to sacrifice for the collective goals (Japan). This is consistent with the characteristics of the vertical collectivism, in which people are anticipated to sacrifice their personal preferences and make evaluations to enhance group interest.

In the advertising domain, the efficacy of an advertising campaign with ethnocentrism appeal is more likely to be effective in a collectivist (versus individualist) culture or used together with claims that highlight an interdependent (versus independent) self-construal. Agrawal and Maheswaran (2005) examined the effect of self-construal on the persuasive efficacy of various advertising appeals. They found that advertising appeals that were consistent with consumers' chronically accessible (chronic) self-construal as well as with appeals that are consistent with the temporarily accessible (latent) self-construal were both persuasive. More importantly, they identified brand commitment as a critical moderating variable that determines the effectiveness of the appeals consistent with consumers' chronic or latent self-construal. These findings suggest that for high commitment/involvement product categories (e.g., cars, home appliances), ethnocentrism appeals may be more effective in collectivist cultures than individualist cultures. For low commitment/involvement or mature products, however, there is larger flexibility to leverage the ethnocentrism appeals if an interdependent self-construal can be made salient among consumers.

Cultural differences may also determine when consumers are more likely to be ethnocentric in choice situations. Na and Kitayama (2008) demonstrated that culture interacts with public scrutiny to influence consumer priorities in the choice context. They demonstrated that North Americans were most motivated to engage in a task they had chosen in private without any perceived public scrutiny. They were thought to be "self-expressive" in prioritizing the input for making the choice. In contrast, in interdependent cultures (e.g., East Asians) individuals were normatively expected to perceive the self as interdependent. These findings extend the observations from Gürhan-Canli and Maheswaran (2000a; b) and suggest that consumers from interdependent cultures are more likely to be ethnocentric and prefer home country products especially when the choice is made under public scrutiny or the product is going to be consumed in public. In contrast, in independent cultures such ethnocentrism would only be evident as a form of self-expression rather than an outcome of public scrutiny. For example, consumers would buy Apple products because they facilitate self-expression rather than because Apple is an American brand.

Previous research has shown that consumers from interdependent cultures have a higher concern for face than consumers from independent cultures. The social need for face is a cornerstone of Asian, collectivist cultures (Hwang, Franscesco, & Kessler, 2003). A collectivist culture tends to view self as interdependent with others. They view face as a socially defined aspect of self that has a more significant role in collectivist cultures than individualist cultures. Especially in public settings, this concern for face makes Asian consumers much less tolerant and more dissatisfied with social failures than Western consumers (Chan, Wan, & Sin, 2009).

This has dual implications for products from home and foreign countries. If a product of foreign origin is not of good quality or associated with negative nation equity (such as a Japanese product in China during political conflict), it may encounter serious obstacles when targeting consumers from interdependent cultures. This effect may be more pronounced if this product were to be consumed publicly since using this product in public may lead to loss of face. Alternately, a home country product that is not competitive in terms of quality compared to foreign brands may also be shunned because an inferior home country brand may lead to a loss of face in a public setting. In other words, when country-of-origin information of a product makes the user lose face in a public setting, then it is likely to be weighted more in their decisions to reject the product in an interdependent culture.

Animosity effects

Previous research has also documented some evidence suggesting the influence of culture on the animosity effect. For example, Chen et al. (1998) found that cultural tendency is believed to moderate the tendency of exhibiting in-group favoritism or out-group discrimination. People with individual-primacy orientation are more motivated to engage in in-group favoritism to achieve personal self-enhancement. If the intragroup comparison is unfavorable to their own group, however, they are more inclined to distance themselves psychologically from members of the in-group, which in turn leads to less in-group favoritism. For collective-primacy people, when the intragroup comparison is unfavorable to their group, they may feel more motivated to protect their in-group (Markus & Kitayama, 1991) and maintain their expression of in-group favoritism. Chen, Brockner, and Chen (2002) further examined this phenomenon and manipulated the feedback of both in-group performance and out-group performance orthogonally. They found that when the in-group performed was better or worse than the out-group, collective primacy was positively related to in-group favoritism. These findings suggest that in collective (versus. individualist) culture, a stronger animosity effect is more likely to occur: they might exhibit higher in-group favoritism (ethnocentrism) or higher out-group discrimination (animosity) as a way to maintain a desirable social identity.

Coexistence of multiple effects

We have so far examined the effect of culture on how consumers perceive specific effects of nation equity. However, there may be situations when multiple effects coexist and simultaneously influence product evaluations. This has been observed among some American consumers who have favorable emotions toward China's culture and tourism, but are also concerned by the recall of products made in China because of quality or safety concerns. Hong and Kang (2006) examined this situation using Japan and Germany as two examples. These two countries both have reputations for manufacturing high-quality products, but are also associated with animosity for their deeds during the World War II. They found that the country of origin had a positive effect on product evaluations when a favorable subset of the stereotype (i.e., produce high-quality products) was activated, but a negative effect when an unfavorable subset (i.e., animosity) was activated. However, such effect would occur only when the product was atypical and not strongly associated with the functional aspects of the country-of-origin stereotypes (e.g., dress shoes made in Japan).

An interesting finding in culture research suggests that consumers from interdependent culture may be more likely to balance both positive and negative attitudes. Previous research has shown that Easterners are more tolerant of ambiguity and less compelled to resolve incongruity (Nisbett, Peng, Choi, & Norenzayan, 2001). Ng (2010) demonstrated that Eastern consumers often consider both positive brand attitude and negative brand extension information when evaluating the parent brand, while Western consumers would either choose the more diagnostic information or discount the information that can be subtyped. Therefore, the effect of nation equity may be more complicated in interdependent culture than in independent culture.

It is possible that in an interdependent culture, traditional nation equity and emotional nation equity (e.g., animosity) jointly influence product evaluations. In an independent culture, in contrast, consumers are more influenced by the dimension of nation equity that is more salient, either chronically or temporarily. Another implication of cultural differences has on nation equity is that it may be more challenging to promote products in an interdependent culture solely based on one type of equity. For example, consumers may have no difficulty in maintaining a positive attitude based on traditional nation equity but show little purchase intention as a result of emotional nation equity. Similarly, it is also possible for consumers to have a positive attitude toward the brand based on ethnocentric advertising campaigns but low trust for its quality.

NATION EQUITY AND EMOTION

The nation equity framework proposes that emotions toward a country would also influence the product evaluations and choice decisions, as summarized in the emotional effect of country of origin. These effects differ considerably from the traditional country-of-origin research that focuses on its role as an information cue that affects judgments of product quality. There are several implications related to consumer emotions toward the country. First, specific emotional states that are induced by cultural or individual characteristics may influence how consumers feel about the product and its country of origin differently. Second, consumers may have mixed emotions toward a country that has conflicting implications on the product evaluations. We need to understand how mixed emotions of opposite valence extend effects on the decision-making process. Finally, consumer emotions toward a country that is generated by nonproduct-related aspects (e.g., history, culture, and tourism) may be considered as irrelevant to product evaluations. It is important to understand when these incidental emotions may have an influence on product evaluations.

Specific emotional state

Consumers may try to forecast the emotional consequences of their decision outcomes. Recent research has shown that anticipated emotions influence consumers' control on their own behaviors. In general, anticipated positive emotions can facilitate self-control (Bagozzi, Baumgartner, & Pieters, 1998). Patrick, Chun, & Macinnis (2009) found that when consumers are exposed to tempting stimulus, anticipating pride facilitated self-control thoughts and behaviors, relative to anticipating shame or no anticipated emotions.

Examining the impact of emotional nation equity will provide a broader understanding of consumer behavior in the global context. First, Patrick et al.'s

(2009) findings suggest that ethnocentrism may be more effective than animosity in hedonic product categories or impulse purchase incidents. The pride from the ethnocentrism effect can facilitate a shift of attention away from the tempting stimulus itself to consumers themselves. Consumers can actually experience the pride if they do choose their home country products. The shame anticipated from choosing products from an animosity country, however, cannot effectively shift consumers' attention away from the tempting products. As a result, consumers may still give in to the temptations and the animosity effect would have little impact.

Second, the ethnocentrism effect would influence consumers' attitudes toward the products but animosity normally would not influence the product evaluations. This is because the anticipated pride from the ethnocentrism effect shifts the attention from product attributes to consumers themselves. The positive feeling of pride about self should enhance product evaluations (Isen & Simmonds, 1978). However, when animosity is generated the attention should still be on the product and the evaluation should still mainly be influenced by product attributes.

Chentsova-Dutton and Tsai (2010) compared the emotional reactivity and found that people from independent culture have more intensive emotional reactivity when attention is shifted to individual aspect of self. People from interdependent culture, in contrast, have more intensive emotional reactivity when attention is focused on relational aspect of self. For example, in European American contexts, noticing one's own reflection in a shop window increases emotional reactivity more than in Asian American contexts, whereas in Asian American contexts, noticing a family picture increases emotional reactivity more than in European American contexts.

These findings suggest that in independent cultures, consumers are more likely to generate strong affective reactions toward a country when their knowledge or experience with the country validates or violates their personal value system (e.g., lack of democracy in African countries may be at odds with some Western consumers' value in freedom). In interdependent cultures, however, consumers may be more likely to have strong affective reactions toward a country when the knowledge or experience with a country is relevant to their collective benefits (e.g., Japanese government's claim of sovereignty to the Senkaku Islands).

Kitayama, Mesquita, & Karasawa (2006) examined the effect of culture on emotion experiences by comparing Japanese and American self-reports of emotions across different social situations and differentiated emotions in the dimensions of pleasantness and social orientation. Social orientation is anchored on a socially engaging end that is derived from and affirming the interdependence of self, and a socially disengaging end that is grounded in independence and autonomy of self and its separateness from others in a relationship. Thus, emotions can be positive and engaging (e.g., friendly feelings and respect), positive and disengaging (e.g., pride and feelings of superiority), negative and engaging (e.g., guilt and shame), or negative and disengaging (e.g., anger and frustration). There is a systematic tendency for Japanese to experience engaging emotions more strongly than Americans do and, conversely, for Americans to experience disengaging emotions more strongly than Japanese do. This finding has implications on those products originating from countries with negative emotional nation equity. For countries with independent (versus interdependent) culture, consumers are more prone to experience strong disengaging emotions like anger, which according to Maheswaran and Chen (2006), will enhance the impact of the country of origin.

Mixed emotions

As noted earlier, the traditional product-related equity can coexist with emotional, nonproduct-related equity toward a country, but are inconsistent with each other in terms of valence. In fact, mixed emotions may also coexist for many countries in the world. Culture, history, tourism, news, or media coverage can create positive or negative emotions toward a country. For example, many Asian consumers may have animosity toward Japan because of its military history during the WWII. These emotions, however, may be dormant most of the time. When these consumers travel to Japan and are impressed by the hospitality, the beautiful scenery, and amazing culture, many positive emotions can be experienced and these emotions may contribute to the purchase of cosmetics, electronics, food, or other souvenirs. When a situation arises and negative emotions or animosity are activated, it may trigger a boycott of products from Japan. Thus, when mixed emotions exist toward a country, a product originating from that country can benefit from a positive halo effect or suffer from a negative halo effect, depending on the feelings that situations call attention to.

Williams and Aaker (2002) demonstrated that mixed emotions could peacefully coexist among consumers, especially for consumers from Eastern countries or collectivist cultures. It is important to understand that to market a product in a country where the local consumers have mixed emotions toward the product's country of origin, the product may be more vulnerable to scandals or rumors. For example, when a few consumers complained about allergic reactions toward SK-II products, a rumor was disseminated about how SK-II products in China are of inferior quality than those sold in other countries. The rumor quickly generated waves of product returns in many cities of China and eventually led to the temporary withdrawal of SK-II from Chinese market.

Incidental emotions

Since country-related emotions are not considered as directly relevant to product performance, the appraisal-tendency framework (ATF) should be important to understand and predict the influence of emotional nation equity on consumer decision making. ATF is focused on studying the incidental emotions and proposes that emotions generated by previous incidents give rise to specific cognitive and motivational processes, which in turn influence subsequent judgment and decision making (e.g., Han, Lerner, & Keltner, 2007). ATF differentiates six cognitive dimensions: certainty, pleasantness, attentional activity, control, anticipated effort, and responsibility (Smith & Ellsworth, 1985). For example, anger is associated with high certainty about what happened and individual, human control for negative events, whereas fear is associated with uncertainty about what happened and situational control for negative events.

Maheswaran and Chen (2006) have applied the ATF framework to study nation equity and found that incidental emotions that consumers experience before product evaluations can influence the use of country-of-origin information in the decision-making process. Specifically, angry consumers are found to be more likely to use the country of origin in product evaluations than sad consumers. In addition, they identify agency control associated with the emotion as the underlying dimension that determines whether and how the country of origin is used in product evaluations. Country of origin has a strong effect on product evaluations only when the incidental emotions are associated with human control (e.g., anger). Their findings suggest that animosity toward a country based on historical, military or economic reasons may influence consumers' reactions toward products from the target countries if the event that generates the animosity is attributed to the country instead of to chances or uncontrollable factors.

In the context of nation equity, the country-related emotions are an interesting case. It is not an integral emotion in the sense that the emotion is toward the country and generated by country-related events, not by the product evaluation process. However, it is not completely irrelevant because the emotional reactions toward the country will naturally influence consumers' intention to buy products associated with such a country. Future research should examine the path and the underlying mechanism through which the emotional nation equity influence the evaluations for products or services originating from the country.

FUTURE RESEARCH: BUILDING AND MANAGING NATION EQUITY

Building nation equity

Previous research suggests that the challenge of building nation equity may differ as a function of cultural differences. Western cultures are characterized by the focus on the self whereas Eastern cultures emphasize collective values. This suggests that compared with those from Eastern culture, people who originate from or are deeply influenced by Western culture may be less likely to identify business practices (or product quality) with a nation (Gürhan-Canli & Maheswaran, 2000a; b). A product should be judged based on its own merits regardless of the country it originates from. Therefore, some emotional nation equity (e.g., ethnocentrism, animosity) may exert a stronger effect in Eastern (versus. Western) culture. In addition, in modern society, people have become more internation-ally mobile and may not easily identify themselves with any one single nation. Similarly, we would expect a weaker effect for emotional nation equity effects such as ethnocentrism or animosity.

Previous research also suggests that the path to build up nation equity may dif-fer by culture. Western culture is dominated with recognition of self-worth and pleasure seeking, whereas Eastern culture is motivated by balancing the envi-ronment, maintaining social harmony, acquiring control, and preventing losses. For example, Valenzuela, Mellers, & Strebel (2010) showed that the momentary feelings of pleasure from an unexpected gift are stronger for Westerners than for Easterners. Chen, Ng, & Rao (2006) also showed that Western consumers are more motivated to fulfill promotional goals (e.g., expend monetary resources to achieve a desirable outcome) whereas Eastern consumers are more motivated to fulfill prevention goals (e.g., avoid an undesirable outcome).

Future research should examine the implications of such cultural differences on how to build nation equity. For example, the nature of product (hedonic ver-sus utilitarian) may influence the salient goals related to it. Hedonic products (e.g., a stylish car) may be more associated with promotion goals (e.g., pleasure seeking). Thus, countries with current negative or weak nation equity can focus on developing or promoting hedonic product categories (tourism, lifestyle prod-ucts) to build up positive nation equity among target consumers from indepen-dent cultures. However, this may not be a viable strategy for consumers from interdependent cultures. For them, heavy promotion on product categories that prevent losses (either socially or financially) may be more effective.

Past research on culture suggests that cognitive dissonance can be another way to enhance nation equity. Individuals may justify their choices and give more favorable product evaluations in order to eliminate cognitive dissonance. Kitayama, Snibbe, Markus, & Suzuki (2004) demonstrated that Japanese consum-ers justified their choices (by increasing the liking of the chosen item) only when self-relevant others were made salient (i.e., social cues were present). European Americans justified their choices regardless of the presence of social cues. This finding suggests favorable emotional nation equity can be leveraged to enhance the traditional product-related nation equity. For example, if a consumer pur-chases a less preferred product out of temporary positive emotions generated for the country of origin, the consumer may experience some cognitive dissonance and thus increase the evaluations of the chosen product because of dissonance effect. However, when the original product choice is private and the product is not consumed publicly, consumers from interdependent culture may feel less dissonance and the above strategy would be less likely to be effective.

Managing nation equity

Managing nation equity involves leveraging positive and overcoming nega-tive nation equity. Cayla and Eckhardt (2008) examined how brand managers contributed to create a sense of belonging and shared consciousness in the Asian region. The symbolic approach to brands highlights a social linking value of brands and allows an understanding on how marketers weave stories that connect people who may never meet each other, such as the Harley Davidson community or Macintosh enthusiasts. One of the symbolic forms of brands is to forge a collective identity around the brand and create a national consciousness by helping people think of themselves as living in the same time and sharing the same history. For example, OCBC Bank strives to maintain its strong image of a regional brand by propagating Chinese heritage and global presence.

This research brings out an important perspective of overcoming negative nation equity. Brands influenced by the animosity effect may look into positioning themselves as regional (versus national) brands. For example, an electronic brand from Japan can build up a transnational brand image by associating with values and cultures endorsed by most Asian countries and thus decrease the sporadic country-specific animosity effect to the minimum. This is consistent with past research on "in-group" and "out-group" effects that demonstrated people tend to respond more positively to their in-group (the group of people that one feels a sense of belonging) than to their out-group (Escalas & Bettman, 2003; Tajfel & Turner, 1979). The in-group preference is also demonstrated in marketing and consumer behavior research (Berger & Heath, 2007). For example, Japanese brands such as Shisheido and Kao often highlight their Japanese origin in Japan and benefit by the "in-group" associations.

Zhang and Khare (2009) provided further understanding to the regional or global strategy in managing nation equity. A global product, which is positioned for consumers from around the world, may be more preferred by consumers with chronically more salient global identity. In contrast, a local product tailored for local market may be more preferred by consumers with chronically salient local identity. This effect can be moderated by culture: for individualist culture where individuals strive to be different from others, there may be a contrastive effect where a local brand positioning becomes appealing to consumers with a global identity. Thus, those brands that take the global positioning strategy in order to overcome the associations with negative nation equity should be cautious when applying this strategy in individualist cultures.

Small and Verrochi (2009) examined charity advertisement and found that participants feel sadder when viewing a sad-faced victim. Contagion effects are automatic and noninferential. The shared experience of sadness made them particularly sympathetic and become more likely to donate than when they see happy or neutral faces. In most nation equity campaigns, people's stories and facial expressions are only secondary to the grand scenes of achievements of the country. However, consumers are most interested in people and also media prefers a human story. An effective strategy would be to present more human stories and evoke automatic and noninferential emotions of the target foreign consumers. For some relatively unknown countries, featuring celebrities in areas like sports, music, and movies may be a productive option to enhance nation equity. For example, the Barbados tourism commercial features Rihanna who happens to be a native of Barbados.

Emotion literature also suggests that rich associations should be built around a country to enhance the nation equity and provide a buffer for publicity crisis. Fedorikhin, Park, and Thomson (2008) examined the effect of emotional attachment on consumer responses to brand extensions. The attachment to a brand is considered as "hot" stimulus-induced affect that describes certain emotion-laden relationships between consumers and brands while brand attitude is relatively "cold". A country can be viewed as a parent brand, and the brands of products originating from this country accordingly are analogous to brand extensions. If there is a high level of attachment to the country, there will be greater accessibility of the nation equity knowledge, stronger motivation to categorize products from this country with this nation equity.

Nation equity "attachment" is accumulated through every available channel of public and private diplomacy, educational and cultural exchanges, foreign investment and export promotion, foreign aid, tourism, sport, and politics. If the attachment is rich and multidimensional, there will be more ways to enhance the nation equity and the equity will also be less susceptible to negative influences. The most obvious example is the United States, a country "whose image repeatedly does not collapse in the face of quite extraordinary international opprobrium, a country that sometimes seems almost to be trying to destroy its good name, but never really gets anywhere near succeeding" (Anholt, 2009). The reason could be that the negative stories are never more than a fraction of the sizable amount of positive nation equity in people's mind.

In summary, it is important to develop a systematic strategy to build, improve and manage the overall nation equity. First, a coherent, unique nation equity should be designed to help the country stand out and to be differentiated from other countries. The equity can be built up most effectively based on the inherent characteristics of each country. For example, past research has shown that emotions toward other groups (or countries) can be categorized along the dimensions of warmth and competence (Fiske, Xu, Cuddy, & Glick, 1999). If a country is in general to be perceived as more warm than competent, based on its history, culture or tourism, a focus on improving the emotional equity may be appropriate. If, however, a country is felt to be primarily competent rather than warm, the country may consider a focus on enhancing the traditional, product-related equity. A coherent equity would be easier to retrieve and more likely to have a stronger impact. Second, there should be a multidimensional perspective in designing strategies to build up or enhance nation equity. A coordinated effort on planning, spending, innovation, marketing, and messaging between different sectors, public and private, would be necessary to create a rich set of associations or perceptions about the country, which can provide a strong buffer for national reputation crises.

REFERENCES

Agrawal, N., & Maheswaran, D. (2005). The effects of self-construal and commitment on persuasion. *Journal of Consumer Research, 31*, 841–849.

Anholt, S. (2009).The media and national image. *Place Branding and Public Diplomacy, 5*, 169–179.

Bagozzi, R. P., Baumgartner, H., & Pieters R. (1998). Goal-directed emotions. *Cognition and Emotion, 12*, 1–26.

Batra, R., Ramaswamy, V., Alden, D. L., Steenkamp, J.-B. E. M., & Ramachander, S. (2000). Effects of brand local and nonlocal origin on consumer attitudes in developing countries. *Journal of Consumer Psychology, 9*, 83–95.

BBC News. (2006). Arla predicts £37m boycott cost, BBC. com, March 6, 2006.

Berger, J., & Heath, C. (2007). Where consumers diverge from others: Identity signaling and product domains. *Journal of Consumer Research, 34*(August), 121–134.

Bilkey, W. J., & Nes, E. (1982).Country-of-origin effects on product evaluations. *Journal of International Business Studies, 13*, 89–99.

Cayla, J., & Eckhardt, G. M. (2008). Asian brands and the shaping of a transnational imagined community. *Journal of Consumer Research, 35*, 216–230.

Centerbar, D. B., Clore, G. L., Schnall, S., & Garvin, E. (2008). Affective incoherence: When affective concepts and embodied reactions clash. *Journal of Personality and Social Psychology, 94*, 560–578.

Chan, H., Wan, L. C., & Sin, L. Y. M. (2009). The contrasting effects of culture on consumer tolerance: Interpersonal face and impersonal fate. *Journal of Consumer Research, 36*, 292–304.

Chen, H., Ng, S., & Rao, A. R. (2006).Cultural differences in consumer impatience. *Journal of Marketing Research, 42*, 291–301.

Chen, Y., Brockner, J., & Chen, X. (2002). Individual–collective primacy and ingroup favoritism: Enhancement and protection effects. *Journal of Experimental Social Psychology, 38*, 482–491.

Chen, Y., Brockner, J., & Katz, T. (1998). Toward an explanation of cultural differences in in-group favoritism: The role of individual versus collective primacy. *Journal of Personality and Social Psychology, 75*, 1490–1502.

Chentsova-Dutton, Y. E., & Tsai, J. L. (2010). Self-focused attention and emotional reactivity: The role of culture. *Journal of Personality and Social Psychology, 98*, 507–519.

Chiu, C. Y., & Hong, Y. Y. (2006). *Social psychology of culture*. New York, NY: Psychology Press.

Escalas, J. E., & Bettman, J. R. (2003). You are what they eat: The influence of reference groups on consumer connections to brands. *Journal of Consumer Psychology, 13*(3), 339–48.

Fedorikhin, A., C., Park, W., & Thomson, M. (2008). Beyond fit and attitude: The effect of emotional attachment on consumer responses to brand extensions. *Journal of Consumer Psychology, 18*, 281–291.

Fiske, S. T., & Taylor, S. (1991). Social cognition, 2nd Edition, McGraw-Hill Humanities/ Social Sciences/Languages; New York.

Fiske, S. T., Xu, J., Cuddy, A., & Glick, P. (1999). (Dis)respecting versus (dis)liking: Status and interdependence predict ambivalent stereotypes of competence and warmth. *Journal of Social Issues, 55*, 473–491.

Gürhan-Canli, Z., & Maheswaran D. (2000a). Cultural variations in country-of-origin effects. *Journal of Marketing Research, 37,* 309–317.

Gürhan-Canli, Z., & Maheswaran D. (2000b). Determinants of country-of-origin evaluations. *Journal of Consumer Research, 27,* 96–108.

Han, S., Lerner, J. S., & Keltner, D. (2007). Feelings and consumer decision making: The appraisal-tendency framework. *Journal of Consumer Psychology, 17,* 158–168.

Hofstede, G. (1980). *Culture's consequences: International differences in work related values.* Beverly Hills, CA:SAGE.

Hong, S. -T., & Kang, D. K. (2006). Country-of-origin influences on product evaluations: The impact of animosity and perceptions of industriousness on judgments of typical and atypical products. *Journal of Consumer Psychology, 16,* 232–239.

Hwang, A., Franscesco, A. M., & Kessler, E. (2003). The relationship between individualism-collectivism, face, and feedback and learning processes in Hong Kong, Singapore, and the United States. *Journal of Cross-Cultural Psychology, 34,* 72–91.

Isen, A. M., &Simmonds, S. F. (1978). The effect of feeling good on a helping task that is incompatible with good mood. *Social Psychology, 41,* 346–349.

Kitayama, S., Markus, H. R., Matsumoto, H., & Norasakkunkit, V. (1997). Individual and collective processes in the construction of the self: Self-enhancement in the United States and self-criticism in Japan. *Journal of Personality and Social Psychology, 72,* 1245–1267.

Kitayama, S., Mesquita, B., & Karasawa, M. (2006). Cultural affordances and emotional experience: Socially engaging and disengaging emotions in Japan and the United States. *Journal of Personality and Social Psychology, 91,* 890–903.

Kitayama, S., Snibbe, A. C., Markus, H. R., & Suzuki, T. (2004). Is there any "free" choice? Self and dissonance in two cultures. *Psychological Science, 15,* 527–533.

Klein J. G., Ettenson R., & Morris, M. D. (1998). The animosity model of foreign product purchase: An empirical test in the people's republic of China. *Journal of Marketing, 62,* 89–100.

Klein, J. G. (2002). Us versus them, or us versus everyone? Delineating consumer aversion to foreign goods. *Journal of International Business Studies, 33,* 345–363.

Leclerc, F., Schmitt, B. H., & Dubé, L. (1994). Foreign branding and its effects on product perceptions and attitudes. *Journal of Marketing Research, 31,* 263–270.

Lerner, J. S., & Keltner, D. (2000). Beyond valence: Toward a model of emotion-specific influences on judgment and choice. *Cognition and Emotion, 14,* 473–493.

Maheswaran, D., & Chen C. Y. (2006). Nation equity: Incidental emotions in country-of-origin effects. *Journal of Consumer Research, 33,* 370–376.

Markus, H. R., & Kitayama, S. (1991). Culture and the self: Implications for cognition, emotion, and motivation. *Psychological Review, 98,* 224–253.

Na, J., & Kitayama, S. (2008). Unconscious Influences of Social Eyes: Choice and Motivation in the U.S. and Korea. Working Paper, University of Michigan.

Ng, S. (2010). Cultural orientation and brand dilution: Impact of motivation level and extension typicality. *Journal of Marketing Research, 47,* 186–198.

Nisbett, R. E., Peng, K., Choi, I., & Norenzayan, A. (2001). Culture and systems of thought: Holistic vs. analytic cognition. *Psychological Review, 108,* 291–310.

Oyserman, D. (2006). High power, low power, and equality: Culture beyond individualism and collectivism. *Journal of Consumer Psychology, 16,* 352–356.

Patrick, V. M., Chun, H. E. H., & Macinnis, D. J. (2009). Affective forecasting and self-control: Why anticipating pride wins over anticipating shame in a self-regulation context. *Journal of Consumer Psychology, 19*, 537–545.

Peabody, D. (1985). *National characteristics.* Cambridge, England: Cambridge University Press.

Roth, M., & Romeo, J. (1992). Matching product category and country image percep-tions: A framework for managing country of origin effects. *Journal of International Business Studies, 23*, 477–49.

Schooler, R. D. (1971). Bias phenomena attendant to the marketing of foreign goods in the US. *Journal of International Business Studies, 2*, 71–80.

Shimp, T. A., & Sharma, S. (1987). Consumer ethnocentrism: Construction and valida-tion of the CETSCALE. *Journal of Marketing Research, 24*, 280–289.

Small, D. A., & Verrochi, N. M. (2009). The face of need: Facial emotion expression on charity advertisements. *Journal of Marketing Research, 46*, 777–787.

Smith, C. A., & Ellsworth, P. C. (1985). Patterns of cognitive appraisal in emotion. *Journal of Personality and Social Psychology, 48*, 813–838.

Tajfel, H., &. Turner, J. C. (1979). An integrative theory of intergroup conflict. In *The social psychology of intergroup relations.* Monterey, CA: Brooks/Cole.

Torelli, C. J. (2006). Individuality or conformity? The effect of independent and inter-dependent self-concepts on public judgments. *Journal of Consumer Psychology, 16*, 240–248.

Valenzuela, A., Mellers, B., & Strebel, J. (2010). Pleasurable surprises: A cross—cul-tural study of consumer responses to unexpected incentives. *Journal of Consumer Research, 36*, 792–805.

Verlegh, P. W. J., & Steenkamp, J.-B. E. M. (1999). A review and meta-analysis of country-of-origin research. *Journal of Economic Psychology, 20*, 521–546.

Williams, P., & Aaker, J. L. (2002). Can mixed emotions peacefully co-exist? *Journal of Consumer Research, 28*, 636–649.

Zhang, Y., & Khare, A. (2009). The impact of accessible identities on the evaluation of global versus local products. *Journal of Consumer Research, 36*, 524–537.

10

Globalization and Exclusionary Responses to Foreign Brands

DONGMEI LI, ROBERT KREUZBAUER,
AND CHI-YUE CHIU ■

There are many examples of inflow of global corporate culture into local markets. For example, in 2009, McDonalds—an icon of global corporation—planned to open a new cafe at the Louvre Museum in Central Paris. In China, during the Chinese New Year, Coca-Cola—another iconic global business—often incorporate Chinese and Western cultural symbolisms in its advertisements. Also in the China markets, during the Chinese Moon Festival, Starbucks and Häagen-Dazs would promote its Chinese culture-inspired coffee moon cakes or moon cake ice cream. One consequence of the massive inflow of global corporate culture into local consumer communities is the increased prevalence of culture mixing—elements of local and global cultures coexist and sometimes fuse in the same space. Some globalization scholars have used the expression "experiential compression of time and space" to characterize this cultural phenomenon (Castells, 1998; Giddens, 1985; Robertson, 1992). With the advance of globalization, individuals living in a globalized environment would frequently experience traditional and modern cultures at the same time and local and foreign cultures in the same space.

Globalization is a complex phenomenon that involves cultural, political, economic, environmental, and many other aspects. It is often defined as the "acceleration and intensification of economic integration among the people, companies, and governments of different nations" (Carnegie Endowment for International Peace, 2007). In the present chapter, given the theme of this volume, we are primarily concerned with consumers' reactions to the cultural implications of globalization.

GENERAL ATTITUDES TOWARD GLOBALIZATION

Aside from promoting global integration of local economies through the establishment of multinational corporations, international trade, and enhanced global connectivity mediated by the Internet, globalization has also increased the popularity of science and innovation-based, results-driven, and efficiency-focused social and business practices in local economies (Chiu & Hong, 2006). Because most global businesses originated in Western developed countries, global business practices and consumer products often embody Western social-moral values such as individuality, freedom, immediate gratification, and hedonism (Chiu, Gries, Torelli, & Cheng, 2011). Some prominent examples of such value embodiment are the embodiment of the value of "Just do it" in Nike, "Think different" in Apple Computers, "Enjoy life" in Coca-Cola, "I'm lovin it" in McDonald's, and "My life, my card" in American Express.

The success of global brands rests in part on their ability to capitalize on economy of scale, marketing standardized products to consumers around the globe. This requires homogenization of consumption patterns across countries, which may be attainable through global marketing strategies such as worldwide advertising that aims to evoke similar consumption desires and create similar lifestyles (Parameswaran, 2002).

Thus, it is not surprising that consumers who are wary of the potential cultural erosion effects of globalization may see global brands as carriers of Western material and cosmological values (Lal, 2000), and perceive the spread of these brands and their embodied values as a potential threat to the purity, integrity, and vitality of local culture (Cheng, 2010; Torelli, Chiu, Tam, Au, & Keh, 2011). A recent study (Yang et al., 2011) shows that in both the United States and Greater China (Mainland China, Hong Kong, and Taiwan), people associate globalization with both modernization (the process of incorporating results-based, scientific, instrumental knowledge and practices into existing educational, knowledge production and management practices) and Westernization (the process of assimilating popular Western social-moral ideals such as individual freedom, human rights, and democracy into local cultural value systems). Furthermore, in Hong Kong, people welcome modernization because of its positive effect on the region's global competitiveness, but are ambivalent about Westernization because of its potential erosive effects on local social-moral values (Fu & Chiu, 2007). Yang and colleagues also found that in both the United States and Greater China, people perceive globalization to have more positive impact on people's competence than on their warmth (Yang, Chiu, Chen, Cheng, Kwan, Tam, & Yeh, 2011). Other researchers also reported that people in Japan, China, and Australia generally believe globalization to have positive effects on people's competence and negative effects on people's warmth (Kashima, Bain, Haslam, Peters, Laham, Whelan, Bastian, Loughnan, Kaufmann, & Fernando, 2009; Kashima, Shi, Tsuchiya, Kashima, Cheng, Chao, & Shin, 2011). On the one hand, they acknowledge that globalization has increased the society's effectiveness and efficiency in attaining material goals. On the other hand, they are wary that globalization would break up communities, creating colder and more dehumanized social milieus (Cheng, Chao, Kwong, Peng, Chen, Kashima, & Chiu, 2010; Kashima et al., 2009, 2011).

EXCLUSIONARY RESPONSES TO INFLOW OF GLOBAL AND FOREIGN CULTURES

Among those consumers who are concerned about the potential cultural impact of globalization, inflow of global business into local markets may evoke fear of cultural contamination or erosion, and incite exclusionary reactions toward global and foreign culture. Following Chiu et al. (2011), we define exclusionary reactions as emotional, reflexive responses directed toward protecting the integrity and vitality of heritage cultures by limiting the spread of global and foreign cultures in local culture. Exclusionary reactions are culturally motivated reactions. Individuals who exhibit exclusionary reactions worry that cultural inflows from foreign countries could lead to contamination and erosion of heritage cultures, and hence perceive such cultural inflows as cultural threats. Exclusionary reactions include behavioral attempts to isolate, reject, and even attack foreign cultural intruders.

It is important to emphasize that exclusionary reactions are not necessarily "bad" reactions. These reactions can increase intercultural tension and discourage intercultural learning. Nonetheless, at times, these reactions can mobilize people to preserve the integrity and vitality of heritage cultures by minimizing cultural erosion resulting from globalization and commercialization. Culturally motivated exclusionary reactions may also invite critical reflections on the cultural effects of globalization and lead to greater respect for cultural diversity (Yang, 2011).

Examples of exclusionary reactions to global and foreign cultures abound. In 2004, Mexicans angrily campaigned to stop Wal-Mart from opening a store near the ruins of Teotihuacan. In 2009, the plan to open a McDonald's restaurant at the Louvre Museum in Central Paris ignited a commotion among the Parisians in the Grande Nation. In January 2007, Chenggang Rui, Director and Anchor of *BizChina*, the prime-time daily business show on China Central Television International, led an online campaign to have Starbucks Coffee removed from Beijing's Imperial Palace Museum. In his online article, Rui (2007) wrote, "The Forbidden City is a symbol of China's cultural heritage. Starbucks is a symbol of lower middle-class culture in the West. We need to embrace the world, but we also need to preserve our cultural identity. There is a fine line between globalization and contamination. . .But please don't interpret this as an act of nationalism. It is just about we Chinese people respecting ourselves. I actually like drinking Starbucks Coffee. I am just against having one in the Forbidden City." Within a few months, this article has attracted more than half a million readers and inspired more than 2700 commentaries, most of which were written in Chinese and were sympathetic to Rui's cause.

These three examples of exclusionary reactions share the following characteristics.

1. they all involve intrusion of a foreign business into the space of a local community
2. the space is regarded by the local community as a respected or scared cultural space
3. such intrusion has evoked negative, exclusionary reactions
4. the intruder is seen as a representative of its culture
5. the intruder is perceived to have the intention of trampling local culture
6. the negative reactions are directed toward both the intruder and the cultural group to which it belongs.

Existing theories of exclusionary reactions

Several theories can account for some aspects of this phenomenon. First, the social identity theory (Tajfel & Turner, 1979) argues that group membership is a part of personal identity and people are motivated to feel good about the self. Therefore, people are motivated to view their in-group as positive and superior to out-groups. One way to maintain this perception is via out-group derogation. Thus, individuals who strongly identify with their own culture are more motivated to evaluate out-group culture and their representatives negatively.

Second, politically conservative individuals are motivated to follow conventional norms in their own culture and not open to ideas and practices from other cultures (Jost, Glaser, Kruglanski, & Sulloway, 2003). Thus, politically conservative individuals are particularly likely to perceive foreign businesses (e.g., American companies for the Chinese) as representative of the foreign culture and to resist cultural inflows from other countries.

Finally, the realistic conflict theory (Sherif, 1966) assumes that people in a certain community will negatively evaluate a competitive out-group when they perceive the out-group to be a realistic threat to the in-group. The realistic conflict theory predicts negative evaluation of an out-group culture and its representatives when the perceivers feel that the out-group culture may outcompete the in-group.

Limitations of existing theories

The social identity theory, the theory of political conservatism, and the realistic conflict theory do not fully account for the contextualized nature of culturally motivated exclusionary reactions. For example, the social identity theory predicts that individuals would react negatively to a foreign culture when in-group cultural identity is salient, either because the individuals have chronic high levels of cultural identification, or because the situation renders the in-group cultural identity salient. For example, in-group cultural identity is rendered salient when reminders of the contrast between in-group and out-group cultures are present (Turner, Hogg, Oakes, Reicher, & Wetherell, 1987). Figure 10.1a shows the Starbucks Coffee at the Imperial Palace Museum in Beijing before it was forced to move out of the Museum. It is possible that this shop evoked strong negative reactions from the Chinese because its architectural style mixes elements of global culture with Chinese culture. Such culture mixing could increase the perceptual salience of the contrast between in-group and out-group cultures and hence the salience of the in-group cultural identity.

Moreover, culture mixing itself does not always increase the likelihood of exclusionary reactions from the local community. The Starbucks Coffee in a tourist area in Beijing (as shown Figure 10.1b) has the same architectural style as the one at the Imperial Palace Museum but does not evoke negative reactions from the Chinese.

Figure 10.1 Starbucks Coffee in different locations in Beijing, China. (a) Starbucks Coffee at the Imperial Palace Museum. (b) A Starbucks Coffee in a tourist area in Beijing. (c) A Starbucks Coffee in a popular shopping area in Beijing.

Furthermore, in-group love does not always automatically translate into out-group hate. In fact, there is evidence that in-group identification is independent of negative attitudes toward out-groups. Furthermore, intergroup conflict is primarily motivated by preferential treatment of in-group members rather than direct hostility toward out-group members (Brewer, 1999).

The theory of political conservatism predicts a generalized negative attitude toward foreign cultures, particularly when elements of foreign cultures are perceived to have contaminated traditional culture. However, negative reactions toward foreign cultural intrusion of local space do not reflect blanket hostility of the local community toward the intruder. Although Wal-Mart in the ruins of Teotihuacan, McDonald's at Louvre, and Starbucks at the Imperial Palace Museum evoked strong negative reactions from the local communities, in 2010, there were 175 Wal-Mart's in Mexico, 1161 McDonald's in France, and 230 Starbucks in China, and the numbers have been increasing.

Politically conservative individuals may be particularly concerned about preserving the purity of traditional cultures. Thus, they may react negatively to culture mixing. Although political conservatism can explain individual differences in negative reactions toward culture mixing, it does not explain its contextual variations (e.g., why the Starbucks at the Imperial Palace Museum evoked negative reactions but the one shown in Figure 10.1b does not).

The realistic conflict theory also does not account for the contextual variations in exclusionary reactions toward culture mixing, because it does not explain why the Starbucks at the Imperial Palace Museum will present a greater realistic threat to China than the ones shown in Figure 10.1b, or the one shown in Figure 10.1c, which is located in a popular shopping area in Beijing.

SYMBOLIC EXCLUSIONISM THEORY

The symbolic exclusionism theory (Chiu, Wan, Cheng, Kim, & Yang, 2010; Yang, 2011) is proposed to account for contextual variations in exclusionary reactions to inflow of foreign cultures in global business settings. According to this theory, consumers in local marketplaces will exhibit exclusionary reactions toward global or foreign businesses when the following six conditions are met:

1. The foreign or global businesses are perceived to be symbols or representatives of foreign or global culture (e.g., when McDonald's is perceived to be a symbol of "coca-colonialism" instead of a fast food restaurant chain, and when Starbucks is perceived to be a symbol of Western middle-class culture). That is, exclusionary reactions are unlikely when cultural significance is not attributed to a global or foreign business entering the local market.
2. The perceptual contrast between local and global/foreign cultures is rendered salient. Accordingly, exclusionary reactions would be attenuated

when the consumers' attention focuses on a foreign/global culture but not on its difference from local culture.

3. The spread of foreign/global brands in the local market is perceived (versus not) to be a threat to the integrity or vitality of local culture or an impolite intrusion into local cultural space.

4. The consumers have (versus do not have) personal motivation to preserve the integrity or vitality of local culture; and

5. The consumers take an essentialist perspective to culture and see cultures as bounded categories with fixed characteristics (i.e., categorical perception of culture), instead of taking a dynamic perspective to cultures, viewing cultures as interrelated complex systems with many connections (Hong & Chiu, 2001; Rosenthal & Levy, 2010).

We will elaborate on these conditions below.

Perceived cultural symbolism of foreign or global Brand

Consider the two advertisements shown in Figure 10.2. In the lower panel of the figure, the logo of McDonald's (the Golden Arch) is superimposed on the Great Wall. This image would likely evoke the perception that McDonald's has intruded into a space that symbolizes Chinese culture. In the upper panel of the figure, the Golden Arch stays outside the picture of the Great Wall. This image should create the perception that McDonald's has not entered the highly symbolic space of Chinese culture. The pictures are experimental stimuli used in a series of studies Yang (2011) conducted in China.

The participants in the Yang (2011) studies were Chinese consumers in Beijing or Shanghai; both are global cities in China that have received massive inflows of global and foreign brands. All consumers in these studies agreed strongly that the Great Wall is a symbol of Chinese culture. Across several studies, when Chinese consumers were presented with the advertisement shown in the upper panel of Figure 10.2, in which McDonald's logo was placed outside the picture of the Great Wall, they evaluated McDonald's relatively favorably. However, when presented with the advertisement shown in the lower panel of Figure 10.2, their evaluations varied depending on the perceived cultural significance of McDonald's. Perception of McDonald's as a symbol of American culture was measured in one study, and manipulated in another study. In the study where perception was measured (Yang, 2011, Study 2), Chinese consumers who perceived McDonald's to be a symbol of American culture reacted more negatively toward McDonald's than those who perceived McDonald's to be a restaurant chain. In the manipulation study (Yang, 2011, Study 1), the cultural symbolism of McDonald's was experimentally manipulated by adding one of the following tag lines to the advertisement: (a) *Freedom, Independence, American Culture: All in McDonald's*; and (b) *Fast, Convenient, Delicious: All in McDonald's*. The first tag line highlighted the American cultural symbolism of McDonald's, whereas the

Figure 10.2 Placement of a foreign business logo next to or on the top of a local cultural space.

second one positioned McDonald's as a fast food restaurant chain. The Chinese consumers reacted negatively to the McDonald's advertisement only when the McDonald's logo was superimposed on the picture of Great Wall (i.e., spatial intrusion) and when the cultural symbolism of McDonald's was highlighted in the tag line. In both studies, cultural identification was also measured. However, the strength of cultural identification did not moderate or mediate the joint effect of McDonald's cultural symbolism and spatial intrusion on the evaluation of McDonald's, indicating that the exclusionary reactions toward culture mixing observed in these studies were not driven by cultural identification.

This result is not limited to Chinese consumers. In a conceptual replication of these studies, Yang (2011, Study 3) had American consumers react to an advertisement of a Mao Zedong memorabilia exhibition in New York City. Half of the participants saw an advertisement with a portrait of Mao Zedong superimposed on a picture of the Statue of Liberty, and the remaining participants saw an advertisement with the Mao portrait placed outside the Statue of Liberty photograph. All American consumers in this study perceived the Statue of Liberty to be a symbol of American culture. In this study, American consumers evaluated the advertisement negatively only when the Mao picture was superimposed on the Statue of Liberty photograph and when they viewed Mao as a symbol of Chinese political culture. These results show that exclusionary reactions to global/foreign brands could be culturally motivated—consumers evaluated the inflow of foreign/global brands negatively when they viewed it as a symbol of foreign culture invading respected local cultural space.

All stimulus advertisements in the Yang (2011) studies presented McDonald's and the Great Wall together. Nonetheless, culturally motivated exclusionary reactions were observed only when the image of McDonald's was superimposed on that of the Great Wall. This result and the other results reviewed below together indicate that evocation of exclusionary reactions requires the perception that a representative of foreign culture has intruded into a respected local cultural space, posing a threat to the integrity of the local culture. Indeed, in the Yang (2011) studies, an independent measure of perceived cultural intrusion mediated consumers' negative evaluations of foreign business (a proxy for exclusionary reactions).

Bicultural priming

There is consistent evidence that presenting symbols of two dissimilar cultures simultaneously in the same space can lead to a perceptual contrast, drawing consumers' attention to the differences in ideas and practices between cultures (intergroup heterogeneity effect), as well as similarities in ideas and practices among members of the same culture (in-group homogeneity effect; Chiu & Cheng, 2007, 2010). That is, the copresence of cultures increases the tendency to: (a) attribute essential qualities that are stereotypically associated with a culture to its members; (b) exaggerate the differences between cultures; and (c) be pessimistic about harmonious integration of cultures. These perceptual effects are referred to as *bicultural priming effect* (Chiu, Mallorie, Keh, & Law, 2009; Leung, Qiu, & Chiu, 2014).

We posit that the bicultural priming effect reflects a basic perceptual tendency, rather than the motivation to differentiate the in-group culture from the out-group cultures. This is because similar phenomena have been found in consumer evaluations that do not take place in intergroup contexts. For example, when required to evaluate two alternatives in the same category (e.g., BMW and Mercedes-Benz) sequentially, consumers tend to use the common criteria for evaluating different alternatives in the category (e.g., the criteria for evaluating luxurious cars). However, when asked to evaluate the two alternatives simultaneously, consumers tend to base their evaluation on the dimensions that differentiate the two options (Hsee, 1996; Hsee & Leclerc, 1998; Hsee, Loewenstein, Blount, & Bazerman, 1999). Furthermore, when health-conscious consumers evaluate the desirability of a healthy food item (e.g., strawberry) and an unhealthy one sequentially, they like the healthy item more. More importantly, this difference is enlarged when the two food items are evaluated simultaneously (Fishbach & Zhang, 2008).

We further posit that the bicultural priming effect (e.g., categorical perception of culture afforded by copresence of dissimilar cultures in the same space) is *necessary*, albeit not sufficient, for evocation of exclusionary responses. In this section, we will review the evidence that copresence of dissimilar cultures would increase categorical perception of cultures. In the next sections, we will review evidence that shows how the bicultural priming effect may facilitate exclusionary and non-exclusionary reactions to culture mixing depending on a host of other factors.

THE BICULTURAL PRIMING EFFECT

Encountering a symbol of a certain culture (Culture A) will activate the cognitive representation of Culture A, and through spreading activation the attributes associated with Culture A (Fu, Chiu, Morris, & Young, 2007; Sui, Zhu, & Chiu, 2007). This process is known as *culture priming* (Hong, Morris, Chiu & Benet-Martinez, 2000). For example, for a Chinese American bicultural consumer, encountering an iconic symbol of American culture (e.g., Superman, Marilynn Monroe) will increase the cognitive accessibility of American culture and its characteristic cultural practices (e.g., explaining behaviors in terms of the internal qualities of the actor), while encountering an iconic symbol of Chinese culture would increase the cognitive accessibility of Chinese cultures and its characteristic cultural practices (e.g., explaining behaviors in terms of situational inducement; see Hong, Chiu, & Kung, 1997).

Encountering symbols of two cultures (Cultures A and B) simultaneously in the same space, a process that we refer to as *bicultural priming*, would activate the cognitive representations of the two cultures and the qualities that *uniquely* associate with each culture, while attenuating the activation of those qualities shared by the two cultures. Consumers under the influence of bicultural priming would perceive: (a) greater differences between the two cultures; (b) higher levels of internal coherence among the defining attributes within a culture; and (c) greater difficulty in achieving cultural integration. In addition, these consumers expect other consumers to possess the psychological characteristics of their culture.

PERCEIVED CULTURAL DIFFERENCES

Consistent with this idea, a recent study (Torelli et al., 2011, Study 2) shows that similar to the perceptual contrast effect resulting from simultaneous evaluation of healthy and unhealthy food (Fishbach & Zhang, 2008), bicultural priming enlarges the perceived distance between cultures. In this study, American participants were randomly assigned to the bicultural priming condition or the control condition. All participants were asked to evaluate new British products likely to be introduced in the Mexican market. Participants in the bicultural priming condition evaluated two British brands (with typical British names: 'Williams' and 'Jones') of products that were icons of Mexican culture (Tequila and Taco's corn tortilla). In this condition, iconic Mexican products activated the cognitive representation of Mexican culture and British brand names activated that of British culture. Participants in the control condition evaluated two products (with the same British names) that were not Mexican icons (backpack and bread toaster). In this condition, only the cognitive representation of British culture was activated.

Following this manipulation, the participants were asked to draw on a half-a-letter-sized sheet in any way they deemed appropriate a bubble to represent each of the following cultures: Mexican, Puerto Rican, Canadian, and British cultures. The distance, in millimeters, between each pair of cultures, was used to represent the degree of perceived similarity or difference between the culture pair. Participants in the bicultural priming condition drew the bubbles representing dissimilar cultures (e.g., Puerto Rica and Canada) farther apart than did the participants in the control condition. In addition, the experimental manipulation did not affect the distances between the bubbles representing similar cultures (e.g., Canada and the United Kingdom). Furthermore, the bicultural priming effect was equally strong on the perception of the distance between British and Mexican cultures (the two cultures involved in the product evaluation task) and that between Canadian and Puerto Rican cultures (the two cultures not involved in the product evaluation task). Finally, in this study, the American participants were not exposed to symbols of US culture, and the dependent measure did not include perceived distances between American and out-group cultures. Thus, the bicultural priming effect observed in this study suggests that this effect can occur even when the participants are not members of the primed culture(s) and the dependent measure does not involve perceived characteristics of the participants' own culture. That is, bicultural priming effect can occur without involving self-categorization, or perceived competition with or threat to in-group culture.

INTERNAL COHERENCE OF CULTURE

Bicultural priming also increases perceived internal coherence of cultural beliefs. In one study (Torelli et al., 2011, Study 1), American participants were randomly assigned to the bicultural priming condition or the control condition. Participants in the bicultural priming condition were asked to evaluate products that are icons of the United States (e.g., jeans, breakfast cereals) but had Chinese brand names. In this condition, iconic American products activated the cognitive representation of American culture and Chinese brand names activated that of Chinese culture. In the control condition, American participants evaluated products that are not icons of any culture (e.g., bread toaster, umbrella) and had Chinese brand names. In this condition, only the cognitive representation of Chinese culture was activated. Following the manipulation, the participants completed a set of items that measured the perceived internal coherence of cultural beliefs. Specifically, they were asked to estimate how likely an American who endorsed a certain American value or belief would also endorse other American values or beliefs, and how likely an American who favored a certain Chinese value or belief would also endorse other Chinese values or beliefs. As expected, relative to the participants in the control condition, those in the bicultural priming participants were more likely to believe that Americans who endorsed a certain American value would also endorse other American values, and that Americans who endorsed a certain Chinese value would also endorse other Chinese values. Participants' identification with American culture was also measured after the experimental manipulation and bicultural priming did not increase participants' identification with American culture. Furthermore, the bicultural priming effect accentuates the perceived coherence of both American and Chinese cultures, suggesting that bicultural priming effect does not result from increased identification with American culture.

PERCEIVED CULTURAL INCOMPATIBILITY

Bicultural priming also reinforces the perception of cultures as distinct, incompatible systems. In the Torelli et al. (2011) study described above, the participants also estimated how likely Americans who endorsed American values or beliefs would also endorse Chinese values or beliefs, and vice versa. Again as expected, relative to the participants in the control condition, those in the bicultural priming condition believed more strongly that Americans who endorsed American values would not endorse Chinese values, and vice versa.

The effect of bicultural priming on perception of cultures as incompatible systems was replicated in another study (Chiu et al., 2009, Study 2) that used a different measure of perceived incompatibility of culture. In this study, American undergraduates were first randomly assigned to the bicultural priming condition or the control condition. Next, participants were asked to indicate their extent of agreement with a statement that expressed persistence of cultural differences despite intercultural interactions ("You can learn new things from different cultures, and even after a long time, you can still separate unique cultural information and apply different knowledge in different cultural settings."), and a statement that expressed integration of cultures through intercultural interactions ("You can learn different things from different cultures, but after a while the information becomes integrated, and it is no longer possible to separate unique cultural information."). As expected, compared to the participants in the control condition, those in the bicultural priming condition agreed more with the persistence of cultural differences item and disagreed more with the cultural integration item.

ATTRIBUTION OF CULTURE-TYPICAL CHARACTERISTICS

Finally, bicultural priming also promotes attribution of culture-typical qualities to members of culture. In the Torelli et al. (2011) study described above, following the bicultural priming manipulation, American participants evaluated two commercial messages for Timex, one appealing to collectivist values, and one to individualist values. They rated how likely an American advertising student would adopt the collectivist or individualist message when designing a Website for Timex. Past research (Aaker & Schmitt, 2001) showed that American consumers prefer the individualist message and Asian consumers prefer the collectivist message. If bicultural priming increases the tendency to attribute culture-typical values to Americans, the participants in the bicultural priming condition (versus control condition) should expect the American advertisement student to choose the individualist message. As predicted, bicultural priming increased the perceived likelihood that the individualist (versus collectivist) message would be adopted. This effect was replicated in another study (Chiu et al., 2009, Study 1), in which Beijing Chinese participants reported a stronger expectancy that a Chinese advertising student would choose the collectivist message after bicultural priming.

Parallel results were obtained in a third study (Chiu et al., 2009, Study 2) using more subtle dependent measures. Previous research showed that Americans consistently made stronger internal attributions and weaker external attributions than did the Chinese (Hong, Benet-Martinez, Chiu, & Morris, 2003; Hong et al., 1997; Hong et al., 2000; Morris & Peng 1994), and they tended to reason analytically and were hence not influenced by exemplar prototypicality in reasoning than did East Asians (Nisbett, 2003; Nisbett, Peng, Choi, & Norenzayan, 2001; Norenzayan, Smith, Kim, & Nisbett, 2002). Consistent with the expectation that bicultural priming would increase the tendency to attribute culture-typical behaviors to members of a culture, in this study (Chiu et al., 2009, Study 2), American participants in the bicultural priming condition (versus control condition) believed that Americans would be more likely to make internal (versus external) attribution. In addition, in the control condition, the participants expected other Americans to find the high exemplar prototypicality argument to be more convincing than the low exemplar prototypicality argument. However, in the bicultural priming condition, the participants expected other Americans to find the two arguments equally convincing.

Note that in the studies that examined the effect of bicultural priming on the attribution of culture-typical attributes to a cultural group, participants were not asked to report their personal preferences (e.g., how much they personally endorse culture-typical values or beliefs). Instead, they were asked to estimate the preferences of other people in their culture. Previous research has shown that personal preferences and perceived preferences of other cultural members capture different psychological processes (Chiu, Gelfand, Yamagichi, Shteynberg, & Wan, 2010). Whereas personal preference measures capture values and beliefs that are important to the self, perceived preferences of others capture perceived norms in the culture. Past studies have found consistent effect of culture priming on personal preferences and cultural identification (Oyserman & Lee, 2008). In contrast, bicultural priming has little effect on personal preference or cultural identification, but has consistent effect on the perceived norms of a culture.

In short, there are studies that have used different procedures of bicultural priming, different national samples and different dependent measures to assess different aspects of the bicultural priming effect. Across these studies, the results consistently show that bicultural priming promotes categorical perception of culture.

Cultural intrusion or symbolic threat

FEAR OF CULTURAL EROSION

A major proposition of the symbolic exclusionism theory is that categorical perception of cultures induced by bicultural priming is a necessary but not sufficient condition for the evocation of exclusionary reactions. There is initial evidence for this proposition from the Yang (2011) studies reviewed above. Presenting symbols of two cultures simultaneously evoked exclusionary responses from the Chinese consumers only when the McDonald's logo was superimposed on a picture of the Great Wall, and this effect was mediated by perception of cultural intrusion. Thus, it seems that exclusionary responses would be evoked only when bicultural priming is accompanied by perception of cultural intrusion or other cultural threat.

A series of studies (Cheng, 2010) have provided direct evidence for this proposition. In one study (Cheng, 2010, Study 1), an American sample and a Chinese sample received American culture priming, Chinese culture priming, bicultural priming, or no priming. The priming manipulation was introduced via a multitrial "short-term memory task." In each trial of the task, two pictures were presented side by side for a brief duration on a computer screen. After the two pictures had disappeared, one of them (randomly selected) reappeared on the screen and the participants were asked to decide whether this picture previously appeared on the left or the right. In the American culture priming condition, each pair of pictures consisted of a picture of an American cultural symbol (e.g., the American eagle) and a culture-neutral picture (e.g., a picture of cloud formation). In the Chinese culture priming condition, each pair of pictures consisted of a picture of a Chinese cultural symbol (e.g., the Chinese dragon) and a culture-neutral picture. In the bicultural priming condition, each pair of pictures consisted of a picture of an American cultural symbol and a picture of Chinese cultural symbol. In the no priming condition, each pair of pictures consisted of two culture-neutral pictures.

Following this manipulation, in an allegedly unrelated study, the Chinese participants read an article about an American children's book publisher planning to open business in Beijing to promote American folklore to the Chinese, whereas the American participants read an article about a Chinese children's book publisher planning to open business in New York to promote Chinese folklore to Americans. Participants were asked to indicate the level of support or resistance to this plan by reporting the extent to which they would support tax benefits for the foreign company or lobby to exclude the company from their community. Additional measures included the extent to which the participants had a chronic concern that globalization would result in erosion of local culture, and the extent to which the foreign publisher had the intention to spread foreign culture to the local community.

Compared to the American participants, the Chinese participants had significantly more severe chronic concern over the potential cultural erosion effect of globalization. This is not surprising because most Western countries, being global economic powers, have been major exporters of global capitalism. The economic and military superiority of the Western powers and the largely unidirectional flow of cultural influence, when interpreted in the context of China's past experiences with Western imperialism, may evoke strong exclusionary reactions toward foreign, global cultures among the Chinese (Leung et al., 2014). In fact, in a 2012 edition of the Communist Party periodical *Seeking the Truth*, Chinese President Hu Jintao had warned the country that, "hostile international powers are strengthening their efforts to Westernize and divide us," and as he sees it, these hostile forces are particularly targeting the ideological and cultural domains of the Chinese community. In contrast, Americans are relatively confident that globalization would more likely lead to export of American culture rather than its erosion.

Not surprisingly, among the Chinese participants, when placed under the influence of bicultural priming, those who perceived that the American publisher intended to spread American culture in China displayed strong exclusionary reactions against the publisher. This effect was not observed among the Chinese participants in other culture priming conditions. This result indicates that consumers would be likely to exhibit culturally motivated exclusionary reactions when bicultural priming is accompanied by perception of cultural intrusion.

In this study, the American participants did not exhibit exclusionary responses to the Chinese publisher. Given their relatively low level of chronic concern over cultural erosion, they did not anticipate that the Chinese publisher in New York would be a threat to the continuity of American culture. In a follow-up study (Cheng, 2010, Study 2), American participants read the synopsis of a social science study that reported evidence for the erosion of core American values under the influence of globalization before responding to the case of the Chinese publisher opening its business in New York. Reading the synopsis effectively raised the participants' concern over cultural erosion. Furthermore, like the Chinese participants, the American participants in this study exhibited strong exclusionary responses to the Chinese publisher if they felt that the Chinese publisher intended to spread Chinese culture in the United States, but only when they were under the influence of bicultural priming.

CULTURAL POLITENESS

Exclusionary responses are culturally motivated negative reactions toward impolite intrusions of global or foreign businesses into local cultural space, and these reactions occur only when consumers perceive cultures categorically. From this perspective, it is possible for foreign or global businesses to mitigate exclusionary reactions from local consumers by turning the perception of an impolite foreign intrusion into one of a polite visit.

According to the theory of interpersonal politeness (Brown & Gilman, 1989; Brown & Levinson, 1987), people from all societies have a need for a positive public self-image (Brown & Levinson, 1987). Politeness, which refers to the speaker taking into account the hearer's feelings when phrasing utterances in interpersonal communication, is a social lubricant that serves to establish rapport and allows both the speaker and the hearer to maintain their face in social interactions. When a speaker addresses somebody, the speaker would choose a form that will not result in uncomfortable feelings for the addressee. For example, a student who writes to a professor the first time will use a more polite form—such as "Dear Professor" rather than more informal expressions "Bing! Hello there"—to convey an adequate level of politeness and respect to the professor.

As an extension of the personal politeness theory, we posit that in intercultural communication, consumers may read a polite (impolite) gesture extended from a foreign/global brand to the local culture as a polite (impolite) gesture to the self as members of the local culture. Thus, cultural politeness could attenuate exclusionary reactions to inflow of foreign cultures.

As a working definition, cultural politeness refers to a collection of gestures in marketing communication through which foreign or global brands tactfully communicate respect and courtesy to local culture. Such gestures include featuring the positive elements of local culture (values, beliefs, practices, and rituals); putting emphasis on the common ground of local and foreign cultures by highlighting the practices or values that are shared in both cultures; emphasizing the equality of different cultures; and presenting the weaknesses of local cultures in positive light.

To investigate the role of polite marketing communication in mitigating exclusionary reactions, the authors of the present chapter developed a measure of perceived cultural politeness of marketing communication. In one study (Li, 2013), American consumers were asked to recall a marketing communication in which the advertiser was impolite or polite to the consumers' culture or the consumer as a person. Next, the participants rated the recalled communication using the cultural politeness scale and a personal politeness scale. The result provided evidence for the validity of the cultural politeness scale, showing that culturally polite communication elicited higher politeness than did the personally polite communication on the cultural politeness scale only.

Another study (Li, 2013) shows that cultural politeness in marketing communication can attenuate exclusionary reactions toward a foreign brand. In this study, Indian consumers were presented with a print advertisement for a foreign brand of mineral water. The advertisement showed a picture of the polluted River Ganges—a symbol of Indian culture—or a picture of another river in India. Half of the participants in each condition read a respectful tag line ("Water of life"), and the remaining participants read a disrespectful one ("Only from clean water"). The respectful tag line in the context of the River Ganges was intended to elicit feelings of cultural politeness, whereas the disrespectful tag line in the same context was intended to elicit feelings of cultural impoliteness. The tag line manipulation was expected to have no effect on the perceived cultural politeness of the advertisement that depicted a culturally noniconic river.

As expected, when the advertisement depicted a Ganges River scene, Indian consumers perceived the advertisement to be more culturally polite and rated the foreign brand more favorably when the tag line was respectful than when it was not. The tag line had no effect on the cultural politeness perception of the advertisement when it depicted a picture of a noniconic Indian river. Furthermore, perceived cultural politeness mediated the differences in the evaluation of the foreign brand across the four experimental conditions. These findings highlighted how cultural politeness in foreign brands' marketing communication could mitigate exclusionary responses to inflow of foreign businesses. Showing respect to local culture could increase local consumers' acceptance of foreign brands' communication.

The benefits of culturally polite marketing communication are particularly pronounced for foreign brands at the early stage of entering a local market. Because local consumers have fewer direct experiences with the foreign brand, they expect a foreign brand to relate to the local community in a polite manner. However, the positive effect of cultural politeness would decrease when the local market has gradually accepted the foreign brand. According to Brown and Levinson (1987), the demand for politeness varies with social distance. People are expected to use more polite language when addressing strangers than familiar people. Stephan, Liberman, and Trope (2010) also found that the expectation to follow politeness norms in interpersonal communication varies with psychological distance—there is a stronger expectation to follow politeness norms and to use more polite language when interacting with someone who is more socially, temporally or physically farther away from the self. By the same argument, in intercultural marketing communication, foreign brands are more strongly expected to comply with the politeness norm when the local consumers feel that foreign brand is more psychologically distant from the local culture. In another study (Li, 2013), the investigators measured individual differences among Chinese consumers in the perceived psychological distance between the KFC (an American brand) and the Chinese communities, using the following item: "KFC is perceived as Chinese people's KFC." In addition, the investigators had Chinese consumers rated ten KFC television commercials in China on (a) how much they liked each commercial and (b) the level of politeness of each commercial to Chinese culture. The dependent variable was the strength of association between liking and perceived politeness (as measured by the within-participant slope relating perceived cultural politeness to liking in a random coefficient model). Results from random coefficient modeling reveal that perceived politeness of a KFC commercial to Chinese culture was positively related to liking for the commercial only among Chinese consumers who did not feel that KFC is psychologically close to Chinese culture. In fact, among Chinese consumers who had accepted KFC as the Chinese people's brand, higher levels of cultural politeness in the commercials were accompanied by less favorable evaluations, suggesting consumers like a culturally polite commercial *less* if the foreign brand is already accepted by the local consumers as an in-group brand.

If cultural politeness can mitigate the negative effects of cultural intrusion on exclusionary responses at least for newly arrived foreign brands, what kind of marketing communication strategies would be accompanied by higher levels of perceived cultural politeness? To provide an initial answer to these questions, Li (2013) had Chinese undergraduates in Singapore watch ten KFC commercials that were launched in China. The participants were asked to rate the level of similarity between each pair of the commercials and evaluated the level of cultural politeness of each commercial. Results from multidimensional scaling and cluster analysis performed on the similarity ratings identified four clusters of commercials: (a) commercials with no cultural themes and no references to consumers' feelings about their culture; (b) commercials that emphasize the benefits of foreign culture to Chinese consumers; (c) commercials that showcase how Western cultural elements can be applied to improve Chinese cultural practices; and (d) commercials that present examples of integrating the strengths of Western and Chinese cultures. The last category received the highest cultural politeness ratings from the Chinese consumers in Singapore.

Existential motivation

If exclusionary reactions are directed toward preserving the integrity of one's heritage culture, the presence of personal motives to protect the vitality of one's culture is another factor that would channel the bicultural priming effect into exclusionary reactions. One robust finding in social psychology is that people are motivated to protect the vitality of their culture when they experience existential anxiety (Greenberg, Pyszczynski, Solomon, Rosenblatt, Veeder, Kirkland, & Lyon, 1990). According to the terror management theory (Greenberg, Porteus, Simon, & Pyszczynski, 1995), humans have both a strong desire for self-preservation and the species-specific capability to anticipate the finitude of their physical existence. These two human characteristics generate existential terror—when reminded of their inevitable mortality, individuals start to question the meanings of their existence and those of their personal strivings.

When mortality concern is salient, people would experience existential anxiety. To manage existential anxiety, people would adhere to their culture and defend their cultural worldview (Greenberg et al., 1995). Accordingly, when mortality is salient, bicultural priming, which promotes categorical perceptions of culture, would likely evoke resistance to any actions that would undermine the integrity and vitality of one's culture.

By trying to be good or accomplished members of their culture, mortality salient individuals can manage their existential anxiety by convincing themselves that even when their physical existence has terminated, they will still live on in the memory of their cultural community. Individuals can become good members of their culture by defending its worldview, and research has shown that mortality salient individuals are motivated to defend the worldview in their culture (Burke, Martens, & Faucher, 2010; Vail, Rothschild, Weise, Solomon, Pyszczynski, & Greenberg, 2010). Mortality salient individuals are also motivated to protect the vitality and integrity of their culture because cultural worldview defense can assuage mortality concerns only when one's culture will live long.

Consistent with this idea, Torelli et al.'s (2011, Study 3) found that rendering mortality salient increases exclusionary reactions when consumers have been induced to think about culture categorically after having gone through a bicultural priming procedure. In this experiment, European American undergraduates were randomly assigned to vividly imagine what would happen to their body as they died and after they died (mortality salience condition) or to describe an anxiety-provoking dental work experience (control condition). This manipulation is an established technique designed to increase accessibility of death-related thoughts (Arndt, Greenberg, Solomon, Pyszczynski, & Simon, 1997). Next, participants were assigned to the bicultural priming or the control condition. In the bicultural priming condition, participants were instructed to evaluate three Chinese brands of products that are icons of American culture (running shoes, jeans, breakfast cereal). In the control condition, participants evaluated three Chinese brands of products that are not icons of American culture (desk lamp, toaster, umbrella).

Next, participants responded to a "marketing plan" from Nike (an iconic American brand) to expand its sales in the Middle East. According to this plan, the brand name "Nike" would be replaced by an Arabic brand name. The "Swoosh" mark would be removed, and a well-known local soccer player, dressed in traditional Islamic attire, would be chosen as the endorser for the new brand. The brand's slogan in marketing communication would be "Dress modestly, the Islamic spirit." This marketing plan was created to evoke a feeling of symbolic intrusion of Islamic culture into American culture via its representative, Nike.

As expected, mortality salience (versus dental work control) increased exclusionary reactions toward Nike's marketing plan, but only for participants in the bicultural priming condition. Mortality salient participants in the bicultural priming condition expected Nike's campaign to fail in the Middle East, anticipated the stock price of Nike to drop in the New York Stock Exchange, and were reluctant to buy sports apparels from Nike. This result confirmed one more time that categorical perception of cultures induced by bicultural priming is a necessary condition for evocation of exclusionary reactions.

In another study (Torelli et al., 2011, Study 4), participants received either the mortality salient manipulation or the dental work manipulation, went through bicultural priming, and responded to a marketing plan. The mortality salient manipulations and the bicultural priming procedures were the same as those used in the Torelli et al. (2011, Study 3) experiment. However, following these manipulations, the participants responded either to the Nike marketing plan described above or to a similar plan from Proctor-Silex, a noniconic American brand of bread toasters. After reading the marketing plan, participants were instructed to write a message supporting the marketing plan. Again, participants under the influence of bicultural priming wrote a less enthusiastic support statement for the Nike plan after having thought about their mortality than an anxiety-provoking dental work experience. The mortality salience manipulation did not affect the level of enthusiasm for the

Proctor-Silex plan. This result shows that perception of cultural intrusion (the intrusion of foreign culture into local culture through its iconic representative) is also a necessary condition for the evocation of exclusionary reactions. Results from these two mortality salience experiments also reveal that the personal motivation to protect the continuity of one's culture would incite exclusionary reactions, but only after the consumers have been induced to think about cultures categorically.

If invoking existential anxiety can increase exclusionary responses, attenuating such anxiety should reduce them. Past research has found that self-affirmation could attenuate the negative effect of existential anxiety (Schmeichel & Martens, 2005). Accordingly, providing consumers with the opportunity to affirm the importance and viability of their personal values could also attenuate exclusionary reactions toward foreign brands. Similarly, if exclusionary reactions are directed toward protecting the continuity of one's culture, providing consumers with an assurance that one's culture will survive the erosive effect of globalization will also attenuate exclusionary reactions (Cheng, 2010).

This idea was tested in a study conducted in Hong Kong (Cheng, 2010, Study 3). To ensure that the participants would exhibit exclusionary reactions, Hong Kong consumers went through the bicultural priming procedure designed to activate categorical perceptions of cultures and were asked to respond to the case in which an American children's book publisher intended to start its business in China. Before they responded to the case, the participants were randomly assigned to the self-affirmation or no self-affirmation condition. In the self-affirmation condition, participants were given the opportunity to affirm their values and personal qualities by ranking the importance of a list of values and personal characteristics and writing a short essay to "explain how the most important items would prevail over time and give them a sense of self-continuity." In the no self-affirmation condition, the participants did not receive this opportunity. Next, half of the participants in the self-affirmation and the no self-affirmation conditions received a cultural continuity assurance while the remaining participants received a cultural continuity threat. Participants in the cultural continuity assurance condition read a magazine story that described the continued popularity of traditional Chinese folk arts in modern Chinese people's life. In the cultural continuity threat condition, the participants read a magazine story that described the decline and extinction of traditional Chinese folk arts due to the lack of interest among the younger generations to learn them. Exclusionary reactions were observed only when the participants did not receive an opportunity to affirm their personal values or personal qualities and had experienced a cultural continuity threat. When given either a self-affirmation opportunity or a cultural continuity assurance, exclusionary responses were attenuated. These results confirm the symbolic exclusionism theory prediction that the existential motivation to protect the continuity of one's culture drives exclusionary reactions.

Thinking about cultures categorically

CATEGORICAL MINDSET

We argue that thinking categorically versus complexly about cultures is a necessary condition for the evocation of exclusionary reactions. Thus far, we have provided evidence of this argument indirectly through the effect of bicultural priming. More direct evidence of this argument comes from a set of studies on the effect of mindset priming on exclusionary reactions (Tong, Hui, Kwan, & Peng, 2011). In these studies, prior to responding to measures of exclusionary reactions, participants went through a set of procedures that activate a categorical mindset, a transactional mindset, or no mindset. The assumption being made in these studies is that participants under the influence of a categorical mindset would encode an international business opportunity as an interaction between *cultures*, whereas those under the influence of a transactional mindset would encode the same opportunity as a business transaction.

To manipulate mindsets, participants in the transaction mindset condition answered five questions pertaining to general cost-benefit calculations that were unrelated to the dependent measure. An example question is: Mrs. Lim earns $12/hour sewing at home. Today she will go to the wet market to buy fish. For each five minutes she bargains with the vendor she can save $1.25. Which is a better deal for her: (a) Bargain for 5 minutes; or (b) No bargain and work for extra 5 minutes? Participants in the categorization mindset condition answered five questions that required stereotype matching. An example question is: Alvin wears t-shirts and jeans to work every day. What occupation do you think he is in: (a) Marketing executive; or (b) software engineer? In the no prime control condition, participants proceeded to the dependent measure without answering any questions.

The manipulation was successful. In a manipulation check, participants were given three round stickers with the names "Lexus," "BMW," and "Nissan" to represent three commonly known automobile brands. Participants were instructed to freely arrange the stickers on a piece of paper to represent their perceived relationships among the brands. Participants in the transaction mindset condition tended to classify the three brands by the economic value of the products, placing Lexus and BMW close to each other and farther away from Nissan. In contrast, participants in the categorization mindset condition tended to classify the three brands by their country of origin, placing Lexus and Nissan close to each other and farther way from BMW.

In the first experiment in this series (Tong et al., 2011, Study 1), Singaporean and non-Singaporean undergraduates residing in Singapore read a fictitious case of "McDonald's takeover of Ya Kun Kaya Toast." The case described McDonald's plan to acquire Ya Kun Kaya Toast, which is a local iconic breakfast chain in Singapore. The possible economic benefits for both companies in this acquisition were emphasized in this scenario, and so was the cultural incompatibility between the typical American management style in McDonald's and the typical

Singaporean management culture in Ya Kun. Participants were asked to report their impression toward Ya Kun if the acquisition materialized, and rate the similarity between McDonald's and Ya Kun Kaya Toast. Participants in the transaction mindset condition were expected to attend to the potential benefits of the acquisition, whereas those in the categorization condition were expected to focus on the categorical differences in the cultures of the two companies.

Among Singaporean participants, priming a categorization (versus transaction) mindset intensified negative impression toward Ya Kun if the acquisition took place when the two companies were perceived to be dissimilar. This pattern of result was not found among non-Singaporeans, probably because they did not perceive the acquisition to yield benefits for their country or pose a threat to their culture.

A conceptually similar experiment (Tong et al., 2011, Study 2) was carried out with American participants using the same mindset manipulation. The acquisition case was changed to one in which India's Tata Motors planned to acquire General Motors, an iconic American company. Again, the case contained information on the economic benefits of the acquisition for General Motors and Tata. It also mentioned concerns for possible cultural clashes between the two companies. As in the Singaporean study, participants with categorization (versus transactional) mindset felt more negatively toward General Motors if the acquisition materialized, particularly when the two companies were perceived to be more dissimilar. In addition, participants with categorization mindset were more negative toward the acquisition if the perceived similarity between organizations was lower. The association between perceived similarity of the two companies and responses to the acquisition was not significant in the transaction mindset priming or no priming conditions. In sum, these studies provided evidence for the idea that categorical thinking about culture is necessary for the evocation of exclusionary reactions.

THOUGHTFUL ELABORATION

If categorical thinking about culture is necessary for the evocation of exclusionary reactions, thoughtful elaboration of cultural differences should attenuate exclusionary reactions. According to the elaboration likelihood model (Cacioppo & Petty, 1982), engaging in thoughtful elaboration of the pertinent issues can attenuate the impact of heuristic reasoning on judgment. Consistent with the elaboration likelihood model, past research has shown that culture's influence on judgments and behaviors is stronger when people process information in a cursory, spontaneous manner, but dissipates when people engage in more deliberative thought processes (Briley & Aaker, 2006). By extension, engaging in thoughtful elaboration about cultural complexities can attenuate the bicultural exposure effect and hence its attendant exclusionary reactions. Elaborate thoughts on cultural similarities and differences could reduce categorical perceptions of cultures and diminish perceived incompatibilities between cultures. Need for cognition is an individual difference variable reflecting the extent to which people engage in and enjoy effortful cognitive activities (Cacioppo &

Petty, 1982). Because individuals high in need for cognition engage in thoughtful elaborations, they are likely to think deeply about cultural similarities and differences and correct the spontaneous cultural inferences produced by the dual activation of cultures. Thus, thoughtful elaboration about cultural complexities (either measured as a chronic individual difference or induced in the experimental setting) should be able to attenuate the effect of bicultural priming and its attendant exclusionary reactions to foreign culture.

This inference has also received consistent empirical support. In one study (Torelli et al., 2011, Study 6), European American participants were first exposed to bicultural priming; they were asked to rate British brands of iconic Mexican products. Next, the participants were asked to draw on a sheet of paper a bubble to represent each of the following cultures: Mexican, Puerto Rican, Canadian, and British cultures. Half of the participants were told to think carefully about the complexity of intercultural relationships during the drawing task; the remaining participants were not. Participants in the complex thinking condition drew the bubbles representing dissimilar cultures closer to each other than those in the control condition. The complex thinking manipulation did not affect the distances drawn between the bubbles representing similar cultures. This study shows that the instruction to think about culture complexly can reduce one manifestation of categorical perception of culture—perceived distance between dissimilar cultures.

Some individuals are more inclined to think about cultures complexly than others. As mentioned earlier, one construct that captures this individual difference is the need for cognition (Cacioppo & Petty, 1982). Individuals with a high need for cognition tend to think deeply about cultural similarities and differences and not to exhibit categorical perceptions of culture. This idea was tested in a study (Torelli et al., 2011, Study 5), in which Hong Kong Chinese undergraduate students were randomly assigned to evaluate two print advertisements of a Chinese product (moon cake; Chinese culture priming), two print advertisements of an American product (hamburger; American culture priming), or one print advertisement of a Chinese product and one print advertisement of an American product (bicultural priming). Following this manipulation, they estimated the extent to which Hong Kong people would agree with a statement depicting the idea of disposition determinism and one depicting the idea of situation determinism. Disposition determinism refers to the idea that personality determines behaviors. This idea is more popular in the United States than in Asia. Situation determinism refers to the idea that situation determines behaviors. This idea is more popular in Asia than in the United States (Norenzayan, Choi, & Nisbett, 2002). In this study, individual differences among the participants in the need for cognition were also measured using the Need for Cognition Scale (Cacioppo, Petty, & Kao, 1984).

The results showed that when participants had low need for cognition, compared to the other two conditions, participants in the bicultural priming condition displayed a greater tendency to attribute culture-typical characteristics to members of a culture; they were more inclined to attribute situation determinism (versus disposition determinism) to other Chinese. However, when participants had high need for cognition, the bicultural priming manipulation did not affect estimated responses of the Chinese; the high need for cognition participants did not attribute a stronger belief in situation determinism (versus disposition determinism) to other Chinese. These results indicate that need for cognition can override the bicultural priming effect on categorical perceptions of culture.

Finally, in a third study (Torelli et al., 2011, Study 7), European American participants received a bicultural priming manipulation. They were presented with a slide named "artsy collage" that depicted symbols of the United States and China side by side. Next, the participants received either the mortality salience manipulation or the dental work manipulation. Following this manipulation, they read the Nike marketing plan to expand its business in the Middle East by mixing elements of Middle East culture with the American brand image of Nike. In addition, the level of Need for Cognition was measured in the study.

As shown in other studies (Torelli et al., 2011, Studies 3 and 4), the combination of bicultural priming and mortality salience manipulation should evoke the strongest exclusionary reactions to the marketing plan. This indeed happened, but for participants with low need for cognition only. Among higher need for cognition participants, exclusionary responses were relatively uncommon in all experimental conditions. Again, these results show that thoughtful elaboration can attenuate the joint effect of bicultural priming and existential motivation on the likelihood to display exclusionary reactions.

SUMMARY AND CONCLUSIONS

With the advance of globalization, inflow of brands, products, symbols, and icons from foreign cultures has become a ubiquitous phenomenon in many societies. Although many global brands have successfully been assimilated into local markets, occasionally, massive exclusionary responses from local consumers are made to limit the spread of global or foreign brands in local markets. Indeed, exclusionary reactions, in their extreme forms, involve isolation of, rejection of, or even attack on foreign cultures and their representatives. These forms of exclusionary reactions may arise from the worry that foreign cultures could through inflow of their brands contaminate and pose a threat to the continuity of heritage cultures (Chiu & Cheng, 2007).

In this chapter, we have reviewed evidence for the symbolic exclusionism theory, which posits that exclusionary responses, in addition to being motivated by political conservatism, strong identification with local culture or realistic conflicts between global and local brands in the marketplace, are directed to maintain the integrity and vitality of heritage cultures. The culturally motivated exclusionary responses are initiated to protect heritage cultures from the erosive effects of globalization.

We have identified some conditions that would facilitate or attenuate exclusionary reactions. These conditions are summarized in Figure 10.3.

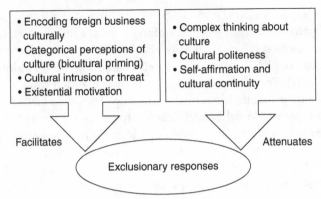

Figure 10.3 Symbolic exclusionism theory. Conditions that facilitate or attenuate exclusionary responses to foreign or global influence.

Exclusionary reactions are likely to occur when consumers encode business transactions culturally; view cultures as discrete homogeneous categories; and see intercultural business transactions as attempts by global or foreign cultures to spread their influence in local culture. Exclusionary responses could be further intensified if consumers are motivated by existential motivation to protect the vitality and integrity of their own culture. In contrast, exclusionary reactions could be attenuated when consumers engage in thoughtful elaborations on pertinent cultural issues; if foreign or global brands would adopt appropriate cultural politeness communication strategies when they market their brands to local communities; and if the consumers could affirm their personal values or are assured of the continued vitality of their culture despite globalization.

Because multiple conditions have to be met for strong exclusionary responses to be evoked, and these responses can be attenuated in multiple ways, strong exclusionary responses are relatively uncommon in global markets. Nonetheless, once evoked, these reactions could be contagious, leading to massive collective actions against certain global businesses. Furthermore, globalization, which has led to experiential compression of time and space (Giddens, 1985; Robertson, 1992), confer many opportunities of bicultural priming in globalized environment. As the evidence reviewed in this chapter clearly indicates, bicultural priming tends to promote categorical perceptions of culture, one of the necessary conditions for the evocation of exclusionary responses. From this perspective, the need to understand exclusionary responses has become more urgent as globalization proceeds.

A couple of caveats are in order. First, as mentioned in the outset, exclusionary responses are not always bad responses. At times, these reactions can motivate collective effort to preserve the integrity and vitality of heritage cultures that are at risk because of the hegemonic influence of globalization and commercialization. Examples of such effort include collective actions organized by the locals to rally against demolition of local heritage landmarks to create space for business expansion, and protest against opening of chain superstores that symbolize global capitalism (e.g., Wal-Mart) in local communities. Culturally motivated exclusionary reactions may also inspire critical reflections on the cultural effects of globalization and as well as appreciation for cultural diversity (Yang, 2011). For example, to express their opposition toward the global cultural meanings that multinational chains (e.g., Starbucks Coffee) represent, some consumers would deliberately choose to patronize stores that embody oppositional local cultural meanings (e.g., local coffee shops) (Thompson & Arsel, 2004). Such critical reflections on the cultural erosive effect of globalization could also generate countervailing market responses that promote consumer behaviors that have previously been attenuated in the process of commercial mainstreaming. For example, to express their opposition to global corporate capitalism, more consumers now prefer to buy foods from local farmers markets. Countervailing market responses like this have fueled the organic food movement and promoted community-supported agriculture (Thompson & Coskuner-Balli, 2007).

Second, globalization or bicultural priming does not always lead to exclusionary reactions. There is evidence that bicultural priming can enhance creativity (Cheng, Leung, & Wu, 2011; Leung & Chiu, 2010). When individuals are exposed to two cultures simultaneously, they become aware of the differences between cultures and how the strengths of different cultures can complement each other. Individuals who are motivated to learn from other cultures are inclined to see dissimilar cultures as valuable cognitive resources for expanding their intellectual horizon (Leung, Maddux, Galinsky, & Chiu, 2008; Maddux, Adam, & Galinsky, 2010). They are inclined to synthesize seemingly incompatible ideas into new ideas (Cheng et al., 2011; Leung & Chiu, 2010; Wan & Chiu, 2002; Ward, Patterson, Sifonis, Dodds, & Saunders, 2002).

Nonetheless, evocation of exclusionary responses could suppress the motivation to learn from other cultures. A recent study (Morris, Mok, & Mor, 2011) showed that exposure to culture mixing could increase cognitive rigidity, reducing the potential creative benefits of intercultural learning. This study shows that in Hong Kong, unless people strongly identify with Western culture, simply reviewing books on Asian cultures written in English or books on Western cultures written in Asian languages would increase close-mindedness.

In light of the tension between exclusionary responses and the potential creative benefits of globalization, a critical question to be addressed in future research is the social psychological conditions that would evoke exclusionary responses and those that would discourage these responses and support creativity through intercultural learning (Chiu et al., 2011; Gelfand, Lyons, & Lun, 2011; Leung et al., 2014). In this chapter, we have provided some preliminary answers to this important question. We anticipate that future research will build on these answers and further illuminate the psychological science of people's responses to the cultural implications of globalization.

REFERENCES

Aaker, J., & Schmitt, B. (2001). Culture-dependent assimilation and differentiation of the self. *Journal of Cross-Cultural Psychology, 32*, 561–576.

Arndt, J., Greenberg, J., Solomon, S., Pyszczynski, T., & Simon, L. (1997). Suppression, accessibility of death-related thoughts, and worldview defense: Exploring the psychodynamics of terror management. *Journal of Personality and Social Psychology, 73*, 5–18.

Brewer, M. B. (1999). The psychology of prejudice: Ingroup love or outgroup hate? *Journal of Social Issues, 55*, 429–444.

Briley, D. A., & Aaker, J. L. (2006). When does culture matter? Effects of personal knowledge on the correction of culture-based judgments. *Journal of Marketing Research, 43*, 395–408.

Brown, R., & Gilman, A. (1989). Politeness theory and Shakespeare's four major tragedies. *Language in Society, 18*,159–212.

Brown, P., & Levinson, S. (1987). *Politeness: Some universals in language usage.* Cambridge, England: Cambridge University Press.

Burke, B. L., Martens, A., & Faucher, E. H. (2010). Two decades of terror management theory: A meta-analysis of mortality salience research. *Personality and Social Psychology Review, 14*, 155–195.

Cacioppo, T. J., & Petty, R. E. (1982). The need for cognition. *Journal of Personality and Social Psychology, 42*, 116–131.

Cacioppo, J. T., Petty, R. E., & Kao, C. E. (1984). The efficient assessment of need for cognition. *Journal of Personality Assessment, 48*, 306–307.

Carnegie Endowment for International Peace (2007). *Culture and globalization.* Retrieved on April 28, 2007 from http://www.globalization101.org/issue/culture/

Castells, M. (1998). *The end of millennium.* Oxford: Blackwell.

Cheng, C-y., Leung, A. K.-y., & Wu, T-Y. (2011). Going beyond the multicultural experience-creativity link: the mediating role of emotions. *Journal of Social Issues, 67*, 806–824.

Cheng, S. Y-y. (2010). *Social psychology of globalization: Joint activation of cultures and reactions to foreign cultural influence* (Doctoral dissertation). University of Illinois at Urbana-Champaign.

Cheng, S. Y-y., Chao, M. M., Kwong, J., Peng, S., Chen, X., Kashima, Y., & Chiu, C-y. (2010). The good old days and a better tomorrow: Historical representations and future imaginations of China during the 2008 Olympic Games. *Asian Journal of Social Psychology, 13*, 118–127.

Chiu, C-y., & Cheng, S. Y-y. (2007). Toward a social psychology of culture and globalization: Some social cognitive consequences of activating two cultures simultaneously. *Social and Personality Psychology Compass, 1*, 84–100.

Chiu, C-y., & Cheng, S. Y-y. (2010). Cultural psychology of globalization. In R. Schwarzer & Peter A. French (Ed.), *Personality, human development, and culture: International perspectives on psychological science* (Vol. 2, pp. 199–212). New York: Psychology Press.

Chiu, C-y., Gelfand, M., Yamagichi, T., Shteynberg, G., & Wan, C. (2010). Intersubjective culture: The role of intersubjective perceptions in cross-cultural research. *Perspectives on Psychological Science, 5*, 482–493.

Chiu, C.-y., Gries, P., Torelli, C. J., & Cheng, S. Y-y. (2011). Toward a social psychology of globalization. *Journal of Social Issues, 67,* 663–676.

Chiu, C-Y., & Hong, Y-Y. (2006). *Social psychology of culture.* New York: Psychology Press.

Chiu, C-y., Mallorie, L., Keh, H. T., & Law, W. (2009). Perceptions of culture in multicultural space: Joint presentation of images from two cultures increases in-group attribution of culture-typical characteristics. *Journal of Cross-Cultural Psychology, 40,* 282–300.

Chiu, C-y., Wan, C., Cheng, S. Y-y., Kim, Y-h., & Yang, Y-j. (2010). Cultural perspectives on self-enhancement and self-protection. In M. Alicke & C. Sedikides (Eds.), *The handbook of self-enhancement and self-protection* (pp. 425–452). New York: Guilford.

Fishbach, A., & Zhang, Y. (2008). Together or apart: When goals and temptations complement versus compete. *Journal of Personality and Social Psychology, 94,* 547–559.

Fu, H-y., & Chiu, C-y. (2007). Local culture's responses to globalization: Exemplary persons and their attendant values. *Journal of Cross-Cultural Psychology, 38,* 636–653.

Fu, H-y., Chiu, C-y., Morris, M. W., & Young, M. (2007). Spontaneous inferences from cultural cues: Varying responses of cultural insiders and outsiders. *Journal of Cross-Cultural Psychology, 38,* 58–75.

Gelfand, M. J., Lyons, S. L., & Lun, J. (2011). Toward a psychological science of globalization. *Journal of Social Issues, 67,* 841–853.

Giddens, A. (1985). *The nation state and violence.* Cambridge: Polity Press.

Greenberg, J., Porteus, J., Simon, L., & Pyszczynski, T. (1995). Evidence of a terror management function of cultural icons: The effects of mortality salience on the inappropriate use of cherished cultural symbols. *Personality and Social Psychology Bulletin, 21,* 1221–1228.

Greenberg, J., Pyszczynski, T., Solomon, S., Rosenblatt, A., Veeder, M., Kirkland, S., & Lyon, D. (1990). Evidence for terror management theory: II. The effects of mortality salience on reactions to those who threaten or bolster the cultural worldview. *Journal of Personality and Social Psychology, 58,* 308–318.

Hsee, C. K. (1996). The evaluability hypothesis: An explanation for preference reversals between joint and separate evaluations of alternatives. *Organizational Behavior and Human Decision Processes, 67,* 247–257.

Hsee, C. K., & Leclerc F. (1998). Will products look more attractive when presented separately or together? *Journal of Consumer Research, 25,* 175–186.

Hsee, C. K., Loewenstein, G. F., Blount, S., & Bazerman, M. H. (1999). Preference reversals between joint and separate evaluations of options: A review and theoretical analysis. *Psychological Bulletin, 125,* 576–590.

Hong, Y- y., Benet-Martinez, V., C-y. Chiu, & Morris, M. W. (2003). Boundaries of cultural influence: Construct activation as a mechanism for cultural differences in social perception. *Journal of Cross-Cultural Psychology, 34,* 453–464.

Hong, Y., & Chiu, C-y. (2001). Toward a paradigm shift: From cultural differences in social cognition to social cognitive mediation of cultural differences. *Social Cognition, 19,* 118–196.

Hong, Y., Chiu, C-y., & Kung, M. (1997). Bringing culture out in front: Effects of cultural meaning system activation on social cognition. In K. Leung, Y. Kashima, U. Kim & S. Yamaguchi (Eds.), *Progress in Asian social psychology* (Vol. 1, pp. 139–150). Singapore: Wiley.

Hong, Y. Y., Morris, M. W., Chiu, C. Y., & Benet-Martinez, V. (2000). Multicultural minds: A dynamic constructivist approach to culture and cognition. *American Psychologist, 55*, 709–720.

Jost, J. T., Glaser, J., Kruglanski, A. W., & Sulloway, F. J. (2003). Political conservatism as motivated social cognition. *Psychological Bulletin, 129*, 339–375.

Kashima, Y., Bain, P., Haslam, N., Peters, K., Laham, S., Whelan, J., Bastian, B., Loughnan, S., Kaufmann, L., & Fernando, J. (2009). Folk theory of social change. *Asian Journal of Social Psychology, 12*, 227–246.

Kashima, Y., Shi, J., Tsuchiya, K., Kashima, E. S., Cheng, S. Y-y., Chao, M. M., & Shin, S-h. (2011). Globalization and folk theory of social change: How globalization relates to societal perceptions about the past and future. *Journal of Social Issues, 67*, 696–715.

Lal, D. (2000). Does modernization require westernization? *The Independent Review, 5*, 5–24.

Leung, A. K-y., & Chiu, C-y. (2010). Multicultural experience, idea receptiveness, and creativity. *Journal of Cross-Cultural Psychology, 41*, 723–741.

Leung, A. K-y., Maddux, W. W., Galinsky, A. D., & Chiu, C-y. (2008). Multicultural experience enhances creativity: The when and how? *American Psychologist, 63*, 169–181.

Leung, A. K-y., Qiu, L., & Chiu, C-y. (2014). Psychological science of globalization. In V. Benet-Martinez & Y-y. Hong (Eds.), *Oxford handbook of multicultural identity: Basic and applied perspectives* (pp. 181–201). Oxford University Press.

Li, D. (2013). *Cultural politeness in international marketing* (Doctoral dissertation). Nanyang Technological University.

Maddux, W. W., Adam, H., & Galinsky, A. D. (2010). When in Rome learn why the Romans do what they do: How multicultural learning experiences enhance creativity. *Personality and Social Psychology Bulletin, 36*, 731–741.

Morris, M. W., Mok, A., & Mor, S. (2011). Cultural identity threat: The role of cultural identifications in moderating closure responses to foreign cultural inflow. *Journal of Social Issues, 67*, 760–773.

Morris, M. W., & Peng, P. (1994). Culture and cause: American and Chinese attributions for social and physical events. *Journal of Personality and Social Psychology, 67*, 949–971.

Nisbett, R. E. (2003). *The geography of thought: How Asians and Westerners think differently.* New York: Free Press.

Nisbett, R. E., Peng, P., Choi, I., & Norenzayan, A. (2001). Culture and systems of thought: Holistic versus analytic cognition. *Psychological Review, 108*, 291–310.

Norenzayan, A., Choi, I., & Nisbett, R. E. (2002). Cultural similarities and differences in social inference: Evidence from behavioral predictions and lay theories of behavior. *Personality and Social Psychology Bulletin, 28*, 109–120.

Norenzayan, A., Smith, E. E., Kim, B. J., & Nisbett, R. E. (2002). Cultural preferences for formal versus intuitive reasoning. *Cognitive Science, 26*, 653–684.

Oyserman, D., & Lee, S. W. S. (2008). Does culture influence what and how we think? Effects of priming individualism and collectivism. *Psychological Bulletin, 134*, 311–342.

Parameswaran, R. (2002). Local culture in global media: Excavating colonial and material discourses in National Geographic. *Communication Theory, 12*, 287–315.

Robertson, R, (1992). *Globalization: Social theory and global culture.* London: Sage.

Rosenthal, L., & Levy, S. (2010). The colorblind, multicultural, and polycultural ideological approaches to improving intergroup attitudes and relations. *Social Issues and Policy Review, 4,* 215–246.

Rui, C. (2007). *Why Starbucks needs to get out of the Forbidden City?* Retrieved from http://blog.sina.com.cn/u/4adabe27010008yg.

Schmeichel, B. J., & Martens, A. (2005). Self-affirmation and mortality salience: Affirming values reduces worldview defense and death-thought accessibility. *Personality and Social Psychology Bulletin, 31,* 658–667.

Sherif, M. (1966). *In common predicament: Social psychology of intergroup conflict and cooperation,* Boston: Houghton Mifflin.

Stephan, E., Liberman, N., & Trope, Y. (2010). Politeness and psychological distance: A construal level perspective. *Journal of Personality and Social Psychology, 98,* 268–280.

Sui, J., Zhu, Y., & Chiu, C-y. (2007). Bicultural mind, self-construal, and recognition memory: Cultural priming effects on self- and mother-reference effect. *Journal of Experimental Social Psychology, 43,* 818–824.

Tajfel, H., & Turner, J. (1979). An integrative theory of intergroup conflict. In W. G. Austin & S. Worchel (Eds.), *The social psychology of intergroup relations* (pp. 94–109). Monterey, CA: Brooks-Cole.

Thompson, C. J., & Arsel, Z. (2004). The Starbucks brandscape and consumers' (anit-corporate) experiences of glocalization. *Journal of Consumer Research, 31,* 632–642.

Thompson, C. J., & Coskuner-Balli, G. (2007). Countervailing market responses to corporate co-optation and the ideological recruitment of consumption communities. *Journal of Consumer Research, 34,* 135–152.

Tong, Y-y., Hui, P. P-Z., Kwan, L., & Peng, S. (2011). National feelings or rational dealing? The role of procedural priming on the perceptions of cross-border acquisitions. *Journal of Social Issues, 67,* 743–759.

Torelli, C. J., Chiu, C-y., Tam, K-p., Au, A. K. C., & Keh, H. T. (2011). Exclusionary reactions to foreign cultures: Effects of simultaneous exposure to cultures in globalized space. *Journal of Social Issues, 67,* 716–742.

Turner, J. C., Hogg, M. A., Oakes, P. J., Reicher, S. D., & Wetherell, M. (1987). *Rediscovering the social group: A self-categorization theory.* Oxford, England: Basil Blackwell.

Vail, K. E. III, Rothschild, Z. K., Weise, D. R., Solomon, S., Pyszczynski, T., & Greenberg, J. (2010). A terror management analysis of the psychological functions of religion. *Personality and Social Psychology Review, 14,* 84–94.

Wan, W., & Chiu, C-y. (2002). Effects of novel conceptual combination on creativity. *Journal of Creative Behavior, 36,* 227–241.

Ward, T. B., Patterson, M. J., Sifonis, C. M., Dodds, R. A., & Saunders, K. N. (2002). The role of graded category structure in imaginative thought. *Memory and Cognition, 30,* 199–216.

Yang, Y-J. (2011). *Some conditions for evocation of negative reaction toward foreign intrusion of local cultural space* (Doctoral dissertation). University of Illinois at Urbana-Champaign.

Yang, D. Y-J., Chiu, C-y., Chen, X., Cheng, S. Y. Y., Kwan, L., Tam, K-P., & Yeh, K-H. (2011). The lay psychology of globalization and its social impact. *Journal of Social Issues, 67,* 677–695.

11

Culture and Branding

SHARON NG, ROHINI AHLUWALIA,
AND MICHAEL J. HOUSTON ■

INTRODUCTION

The interplay between culture and branding has been of considerable interest to researchers and marketers alike. Products and brands marketed and sold internationally to different geographic markets often face distinct branding challenges across these markets. The source of these challenges often comes from the cultural differences that can exist across international markets. This chapter focuses on research examining this interplay between culture and branding. In this chapter we review the growing literature on the impact of culture on branding issues as well as how branding practices may exert an influence on culture.

We begin with an overview of the effects of culture on the cognitive structure of brands (i.e., how culture influences the types of mental representation and organization of brand knowledge). While culture influences how brand knowledge is organized, we must also consider if cultural variations in the content of that knowledge exist (i.e., does the meaning of a brand differ within and across cultures?). A brand may exist globally but does it have the same meaning in all cultures? The second section reviews research on how culture influences brand meanings. With an understanding of how culture affects brand category structure and meaning, we proceed to discuss the implications of the above cultural differences on how brand extensions are evaluated, including the brand dilution effects of failed extensions. The chapter concludes by discussing the reverse effect of brands on the evolution of culture, with a special examination of the unique case of global brands. First, let us begin by understanding how culture influence consumers' brand cognitive structure.

BRAND COGNITIVE STRUCTURE

Brand cognitive structures refer to the mental representations of brands in the minds of consumers (Christensen & Olson, 2002; Keller, 2003; Sedikides & Skowronski, 1991). They pertain to the manner in which brand knowledge is represented and organized in memory (Ratneshwar & Shocker, 1991). In line with the Associative Network Theory, brand has frequently been viewed as a category where a number of associations are linked to it (Broniarczyk & Alba, 1994; Christensen & Olson 2002; Keller, 2003; Joiner, 1998; Lawson, 2002; Loken, Joiner, & Peck, 2002). Brand associations are viewed as nodes in an extensive network of information, and the nodes are linked to one another. It is generally assumed that activating a piece of information in the network would send excitatory forces to concepts that are linked to the activated node, thereby increasing the probability that the linked concepts would come to mind (Barsalou, 1992). The strength of the linkages depends on the extent consumers elaborate on the information during encoding and the number of cues that are linked to the piece of information (van Osselaer & Janiszewski, 2001; Wyer & Srull, 1989). If sufficient excitation accumulates at these other nodes, these concepts are activated as well.

Brand cognitive structure is multidimensional. It may include descriptive and evaluative information about the brand, such as attitudes, emotions and feelings, symbols, memories of past consumption events, and consumption visions of anticipated experiences (Christensen & Olson, 2002; Keller, 2003). It is both a result of one's prior processing of information and a determinant of the way one processes information in the future (Sujan, 1985; Wyer & Srull, 1989). Information can only be processed if the perceiver has some type of internal knowledge structure to receive and organize it (Joiner, 1998; Lawson, 2002; Markus & Zajonc, 1985; Wyer & Srull, 1989). As people acquire new information and interrelate it with existing knowledge in memory, the encoded information is stored in an organized network and subsequent retrieval from long-term memory should reflect the way information is organized in memory (Christensen & Olson, 2002; John & Whitney, 1986; Kanwar, Olson, & Sims, 1981; Markus & Zajonc, 1985; Sedikides & Skowronski, 1991). The type of information available and the way one organizes the information in his or her mind also affects what consumers pay attention to and the way newly acquired information is represented (Christensen & Olson, 2002; Lawson, 2002; Markus & Zajonc, 1985).

Recent research in culture and branding reveals that consumers brand cognitive structures differ across cultures. The type of information stored and the way associations are structured or categorized is influenced by one's self-construal and processing styles. First, let us consider how brand information is structured and categories are defined in different cultures. Prior research shows that one of the key differences between independents and interdependents is the differential attention to contextual information (Nisbett, Peng, Choi, & Norenzayan, 2001). Specifically, interdependents have been found to pay greater attention to the context and take such information into account when encoding and categorizing information, relative to independents (Jain, Desai, & Mao, 2007; Kühnen, Hannover, Roeder, Shah, Schubert, Upmeyer & Zakaria, 2001; Ng & Houston, 2009; Nisbett et al., 2001). Jain et al. (2007) show that consideration of context information makes interdependents focus more on between category differentiation (versus within-category richness), whereas the more context-independent nature of independents' processing lead them to focus more on within-category richness (versus category differentiation). Specifically, the authors argue that interdependents are more likely to focus on defining (versus characteristic) features of a category, leading to stronger linkages between such features and the category. Defining features refer to those features that are exclusive to the category (e.g., prints documents for computer printers) while characteristic features refer to those features that may be common across multiple categories (e.g., comes in multiple sizes for microwave ovens). Since defining features are exclusive to the category, focusing on defining features also mean that the category structure in the minds of interdependents will be more differentiated. On the other hand, the authors argue that since independents are motivated by within-category richness, they will focus more on characteristic features, which is useful in providing more information about the category. This leads to more broadly defined types of categories. Thus, they concluded that category structure would be more differentiated in the minds of interdependents compared to independents. This is consistent with the findings from Ng and Houston (2009) who argue that since interdependents pay greater attention to contextual information, the stored brand representations should be more context dependent, and individuating or episodic information, such as usage occasion, would be stored and linked to the products and brand. Thus, interdependents are more likely to focus on the differences among the products and are less likely to generalize information across product categories. On the other hand, since independents are more context independent, they are more likely to pay less attention to contextual information and extract and integrate information from exemplars or episodic memories to form overall brand beliefs. To test this hypothesis, the authors examined the extent to which priming interdependents with beliefs (e.g., good quality) of one product by the brand would spread the activation to another product by the same brand, thereby facilitating its response. If the products are linked to the same belief, significant facilitation should be observed. On the other hand, if the products are not linked to the same belief, minimal facilitation should be observed. Examining the time participants take to react to different word pairs, the author found that priming independents with beliefs of another product by the same brand leads to greater degrees of facilitation compared to interdependents. This shows that interdependents possess a more differentiated category structure, with products of a brand categorized into distinct subcategories, and these subcategories may or may not be to the same beliefs. On the other hand, independents possess a less differentiated category structure, with products of a brand being connected to a common set of beliefs. The research further shows that expertise will exacerbate the cultural differences as expertise will magnify the ability to detect similarities or differences among the products.

Building on the above findings, Ng and Houston (2006) further show that the different category structures across cultures also influence the relative accessibility of global beliefs versus exemplars in consumers' minds. Global beliefs refer to general evaluative or descriptive thoughts consumers may have about a brand (e.g., Sony represents good quality). Exemplars, on the other hand, refer to thoughts about specific products or its related categories (an exemplar for Sony may be Sony Vaio or Sony Bravia). The authors argue that since independents pay less attention to context and are inclined to focus on traits, they would focus more on global beliefs (relative to exemplars) as, like individual traits, forming general beliefs about the brand requires one to aggregate information across numerous purchasing contexts. On the other hand, since interdependents focus less on trait information and more on concrete episodic information, exemplars would be relatively more accessible than global beliefs to them. Using a free association task, the authors show that independents tend to retrieve more general beliefs about a brand, whereas interdependents tend to retrieve more exemplars about a brand.

Overall, findings from recent research show that independents and interdependents encode and store brand information differently. Interdependents' attention to contextual information leads them to focus on the situational specificity of each product, leading to more complex and finely differentiated categories. Contextual information is linked to the products and this in turn leads to increased accessibility of exemplars. Independents' inattention to contextual information, on the other hand, leads to broader and more all encompassing brand categories. Beliefs are abstracted from experiences and are more accessible.

After reviewing the impact of culture on the type and way associations are stored in consumers' minds, we now shift our attention to the interplay between culture and the content or meaning contained with brand cognitive structures.

CULTURE AND BRAND MEANING

Brands essentially do not exist until meaning is attached to them. As Keller (2002, p. 3) indicates, many brand managers define a brand as having "a certain amount of awareness, reputation, and prominence in the marketplace." The meaning attached to a brand becomes the foundation for its success in the marketplace. Consequently, much of the marketing effort in support of a brand is designed to establish meaning in the minds of current and prospective buyers of the brand. Brand meaning that resonates with buyers yields greater brand success.

Culture's influence on brand meaning

Although brand name as a signal of quality appears to be a "universal" marketing phenomenon (Dawar & Parker, 1994; data from thirty-eight mostly Western industrialized nations and Japan relating to evaluation of products in consumer electronics), the strength of this signal tends to vary across cultures. For instance, Erdem, Swait and Valenzuela (2006), who collected data on two product categories (orange juice and personal computers) from respondents in Brazil, Germany, India, Japan, Spain, Turkey, and the United States, found that the positive effect of brand credibility (the believability of the brand's product position information or its perceived ability and willingness to deliver on what it promises) on choice is greater for consumers who rate high on either collectivism or uncertainty avoidance. Erdem et al. (2006) suggest that credible brands provide more value to collectivist consumers because such consumers perceive these brands as being of higher quality (i.e., reinforcing group identity). Similarly, credible brands are valued more by high uncertainty-avoidance consumers because such brands have lower perceived risk and information costs.

In addition to the value attached to brand names, the meaning of brands is also likely to be influenced by the consumer's culture. Meanings of a culture typically get embedded in its consumptions symbols, including brands. The effects of culture on brand meaning, however, are more likely to be observed for the symbolic or value-expressive functions associated with a brand (typically communicated via brand personality) than for their utilitarian attributes. As such, a brand's symbolism (and personality) is rooted in individuals' needs, self-views, and socialization—all of which tend to vary across cultures; however, consumers are less likely to exhibit variability in meaning of utilitarian attributes across cultures (Aaker, Benet-Martinez, & Garolera, 2001). Several studies in the literature have examined the differences in brand personality across cultures.

Aaker et al. (2001) studied brand personality in Japan and Spain and compared them to the dimensions obtained in the United States. They found that although some brand personality dimensions were common to Japan and United States (e.g., Sincerity, Excitement, Competence, and Sophistication), there were also some culture-specific dimensions associated with brands in these markets (Japanese: Peacefulness; American: Ruggedness). Spanish brands, on the other hand, exhibited a distinctively different dimension of Passion (traits such as fervent, passionate, spiritual, and bohemian). Additionally, distinct from the American and Japanese markets, for Spanish consumers, the Competence dimension blended into the Sophistication dimension. The emergence of a Peacefulness dimension in Japan and Spain, is consistent with the finding that individuals in these cultures tend to put greater weight on harmony and cooperation than those in the North American culture. Notably, even for the dimensions that emerged across cultures, signifying universally held individual needs (e.g., Excitement and Sophistication), the meaning was somewhat variable across cultures. For instance, although Excitement was associated with being young, contemporary, spirited, and daring across all the cultures, it was also related to imaginativeness, uniqueness, and independence in Spain and North America, but included a "talkativeness" aspect in Japan.

More recently Sung and Tinkham (2005) found that global brands carry different cultural meaning in Korea as compared to the United States. Reflecting the importance of Confucian values in Korea's social and economic systems—two new factors emerged in the brand personality structure of the Korean consumers: Ascendancy (traits such as strict, heavy, intelligent, big, daring; corresponding to Confucian themes of paternalism and Confucian capitalism) and Passive Likeability (defined by traits such as funny, small-town, easy, smooth, family oriented, warm). Passive Likeability appears to be similar to general likeability (as in the US model—e.g., warm, funny, playful, sentimental), but with a blend of traditional values, harmony and gentleness added to it (as opposed to exuberance and outdoorsy). The data also suggest that professional status and gender roles are separated more strongly from other dimensions of brand perception in the United States than in Korea. Particularly interesting in this regard is the difference in the way gender effects emerged across cultures. In the Korean sample, "masculine" and "feminine" traits were prominent attributes, with masculine loading on Ruggedness and feminine loading on Sophistication. In the United States, Sophistication was not as well distinguished by gender associations, instead, masculine and feminine loaded on the Androgyny factor (suggesting that expensive brands, both masculine and feminine, could be associated with high status).

The collective results of the different studies in this area suggest that the meaning associated with brands tends to vary from culture to culture, influenced by themes dominant in each culture. For instance, in Eastern cultures, the themes of obedience, harmony, and family are seen as traits that consumers look for in brands as well (Peacefulness, Passive Likeability). In contrast in the American society, where the focus is on personal achievement and individualism, ruggedness and competence is a common theme found in brand representations. Interestingly, it is possible for the same brand to become associated with differential meanings across cultures despite the parent company's attempt to standardize meaning globally. In this regard, a recent study by Foscht, Maloles, Swaboda, Morschett, and Sinha (2008), which examined brand perceptions for one global brand (energy drink Red Bull) in six different countries (Austria, Germany, Netherlands, Singapore, United Kingdom, and United States) is insightful. The study reveals that the same brand was perceived differently in different cultures in spite of the company's attempt to position the brand similarly across cultures (e.g., more exciting but less rugged in Singapore than in the United States or Germany).

Anthropological studies have also built a strong empirical case that consumers often appropriate the meanings of global brands to their own ends, adding new cultural associations, dropping incompatible ones, and transforming others to fit into the local culture and lifestyle (Miller, 1998). As such, global brands seem to take on a variety of localized meanings (Ger & Belk, 1996; Miller, 1998).

More generally, these theorists contend that local cultures and the forces of globalization coshape each other; hence, they describe the effects of globalization on everyday cultural life—via global brands, fashion, and mass media—as a process of "glocalization" (Robertson, 1995; Thompson & Arsel, 2004; Wilk, 1995).

Malleability of brand meaning

There is some evidence that Asian cultures, especially Chinese, do not necessarily attach consistent meaning to a brand. Rather, as a culture that values public meanings or those assigned to the object by the society at large (Eckhardt & Houston, 2008), and emphasizes malleability, change, and holistic, Yin/Yang outlooks (Tse, 1996), buyers in the Chinese culture would attach less consistent, more dynamic meanings to brands. Malleability in brand meaning stems from the interdependent self and, therefore, is likely to extend beyond the Chinese culture to include consumers in other Asian countries. The interdependent self emphasizes social relationships as the source of identity for an individual. Each social relationship exists within its own context and the context-driven nature of processing by individuals with a chronic interdependent self suggests that the meaning of a brand from one social relationship to another can differ.

In research specific to the Chinese culture, Eckhardt and Houston (2008) found that the meaning of a product or brand changes based on context and the nature of the interpersonal relationship in which product or brand usage occurs. Using qualitative methods, they examined how Chinese consumers going through everyday lives attach different meanings to a product or brand as they switch from one social relationship to another. In essence, the symbolism of a brand to an individual can change depending on the social situation and dynamics of the context the individual is experiencing. The meaning can change even to the point that opposite meanings for the same brand can occur. Such a finding is consistent with research reported by Aaker and Sengupta (2000). They found that members of an Asian culture react differently to incongruent information than do members of Western cultures. When presented with information that is incongruent, members of Western cultures engage in elaboration in an attempt to resolve the incongruency, while Asians are more comfortable with the incongruency and are not motivated to resolve it. Rather, they accommodate both pieces of information in their judgments. Thus, they are comfortable with having different meanings for the same brand in different contexts.

So far, the review has focused on the impact of culture on how people view brands and store brand information. A next logical question would be—so what? So what if people across cultures view brands differently? In the next section, we will examine how these differences will affect the way consumers evaluate brands—brand extension, brand dilution, and culturally symbolic brands. In particular, most research in culture and branding has focused on brand extension and this will be the focus of the next section.

BRAND EXTENSION

Brand extension is a tactic widely used to leverage a brand's positive equity (Keller, 2003). In the cross-cultural context, the main bulk of the research done in this area has been to identify the impact of culture on consumers' perception of fit between a new product and the parent brand (Ahluwalia, 2008; Monga & John, 2007; Ng & Houston, 2006). Fit refers to the extension's perceived similarity to the parent brand (Aaker & Keller, 1990; Boush & Loken, 1991). Conventionally, it is assumed that fit evaluation is based on product category similarity or attributes (e.g., benefits, brand image) (Broniarczyk & Alba, 1994; Keller, 2002; Park, Milberg, & Lawson, 1991). Extensions that do not belong to the same product category or evoke similar benefits or image associations would be considered a bad fit to the parent brand and therefore, evaluated unfavorably.

However, Eastern societies are replete with stories of successful extensions that may be considered to be a "bad fit" by conventional standard. For example, the big conglomerates in Korea such as Samsung own products in a variety of product categories (such as electronics, life insurance, ship building) that are barely related to one another. Yet, these extensions are well received by the consumers. Similar stories can be found in Japan (e.g., Mitsubishi). Such anecdotal evidence seems to suggest that extension evaluations in Eastern societies are more flexible than what existing theories prescribed. Recent findings show that differences in category definition and processing styles are two main factors leading to extension evaluation differences across cultures (Ahluwalia, 2008; Monga & John, 2007; Ng & Houston, 2006). In the following sections, we will review existing findings on how type of associations (exemplars versus beliefs) and processing styles (relational versus non-relational) may moderate consumers' extension evaluations.

Category definition and association accessibility

As reviewed earlier, Easterners and Westerners differ in the way categories are defined and information is structured in their mind (Ng & Houston, 2009). Since brand are viewed as categories and extension evaluation depends in large part on whether the new product is seen to belong to the same category as the parent brand, such structural difference would have important implications on how consumers evaluate brand extensions.

Research shows that the relative accessibility of the different types of associations connected to the focal brand affects one's assessment of fit and perception of a new product. Brand associations that are more accessible will have a higher probability of being used to evaluate the fit of new products. Findings from Ng and Houston (2006) show that exemplars (e.g., computer) should exert a stronger influence on fit perception for interdependents, whereas beliefs (e.g., creative) should exert a stronger influence on fit perception for independents.

Table 11.1 Findings on impact of culture on brand structure and evaluations

	Interdependent	Independent
Processing style	Context dependent	Context independent
Brand cognitive structure	Category is fine tune • Store episodic information • Separate sets of beliefs for each sets of products • Focus on defining features	Category is broad • Store abstract beliefs • Most products of the same brand linked to the same sets of beliefs • Focus on characteristics features
Brand associations	Exemplars more accessible	Beliefs more accessible
Brand Extension	Bases of fit: Focus on relational fit Relational processing advantage	Bases of fit: Focus on taxonomic or attribute fit No relational processing advantage

(See Table 11.1 for a summary of the findings.) For example, if the most accessible association of Apple is "creative," new extensions will be judged on its fit to the creative concept. On the other hand, if the most accessible association of Apple is "computer," new extensions will be judged on its category fit to the brand.

Though at first glance the predominance of exemplars in influencing consumers' extension evaluations would imply a more restrictive extension list as exemplars are more concrete than beliefs, and prior research has shown that concrete associations are less extendable than abstract associations (Broniarczyk & Alba, 1994; Jain et al., 2007; Keller, 2002), this is not necessarily the case. How exemplars are used to assess fit is also influenced by the way categories are defined. One may consider how the new product belongs to the same product category as the exemplar (which may lead to a more restrictive list of possible extensions) or how it may be related to the exemplars on a broader level (e.g., usage occasion, which may lead to a more expansive list of possible extensions). Which fit assessment prevails is in turn influenced by one's processing styles. For example, Monga and John (2010) show that all is not lost for brands with more dominant concrete associations (e.g., brands tied to specific attributes or product categories). They argue that brands with concrete associations may also enjoy success in a distant extension if consumers are more interdependent or are primed to think more holistically as a holistic thinking style will encourage consumers to focus on relational similarity and uncover alternative ways to connect the extension to the parent brand. Thus, processing styles can exert a significant effect on how consumers may perceive the same extension. This brings us to the next section.

Relational processing by interdependents

Another stream of research on culture and brand extension focuses on how differences in processing styles across cultures may influence consumers' extension evaluations. Prior research in the psychology literature shows that interdependents tend to group together objects based on relationships, such as functional (e.g., pencil and notebook) or social relationships (e.g., mother and children) (Ahluwalia, 2008; Nisbett et al., 2001). Independents, on the other hand, tend to focus on the attributes of the products and group together objects that belong to the same taxonomic category (e.g., newspaper and magazine; Nisbett et al., 2001). For instance, Chiu (1972) shows that Chinese children are more likely to group objects that share thematic or functional similarities together whereas American children are more likely to group objects that either possess similar attributes or belong to the same product category together. Since favorability of an extension depends on a consumer's ability to connect the new product to the parent brand, interdependents' tendency to engage in relational processing provides them with a greater ability to detect to uncover relationships between objects (Ahluwalia, 2008; Nisbett et al., 2001). For example, Ji, Peng, and Nisbett (2000) shows that holistic thinkers possess greater ability to detect covariation between distant objects. In the marketing context, research has shown that the propensity to engage in relational processing filters down to influence consumers' evaluation of ads and products (e.g., Aaker & Maheswaran, 1997; Han & Shavitt, 1994; Zhang & Shavitt, 2003).

Recent findings show that this ability to detect greater relationship between distant objects has important implications on how consumers view extensions by brands. Specifically, recent research shows that the attention to relationship by interdependents (as opposed to independents) allow them to detect more and varied ways (e.g., usage occasion) to connect new products to the parent brand. They may also engage in more in-depth analysis of each connection (Ahluwalia, 2008; Ji et al., 2000; Monga & John, 2007). Ahluwalia (2008) argues that individuals high in interdependence possess a "relational processing advantage" (p. 338) relative to those low in interdependence. Specifically, the author argued that consumers' self-construal will affect their ability to resolve the deviation presented by a brand stretch. High interdependents tend to engage in a wider and deeper processing of relational bases of similarity. By considering more ways to connect two disparate objects, relational thinking allows consumers to perceive a better fit between two objects that are conventionally considered different. Ahluwalia (2008) also shows that when interdependents are presented with a moderate extension (e.g., Johnson and Johnson stuffed toys and Adidas brown shoes), interdependents exhibited significantly more positively evaluation of the new products relative to independents. Subsequent experiments show that this may be attributed to interdependents' greater ability to generate more relational thoughts to connect the new product that the parent brand. A similar pattern of results was also found in Monga and John (2007) who show that Indian students, who are more holistic thinkers, were more favorable toward Kodak shoes and

Kodak filing cabinets than American students. They were more likely to consider how these products may be used with other Kodak's products. Ng and Houston (2006) also show that interdependents exhibit more favorable attitude toward a brand extension when relational similarity is high (e.g., gym equipment and heart rate monitor) while independents exhibit more favorable attitude toward a brand extension when the taxonomic similarity is high (e.g., gym equipment and other sports equipment).

Though it is argued that interdependents may evaluate a moderately distant extension more favorably, further research shows that the extent to which this difference emerges may depend on a number of brand and individual character-istics. For instance, research shows that the cultural difference discussed may not be evident when the extension is highly similar (in terms of product category). When an extension is categorically very similar to existing products owned by the parent brand (e.g., onion ring for McDonald), consumers can relate the new product to the parent brand easily (Ahluwalia, 2008; Monga & John, 2007). Thus, any advantage relational processing interdependents may enjoy is nullified, as at this level of similarity, even independents can relate the new product to the parent brand. It is argued that the impact of culture on consumers' fit percep-tion and evaluation of a brand extension should be most prominent when the extension is moderately dissimilar (Ahluwalia, 2008). Moderate incongruity has been shown in other literature to stimulate greater processing (e.g., Meyers-Levy, Louie, & Curren, 1994). Consistent with this literature, it is argued that moderate incongruity is where consumers have the most leeway and opportunity to search for possible relationships between the new product and the parent brand. The relational processing advantage interdependents enjoy will allow them to make full use of such opportunities.

Though there is no quibble on how independents and interdependents will behave when extension is categorically very or moderately similar, findings on how independents and interdependents behave when extension is highly dissimilar differ. Monga and John (2007) found that holistic thinking style generally leads to more positive evaluation of very dissimilar extensions. Examining Indians and American's evaluation of Kodak extending into shoes and McDonald's extending into razors, they found that even for very dissimilar extensions, Indians are still more favorable toward these products compared to Americans. On the other hand, Ahluwalia (2008) argues that when an extension is highly dissimilar, interdependents may not exhibit any significant evaluation advantage relative to independents. It is argued that farther brand extensions require much effort to reconcile the incongruities and unless interdependents are extrinsically motivated to engage in increased elaboration, relational processing does not accord them any special advantage. The author argues that higher moti-vation level is an important prerequisite for interdependents to uncover some ways to connect a highly dissimilar extension to the parent brand. Though the conclusions reached are slightly different, the different conclusions reached may be a function of a difference in the samples used. Several factors (other than just self-construal) may influence the acceptance of low-fit brand extensions across cultures. Several of the interdependent Eastern cultures/countries used in past brand extension research (e.g., India) are bureaucratic and hierarchical, which are more likely to be cautious and risk averse (e.g., Douglas & Wildavsky, 1982; Zhou, Su, & Bao, 2002) than the more independent cultures (e.g., United States). They are likely to be less risk taking in their product-related behaviors than their more independent counterparts. Therefore, consumers from these countries may be more open to farther extensions from reputable brands since a strong brand reputation can lower the risk associated with product failure.

Reconciliation

Overall, findings from various streams of research seem to converge on the conclusion that interdependents are more able to detect similarities or connections between an extended product and the parent brand, leading to greater acceptance and more favorable attitude toward the new product. A couple of things might be worth mentioning though.

First, though differences in cognitive structure and processing styles are examined as two factors that may influence brand extension, in reality it is very hard to disentangle both constructs (Wyer & Srull, 1989). Cognitive structures will influence the type of processing one employs and vice versa. Moreover, the prescription from both mechanisms appeared to be the same, making it even harder to tease both explanations apart. Nonetheless, the underlying mechanism for both explanations is the same—that is, the difference is a result of independents and interdependents' differential attention to contextual information.

Second, the preceding review has focused primarily on how culture influences brand extension evaluation through its impact on consumers' fit perception. An alternative perspective that has received somewhat lesser attention is the argument that fit may not be as important in dictating the success of an extension in other cultures. An increasing number of articles in the literature have proposed that the importance of fit assessment is overly hyped and fit may not be the most important element affect consumers' brand extension evaluations (e.g., Bridges, Keller, & Sood, 2000; Hagtvedt & Patrick, 2008). Though no research has been done on this, it is highly possible that culture may influence extension evaluation through other routes and bypass fit perception.

Third, the findings reviewed earlier also raise the question—what does fit mean? In a typical brand extension research, authors would frequently argue that interdependents have more favorable attitude toward a "low-fit" product (e.g., Monga & John, 2007). However, the product is considered to be of a low fit because it is evaluated by the Western society's benchmark. Usually, participants are asked to indicate how similar or consistent a new extension is to the parent brand in terms of product category or attributes. This is more akin to taxonomic similarity. However, as pointed out by Ahluwalia (2008), there are so many bases of fit—category, attribute, usage occasion, and target market. An extension viewed to be a low fit based on categorical similarity may be a good fit based on other fit assessment. As Ahluwalia (2008) said, "reaction to a brand stretch is determined by the extent to which the consumer can resolve the presented deviation" (p. 338). It might be more accurate to classify extensions on a continuum of resolvability. Thus, more precise language may be needed in future research. Instead of simply stating that the new extension is a bad fit, it should be clear on what dimension this judgment is based on. The key is to identity which fit dimension matters most to the consumers, as whichever dimension they use to determine fit will be the dimension that affects brand choice.

Brand feedback effect

Though engaging in brand extension is a popular way companies used to leverage their brand equity, it is not without its downside. Extension failure has been shown to have a negative feedback effect on the parent brand (John, Loken, & Joiner, 1998; Loken & John, 1993). Research done in Western cultures shows that when an extension fails to live up to consumers' expectations, the negative attitude generated by the failed product will feedback to the parent brand, leading to lower parent brand equity (Loken & John, 1993; Milberg, Park, & McCarthy, 1997). However, does extension failure have similar effects in different cultures?

Contrary to conventional wisdom that a negative extension would automatically lead to negative feedback to the parent brand, recent findings show that interdependents or holistic thinkers are relatively immune to such dilution effects (Monga & John, 2008; Ng, 2010). Ng (2010) shows that in the event of an extension failure by a positively viewed brand, interdependents experience lesser decline in the parent brand's equity, relative to independents. Since negative information from an extension failure contradicts any positive perception one may have of the parent brand (especially since most extension comes from parent brands with positive brand equity), Ng (2010) argues that people in different cultures deal with such contradiction differently. Research in psychology and marketing has shown that interdependents possess a "more dialectic way of thinking," which "involves reconciling, transcending, or even accepting apparent contradictions" and the search for the "Middle Way" (Nisbett et al., 2001, p. 294). This originates from their view that the world is ever changing and it is important to understand how things are related. Constant change also implies constant contradiction. Such beliefs promote a greater tolerance of conflict and incongruity and a search for a compromise (Aaker & Sengupta, 2000; Peng & Nisbett, 1999). Thus, unlike Westerners, who are chronically more likely to reject one of the propositions and focus on the piece of information they consider more plausible or diagnostic, Easterners believe that they can find truth in each perspective and should seek a balance between extreme views. Thus, in the event of an extension failure, independents are more likely to zoom in on the failure information since negative information is generally more salient and carries greater weight in a judgment. Interdependents, on the other hand, are more likely to take the parent brand's prior success into account and thereby, exhibit a more moderate attitude toward the parent brand. Since focusing solely on the negative extension failure information should result in a more negative attitude than a judgment that also take into account the brand's positive equity, independents should exhibit greater degree of dilution than interdependents.

Consistent with the above finding, Monga and John (2008) also show that interdependents, compared to independents, are more able to protect their existing beliefs about a positive-viewed brand, making it relatively immune to extension failure influence. Drawing from findings on attribution differences across cultures, they show that since interdependents tend to take into account contextual factors, they are more likely to attribute the negative extension to external causes. Specifically, they show that holistic thinkers were more likely to endorse external context-base explanation for a failed extension by Mercedes-Benz, relative to analytic thinkers. Attributing the failure to an external cause in turn allows interdependents to protect their existing beliefs about the parent brand. Thus, they are less likely to exhibit decline in parent brand's equity in the event of a negative publicity about a new product. On the other hand, analytic thinkers were less likely to consider contextual factors and were more likely to attribute any failure to the parent brand and exhibit greater decline in the parent brand's equity.

However, the above mitigating effect of an interdependent self-construal has its boundary conditions. Ng (2010) argues that though interdependents are chronically inclined to take into account conflicting information, such tendency will be reversed when motivation is high. Elevated motivation prompts one to examine the information in greater detail and focuses one attention to information that is perceived to be more diagnostic. In the case of a typical extension, failure in a product that the company is supposed to do well in would be considered to be a piece of diagnostic information and given greater weight in the judgment, leading to significant dilution. Conversely, in the case of an atypical extension, failure in the new product would not be considered to be diagnostic of the firm's ability and would thus be given minimal weight in the judgment. In such situations, lower degree of dilution would be expected. The opposite pattern of results is expected for independents since independents are chronically inclined to resolve incongruity by focusing on one aspect of the argument. The author further shows that such differences are not observed when an extension succeeds, as information about a successful extension is consistent with one's expectation of a positively viewed brand and thus, no conflict resolution is required.

Monga and John (2008) also argue that though interdependents are chronically inclined to take contextual information into account, such processes require a minimum level of cognitive resources, without which interdependents would be expected to behave like independents. By asking participants to memorize a list of one (versus ten) words, the authors show that holistic thinkers who were subjected to the high cognitive load manipulation exhibited significantly greater degree of dilution of the parent brand's equity, relative to those who were subjected to a low cognitive load.

Findings from both sets of studies suggest that greater attention to contextual information (which may be one's internal prior beliefs about the brand or external environmental factors) may allow interdependents to buffer their existing brand beliefs but too much or too little an opportunity to do so will nullify the effect. An inability to take into account contextual information due to a lack of cognitive resources or an overly enthusiastic scrutiny of the information given will make interdependents focus on the negative extension failure information (without taking into account the positive parent brand equity or other contextual information), leading to greater brand dilution. Thus, it appears that the advantage of an interdependent self-construal in mitigating negative feedback effect from a failed extension follows an inverted-U curve (see Figure 11.1). These findings suggest that to some extent, companies can be a little more risk taking when introducing new products in the Orient. A more interdependent self-construal allows people in Eastern cultures to protect and defend their existing attitude toward the parent brand should the new product fails.

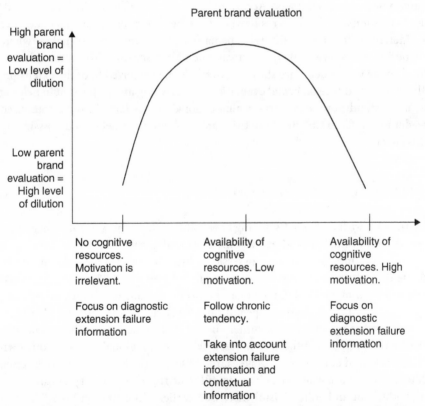

Figure 11.1 Impact of failure of typical extension on *interdependents*' parent brand equity.

Culturally symbolic brands

Culture may also affect consumers' brand evaluation through its strength of association. Brands and products that are highly representative of the abstract characteristics that define a culture or country tend to have strong associations with the culture and are considered to be "culturally symbolic" (Torelli, Keh, & Chiu, 2009). A recent study in the domain of brand extensions (Torelli & Ahluwalia, 2012), reveals a relatively automatic mechanism by which the cultural associations of global brands may influence product evaluations. Torelli and Ahluwalia's research demonstrates that exposure to well-known, culturally symbolic brands (e.g., Sony, Giorgio Armani) spreads activation within the associated cultural schema (e.g., Japanese or Italian) and makes other concepts, including products categories, associated with the cultural schema more accessible (e.g., sushi, cappuccino-macchiato maker) and, hence, processed more fluently. As a consequence, brand extensions that may be low on perceived fit, but belong to the cultural schema activated by the brand (e.g., Sony Sushi serving sets) are evaluated more favorably due to their enhanced conceptual fluency. This fluency advantage only emerges for culturally symbolic brands, and not for all global brands, even if they are associated with the same country of origin (e.g., Panasonic Sushi serving sets). Additionally, disfluency effects, which lower product evaluations, are likely to result when the extension product category activates a different, incongruent cultural schema (e.g., Sony cappuccino maker, where cappuccino makers are likely to activate the Italian schema). The automatic cultural congruency effects are shown to override the perceived fit of the extension. This effect of culture on brand evaluation is interesting and important in helping us understand how consumers evaluate global versus local brands. Interested reader may refer to Chapter 13 in this handbook for more detailed discussion on this effect.

INFLUENCE OF BRANDS ON CULTURE

Up till now, we have been discussing how culture affects the way consumers view brands and evaluate brand extensions. However, given that brands comprise a significant component of our possessions, brands can also have the ability to shape the culture itself. As Belk asserted in his seminal 1988 article, "our possessions are a major contributor to and reflection of our identities". Brands can influence not only the brandscape but can also create unique cultural identities.

A stream of research in consumer culture theory has shown that brand stories increasingly frame the way we view the global, regional and even our own local world and cultures (e.g., Askegaard, 2006; Holt, 2004; Thompson & Arsel, 2004). Note that consumer culture is different from the country culture (e.g., individualism and collectivism) discussed earlier. Consumer culture "denotes a social arrangement in which the relations between lived culture and social resources, and between meaningful ways of life and the symbolic and material resources on which they depend, are mediated through markets" (Arnould & Thompson, 2005, p. 869). Consumer culture theory focuses on how people may use consumptions to construct or experience realities. This may, in turn, feed back to affect social norms and people's values and ideals (i.e., culture of the society). For instance, Holt (2004) reveals how Mountain Dew's advertising and branding efforts attempt to create an alternative model of masculinity that attempts to integrate societal demands for achievement, while at the same time recognizing the reality of American working-class lives. Similarly the Starbucks revolution has transformed gourmet coffee from a yuppie status symbol into a mainstream consumer good, and has been credited for creating the American coffee shop market. Thompson and Arsel (2004) demonstrate how the mythology of Starbucks as a massive, hostile competitor fuels antibig business and anticorporate sentiment in the United States, while also at the same time shaping the meaning of the coffeehouse as a personal, intimate space. Through their anticorporate identifications, consumers can experience the local coffee shops as aesthetic, social, and political alternatives to corporate hegemony. In this way, the patronage of local coffee shops provides "a symbolic anodyne" for the feelings of cynicism, alienation, disenchantment, and disempowerment that could result from the increasing presence of corporate influence in everyday life (Thompson & Arsel, 2004).

Brands and their advertising campaigns have also been known to help in the creation of cultural identities such as the global consumer (Alden, Steenkamp, & Batra, 1999) or the Mediterranean consumer (Cova, 2005). More recently, Cayla and Eckhardt (2008) demonstrate how brands can function as symbolic devices for the creation of transnational imagined worlds, such as the "imagined Asia". Cayla and Eckhardt (2008) examine marketers' attempts to create the cultural myth of "transnational imagined Asia" which is cosmopolitan, urban, and modern with a global status and influence, steeped with images of megalopolises such as Tokyo, Shanghai, Singapore, or Hong Kong, characterized by the absence of references to a specific past, but with a focus instead on the present and the future. In other words, these brands (e.g., Tiger Beer, Zuji) attempt to construct a new identity myth for Asian consumers that is more appealing than the depiction of an exotic Asia, by weaving together tradition and modernity, East and West, to construct a new type of modernity that does not mimic the West or represent Asia as exotic (Cayla & Eckhardt, 2008).

Brands can also mediate new kinds of social relations, enabling connections between people who may have never seen each other yet share a sense of responsibility toward a brand and the community formed by it (McAlexander, Schouten, & Koenig, 2002; Muniz & O'Guinn, 2001), such as the Harley Davidson or Apple enthusiasts. Brand communities are not geographically bound and link people who may have never met but feel they somehow know one another (Muniz & Schau, 2005). The effect of brands on the building of connections and relationships is particularly applicable for global brands.

Thus, branding activities may feedback to affect a society's norms and values. However, research on this reverse effect of consumption on social culture is still at its infancy. It would be great if future research can shed more light in this area as greater understanding of the social impact of consumption would be of great importance to marketers and policy makers alike.

CONCLUSION

Considerable research has now appeared in the literature on culture and branding. Distinct patterns of brand cognitive structures, brand meanings and their impact on brand extension evaluations appear to differ across cultures. The meaning of the same brand can vary within and across cultures to differing degrees. Brands can also affect cultures. This interplay between culture and brands is ongoing and we are only beginning to develop a more in-depth understanding of this dynamic. We hope that this chapter has provided some guidance as to what has been done so far and stimulate greater interest in this area.

REFERENCES

Aaker, D. A., & Keller, K. L. (1990). Consumer evaluations of brand extensions. *Journal of Marketing*, 54(1), 27–41

Aaker, J. L., Benet-Martinez, V., & Garolera, J. (2001). Consumption symbols as carriers of culture: A study of Japanese and Spanish brand personality constructs. *Journal of Personality and Social Psychology*, 81(3), 492–508.

Aaker, J., & Sengupta, J. (2000). Additivity versus attenuation: The Role of Culture in the resolution of information incongruity. *Journal of Consumer Psychology*, 9(2), 67–82.

Aaker, J. L., & Maheswaran, D. (1997). The effect of cultural orientation on persuasion. *Journal of Consumer Research*, 24(December), 315–328.

Ahluwalia, R. (2008). How far can a brand stretch? Understanding the role of self-construal. *Journal of Marketing Research*, 45(3), 692–705.

Alden, D. L., Steenkamp, J. B. E. M., & Batra, R. (1999). Brand positioning through advertising in Asia, North America, and Europe: the role of global consumer culture. *Journal of Marketing*, 63, 75–87.

Arnould, E. J., & Thompson, C. J. (2005). Consumer culture theory (CCT): Twenty years of research. *Journal of Consumer Research*, 31(4), 868–882.

Askegaard, S. (2006). Brand as a global ideoscape. In M. Featherstone (Ed.), *Global Couture: Nationalism, Globalization and Modernity* (pp. 295–310). London, UK: Sage.

Barsalou, L. W. (1992), *Cognitive Psychology: An Overview for Cognitive Scientists*. Hillsdale, NJ, USA: Lawrence Erlbaum Associates Inc.

Boush, D. M., & Loken, B. (1991). A process-tracing study of brand extension evaluation. *Journal of Marketing Research*, XXVIII (February), 16–28.

Bridges, S., Keller, K. L., & Sood, S. (2000). Communication strategies for brand extensions: Enhancing perceived fit by establishing explanatory links. *Journal of Advertising, 29*(4), 1–11.

Broniarczyk, S. M., & Alba, J. W. (1994). The importance of the brand in brand extension. *Journal of Marketing Research, 31*(May), 214–228.

Cayla, J., & Eckhardt, G. M. (2008). Asian brands and the shaping of a transnational imagined community. *Journal of Consumer Research, 35*(2), 216–230.

Chiu, L. -H. (1972). A cross-cultural comparison of cognitive styles in Chinese and American children. *International Journal of Psychology, 8*, 235–242.

Christensen, G. L., & Olson, J. C. (2002). Mapping consumers' mental models with ZMET. *Psychology and Marketing, 19*(6), 477–502.

Cova, B. (2005). Thinking of marketing in meridian terms. *Marketing Theory, 5*(2), 205–214.

Dawar, N., & Parker, P. (1994). Marketing universals: consumers' use of brand name, price, physical appearance, and retailer reputation as signals of product quality. *Journal of Marketing, 58*(2), 81–95.

Douglas, M., & Wildavsky, A. (1982), *Risk and culture: an essay on the selection of technical and environmental dangers*, Berkeley: University of California Press.

Eckhardt, G. M., & Houston, M. J. (2008). On the malleable nature of product meaning in China. *Journal of Consumer Behaviour, 7*(6), 484–495.

Erdem, T., Swait, J., & Valenzuela, A. (2006). Brands as signals: a cross-country validation study. *Journal of Marketing, 70*(1), 34–49.

Foscht, T., Maloles, C., Swaboda, B., Morschett, D., & Sinha, I. (2008). The impact of culture and brand perceptions: a six-nation study. *Journal of Product and Brand Management, 17*(3), 131–142.

Ger, G., & Belk, R. W. (1996). I'd like to buy the world a coke: Consumptionscapes of the "less affluent world. *Journal of Consumer Policy, 19*(3), 271–304.

Hagtvedt, H., & Patrick, V. M. (2008). Art and the brand: The strategic role of art in enhancing brand extendibility. *Journal of Consumer Psychology, 18*, 212–222.

Han, S. -P., & Shavitt, S. (1994). Persuasion and culture: advertising appeals in individualistic and collectivistic societies. *Journal of Experimental Social Psychology, 30*(July), 326–350.

Holt, D. B. (2004), *How Brands Become Icons: The Principles of Cultural Branding*, Cambridge, MA: Harvard Business School Press.

Jain, S. P., Desai, K., & Mao, H. (2007). The influence of chronic and situational self-construal on categorization. *Journal of Consumer Research, 34*(1), 66–76.

Ji, L. -J. Peng, K., & Nisbett, R. E. (2000), Culture, control, and perception of relationships in the environment, *Journal of personality and Social Psychology, 78*, 943–955.

John, D. R., & Whitney, J. C. (1986). The development of consumer knowledge in children: A cognitive structure approach. *Journal of Consumer Research, 12*(March), 406–417.

John, D. R., Loken, B., & Joiner, C. (1998). The negative impact of extensions: Can flagship products be diluted. *Journal of Marketing, 62*(January), 19–32.

Joiner, C. (1998). Concept mapping in marketing: A research tool for uncovering consumers' knowledge structure associations. *Advances in Consumer Research, 25*, 311–317.

Kanwar, R., Olson, J. C., & Sims, L. S. (1981). Toward conceptualizing and measuring cognitive structures. *Advances in Consumer Research, 8*(1), 122–127.

Keller, K. L. (2002). *Branding and Brand Equity.* Cambridge, Mass.: Marketing Science Institute.

Keller, K. L. (2003). Brand synthesis: The multidimensionality of brand knowledge. *Journal of Consumer Research, 29*(March), 595–600.

Kühnen, U., Hannover, B., Roeder, U., Shah, A. A., Schubert, B., Upmeyer, A., & Zakaria, S. (2001). Cross-cultural variations in identifying embedded figures: Comparisons from the United States, Germany, Russia, and Malaysia. *Journal of Cross-Cultural Psychology, 32*(3), 365–371.

Lawson, R. (2002). Consumer knowledge structures: Background issues and introduction. *Psychology and Marketing, 19*(6), 447–456.

Loken, B., & John, D. R. (1993). Diluting brand beliefs: When do brand extensions have a negative impact? *Journal of Marketing, 57*(3), 71–84.

Loken, B., Joiner, C., & Peck, J. (2002). Category attitude measures: Exemplars as inputs. *Journal of Consumer Psychology, 12*(2), 149–161.

Markus, H., & Zajonc, R. B. (1985). The cognitive perspective in social psychology. In L. Gardner & E. Aronson (Eds.), *Handbook of social psychology,* 3rd Edition (pp. 137–230). New York, NY, USA: Knopf.

McAlexander, J. H., Schouten, J. W., & Koenig, H. F. (2002). Building brand community. Journal of Marketing, 66(1), 38–54.

Meyers-Levy, J., Louie, T., & Curren, M. (1994). How does the congruity of brand names affect evaluations of brand name extensions?" *Journal of Applied Psychology, 79*(February), 46–53.

Milberg, S. J., Park, C. W., & McCarthy, M. S. (1997). Managing negative feedback effects associated with brand extensions: The impact of alternative branding strategies. *Journal of Consumer Psychology (Lawrence Erlbaum Associates), 6*(2), 119–140.

Miller, D. (Ed.). (1998). Material cultures: why some things matter. Chicago, IL, USA: University of Chicago Press.

Monga, A. B., & John, D. R. (2007). Cultural differences in brand extensions evaluation: The influence of analytic versus holistic thinking. *Journal of Consumer Research, 33*(4), 529–536.

Monga, A. B., & John, D. R. (2008). When does negative brand publicity hurt? The moderating influence of analytic versus holistic thinking. *Journal of Consumer Psychology, 18*(4), 320–332.

Monga, A. B., & John, D. R. (2010). What Makes Brands Elastic? The Influence of Brand Concept and Styles of Thinking on Brand Extension Evaluation. *Journal of Marketing, 74*(3), 80–92.

Muniz, A. M. Jr., & O'Guinn, T. C. (2001). Brand community. *Journal of Consumer Research, 27*(4), 412–432.

Muniz, A. M. Jr, & Schau, H. J. (2005). Religiosity in the abandoned Apple Newton brand community. *Journal of Consumer Behavior, 31*(3), 737–747.

Ng, S. (2010). Cultural orientation and brand dilution: Impact of motivational level and extension typicality. *Journal of Marketing Research, XLVII* (February), 186–198.

Ng, S., & Houston, M. (2006). Exemplars or beliefs? The impact of self-view on the nature and relative influence of brand associations. *Journal of Consumer Research, 32*(March), 519–529.

Ng, S., & Houston, M. (2009). Field dependency and brand cognitive structures. *Journal of Marketing Research, XLVI* (April), 279–292.

Nisbett, R. E., Peng, K, Choi, I., & Norenzayan, A. (2001). Culture and systems of thought: Holistic vs. analytical cognition. *Psychological Review, 108*(2), 291–310.

Park, C. W., Milberg, S., & Lawson, R. (1991). Evaluations of brand extensions: The role of product feature similarity and brand concept consistency. *Journal of Consumer Research, 18*(September), 185–193.

Peng, K., & Nisbett, R. E. (1999). Culture, dialectics, and reasoning about contradiction. *American Psychologist, 54*(9), 741–54.

Ratneshwar, S., & Shocker, A. D. (1991). Substitution in use and the role of usage context in product category structures. *Journal of Marketing Research, 28*(August), 281–295.

Robertson, R. (1995). Glocalization: Time-space and homogeneity-heterogeneity. Los Angeles, CA, USA: Global Modernities.

Sedikides, C., & Skowronski, J. J. (1991). On the law of cognitive structure activation. *Psychological Inquiry, 2*(2), 169–184.

Sujan, M. (1985). Consumer knowledge: Effects on evaluation strategies mediating consumer judgments. *Journal of Consumer Research, 12*(June), 31–46.

Sung, Y., & Tinkham, S. F. (2005). Brand personality structures in the United States and Korea: common and culture-specific factors. *Journal of Consumer Psychology, 15*(4), 334–350.

Thompson, C. J., & Arsel, Z. (2004). The Starbucks brandscape and consumers' (anticorporate) experiences of globalization. *Journal of Consumer Research, 31*(3), 631–642.

Torelli, C. J., & Ahluwalia, R. (2012). Extending culturally symbolic brands: A blessing or a curse? *Journal of Consumer Research, 38*(5), 933–947.

Torelli, C. J., Keh, H. T., & Chiu, C. -Y. (2009). Cultural symbolism of brands. In B. Loken, R. Ahluwalia, & M. J. Houston (Eds.), *Brands and brand management: Contemporary research perspectives* (pp. 113–132). New York, NY, USA: Routledge.

Tse, L. (1996). *Culture, Language, and Literacy: The Effects of Child Brokering on Language Minority Education.* McQuillan, Jeff.

van Osselaer, Stijn M., & Janiszewski, C. (2001). Learning brand associations. *Journal of Consumer Research, 28*(September), 202–223.

Wilk, R. (1995). Learning to be local in Belize: global structures of common difference. In D. Miller (Ed.), *Worlds apart: Modernity through the prism of the local* (pp. 110–133). London, UK: Routledge.

Wyer, R. S. Jr, & Srull, T. J. (1989), *Memory and cognition in its social context,* Hillsdale, NJ, USA: Lawrence Erlbaum Associates Inc.

Zhang, J., & Shavitt, S. (2003). Cultural values in advertisements to the Chinese X-generation: Promoting modernity and individualism. *Journal of Advertising, 32*(1), 23–33.

Zhou, K. Z., Su, C. T., & Bao, Y. Q. (2002). A paradox of price-quality and market efficiency: a comparative study of the US and China markets. *International Journal of Research in Marketing, 19*(4), 349–365.

12

Culture and Brand Relationships

ZEYNEP GÜRHAN-CANLI AND GÜLEN SARIAL-ABI ■

Consumers form relationships with brands in much the same way as they form relationships with other individuals. Brand relationship concept has become important, mostly because of the economic advantages that firms are assumed to enjoy such as reduced marketing costs, ease of access, customer retention, brand equity, and increasing profits (Blackston, 2000; Dowling, 2002). Relationships are thought to improve the position of firms by enhancing cash flows, establishing entry barriers, and offering the possibility of increased prices and market share (Srivastava, Shervani, & Fahey, 1998). Hence, previous research suggests that the strength of consumer relationships is a commercial asset that is predictive of performance and resilience to competition (Ashworth, Dacin, & Thomson, 2009).

Culture seems to play an important role in portraying brands and developing relationships with brands (Fournier, 1998). For example, take-out coffee is the dominating coffee culture in the United States. In China, young professionals drink coffee to show their international attitude. In Europe and China, take-out coffee appeals to young people who are attracted by the mythical value of American coffee culture, while it is incompatible on the cultural level (Gagliardi, 2001). This example illustrates that while US consumers may have strong brand relationships with the take-out coffee brands, consumers in other cultures may have different types of relationships. Given the interaction between culture and brand relationship, the objective of this chapter is to provide an understanding of the concept of brand relationships, cultural factors affecting the formation and management of brand relationships and providing insights for further research.

WHAT IS BRAND RELATIONSHIP?

The nature of the brand relationships varies across different consumers (Fournier, 1998; Muniz & O'Guinn, 2001) and the construct of brand relationship is complex (MacInnis, Park, & Priester, 2009). In defining the functions that brand relationships serve, one must not forget that relationships are multiplex phenomena, which range across several dimensions and take many forms (Fournier, 2009). Relationships can be defined in terms of strong versus weak relationships, but they can also be distinguished as hierarchical versus egalitarian or forced versus voluntary relationships. Moreover, relationships are not static, but they rather evolve and change over a series of interactions (Fournier, 1998).

One stream of research characterizes brand relationships by feelings such as love and passion, intimacy, and commitment (Fournier, 1998). Other researchers conceptualize brand relationships in terms of satisfaction, trust, and commitment (Gregoire & Fisher, 2008). None of these perspectives seem to be adequate on their own. For example, it is possible that consumers may be satisfied with a brand but switch to another brand when an opportunity arises (Liljander & Roos, 2002).

Recent research explored the concepts of identification and attachment within brand relationship context. Attachment has been used to describe a person's emotional bond with a particular object or a person that he or she perceives as special and irreplaceable (Bowlby, 1979; Kleine & Baker, 2004). Attachments provide a good indication of strong brand relationships (Keller, 2001). Whereas attachment has been defined as an emotional bond, identification has been used to refer to the sense of connection between a consumer and some entity. Identification is the degree to which consumers define themselves by the same attributes they believe define the target entity (Aqueveque, 2005; Einwiller, Fedorikhin, Johnson, & Kamins, 2006). Several other researchers used concepts such as brand connectedness (Winterich, 2007), brand evangelism (Matzler, Pichler, & Hemetsberger, 2007), brand love (Ahuvia, 2005), brand loyalty (Chaudhuri & Holbrook, 2001), brand passion (Bauer, Heinrich, & Martin, 2007), and brand trust (Chaudhuri & Holbrook, 2001) to categorize consumers based on the intensity of these consumer-brand relationships.

According to the social relationship theory, relationships carry norms of behavior that guide individuals' evaluations of their relationship partner (Aggarwal, 2004). Brands are evaluated by the rules that govern the society when they behave like members of a culture. There are two types of relationships: exchange and communal (Clark & Mills, 1993). In exchange relationships, the motivation for giving a benefit to the partner is to get something back in return. Relationships between strangers and people who interact for business purposes are typical exchange relationships. Individuals in an exchange relationship expect to receive monetary payments for providing help, prefer to get comparable benefits in return, and expect prompt repayment for benefits given to a partner. On the other hand, in communal relationships people give benefits to others to demonstrate a concern for them and to attend to their needs. Most family relationships, romantic relationships, and friendships have communal relationships. Individuals in a communal relationship do not expect monetary payment for helping their partner. They prefer to get noncomparable benefits in return and do not expect prompt repayment for benefits given (Clark, 1981; Clark & Mills, 1993; Clark, Mills, & Corcoran, 1989). Exchange and communal norms are likely to vary in different cultures. For example, as we will subsequently discuss in detail, collectivist (versus individualist) consumers are more likely to emphasize communal norms than exchange norms. Consequently, collectivist consumers are likely to form relationships with brands that emphasize communal concerns such as online communities or corporate social responsibility activities.

MOTIVES TO FORM BRAND RELATIONSHIPS

Brand relationships are motivating because they help consumers to fulfill their goals (MacInnis et al., 2009). Brands help consumers to construct and expand their identities. For example, Reimann and Aron (2009) suggest that individuals are motivated to expand themselves by enhancing their ability to achieve higher and lower order goals, and brand relationships are important ways to fulfill these goals. Consumers may also form brand relationships because they see similarities between their self-concept and the brand (Dolich, 1969). In other words, consumers can verify their self through forming relationships with brands consistent with their self-concept. Consumers also use brands to express their identities to other individuals (Fournier, 1998). These motives of self-expansion, self-verification, and self-expression are partly rooted in individual's concerns with social acceptance and approval. Hence, these motives are mainly for facilitating individual's social interactions and relationships, which may vary depending on the culture (Leary, 2007). In the next section, we will briefly review these three important motives (e.g., self-construction/expansion, self-verification, and self-expression) separately and discuss how culture may influence these motives.

Self-construction and expansion motives and the role of culture

According to the self-expansion model, there is a general motivation to expand the self and inclusion of close others in the self (Aron & Aron, 1986). The model emphasizes the central human motive of the desire to expand the self by acquiring perspectives, resources, and identities that enhance one's ability to accomplish goals (Aron, Aron, & Norman, 2003). As such, developing a new relationship is thought to expand the self. Reimann and Aron (2009) applied this model to brand relationships. They suggest that the rapid expansion of the self takes place for the newly acquired brands. When a consumer buys a Rolex watch, the purchase and ownership can lead to the formation of a new, close relationship between brand and consumer. If the consumer loses the watch, this can lead to a rapid de-expansion of the self. Furthermore, this effect is stronger for brands of high-involvement products and weaker for brands of low-involvement products. The authors further argue that the rate of self-expansion decreases over time with brands that have been repeatedly purchased, owned, and used (Reimann & Aron, 2009). They also posit that the higher the interaction intensity, the more decrease in self-expansion will be associated with the brand over time.

Culture is likely to influence the way consumers are motivated to expand their selves. One important distinction among cultures is individualism versus collectivism. Hofstede (1980) defined individualism as a focus on rights above duties, a concern for oneself and immediate family. There is an emphasis on personal autonomy and self-fulfillment. One's identity is based on one's personal accomplishments. Schwartz (1990) defined individualistic societies as fundamentally contractual, consisting of narrow primary groups and negotiated social relations. In these societies, there are specific obligations and expectations focusing on achieving status. These definitions all conceptualize individuals as centralizing on personal goals, personal uniqueness, and personal control (Bellah, Madsen, Sullivan, Swidler, & Tipton, 1985; Hsu, 1983; Kagitcibasi, 1994; Markus & Kitayama, 1991; Triandis, 1995).

Individualism implies creating and maintaining a positive sense of self as a basic human endeavor (Baumeister, 1998), feeling good about oneself, personal success, and having many unique or distinctive personal attitudes and opinions as valued features (Oyserman & Markus, 1993; Triandis, 1995). Individualism also entails that open emotional expression and attainment of one's personal goals are important sources of well-being and life satisfaction (Diener & Diener, 1995; Markus & Kitayama, 1991). Moreover, individualism suggests that judgment, reasoning, and causal inference are generally oriented toward the person rather than the situation or social context because the decontextualized self is assumed to be a stable, causal nexus (Choi, Nisbett, & Norenzayan, 1999). Consequently, individualism promotes a decontextualized, as opposed to a situation-specific, reasoning style (Oyserman, Coon, & Kemmelmeier, 2002). Furthermore, with regard to relationality, individualism implies that individuals need relationships and group memberships to attain self-relevant goals, but relationships are costly to maintain (Oyserman, 1993). Accordingly, individuals leave relationships and groups when the costs of participation exceed the benefits and creating new relationships as personal goals shift. Therefore, for individualists, relationships and group memberships are impermanent (Bellah et al., 1985; Kim, 1994; Shweder & Bourne, 1982).

According to Schwartz (1990), collectivist societies are communal societies characterized by diffuse and mutual obligations and expectations based on ascribed statuses. In these societies, social units with common fate, common goals, and common values are centralized. The individual is simply a component of the social. The key unit of analysis is the in-group (Triandis, 1995). Collectivism is a social way of being, oriented toward in-groups and away from out-groups (Oyserman, 1993). It implies that group membership is a central aspect of identity (Hofstede, 1980; Hsu, 1983; Kim, 1994; Markus & Kitayama, 1991). Valued personal traits reflect the goals of collectivism (e.g., sacrifice for the common good and maintaining harmonious relationships with close others; Markus & Kitayama, 1991; Oyserman, 1993; Triandis, 1995). Furthermore, collectivism suggests that important group memberships are ascribed and fixed. Boundaries between in-groups and out-groups are stable, relatively impermeable, and important. In-group exchanges are based on equality or even generosity principles (Morris & Leung, 2000; Triandis, 1995).

Self-expansion is possible by adding new social identity or strengthening existing social identities. Social identity is defined as the actuated perspective or frame of reference that a consumer possesses as part of the repertoire of whom they are or who they want to appear to be. Consumers can have multiple social identities based on demographics (e.g., Asian American), social roles (e.g., parents), and shared consumption patterns (e.g., dieters). They are attracted to products and brands that are linked to their actual and desired social identities (Reed, 2004). Moreover, consumer's identity motivates the formation and expression of identity-oriented beliefs and selection and avoidance of products that reinforces their identity (Berger & Heath, 2007). Consumers can form brand relationships to strengthen their existing social identity by associating the new brand to their existing social identity. For example, Harley Davidson is strongly linked to a social identity of a rebel image (Muniz & O'Guinn, 2001). If a consumer defines himself as a rebellious, marginal, belonging to an outlaw culture, he may form a brand relationship with Harley Davidson rather than other motorcycle brands in order to strengthen his existing social identity. Another way that consumers may be motivated to form brand relationship is to establish a new social identity. For example, a business professional may be drawn to Apple in order to establish a new identity that is more creative, colorful, and different (Berger & Heath, 2007).

We suggest that individuals from different cultures will have different motives to expand their social identities. Collectivists are likely to form relationships with new brands that are congruent with their existing social identity. If the brand is incongruent with their social identity, these individuals will not be motivated to form a relationship with that brand. On the other hand, for individualists, congruency of the brand to the existing social identity may not be important. Individualists are likely to be motivated to form relationships that add new social identities to the extent doing so helps them achieve their self-relevant goals. Hence, we propose:

P1: Collectivists form brand relationships to expand their social identity by approaching new brands that are congruent with their existing social identities. Individualists form brand relationships to expand their social identity by approaching brands that help them achieve their self-relevant goals regardless of the brands' congruity with their existing social identity.

Self-verification motive and the role of culture

Self-concept is the totality of an individual's thoughts and feelings about himself/herself (Rosenberg, 1979). Individuals may verify their self-concepts by forming brand relationships that represent their thoughts and feelings about themselves. At the group level, individuals may verify their self-concepts by forming brand relationships that are congruent with their national identities (e.g., country of origin). In the following section, we will review the relevant literature on self-concept connection and country-of-origin connection with brands and the moderating role of culture in this context.

SELF-CONCEPT CONNECTION AND SELF-VERIFICATION

Individuals value symbolic and psychological benefits of brands because brands construct, cultivate, and express one's self-concept (Fournier, 1998). According to McCracken's (1986) theory of meaning movement, individuals construct their self-concept by using brands. Individuals evaluate the symbolic meanings of brands derived in part from cultural sources of meaning (e.g., celebrities, reference groups). Symbolic properties of the reference group or celebrity first become associated with the brands they use or endorse. Then, these symbolic meanings are transferred to individuals as they select brands with meanings congruent with their self-concept. Consumers are more likely to develop self-brand connection when there is a strong usage association between a reference group and the brand and there is a strong connection between the reference group and the consumer's self-concept (Escalas & Bettman, 2009).

Appropriate use of celebrity endorsers can be highly effective in product promotions (Mitchell &Olson, 1981; Misra & Beatty, 1990). Brands use celebrities both from the same country of origin and different country of origin. For example, Pizza Hut has used Mikhail Gorbachev in one of its recent advertising campaigns in the United States. Recent research suggests that while a Western figure is usually employed by local and foreign brands to create an image of international sophistication, homegrown Chinese talent continues to be used to build a solid connection with consumers in China (Blecken, 2009).

In individualistic cultures, any celebrity, regardless of country of origin may be effective depending on the consistency of the celebrity's image with the target consumer's self-concept. However, celebrities from different cultures may not always be effective in collectivistic societies. Celebrity endorsers should be carefully chosen based on how compatible they are with in-group identities and aspirations.

> P2: Individualists are more likely to form brand relationships with brands that use celebrities consistent with their self-concept. On the other hand, collectivists are more likely to form brand relationships with brands that use celebrities who are consistent with their group identity.

There are at least two different selves that individuals, in each culture, possess: independent and interdependent self (Gudykunst, Matsumoto, Ting-Toomey, Nishida, Kim, & Heyman, 1996; Markus & Kitayama, 1991). A growing body of work suggests that the self is a complex structure with multiple manifestations (Singelis, 1994). An individual's construal of the self is frequently defined as a "constellation of thoughts, feelings, and actions concerning one's relationship to others such as the self being distinct from others or connected to others" (Singelis,

1994, p. 581). While self-construal is often considered to be based on cultural orientation (Markus & Kitayama, 1991), research has found that self-construal can be activated through situational priming (Agrawal & Maheswaran, 2005; Ng & Houston, 2006; Triandis, 1995). According to Markus and Kitayama (1991, p. 226), the independent self-construal is characterized by "an individual whose behavior is organized and made meaningful primarily by reference to one's own internal repertoire of thoughts, feelings, and actions, rather than by reference to the thoughts, feelings, and actions of others." This implies that an independent self-construal should cause one's opinions to be altered by individual thoughts and personal opinions. Conversely, those with an interdependent construal of self base their attitudes and behavior on the thoughts, feelings, and actions of others in the relationship (Markus & Kitayama, 1991). The independent self involves cognitions concerning individual personality traits. The interdependent self, on the other hand, involves cognitions concerning characteristics that are inherently more indicative of how one relates to others (Greenwald & Pratkanis, 1984).

Individuals' construal of self (independent or interdependent) can also influence brand meaning (Escalas & Bettman, 2005), the persuasiveness of various advertising appeals (Agrawal & Maheswaran, 2005), and brand extension evaluations (Ng & Houston, 2006). Consumer's self-concept connection is likely to be important when an independent self-construal becomes salient (Swaminathan, Page, & Gürhan-Canli, 2007). The self-concept connection is based on consumers' desires to express their individuality and their self as distinct from others. Therefore, the impact of self-concept connection is greater when an independent self-construal is primed. On the one hand, if an independent self-construal is relatively salient and there is high self-concept connection with the brand, the individual is more likely to refute any negative information challenging his or her self-concept connection with the brand by counterarguing the negative information (Ahluwalia, Burnkrant, & Unnava, 2000). Such counterarguments will minimize any brand attitude change caused by negative information. However, if an independent self-construal is relatively salient and there is low self-concept connection with the brand, then brand attitude change occurs, since there is no refutation of negative information. In contrast, when an interdependent self-construal is made salient, self-concept connection is likely to be less important when evaluating a brand. For instance, Markus and Kitayama (1991, p. 236) suggest that, "among those with more interdependent selves, one's inner feelings may be less important in determining one's consequent actions." However, one can also argue that because interdependents are more likely to define their selves with the group they belong to, by emphasizing group-based connection, they may also satisfy their self-concepts, which are congruent with their groups. Moreover, the impact of self-concept connection varies based on self-construal, such that changes in brand attitude are greater for low self-concept connection (versus high self-concept connection) brands under independent self-construal (Swaminathan et al., 2007). On the other hand, when an interdependent self-construal is made salient, brand attitude change occurs regardless of whether the individual has a high or low individual-based relationship with the brand.

Individuals from different cultures may also differ in their choices to form self-brand connection. For example, individualists are more likely to experience self-brand connection with brands that emphasize their unique self. On the other hand, collectivists are more likely to experience group-brand connection with brands that emphasize values, and norms of groups that are consistent with the culture they belong to.

COUNTRY-OF-ORIGIN CONNECTION AND SELF-VERIFICATION

National identity is another way by which individuals connect with brands. This effect is most prominently reported in research about country of origin. Country-of-origin effects refer to the extent to which the place of manufacture influences product evaluations. Country of origin is used as a cue in evaluating new products under several conditions. In general, favorable country perceptions lead to favorable inferences about product attributes and subsequent favorable evaluations. However, the weight given to country of origin in product evaluations may not be universal (Bozell-Gallup, 1996). For example, several studies have found that featuring Japan as the country of origin leads to favorable perceptions of product quality (Maheswaran, 1994). However, Klein, Ettenson, and Morris (1998) show that Chinese consumers in Nanjing might not purchase Japanese products because of animosity toward Japan due to prior Japanese occupation.

Shimp and Sharma (1987) found that ethnocentric individuals are more likely to purchase domestic products over foreign products, reinforcing their patriotic identity. Similarly, Klein et al. (1998) found that even when a consumer recognizes a brand as high quality, the consumer may still refuse to purchase the brand if it does not adequately symbolize their group membership. Furthermore, the impact of country of origin on brand evaluations is shown to vary based on a variety of factors, including prior elaboration (Hong & Wyer, 1990), consumer expertise (Maheswaran, 1994), consumer ethnocentricity (Shimp & Sharma, 1987), and culture-specific factors (Klein et al., 1998). The brand country of origin (i.e., whether the brand name is local or foreign), a group-level variable, is particularly meaningful to consumers as it helps differentiate between in-group members and out-group members. Further, brand country-of-origin connection may become more prominent or salient when there is a greater focus on relationships with others. Recall that an interdependent self-construal places greater emphasis on the relationship between self and others, with distinctions made between in-group and out-group members. Consequently, brand country of origin, which distinguishes between local and foreign brands, is likely to have a greater impact when self-construal is relatively more interdependent (Swaminathan et al., 2007). Specifically, consumers are more likely to resist negative information regarding local (versus foreign) brands when an interdependent self-construal is primed. In contrast, since an independent self-construal places greater emphasis on self, brand country of origin has less influence on brand attitudes when an independent self-construal is primed. In support of this, Gürhan-Canli and Maheswaran (2000) show that home country products are evaluated more favorably when the interdependent self-construal is dominant. The impact of brand country-of-origin connection varies based on self-construal, such that changes in brand attitude are greater for foreign (versus local) brands under interdependent self-construal. However, the impact of brand country-of-origin connection is lower in independent self-construal (Swaminathan et al., 2007).

P3: Individualists are more likely to form brand relationships when there is high (versus low) self-concept connection. Collectivists are more likely to form brand relationships when there is high (versus low) group connection.

Self-expression motive and the role of culture

Self-expression can be an important driver of consumer choice and preference (Belk, 1988). Individuals act differently in different situations and self is a malleable construct (Markus & Kunda, 1986). Individuals are influenced by different social roles and cues, and have a need for self-presentation (Aaker, 1999). Hence, self-expressive use of brands is important to consider for brand relationships.

Traditions and religions (e.g., Buddhism versus Islam), life philosophies (e.g., Confucianism), and socialization processes (e.g., child-rearing practices that encourage differentiation versus assimilation) differ from culture to culture. These differences foster the development of interdependent and independent self (Aaker & Schmitt, 2001). Self-view differences are found at the cultural level such that individuals from East Asian cultures are likely to see themselves as more interdependent and less independent than those in North American cultures (Kwan, Bond, & Singelis, 1997; Singelis & Sharkey, 1995). Aaker and Schmitt (2001) suggest that self-expression occurs in both East Asian and North American cultures. However, in North American cultures, traits that emphasize the distinction from others should be expressed. In East Asian cultures traits that emphasize the similarity with others should be expressed. This suggests that the process in which brand relationships are formed may differ among different cultures. We propose:

P4: In individualistic (collectivists) cultures, brands should emphasize how distinctive (similar) the consumer would be when they have relationship with the brand.

Forming brand relationships can also contribute to consumers' identity by focusing on individuals' race, ethnicity, or nationality in general. Symbols encountered elicit emotions and feelings that lead to either comfort or discomfort based on the meanings derived from the symbols (Bitner, 1992). For example, "Got

Milk" campaign for the California Milk Processor Board was altered to meet the symbolic needs of Hispanic cultures, featuring the slogan "Generations" as an alternative. Hence, the Generations campaign featured the nurturing relationships between mothers, grandmothers, and daughters, highlighting the family values and honoring women of the household (Maso-Fleishman, 1997). This shows that consumers are more likely to form brand relationships when they emphasize certain ethnic or national values because they may aid individuals to express their values to others.

There are seven distinct types of cultural-level values organized around two dimensions (Schwartz, 1994). These dimensions are conservatism versus autonomy and hierarchy/mastery versus egalitarian commitment/harmony (Schwartz, 1992). The seven types of values, namely conservatism, intellectual autonomy, affective autonomy, hierarchy, mastery, egalitarian commitment, and harmony, are identified through a procedure involving more than sixty cultural groups (Schwartz, 1994; Schwartz & Bilsky, 1990; Schwartz & Sagiv, 1995). However, there are differences among cultures along these dimensions (Schwartz, 1994). For example, mastery, which is related with getting ahead of other people, is particularly important in the United States. In contrast, harmony, which is related with keeping balance and peace with nature and people, is seen in Asian and Latin cultures.

The attributes that structure the meaning of commercial brands in the United States (Aaker, 1997) seem to align themselves with several of Schwartz's cultural value types. For instance, a close inspection of the attributes that define sincerity (e.g., family oriented, real, small-town), suggests that this dimension may capture brand perceptions associated to conservatism values (e.g., emphasis on family security and safety, being stable and polite). Concepts defining excitement (e.g., unique, exciting, young), on the other hand, suggest a link with affective autonomy values (e.g., valuing novelty and creativity, having an exciting life). Competence (e.g., reliable, successful, intelligent) appears to be related to mastery values (emphasis on being capable and successful, demonstrating competence), and sophistication (e.g., upper class, glamorous). These values are reflected in individuals' preferences among brands that have different brand personalities.

Sincerity, excitement, competence, sophistication, and ruggedness are five dimensions of brand personality (Aaker, 1997). These personality traits provide symbolic benefits for the consumers (Aaker, 1997). Although there are certain dimensions of brand personality that are shared by different cultures, there are also culture-specific dimensions. For example, sincerity, excitement, competence, and sophistication are shared by both Japanese and American cultures. However, peacefulness is specific to Japanese cultures, whereas ruggedness is specific to the American culture. Moreover, sincerity, excitement, and sophistication are shared by Spanish and American cultures. However, passion is specific to the Spanish culture and competence is specific to the American culture (Aaker, Benet-Martinez, & Garolera, 2001). Korean consumers are more likely to place emphasis on two culture-specific brand personality dimensions: passive likeableness and ascendancy (Sung & Tinkham, 2005). In summary, extant research suggests that consumers are likely to form brand relationships with brands that provide culturally symbolic values. Hence, we propose:

P5: Individuals in different cultures will use brands for self-expression consistent with their values.

MANAGING BRAND RELATIONSHIPS AND TRANSGRESSIONS: A CULTURAL PERSPECTIVE

As in one-to-one individual relationships, managing relationships with brands is not easy. At any point of time, one partner may behave destructively, violating the rules guiding the relationship (Rusbult, Verette, Whitney, Slovik, & Lipkus, 1991). Metts (1994) define such potentially destructive acts that violate the implicit or explicit rules guiding relationship evaluation and performance as transgressions. Transgressions also occur in relationships among consumers and brands (Aaker, Fournier, & Brasel, 2004). Effects of transgressions for the consumer-brand relationship are damaging (Gremler, 2004). Folkes (1984) shows that the damaging effects of transgressions depend on how bad consumers perceive the act. As in individual relationships, there are also recovery periods after the transgressions, which the research suggests that under certain conditions a highly satisfactory recovery following a relationship transgression can maintain or increase satisfaction and even loyalty levels (Smith & Bolton, 1998). Additionally, the effect of transgressions is, partly, influenced by how the consumers cope with those transgressions (Rusbult et al., 1991). Similarly, the effect of transgressions depends on personality of the consumer (Aaker et al., 2004).

Individuals respond to transgressions in brand relationships in four ways: (a) exit: ending the relationship; (b) voice: actively working with the relationship partner to remedy problems; (c) loyalty: passively but optimistically waiting for conditions to improve; and (d) neglect: allowing relationship to deteriorate (Paulssen & Bagozzi, 2009). We suggest that individuals belonging to different cultures will also differ in their ways responding to transgressions. For example, individuals from individualistic cultures may be more willing to exit the relationship or neglect the problem to allow the relationship to deteriorate. On the other hand, individuals from collectivist cultures may be more willing to actively working with the partner to remedy the problem or to wait for conditions to improve. This may be because individuals in collectivist (versus individualistic) cultures are more likely to sacrifice for the common good and maintaining harmonious relationships with others (Markus & Kitayama, 1991). Hence, we propose:

P6: Individuals in individualistic cultures will respond to transgressions by exit or neglect ways. On the other hand, individuals in collectivist cultures will respond to transgressions by loyalty or voice ways.

Attribution research in psychology (e.g., Ybarra, 2002) suggests that negative behaviors tend to be attributed to the dispositional qualities of the actor performing the behavior (e.g., the person is not trustworthy). Thus a product-harm crisis is expected to be attributed to the brand by default. However, studies that have examined the impact of negative events on brands show that not all brands are equally affected by these default dispositional attributions. For example, Laczniak, DeCarlo, and Ramaswami (2001) found that consumers make fewer negative attributions about a favorable (versus less favorable) brand when exposed to negative word-of-mouth messages. Similarly, Klein and Dawar (2004) found that consumers blame the firm less for a product-harm crisis when they have positive (versus negative) prior beliefs about the firm's corporate social responsibility. Indeed, anecdotal evidence in the marketplace shows that strong brands survive even severe crises. For example, Tylenol was able to regain nearly all of its lost market share in less than six months after the deadly crisis in 1982 (Lewin, 1986), and 78% of Firestone's sales remained intact in 2001 despite the massive product recall in the same year (Welch, 2001). One explanation for these findings is that, although consumers make initial dispositional attributions to the brand, they may adjust these depending on their prior beliefs (Johar, 1996). Adjustment of attributions to the brand may differ among different cultures. For example, Chinese, as compared to North Americans, assign a greater weight to contextual factors than to dispositional factors when they explain social events (Chiu, Hong, Morris, & Menon, 2000). Hence, Chinese are more likely to focus on situations, rather than the individual actors, when they make attributions.

Individuals adapt to life in other cultures in different ways. Acculturation reflects varying degrees of identification with and attachment to the dominant culture. Ethnic identification refers to the extent to which traits from the original culture are maintained. In contrast to the consumer ethnocentrism, recent research demonstrates a consumer disidentification model, which predicts that consumers' repulsion from their domestic country negatively affects the purchase of products made in the consumer's domestic country or by domestic firms (Josiassen, 2011). Results of the study show that for second-generation Turkish immigrants, acculturation and ethnic identification are important predictors for both consumer ethnocentrism and consumer disidentification.

Consumers also have expectations about the consumer-brand relationships they should experience in different product categories. Closeness can vary not only within interpersonal relationships, but also in how consumers perceive their relationships with brands (Fournier, 1998). One determinant of consumers' expectations regarding closeness in their relationships with brands could be brand type or the product category to which it belongs. Consumers may expect their relationships with brands in some categories (e.g., financial counseling) to be based on closeness, teamwork, or shared goals, whereas relationships with other brands in even very similar categories (e.g., insurance) may be expected to be more distant, based less on mutual goals and more on "zero-sum" behavior. These differences, in turn, could lead message recipients to react differently to the same copy, based on the extent to which the closeness implied in the message matches people's expectations regarding the relationship and its associated norms.

In addition to the brand type or category, a key factor that is likely to influence people's closeness expectations, and hence their reactions to relationship-implying language, is the nature of their affiliation with the brand. Specifically, whereas existing brand customers may expect their relationship with a brand to be either close or distant (e.g., depending on the brand), noncustomers should generally expect their relationship and potential interactions with brands with which they are not affiliated to be relatively distant, in much the same way that people expect distance in their relationships with strangers.

Prior research indicates that people are more sensitive to subtle influences, including linguistic components in a communication, when they are motivated to process the information carefully (McQuarrie & Mick, 1996; Meyers-Levy & Peracchio, 1996; Petty, DeMarree, Briñol, Horcajo, & Strathman, 2008). Recent research expects that the effects of subtle language variations would be moderated by the extent of cognitive elaboration (Sela, Wheeler, & Sarial-Abi, 2012). The hypothesis regarding the moderating role of cognitive elaboration is based on the premise that consumers must first assess the consistency between the specific language used in the communication and representations of the relationship stored in their memory. Then, they must use this assessment to guide judgment and attitudes toward the communicating brand. At each of these two steps, there is reason to believe that effortful cognitive elaboration would increase the effects of language on brand attitudes. Effortful elaboration on brand information is likely to render associated knowledge structures (such as one's relationship expectations toward the brand) more accessible (Petty et al., 2008), and accessible knowledge is more likely to be used as a basis for consistency judgments (Higgins, 1996; Mussweiler, 2003). Further, thoughts taking place under increased cognitive elaboration tend to be better predictors of attitudes than thoughts under low elaboration (e.g., Petty, Schumann, Richman, & Strathman, 1993).

Broadly speaking, people tend to process self-relevant information more effortfully than they do self-irrelevant information (Burnkrant & Unnava, 1995; Wheeler, Petty, & Bizer, 2005). This suggests that brand affiliation should influence not only closeness expectations, but also the likelihood of cognitive elaboration. Specifically, communications should be more self-relevant to brand customers than to noncustomers. Consequently, recent research expects the effects of subtle pronoun variations in marketing communications to be particularly pronounced among brand customers, who are motivated by default to elaborate on brand communications (Sela, Wheeler, and Sarial-Abi, unpublished data). That is, brand customers are expected to respond more favorably to closeness-implying language that matches their expectations from the relationship and less favorably to language that does not match relationship expectations.

Noncustomers, in contrast, should only be affected by pronoun variations when they are induced to elaborate effortfully on the communications. This can happen, for example, when the importance of thinking carefully is emphasized

(Cacioppo, Petty, Feinstein, & Jarvis, 1996; Maheswaran & Chaiken, 1991). In such instances, noncustomers should become more sensitive to subtle pronoun variations than they normally would be. We further propose that the use of closeness-implying language may differ among different cultures. For example, collectivist customers and noncustomers are likely to have positive evaluations of brands that use "we" as a language if the brand is consistent with their group-values. On the other hand, individualists are more likely to have positive evaluations of brands that use "we" as a language when they are customers.

P7: Collectivist customers and noncustomers are more likely to have positive evaluations of brands that use "we" as a language if the brand is consistent with their group-values. Individualists are more likely to have positive evaluations of brands that use "we" as a language when they are customers.

CONCLUSION

Brand relationship has become an important area for research over the last decade. However, relatively little empirical research has investigated this topic from a cross-cultural perspective. In this chapter, we tried to combine the research on brand relationships and culture by focusing on self-related motives. We also discussed how relationships are maintained and managed over time. We provided some propositions that can be investigated in future research. We hope that this chapter helps stimulate further research on this interesting topic.

REFERENCES

Aaker, J. L. (1997). Dimensions of brand personality. *Journal of Marketing Research*, *34*, 342–352.

Aaker, J. L. (1999). The malleable self: The role of self-expression in persuasion. *Journal of Marketing Research*, *36*(February), 45–57.

Aaker, J. L., & Schmitt, B. (2001). Culture-dependent assimilation and differentiation of the self: Preferences for consumption symbols in the United States and China. *Journal of Cross-Cultural Psychology*, *32*(5), 561–576.

Aaker, J. L., Benet-Martinez, V., & Garolera, J. (2001). Consumption symbols as carriers of culture: A study of Japanese and Spanish brand personality constructs. *Journal of Personality and Social Psychology*, *81*, 492–508.

Aaker, J. L., Fournier, S., & Brasel, S. A. (2004). When good brands do bad. *Journal of Consumer Research*, *31*(1), 1–16.

Aggarwal, P. (2004). The effects of brand relationship norms on consumer attitudes and behavior. *Journal of Consumer Research*, *31*(1), 87–101.

Agrawal, N., & Maheswaran, D. (2005). The effects of self-construal and commitment on persuasion. *Journal of Consumer Research*, *31*(March), 841–849.

Ahluwalia, R., Burnkrant, R. E., & Unnava, R. H. (2000). Consumer response to negative publicity: The moderating role of commitment. *Journal of Marketing Research,* 37(May), 203–214.

Ahuvia, A. C. (2005). Beyond the extended self: Loved objects and consumers' identity narratives. *Journal of Consumer Research,* 32(1), 171–184.

Aqueveque, C. (2005). Marketing and market development: Signaling corporate values: consumers' suspicious Minds. *Corporate Governance,* 5(3), 70–81.

Aron, A., & Aron, E. N. (1986). *Love and the Expansion of self: understanding attraction and satisfaction,* New York, NY, USA: Hemisphere.

Aron, A., Aron, E. N., & Norman, C. C. (2003). Self-expansion model of motivation and cognition in close relationships and beyond. In M. B. Brewer & M. Hewstone (Eds.), *Self and social identity* (pp. 100–123). Oxford, UK: Blackwell.

Ashworth, L., Dacin, P., & Thomson, M. (2009). Why on earth do consumers have relationships with marketers? In D. J. MacInnis, C. W. Park, & J. R. Priester (Eds.), *Handbook of brand relationships* (pp. 82–106). New York, NY, USA: M. E. Sharpe.

Bauer, H. H., Heinrich, D., & Martin, I. (2007). How to create high emotional consumer-brand relationships? The causalities of brand passion. In Dr. M. Thyne & K. R. Deans (Eds.), *Australian and New Zealand Marketing Academy (ANZMAC) Conference 2007,* Dunedin, New Zealand, 2189–2198.

Baumeister, R. (1998). The self. In D. Gilbert, S. Fiske, & G. Lindzey (Eds.), *Handbook of social psychology,* Vol. 1 (pp. 680–740). New York, NY, USA: Oxford University Press.

Belk, R. W. (1988). Possessions and the extended self. *Journal of Consumer Research,* 15(2), 139–68.

Bellah, R., Madsen, R., Sullivan, W., Swidler, A., & Tipton, S. (1985). *Habits of the heart: Individualism and commitment in American life,* Berkeley, CA, USA: University of California Press.

Berger, Jonah & Heath, C. (2007). Where consumers diverge from others: Identity signaling and product domains. *Journal of Consumer Research,* 34(2), 121–134.

Bitner, M. J. (1992). Servicescapes: The impact of physical surroundings on customers and employees. *Journal of Marketing,* 56(April), 57–72.

Blackston, M. (2000). Observations: Building brand equity by managing the brand's relationships. *Journal of Advertising Research,* 32(3), 79–84.

Blecken, D. (2009). Can overseas celebrities sell brands in China?. *Media,* September 10, 17.

Bowlby, J. (1979), *The making and breaking of the affectional bonds.* London, UK: Tavistock.

Bozell-Gallup (1996), *The Second Annual Bozell-Gallup Worldwide Quality Poll.* New York: Bozell Worldwide.

Burnkrant, R. E., & Unnava, H. R. (1995). Effects of self-referencing on persuasion. *Journal of Consumer Research,* 22(June), 17–26.

Cacioppo, J. T., Petty, R. E., Feinstein, J. A., & Jarvis, B. W. G. (1996). Dispositional differences in cognitive motivation: The life and times of individuals varying in need for cognition. *Psychological Bulletin,* 119(2), 197–253.

Chaudhuri, A., & Holbrook, M. B. (2001). The chain of effects from brand trust and brand affect to brand performance: The role of brand loyalty. *Journal of Marketing,* 65(2), 81–93.

Chiu, C.-y., Hong, Y.-y., Morris, M. W., & Menon, T. (2000). Motivated cultural cognition: The impact of implicit cultural theories on dispositional attributes varies as a function of need for closure. *Journal of Personality and Social Psychology, 78*(2), 247–259.

Choi, I., Nisbett, R. E., & Norenzayan, A. (1999). Causal attribution across cultures: Variation and universality. *Psychological Bulletin, 125*, 47–63.

Clark, M. S. (1981). Noncomparability of benefits given and received: A cue to the existence of friendship. *Social Psychology Quarterly, 44*(December), 375–381.

Clark, M. S., & Mills, J. (1993). The difference between communal and exchange relationships: What it is and is not. *Personality and Social Psychology Bulletin, 19*(December), 684–691.

Clark, M. S., Mills, J., & Corcoran, D. M. (1989). Keeping track of needs and inputs of friends and strangers. *Personality and Social Psychology Bulletin, 15*(December), 533–542.

Diener, E., & Diener, D. (1995). Cross-cultural correlates of life satisfaction and self-esteem. *Journal of Personality and Social Psychology, 68*, 653–663.

Dolich, I. C. (1969). Congruence relationships between self-images and product brands. *Journal of Marketing, 6*(February), 80–84.

Dowling, G. (2002). Customer relationship management: In B2C markets, often less is more. *California Management Review, 44*(3), 87–106.

Einwiller, S. A., Fedorikhin, A., Johnson, A. R., & Kamins, M. A. (2006). Enough is enough! When identification no longer prevents negative corporate associations. *Journal of the Academy of Marketing Science, 34*(2), 185–194.

Escalas, J. E., & Bettman, J. R. (2005). Self-construal, reference groups, and brand meaning. *Journal of Consumer Research, 32*(December), 378–389.

Escalas, J. E., & Bettman, J. R. (2009). Self-brand connections: The role of reference groups and celebrity endorsers in the creation of brand meaning. In D. J. MacInnis, C. W. Park, & J. R. Priester (Eds.), *Handbook of brand relationships* (pp. 107–123). New York, NY, USA: M. E. Sharpe.

Folkes, V. S. (1984). Consumer reactions to product failure: An attributional approach. *Journal of Consumer Research, 10*(4), 398–409.

Fournier, S. (1998). Consumers and their brands: Developing relationship theory in consumer research. *Journal of Consumer Research, 24*(March), 343–373.

Fournier, S. (2009). Lessons learned about consumers' relationships with their brands. In D. J. MacInnis, C. W. Park, & J. R. Priester (Eds.), *Handbook of brand relationships* (pp. 5–23). New York, NY, USA: M. E. Sharpe.,

Gagliardi, M. (2001). Alchemy of cultures—From adaptation to transcendence in design and branding. *Design Management Review, 12*(4), 32–39.

Gremler, D. D. (2004). The critical incident technique in service research. *Journal of Service Research, 7*(1), 65–89.

Gregoire, Y., & Fisher, R. J. (2008). Customer betrayal and retaliation: When your best customers become your worst enemies. *Journal of the Academy of Marketing Science, 36*(2), 247–261.

Greenwald, A., & Pratkanis, A. (1984). The self. In S. Wyer & T. K. Srull (Eds.), *Handbook of social cognition* (pp. 129–178). Hillsdale, NJ: Lawrence Erlbaum Associates Inc.

Gudykunst, W. B., Matsumoto, Y., Ting-Toomey, S., Nishida, T., Kim, K. S., & Heyman, S. (1996). The influence of cultural individualism-collectivism, self-construal, and values on communications styles across cultures. *Human Communication Research*, 22, 510–543.

Gürhan-Canli, Z., & Maheswaran, D. (2000). Cultural variations in country of origin effects. *Journal of Marketing Research*, 37(August), 309–317.

Higgins, E. T. (1996). Knowledge activation: Accessibility, applicability, and salience. In E. T. Higgins & A. W. Kruglanski (Eds.), *Social psychology: Handbook of basic principles* (pp. 133–168). New York, NY, USA: Guilford Press.

Hofstede, G. (1980). *Culture's consequences*. Beverly Hills, CA, USA: Sage.

Hong, S. -T., & Wyer, R. S. Jr. (1990). Determinants of product evaluation: Effects of the time interval between knowledge of a product's country of origin and information about its specific attributes. *Journal of Consumer Research*, 17(December), 277–288.

Hsu, F. L. K. (1983). *Rugged individualism reconsidered*. Knoxville: University of Tennessee Press.

Johar, G. V. (1996). Intended and unintended effects of corrective advertising on beliefs and evaluations: An exploratory analysis, *Journal of Consumer Psychology*, 5(3), 209–230.

Josiassen, A. (2011). Consumer disidentification and its effects on domestic product purchase: An empirical test in the Netherlands. in *Journal of Marketing* 75(2), 124–140.

Kagitcibasi, C. (1994). A critical appraisal of individualism and collectivism: Toward a new formulation. In U. Kim, H. C. Triandis, C. Kagitcibasi, S. C. Choi, & G. Yoon (Eds.), *Individualism and collectivism: Theory, method, and applications*, (pp. 52–65). Thousand Oaks, CA, USA: Sage.

Keller, K. L. (2001). Building customer-based equity. *Marketing Management*, 10(July/August), 14–19.

Kim, U. (1994). Individualism and collectivism: Conceptual clarification and elaboration. In U. Kim, H. C. Triandis, C. Kagitcibasi, S. C. Choi, & G. Yoon (Eds.), *Individualism and collectivism: Theory, method, and applications* (pp. 19–40). Thousand Oaks, CA, USA: Sage.

Klein, J., Ettenson, R., & Morris, M. D. (1998). The animosity of model of foreign product purchase: An empirical test in the People's Republic of China. *Journal of Marketing*, 62(January), 89–100.

Klein, J., & Dawar, N. (2004). Corporate social responsibility and consumers' attributions and brand evaluations in a product–harm crisis. *International Journal of Research in Marketing*, 21(September), 203–217.

Kleine, S. S., & Baker, S. M. (2004). An Integrative review of material possession attachment. *Academy of Marketing Science Review*, 1, 1–39.

Kwan, V. S. Y., Bond, M. H., & Singelis, T. M. (1997). Pancultural explanations for life satisfaction: Adding relationship harmony to self-esteem. *Journal of Personality and Social Psychology* 73(5), 1038–1051.

Laczniak, R. N., DeCarlo, T. E., & Ramaswami, S. N. (2001). Consumers' responses to negative word-of-mouth communication: An attribution theory perspective. *Journal of Consumer Psychology*, 11(1), 57–73.

Leary, M. R. (2007). Motivational and emotional aspects of the self. *Annual Review of Psychology*, 58, 317–344.

Lewin, T. (1986). Tylenol maker finding new crisis less severe. *New York Times*, February 12.

Liljander, V., & Roos, I (2002). Customer-relationship levels-from spurious to true relationships. *Journal of Services Marketing, 16*(7), 593–614.

MacInnis, D. J., C. Park, W., & Priester, J. (2009). Why brand relationships? In Deborah
J. MacInnis, C. Whan Park, & Joseph R. Priester (Eds.), *Handbook of brand relationships* (pp. ix–xxi). New York, NY, USA: M. E. Sharpe.

Maheswaran, D. (1994). Country-of-origin as a stereotype: Effects of consumer expertise and attribute strength on product evaluations. *Journal of Consumer Research,
21*(September), 354–365.

Maheswaran, D., & Chaiken, S. (1991). Promoting systematic processing in
low-motivation settings: Effect of incongruent information on processing and judgment. *Journal of Personality and Social Psychology, 61*(1), 13–25.

Markus, H. R., & Kitayama, S. (1991). The cultural construction of self and emotion: Implications for social behavior. In S. Kitayama, & H. R. Markus (Eds.), *Emotion
and culture: Empirical studies of mutual influence* (pp. 89–132). Washington, DC,
USA: American Psychological Assoc.

Markus, H. R., & Kunda, Z. (1986). Stability and malleability of the self-concept.
Journal of Personality and Social Psychology, 51(4), 858–866.

Maso-Fleishman, R. (1997). The grandmother: A powerful symbol for Hispanic
women. *Marketing News*, February 3, 13–14.

Matzler, K., Pichler, E. A., & Hemetsberger, A. (2007). Who is spreading the word? The
positive influence of extraversion on consumer passion and brand evangelism. In
2007 AMA Winter Educators' Conference, San Diego, CA, pp. 25–32.

McCracken, G. (1986). Culture and consumption: A theoretical account of the structure and movement of the cultural meaning of consumer goods. *Journal of Consumer
Research, 13*(June), 71–84.

McQuarrie, E. F., & Mick, D. G. (1996). Figures of rhetoric in advertising language.
Journal of Consumer Research, 22(March), 424–437.

Metts, S. (1994). Relational transgressions. In W. R. Cupach & B. Spitzberg (Eds.),
The dark side of interpersonal communications (pp. 217–239). Hillsdale, NJ,
USA: Lawrence Erlbaum Associates Inc.

Meyers-Levy, J., & Peracchio, L. A. (1996). Moderators of the impact of self-reference
on persuasion. *Journal of Consumer Research, 22*(4), 408–423.

Mitchell, A. A., & Olson, J. C. (1981). Are product attribute beliefs the only moderator
of advertising effects on brand attitude? *Journal of Marketing Research, 18*(August),
318–332.

Misra, S., & Beatty, S. E. (1990). Celebrity spokesperson and brand congruence: an
assessment of recall and affect. *Journal of Business Research, 21*(2), 159–173.

Morris, M. W., & Leung, K. (2000). Justice for all? Progress in research in cultural variation in the psychology of distributive and procedural justice. *Applied Psychology: An
International Review, 49*, 100–132.

Muniz, A. M. Jr, & O'Guinn, T. C. (2001). Brand community. *Journal of Consumer
Research, 27*(4), 412–431.

Mussweiler, T. (2003). Comparison processes in social judgment: Mechanisms and
consequences. *Psychological Review, 110*(3), 472–489.

Ng, S., & Houston, M (2006). Exemplars or beliefs? The impact of self-view on the
nature and relative influence of brand associations. *Journal of Consumer Research,
32*(March), 519–29.

Oyserman, D. (1993). The lens of personhood: Viewing the self, others, and conflict in a multicultural society. *Journal of Personality and Social Psychology, 65*, 993–1009.

Oyserman, D., & Markus, H. R. (1993). The sociocultural self. In J. Suls (Ed.), *The self in social perspective* (pp. 187–220). Hillsdale, NJ, USA: Erlbaum.

Oyserman, D., Coon, H. M., & Kemmelmeier, M. (2002). Rethinking individualism and collectivism: Evaluation of theoretical assumptions and meta-analyses. *Psychological Bulletin, 128*(1), 3–72.

Paulssen, M., & Bagozzi, R. P. (2009). Customer coping in response to relationship transgressions: An attachment theoretic approach. In D. J. MacInnis, C. W. Park, & J. R. Priester (Eds.), *Handbook of brand relationships* (pp. 358–375). New York, NY, USA: M. E. Sharpe.

Petty, R. E., DeMarree, K. G., Briñol, P. B., Horcajo, J., & Strathman, A. J. (2008). Need for cognition can magnify or attenuate priming effects in social judgment. *Personality and Social Psychology Bulletin, 34*(7), 900–912.

Petty, R. E., Schumann, D. W., Richman, S. A., & Strathman, A. J. (1993). Positive mood and persuasion: Different roles for affect under high- and low-elaboration conditions. *Journal of Personality and Social Psychology, 64*(1), 5–20.

Reed II, A. (2004). Activating the self-importance of consumer selves: Exploring identity salience effects on judgments. *Journal of Consumer Research, 31*(2), 286–295.

Reimann, M., & Aron, A. (2009). Self-expansion motivation and inclusion of brands in self. In D. J. MacInnis, C. W. Park, & J. R. Priester (Eds.), *Handbook of brand relationships* (pp. 65–81). New York, NY, USA: M. E. Sharpe.

Rosenberg, M. (1979). *Conceiving the self,* New York, NY, USA: Basic Books.

Rusbult, C. E., Verette, J., Whitney, G. A., Slovik, L. F., & Lipkus, I (1991). Accommodation processes in close relationships: Theory and preliminary empirical evidence. *Journal of Personality and Social Psychology 60*(1), 53–78.

Schwartz, S. H. (1990). Individualism–collectivism: Critique and proposed refinements. *Journal of Cross-Cultural Psychology, 21*, 139–157.

Schwartz, S. H. (1992). Universals in the content and structure of values: Theoretical advances and empirical tests in 20 countries. In M. P. Zanna (Ed.), *Advances in experimental social psychology*, Vol. 25 (pp. 1–65). New York, NY, USA: Academic Press.

Schwartz, S. H. (1994). Beyond individualism/collectivism: New cultural dimensions of values. In U. Kim, H. C. Triandis, C. Kagitcibasi, S. Choi, & G. Yoon (Eds.), *Individualism and collectivism: Theory, method, and Applications* (pp. 85–119). Thousand Oaks, CA, USA: Sage.

Schwartz, S. H., & Bilsky, W. (1990). Toward a theory of the universal content and structure of values: Extensions and cross-cultural replications. *Journal of Personality and Social Psychology 58*(5), 878–891.

Schwartz, S. H., & Sagiv, L. (1995). Identifying culture-specifics in the content and structure of values. *Journal of Cross-Cultural Psychology, 26*(1), 92–116.

Sela, A., Wheeler, S. C., & Sarial-Abi, G. (2012). We are not the same as 'you and I': causal effects of minor language variations on consumers' attitudes toward brands. *Journal of Consumer Research, 39*(3), 644.

Shimp, T. A., & Sharma, S. (1987). Consumer ethnocentrism: construction and validation of the CETSCALE. *Journal of Marketing Research, 24*(August), 280–89.

Shweder, R. A., & Bourne, E. J. (1982). Does the concept of the person vary cross-culturally? In A. J. Marsella & G. M. White (Eds.), *Cultural conceptions of mental health and therapy* (pp. 97–137). New York, NY, USA: Reidel.

Singelis, T. M. (1994). The measurement of independent and interdependent self-construal. *Personality and Social Psychology Bulletin, 20*, 580–591.

Singelis, T. M., & Sharkey, W. F. (1995). Culture, self-construal, and embarrassability. *Journal of Cross-Cultural Psychology, 26*, 622–644.

Smith, A., & Bolton, R. (1998). An experimental investigation of customer reactions to service failure and recovery encounters: Paradox or peril. *Journal of Service Research, 1*(1), 5–17.

Srivastava, R. K., Shervani, T. A., & Fahey, L. (1998). Market-based assets and shareholder value: A framework for analysis. *Journal of Marketing, 62*(January), 2–18.

Sung, Y., & Tinkham, S. F. (2005). Brand personality structures in the United States and Korea: Common and culture-specific factors. *Journal of Consumer Psychology, 15*(4), 334–350.

Swaminathan, V., Page, K. L., & Gürhan-Canli, Z. (2007). My brand or our brand: The effects of brand relationship dimensions and self-construal on brand evaluations. *Journal of Consumer Research, 34*(August), 248–259.

Triandis, H. C. (1995). *Individualism and collectivism*, Boulder, CO: Westview.

Welch, D. (2001). Meet the new face of firestone. *BusinessWeek*, April 30.

Wheeler, S. C., Petty, R. E., & Bizer, G. Y. (2005). Self-schema matching and attitude Change: situational and dispositional determinants of message elaboration. *Journal of Consumer Research, 31*(March), 787–797.

Winterich, K. P. (2007). *Self-other connectedness in consumer affect, judgments, and action*. Dissertation, University of Pittsburgh, Joseph M. Katz Graduate School of Business, Pittsburgh, PA.

Ybarra, O. (2002). Naive causal understanding of valenced behaviors and its implications for social information processing. *Psychological Bulletin, 128*(3), 421–441.

13

Culture and Brand Iconicity

CARLOS TORELLI AND SHIRLEY Y. Y. CHENG ■

With globalization, the world is becoming smaller and the consciousness of the world as a whole is intensifying rapidly (Robertson, 1992). With the rapid growth of global linkages and global consciousness, the marketplace is becoming increasingly complex for marketers to navigate. While major American brand names such as Starbucks and Nike have traditionally enjoyed sustained growth in emerging economies such as China, India, and Brazil, brands from these regions have also recently emerged as global challengers. Consider for instance the footprint gained in recent years by Chinese Lenovo Group in the personal computer industry, the recent entry of Indian's Tata Group into the luxury cars segment via the acquisition of the Jaguar and Land Rover brands, or the growth of Brazilian's Embraer in the Western-dominated aerospace industry. In a globalized marketplace, a wide range of brands bring diverse cultures to a consumer population that is also growing ethnically diverse. For example, the 2010 Census showed that the Hispanic population in the United States grew substantially in the last decade (50.5 million Hispanics versus 38.9 million African Americans; Humes, Jones, & Ramirez, 2011). Something similar is happening in Europe, where the Muslim population has more than doubled in the past 30 years and will have doubled again by 2015 (Michaels, 2009).

The need for marketers to better understand how to deepen consumer-brand relationships with *global* consumers has never been more important (Shavitt, Lee, & Torelli, 2008). For many companies, the critical goal is to build iconic brands with distinct, relevant associations that can create deep psychological bonds with multicultural consumers and achieve strong market-leadership positions (Holt, 2003; Keller, 1993; Leibig, 2005). In the pages that follow, we review the latest findings in how consumers react to culturally symbolic brands. Drawing on the notion that brands can be regarded as cultural products, as well as on findings showing that consumers' interactions with brands are often guided by the fulfillment of salient cultural identity needs and the alignment with self-relevant values, we develop a framework for understanding the relationship that multicultural consumers establish with culturally symbolic brands. Our review suggests that, because a culturally symbolic brand can fulfill salient social identity needs, consumers can react positively or negatively to the brand's cultural symbolism depending on the context. We identify factors that moderate these consumer reactions and discuss key issues in building and leveraging brand equity in multicultural markets. In doing so, we highlight the theoretical importance of a brand's cultural symbolism for fulfilling social identity needs and the consequences for brand evaluations and consumer-brand relationships. We also provide marketers with an actionable framework for building iconic brands in multicultural markets.

BRANDS AS CULTURAL SYMBOLS

According to the dynamic constructivist theory of culture (Chiu & Hong, 2007; Hong, Morris, Chiu, & Benet-Martinez, 2000), people with some direct or indirect experiences with a certain culture will develop a cognitive representation of it. Culture is defined here as shared elements that provide the standards for perceiving, believing, evaluating, communicating, and acting among those who share a language, a historical period, and a geographic location (Triandis, 1989, 1995). As a collective phenomenon, culture consists of shared meanings that provide a common frame of reference for a human group to make sense of reality, coordinate their activities, and adapt to their environment (Shore, 2002; Sperber, 1996). Adopting a constructivist approach to culture (Chiu & Hong, 2006; Hong et al., 2000), we consider that shared cultural knowledge is not internalized as an integrated and highly general structure, such as an overall mentality or value orientation (i.e., individualism versus collectivism). Rather, culture is internalized in the form of a loose network of domain-specific knowledge structures consisting of a central concept (e.g., American culture) and its associated categories (e.g., individualist values of freedom and self-reliance), implicit theories (e.g., an individual's behavior originates in internal dispositions), and cultural icons (e.g., the Statue of Liberty or the American flag) (Hong et al., 2000; Torelli & Ahluwalia, 2012; Torelli & Cheng, 2011). These knowledge structures guide cognition and behavior only when they come to the fore in an individual's mind—either because they are chronically accessible or activated by environmental stimuli (Hong et al., 2000; Lau, Chiu, & Lee, 2001; Sechrist & Stangor, 2001; Trafimow, Silverman, Fan, & Law, 1997).

Culture is not only instrumental for human adaptation by facilitating the collective coordination of human activity, it also serves multiple psychological functions for the individual, including providing a sense of epistemic security, a sense of belongingness, and a buffer against existential terror (Chiu & Hong, 2006). Not surprisingly, cultural knowledge is widely disseminated in society and instantiated in social institutions (e.g., family or the workplace), social practices (e.g., division of labor), and a variety of media (e.g., popular songs or news media) and iconic images (e.g., flags, monuments, or consumer products) (Aaker,

Benet-Martinez, & Garolera, 2001; Morling & Lamoreaux, 2008; Morris & Peng, 1994; Torelli & Ahluwalia, 2012; Wan, Torelli, & Chiu, 2010). Unlike other cultural icons, such as a national flag or a commemorative monument, brands are commercial entities that are not created to be symbols of a culture. Marketers create brands to establish certain desirable meanings and unique positioning in the minds of consumers (Keller, 2007). However, through the process of social consensus building (Krauss & Fussell, 1996; McCracken, 1986), some brands acquire cultural meanings and become associated with the abstract characteristics that define a cultural group (Aaker et al., 2001; Han & Shavitt, 1994; Torelli & Cheng, 2011). For instance, hedonic products or automobiles characterize French or Japanese cultures, respectively (Hong & Kang, 2006; Leclerc, Schmitt, & Dubé, 1994), as much as brands like Budweiser or Sony characterize American or Japanese cultures, respectively (Torelli & Ahluwalia, 2012).

A brand's cultural symbolism is defined as perceived consensus of the degree to which the brand symbolizes the abstract image of a certain cultural group (Torelli, Keh, & Chiu, 2010). Because members of a cultural group typically agree on the assumed sharing of culturally relevant beliefs (Wan et al., 2010; Zou, Tam, Morris, Lee, Lau, & Chiu, 2009), cultural symbolism is measured via ratings of the extent to which an average group member perceives that a target brand belongs to the cultural network—using items such as: "the brand embodies [target culture] values," "the brand is an icon of [target culture]," or "the brand is a good example of what it means being a member of [target culture]" (Torelli & Ahluwalia, 2012; Torelli, Keh, et al., 2010; Wan et al., 2010). Notice that cultural symbolism should be distinguished from strong country-of-origin connections (e.g., Gürhan-Canli & Maheswaran, 2000). A country-of-origin connection refers to concrete knowledge about the country in which the headquarters of the brand's parent firm is located (Balabanis & Diamantopoulos, 2008; Johansson, Douglas, & Nonaka, 1985), regardless of the extent to which the brand in question symbolizes an abstract cultural image. In contrast, cultural symbolism emerges, at least in part, from associations with abstract group meanings such as values (Allen, 2002; Holt, 2004). When using nationality as the defining cultural criterion, we are likely to find that iconic brands have strong country-of-origin connections. However, this would not be a sufficient condition to grant a brand an iconic status. For instance, although most Americans undoubtedly recognize Special K and Victoria's Secret as American brands (i.e., strong country-of-origin connection), these brands are rated relatively low in terms of their symbolism of American culture (Torelli, Chiu, Keh, & Amaral, 2010). That is because these brands symbolize feminine values that do not consensually characterize American culture.

As part of the cultural knowledge network, a culturally symbolic brand not only connects to the central concept (e.g., Budweiser's symbolism of American culture), but also to the various elements in the knowledge representation of the culture (e.g., American cultural values of freedom and independence) (Torelli, Keh, et al., 2010). For this reason, a culturally symbolic brand embodies consumers' abstract, consensual view of the cultural group the brand symbolizes (McCracken, 1986), and hence becomes a tangible, public representation of the meanings and ideas shared in the culture (Morling & Lamoreaux, 2008). As such, exposure to culturally symbolic brands should produce cultural priming effects similar to those documented in past research using other cultural products (e.g., national flag; Hong et al., 2000). We review the empirical evidence supporting these ideas next.

Culturally symbolic brands embody abstract cultural characteristics

The notion that consumer brands can symbolize the abstract characteristics that distinguish a culture was first suggested by Han and Shavitt (1994). They demonstrated that magazine advertisements in the United States (an individualist culture) and Korea (a collectivist culture) varied predictably according to the corresponding cultural value priorities in these countries. That is, appeals to individual benefits and preferences, personal success, and independence were more common in the United States, whereas appeals emphasizing in-group benefits, harmony, and family integrity were more common in Korea. Similarly, Aaker et al. (2001) found that brands in a culture embody personality traits unique in the culture. They show that some brands in the United States are associated with ruggedness (i.e., strength, masculinity, and toughness) and some brands in Japan are associated with peacefulness, and ruggedness and peacefulness are dimensions characteristic of American and East Asian cultures, respectively. Torelli and colleagues (Torelli, Chiu, & Keh, 2010; Torelli, Ozsomer, Carvalho, Keh, & Maehle, 2009) more directly demonstrate that cultural symbolism of a brand is positively associated with its embodiment of culture-distinctive values. They presented American (individualist culture) and Venezuelan (collectivist culture) participants with brands that varied in their levels of cultural symbolism (for the corresponding group), and asked them to rate these brands in terms of their embodiment of individualist and collectivist values (Torelli, Ozsomer, et al., 2009). Results showed that Americans perceive that iconic American brands embody individualist values (power, achievement, self-direction, stimulation, and hedonism), whereas Venezuelans perceive that Venezuelan brand icons embody collectivist values (universalism, benevolence, tradition, conformity, and security). These findings are consistent with a view of brands as cultural "products," or as external representations of meanings and ideas shared in a culture (Morling & Lamoreaux, 2008).

Cultural priming effects triggered by exposure to culturally symbolic brands

Priming with cultural icons induces cultural frame switching because icons of a culture are like "magnets of meaning"; they connect many diverse elements of cultural knowledge (Betsky, 1997; Ortner, 1973). When activated, these icons automatically spread activation to other constructs in the cultural knowledge network and increase their cognitive accessibility (Hong et al., 2000). Cultural priming effects are evident in research with bicultural individuals—those having internalized two cultures, either by being of mixed racial heritage (e.g., Asian Americans born in the United States) or born in one culture and raised in a second (e.g., Asian immigrants living in the United States) (LaFromboise, Coleman, & Gerton, 1993; Lau-Gesk, 2003). For these individuals, exposure to symbols of one culture can prime them to adopt its associated cultural frame to the exclusion of the other (also known as "frame switching"; e.g., Briley, Morris, & Simonson, 2005; Hong et al., 2000; Ng, 2010). For instance, Chinese American biculturals primed with American icons (e.g., American flag) exhibit judgments and behaviors aligned with implicit theories of American culture (e.g., lower attribution of behavior to external social pressure), whereas priming with Chinese icons (e.g., Chinese opera singer) leads them to align with Chinese culture (e.g., higher attribution of behavior to external social pressure) (Y.-Y. Hong, Chiu, & Kung, 1997). Priming with cultural icons can also have other effects, such as reminding people of their membership in a larger collective and stimulating the adoption of a group mindset (Briley & Wyer, 2002).

With globalization, the number of individuals with direct or indirect knowledge about two (bicultural) or more cultures (multicultural) as opposed to a single culture (monocultural) is rapidly on the rise (Lau-Gesk, 2003; Maheswaran & Shavitt, 2000). According to the World Tourism Organization (World Travel & Tourism Council, 2011), international arrivals worldwide have more than doubled since 1990, rising from 435 million to 675 million in 2000, and to 940 million in 2010 (approximately 13% of the world population). During the same period, Internet usage has grown at a staggering rate of 75,566 %, as the number of Internet users has risen from about 3 million in 1990 to 361 million in 2000, and to 2267 million in 2010 (approximately 32% of the world population) (Internet World Stats, 2011). This tremendous growth in Internet access increases the availability that people have to information about lifestyles, customs and developments around the world. With increasing exposure to foreign cultures, so-called monocultural individuals that have not lived for extended periods in a foreign culture can internalize certain aspects of these cultures through international travel and media exposure, and hence exhibit cultural priming effects similar to the ones just described among traditional biculturals (Alter & Kwan, 2009).

Like other cultural icons, a culturally symbolic brand can activate its associated cultural knowledge (Chiu, Mallorie, Keh, & Law, 2009; Torelli & Ahluwalia, 2012; Torelli, Chiu, Keh, & Amaral, 2009). Furthermore, this can occur outside of conscious awareness or without conscious deliberation about cultural inferences (Alter & Kwan, 2009; Hong et al., 1997). This is illustrated in a cued recall study (Torelli, Chiu, et al., 2009). European Americans who read a list of important and unimportant values (for American culture) recalled a greater number of culturally important values in a subsequent surprise recall task when shown, as recall cues, images of brands high (versus low) in cultural symbolism (for Americans). The effect occurred presumably because culturally symbolic brands automatically spread activation in the cultural knowledge network and hence facilitated recall of culturally important values encountered earlier (e.g., Uleman, Winborne, Winter, & Shechter, 1986; Winter & Uleman, 1984). The extent to which the brands used as retrieval cues symbolized American culture did not influence recall of culturally unimportant values.

Exposure to iconic brands or products can also induce engaging in culturally appropriate behaviors. Prior studies have shown that Hispanic American women presented with an advertisement in Spanish (versus English) are more likely to endorse self-sufficient descriptors of behavior that reflect what is appropriate among modern Latinas (Luna, Ringberg, & Peracchio, 2008), presumably because the advertisement in Spanish activates Latin culture but the one in English does not. Consistently, Hong Kong Chinese participants presented with a McDonald's advertisement (versus an advertisement containing Chinese symbols) were more likely to prefer an individualist message over a collectivist one (Chiu et al., 2009), presumably because the iconic American brand activated American cultural values (i.e., individualist values) and thus elicited culturally consistent judgments.

In combination, the findings described in this section indicate that: (a) brands can be regarded as cultural symbols; and (b) incidental exposure to culturally symbolic brands can spontaneously activate its associated cultural knowledge, which can in turn trigger culturally appropriate behaviors.

Culturally symbolic brands can fulfill cultural identity needs

Because culturally symbolic brands activate their attendant cultural meanings, consuming these brands can signal one's allegiance to the culture (Oyserman, 2009; Shavitt, Torelli, & Wong, 2009; Stayman & Deshpande, 1989). For instance, an American consumer can favor an American brand of automobiles (e.g., Ford) over a foreign one (e.g., Toyota) as a means of reinforcing his patriotic national identity (Shimp & Sharma, 1987). The usage of a brand associated with an in-group can strengthen the psychological bond with the group and consequently increase perceptions of belongingness to the group (Escalas & Bettman, 2003). This is more likely to occur when the need to reinforce one's cultural identity is chronically or temporarily salient (Turner, Hogg, Oakes, Reicher, & Wetherell, 1987). Thus, consumers develop favorable attitudes toward culturally symbolic brands and establish strong bonds with these brands as a way to fulfill salient cultural identity needs. We review the empirical evidence in support of these premises next.

Liking for culturally symbolic brands

Some recent studies illustrate how people develop favorable attitudes toward culturally symbolic brands (over nonsymbolic ones) to fulfill temporarily or chronically salient cultural identity needs (Torelli, Chiu, et al., 2010; Torelli, Chiu, et al., 2009; Torelli, Chiu, Keh, et al., 2010). In one study (Torelli, Chiu, Keh, et al., 2010), European Americans reminded (versus not reminded) of the positive qualities of the American identity, which increased their identification with American culture, evaluated brands that are symbolic of the American culture (e.g., Budweiser) more favorably, but were indifferent toward brands that, although generally associated with America, are low in cultural symbolism (e.g., New Balance or Special K).

The effects emerge regardless of whether one wants to reinforce a local or a foreign cultural identity, as people who want to express identification with global culture often favor global brands that symbolize Western values of conspicuous consumption and status seeking (Batra, Ramaswamy, Alden, Steenkamp, & Ramachander, 2000; Steenkamp, Batra, & Alden, 2003; Zhang & Khare, 2009). For instance, a study with Indian consumers (Batra et al., 2000) shows that, among consumers with a greater admiration for the lifestyle in economically developed countries, brands perceived as having a nonlocal (Western) country of origin were more favorably evaluated compared to brands perceived to be local. Similarly, Zhang and Khare (2009) demonstrate that consumers with an accessible global identity prefer a global (more than a local) product.

Because social identity goals can potentially substitute one another (Braun & Wicklund, 1989; Wicklund & Gollwitzer, 1981), people can connect with culturally symbolic brands in response to identity threats in contexts unrelated to culture. That is because patronizing culturally symbolic brands may compensate for perceptions of incompleteness in other social identities. Consistent with this idea, Torelli and colleagues (2009) demonstrated that an induced need to repair a tarnished group identity enhanced evaluation of culturally symbolic brands. In their study, the need to repair one's group identity was manipulated by reminding some American college students of a recent ban on their university's mascot (a symbolic marker of their student identity). Compared to those who were not given the reminder, those who were reminded would feel a need to find another group identity to replace the tarnished one, and they might do so by increasing their identification with American culture. As predicted, the ban reminder increased the tendency to favor brands that symbolize American culture.

Bonds that consumers form with culturally symbolic brands

Consumers' continued reliance on culturally symbolic brands for fulfilling salient cultural identity needs should result in the development of strong self-brand relationships. One study demonstrates that consumers form strong bonds with culturally symbolic brands that fulfill chronic cultural identity concerns (Torelli, Chiu, et al., 2010). In the study, European American, and Chinese participants each named their favorite brand. After that, they rated the extent to which they had established a strong bond with the brand (i.e., self-brand connection) as well as the extent to which the brand was widely perceived to be a symbol of their national culture (i.e., cultural symbolism). Results confirmed that the level of self-brand connection increased with the brand's cultural symbolism, but only for participants high in cultural identification. For them, the more a brand symbolizes their culture, the stronger the relationship they form with the brand. In contrast, the level of self-brand connection was unrelated to the brand's level of cultural symbolism among participants low in cultural identification. For these participants, who did not particularly identify with their culture, the extent to which the brand symbolizes their culture was not an important factor in defining their brand relationships.

A key benefit of strong consumer-brand relationships is their ability to protect the brand from negative publicity (Ahluwalia, Burnkrant, & Unnava, 2000; Cheng, White, & Chaplin, 2012). Forming a bond with a culturally symbolic brand, due to its cultural identity meaning, should shield the brand against negative publicity when cultural identity needs are salient. In other words, consumers should be more likely to resist negative information regarding an iconic brand when their cultural identity is salient. We find evidence for this premise in a study about consumers' reactions to negative brand information (Swaminathan, Page, & Gürhan-Canli, 2007). In this study, American participants were exposed to negative information (or no information) about an iconic American brand (Dell) after being primed with either an interdependent or independent self-construal. Participants in the interdependent-prime condition showed no changes in their attitudes toward the brand upon reading (versus. not) about the negative brand information, presumably because the American identity made available by the prime led them to challenge the negative information. In contrast, in the independent-prime condition, in which the collective American identity was less salient, participants exhibited a drop in brand evaluation after reading (versus not) about the negative brand information.

In summary, latest findings showed that consumers can favor and establish strong bonds with culturally symbolic brands. They do so as a way to fulfill identity needs either by reinforcing one's cultural identity or by compensating other threatened social identity. However, consumers can also reject and resist the cultural meanings in brands. We turn to this issue next.

CULTURALLY SYMBOLIC BRANDS AS CULTURAL CONTAMINANTS

It is well known that when consumers dislike the central cultural concept symbolized by a brand, they signal their animosity toward the associated culture by boycotting the brand (Hong & Kang, 2006; Klein, Ettenson, & Morris, 1998). Although such reactions are often evident among consumers of cultures with a history of hostile relations with another culture (e.g., reactions of consumers from the Chinese city of Nanjing toward Japanese brands; Klein et al., 1998), similar reactions are seen when consumers perceive foreign brands or products as threats to the survival of the local culture (Sharma, Shimp, & Shin, 1995;

Shimp & Sharma, 1987; Varman & Belk, 2009). The fear that foreign cultural symbols may contaminate the local culture can escalate to extremes, and even result in violent acts. Recent studies (Chen & Chiu, 2010; Cheng, 2010; Cheng, Rosner, Chao, Peng, Chen, Li, Kwong, Hong, & Chiu, 2011; Chiu & Cheng, 2007; Torelli & Ahluwalia, 2012; Torelli, Chiu, Tam, Au, & Keh, 2011) have uncovered the following contextual and psychological factors that foster negative reactions toward brands that symbolize foreign cultures: (a) Salience of intercultural competition; (b) Simultaneous activation of two cultures; and (c) Evoking a culture defense mindset. We elaborate next on each of these factors.

Salience of intercultural competition

Negative reactions toward foreign icons can be incited by the salience of intercultural competition. Salient intergroup competition highlights in-group–out-group boundary and heightens a sense of distrust of out-groups (Insko & Schopler, 1998; Turner et al., 1987). This should result in more unfavorable attitudes toward brands that symbolize foreign cultures compared to a context in which intercultural competition is not salient. Cheng et al. (2011) investigated this notion with Chinese consumers during the 2008 Beijing Olympics. Mainland Chinese participants evaluated brands that symbolize either Chinese (e.g., LiNing) or American cultures (e.g., Nike), as well as indicated their identification with Chinese culture, immediately before and after the Beijing Olympics. Before the Olympics, only respondents who were highly identified with Chinese culture showed favoritism for Chinese (over American) symbolic brands. However, as the Olympics progressed, presumably because of the salient rivalry between the United States and China, participants who were both high and low in their identification with Chinese culture exhibited favoritism of Chinese (over American) symbolic brands. This finding suggests that, in face of salient intercultural competition, people shifted their preferences in favor of brands that symbolize the local culture over brands that symbolize a competing foreign culture.

Bicultural priming

Several studies demonstrate that simultaneous activation of two cultures (*bicultural priming*) heightens perception of cultural differences and thus increases defensive, exclusionary reactions to brands that are perceived as a threat to the heritage culture (Chen & Chiu, 2010; Cheng et al., 2011; Chiu & Cheng, 2007; Torelli, Chiu, Tam, et al., 2011). This occurs because bicultural (relative to *monocultural*, or single culture activation) priming heightens perceptions of cultural differences and sensitizes about the role of foreign icons as potential sources of cultural contamination. Torelli and Ahluwalia (2012) illustrate how bicultural priming effects operate. In one study, they asked American participants to evaluate either a bicultural (*Sony cappuccino machines*—the Sony brand is iconic of

Japan whereas cappuccino machines are iconic of Italy) or a monocultural product (*Sony toaster oven*—only the Japanese Sony is culturally symbolic). Results showed that although the two products offered the same level of moderate fit with the Sony brand, the bicultural *Sony cappuccino machine* was evaluated less favorably than the monocultural *Sony toaster oven*. Subsequent studies demonstrated that this unfavorable evaluation was driven by the subjective experience of disfluency triggered by the simultaneous activation of two different cultural schemas.

Another study with mainland Chinese participants demonstrates more directly how bicultural (versus monocultural) priming triggers less favorable evaluations of a foreign target perceived as a cultural contaminant (Cheng, 2010). Participants in the bicultural priming condition were presented with symbols of American and Chinese culture side-by-side (versus separately in the monocultural condition) prior to evaluating a fictitious New York-based publisher planning to set up an Asian headquarter in China. Only in the bicultural priming condition participants evaluated the publisher less favorably if they perceived that the publisher intended to promote American culture. This occurs presumably because bicultural priming increases perception of cultural differences, and thus sensitizes participants of the cultural contamination that the publisher potentially brings to the local culture.

Evoking a culture defense mindset

Perception of cultural contamination is also heightened by evoking a culture defense mindset, such as that triggered by thoughts of one's own death (Torelli, Chiu, Tam, et al., 2011). When reminded of their mortality, people adhere to and defend their cultural worldview as a way to achieve symbolic immortality (Greenberg, Porteus, Simon, & Pyszczynski, 1995). This in turn encourages aggression against those who violate the cultural worldview (McGregor, Lieberman, Greenberg, Solomon, Arndt, Simon, & Pyszczynski, 1998) and evokes intolerance of using cultural icons in an inappropriate way (e.g., using the crucifix as a hammer, Greenberg et al., 1995). Extending this notion to the bicultural priming situations discussed earlier, Torelli and colleagues (2011) show that people are particularly intolerant of contamination of brands that symbolize their culture when they are under the joint influence of bicultural priming and mortality salience. Upon inducing (versus not) mortality salience, American participants were asked to evaluate a marketing plan of Nike (an American icon), which involved some questionable actions to increase its competitiveness in a foreign market (e.g., eliminating the "Swoosh" symbol and replacing the Nike brand name with the Arabic word for "Sportsmanship" to penetrate the Middle East market). Results showed that, only upon making mortality salient, participants evaluated the marketing plan less favorably following bicultural priming than following monocultural priming. These findings suggest that bicultural priming and worldview defense can jointly enhance negative reactions to the inappropriate use of a cultural icon.

In summary, there is consistent evidence that people can and would react unfavorably to a culturally symbolic brand that is perceived as a cultural contaminant. Perceptions of cultural contamination are more likely: (a) when intercultural competition is made salient; (b) when people are under the effects of bicultural (versus monocultural) priming; and (c) under the influence of a culture defense mindset, such as that triggered by thoughts of one's own death.

LEVERAGING CULTURALLY SYMBOLIC BRANDS

Given the above review on the positive and negative reactions to culturally symbolic brands, how does a brand's status as a cultural symbol influences its ability to leverage its brand equity through product extensions? Prior research on this topic suggests that for well-known brands, country or culture associations play only a nominal role on attitudes and choices (Balabanis & Diamantopoulos, 2008; Erickson, Johansson, & Chao, 1984; Johansson et al., 1985); however, the discussion in the previous pages suggests that, depending on the context, a culturally symbolic status might be an asset or a liability when leveraging brand equity. We review these issues next.

Exposure to a culturally symbolic brand activates its associated cultural schema. Previous research suggests that cueing of a schema, via the process of spreading activation, can create expectancies by activating other concepts strongly related to it (Whittlesea, 1993). The increased activation of these associated concepts facilitates their identification (Biederman, 1995), making their processing easier or more fluent (i.e., rendering them conceptually fluent, Shapiro, 1999; Shapiro, Macinnis, & Heckler, 1997). Conceptual fluency, or ease with which a target stimuli is processed when primed by an associated concept, is known to enhance stimuli evaluations (Lee & Labroo, 2004; Reber, Schwarz, & Winkielman, 2004; Whittlesea, 1993). Fluency effects are typically driven by the perceiver attributing "ease of processing" to better quality of the target (Avnet & Higgins, 2003; Camacho, Higgins, & Luger, 2003). It stands to reason that when a product extension is associated with the cultural schema activated by the brand (i.e., the brand and extension product category are culturally congruent) the extension is likely to be processed fluently, generating a feeling of ease and leading to a more favorable evaluation of the extension. Importantly, if the context involves lower involvement or motivation conditions, such as those typically prevalent in the marketplace, people are even more likely to rely on this fluency experience for their evaluations (Fang, Singh, & Ahluwalia, 2007).

In a series of studies using familiar culturally symbolic brands from a variety of cultures (Italian, American, British, Mexican, or Japanese), Torelli and Ahluwalia (2012) demonstrate the advantage in terms of favorable evaluations enjoyed by culturally symbolic brands when extending into culturally congruent products, beyond what one might expect given the brand-product fit. These advantages emerged relative to extensions into culturally neutral products with similar levels of fit with the parent brand, as well as relative to product extensions introduced by brands low in cultural symbolism. For instance, in one study (Torelli & Ahluwalia, 2012), participants evaluated more favorably an extension by Sony (a Japanese icon) into the culturally congruent sushi serving set product (a product symbolic of Japan) compared to an extension into the culturally neutral food serving set. This effect emerged in spite of the similar levels of low fit between the Sony brand and the two product extensions (food-related products are incompatible with Sony's image) and after controlling for participants' prior attitudes toward both Sony and the extension product. In another study (Torelli & Ahluwalia, 2009), participants also evaluated more favorably a Sony sushi serving set compared to a similar product extension introduced by Panasonic—a brand that, although associated with Japan, is relatively neutral in terms of its cultural symbolism. Attesting to the generalizability of the *cultural congruity* effect, Torelli and Ahluwalia (2012) demonstrate that this effect emerges for both moderate and low-fit brand extensions, as well as for narrow and broad brands. Furthermore, empirical evidence confirmed that the effect was driven by the processing fluency generated by the simultaneous activation of the same cultural schema by the product and the brand.

What if the brand and the product category activate incongruent or different cultural schemas? As indicated earlier, the simultaneous activation of two different cultural schemas can increase perceptions of cultural contamination. When two contrasting cultural schemas are activated, their incongruency is also likely to result in a decreased fluency or ease in processing the new product. This sense of unease or disfluency generated by the incongruency is likely to make consumers less receptive to the extension, overriding the effects of conscious elaboration on the potential fit between the brand and the extension product. In support of this prediction, Torelli and Ahluwalia (2012) demonstrated that people exhibit more unfavorable evaluations of culturally incongruent brand extensions (e.g., Sony cappuccino makers or Budweiser tequila) compared to culturally neutral ones (e.g., Sony toaster oven or Budweiser brandy) with similar levels of brand-product fit. However, the effects only emerged when *both* the brand and the product were culturally symbolic, likely to automatically activate a cultural schema; but did not emerge for brands low in cultural symbolism (e.g., for Coors tequila–where Coors, although clearly an American brand, is rated relatively low in American culture symbolism). Furthermore, the effects were driven by the processing *disfluency* generated by the simultaneous activation of different cultural schemas by the product and the brand.

In summary, the findings reviewed in this section show that a brand's cultural symbolism can be a liability or an asset, and to harness it profitably, a manager needs to understand the cultural symbolism of the potential extension categories under consideration. Culturally symbolic brands may successfully extend into culturally congruent products regardless of fit and may backfire in culturally incongruent categories, despite their perceived fit. Cultural associations, however, are not likely to be of concern for managers of brands that are neutral or low in cultural symbolism, as these associations are unlikely to drive people's judgments.

CONCLUSIONS AND FUTURE DIRECTIONS

As marketing efforts become increasingly globalized, it is imperative to understand the cultural significance of brands for multicultural consumers. Branding activities aimed at establishing deep self-brand connections will require a thorough understanding of the cultural symbolism of brands. Existing models of brand equity (e.g., Keller, 1993) emphasize that the ultimate level of brand-building activity is frequently characterized by a deep psychological bond between the customer and the brand (Keh, Pang, & Peng, 2008). The discussions in this chapter highlight the theoretical importance of a brand's cultural symbolism for understanding consumer-brand relationships, as well as provide marketers with an actionable framework for building iconic brands in multicultural markets.

As depicted in Figure 13.1, culturally symbolic brands are unique in the sense that they embody abstract cultural characteristics that can be easily brought to mind upon brand exposure. For marketers, this can be an asset or a liability depending on the context. Because culturally symbolic brands serve a cultural identity function, consumers can establish strong bonds with these brands when cultural identity needs are temporarily or chronically salient. This in turn can help to protect the brand from negative publicity and avoid brand dilution. In addition, abstract cultural images brought to mind by a culturally symbolic brand can facilitate successful brand extensions into new products that are also culturally symbolic, even if these products fall outside the brand's perceived area of expertise. However, a brand's cultural symbolism can also be a liability and elicit unfavorable consumer reactions. That is the case when personal experiences or situational factors heighten perceptions of the brand as a cultural contaminant. This is more likely to occur in the face of intercultural competition, under the presence of bicultural priming, or upon activating a culture defense mindset. As a result, culturally symbolic brands are at a disadvantage when leveraging brand equity through extensions into culturally incongruent products, even when these products fall within the brand's perceived area of expertise.

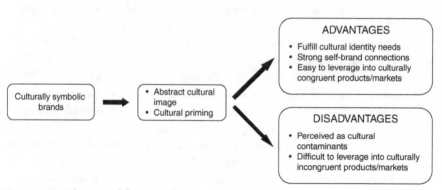

Figure 13.1 Theoretical framework.

Our review suggests that exposure to a culturally symbolic brand can not only activate its associated culture but also trigger the fulfillment of social identity needs. Importantly, these are two different psychological effects that do not need to occur simultaneously. For instance, although people low in cultural identification might not pay attention to a brand's cultural symbolism for their consumer choices, they would still bring to mind the associated cultural representation when exposed to the brand. As a consequence, these consumers would experience the fluency-based effects reported earlier when seeing these brands coupled with other culturally symbolic products. Notably, these effects would occur without triggering social identity needs. These fluency-based effects would also occur among individuals high in cultural identification. However, in this case, the cultural identity needs triggered by the brand could also guide behavior. In certain contexts, these two psychological processes might reinforce each other. For instance, although Americans might evaluate relatively favorably a low fit culturally congruent extension like Nike cola (both the brand and the product are highly symbolic of American culture, but unhealthy colas do not fit Nike's athletic image), those high (versus low) in their identification with American culture might react even more favorably to such extension because it fulfills their chronically salient American identity. Nonetheless, we can also think of situations in which the two psychological forces can oppose each other. For example, although consumers might evaluate relatively favorably a low fit culturally congruent extension like Sony sushi serving set (both the brand and the product are highly symbolic of Japanese culture, but a food serving set does not fit Sony's image), those high (versus low) in their animosity against Japanese culture might react less favorably to such extension. Further investigating the interaction between the fluency- and identity-based processes triggered by exposure to culturally symbolic brands seems a worthy area for future research.

Our review suggests that consumers can develop strong bonds with culturally symbolic brands, and in turn defend these brands from negative publicity when cultural identity needs are salient. However, what would happen when an iconic brand fails in its cultural obligations? As stated earlier, consumers can be critical of the actions from an icon of one's own culture when such actions are perceived to contaminate the culture (e.g., for Americans, Nike's actions to localize their symbols to penetrate Middle Eastern markets). However, this seems more likely to occur when evoking a culture defense mindset, such as that triggered by thoughts of one's own death, which facilitates perceiving such marketing actions as cultural contaminants (Torelli, Chiu, Tam, et al., 2011). These findings suggest that consumers expect culturally symbolic brands to live up to their cultural obligations, which can impose constraints in the kinds of marketing actions that iconic brands can undertake. Further studying failures by iconic brands seems an important research endeavor.

The reactions to culturally symbolic brands documented in this chapter emerged among consumers from East Asian, North American, and South American cultures, which suggests that the importance of cultural symbolism in branding might be a general phenomenon. Furthermore, it is a well-established notion in anthropology that each culture has icons that connect many diverse elements of cultural knowledge (Betsky, 1997; Ortner, 1973). Because iconic brands are cultural icons, it is reasonable to expect that most cultures should have culturally symbolic brands that elicit effects similar to those reported here. However, there might be culture-level variations in the frequency with which these effects emerge in day-to-day consumer decisions. Cultures might vary in the extent to which their members are chronically or temporarily reminded of their cultural identity, which in turn should impact the likelihood of fulfilling cultural identity needs through consumption. For instance, consumer decisions should be more likely to incorporate identity concerns in cultures that foster a stronger level of cultural identification among their members. This might require both a clear notion of what it means to be a group member (i.e., clearly delin- eated in-group–out-group boundaries and widely shared norms and standards of behaviors) as well as a strong sense of pride in group membership. Further exploring these issues seems worthy of research.

The findings reviewed in this chapter have several implications for brand man- agers interested in building iconic brands. As a first step, building a cultural icon requires endowing the brand with abstract characteristics that define the culture. Managers do so by delivering intended communication messages aimed at cre- ating such abstract images. For instance, Harley Davidson (an American icon) continuously strives for communicating the image of freedom and adventure that characterizes American culture. However, because a brand's cultural sym- bolism is the product of social consensus building (Krauss & Fussell, 1996), not all brands that communicate such abstract cultural messages become cultural icons. This level of cultural symbolism is only achieved upon people's consensual interpretation of the abstract meanings carried by these messages in cultural terms (Wan et al., 2010). Further investigating how marketers can promote these consensual interpretations seems a fruitful area for research.

The previous discussion also carries important consequences for managers of global brands operating in multicultural markets. It is a well-known fact that global brands attempting to penetrate a foreign market often succeed by means of adapting their brand communication to match the value priorities in the tar- get market (de Mooij, 2010). This is commonly done by focusing on the broad value dimensions of individualism (i.e., the emphasis on the attainment of values that serve the individual, such as self-direction or power) or collectivism (the emphasis on values that serve the collective, such as concerns for the welfare of others or conformity) (Shavitt, Lalwani, Zhang, & Torelli, 2006; Shavitt et al., 2008; Torelli, Ozsomer, Carvalho, Keh, & Maehle, 2012). Because promoting a brand image that is consistent with culturally defining values facilitates in the process of creating an iconic brand, could a foreign brand imbued with cultural meanings reach the status of a local icon? As stated earlier, country-of-origin associations and a brand's level of cultural symbolism are distinct constructs. With globalization, companies are using multiple countries for sourcing com- ponents and/or assembling products. Moreover, many manufacturers use brand names that suggest language origins dissociated from the brand's true country of origin (Samiee, Shimp, & Sharma, 2005), while others acquire local brands in order to penetrate foreign markets (e.g., Fiat's acquisition of Chrysler brand in the United States). Not surprisingly, consumers' overall ability to identify a brand's country of origin has been shown to be very limited—with overall correct identification rates in the range of 18% to 49% (Balabanis & Diamantopoulos, 2008; Samiee et al., 2005). Thus, we believe that, under certain circumstances, foreign brands can become icons that carry cultural meanings in a foreign culture. This may be more likely to occur when foreign brands imbued with cultural meanings de-emphasize their foreignness and weave themselves within the fabric of the local culture. Some evidence in support of this premise can be found in a study of cultural symbolism among Venezuelan consumers (Torelli, Ozsomer, et al., 2009). In this study, Venezuelan consumers perceived "Heinz" and "Ace" (both American brands with a longstanding presence in the country adopting a "localized" positioning) as higher in cultural symbolism than well-known Venezuelan brands (such as "Mavesa," a very old local brand, or "Movilnet," the largest and government-owned mobile service provider). Another culturally symbolic Venezuelan brand, *Savoy*, is owned by Swiss manufacturer Nestlé, which conspicuously displays its logo in Savoy products. These findings suggest that, at least in developing countries, foreign brands can reach levels of cultural symbolism similar to those of local brands. Because consumers in developing markets have historically being exposed to an inflow of foreign brands, it might be easier for these foreign brands to reach an iconic status in developing markets than the other way around. Further studying these issues seems a fruitful area for research.

When planning global expansions, brand managers might want to pay attention to the cultural similarities between local and foreign markets. To the extent that target culture(s) share the same relevant values (e.g., individualistic values) in both the local and a foreign market, branding professionals may need to do little adjustments to their positioning strategies and still aim at achieving an iconic status in multiple markets. However, an established brand with a strong image that is incompatible with the values symbolized by a target culture may find it difficult to appeal to broader audiences unless it repositions itself. In this context, attempting to turn the brand into a cultural symbol in the target culture would require a departure from the current image (i.e., by embodying the values that are important in the target culture). Because these brand images may be often in conflict with each other (Torelli, Basu-Monga, & Kaikati, 2012), companies may be hesitant to adopt this strategy as it might lead to brand dilution in the markets they currently serve, as well as result in more challenging efforts when coordinating global marketing activities. When the risk for dilution in existing markets outweigh the potential benefits (i.e., gains in market share) from imbuing the brand with novel meanings in the new target culture, the brand manager might opt for keeping the original brand image and try to become an important niche player in the target culture. For example, Harley Davidson is recognized for its consistent brand image of independence and freedom in every country it operates. Although Harley Davidson could be recognized as an iconic brand in America, and perhaps could aspire a similar status in some other countries that are culturally similar like Australia and Canada, it might be difficult for the brand to become a cultural symbol in collectivist countries like Japan or China (where the individualist values associated with Harley Davidson might be in conflict with the collectivist orientation; Torelli, Basu-Monga, et al., 2012; Torelli, Ozsomer, et al., 2012). In these latter countries, the brand might attempt to become a strong niche player by appealing to subcultural segments that endorse individualistic values (e.g., educated young individuals). These are issues worth investigating in the future.

Although most of the discussion in this article refers to cultural groups defined in terms of nationality, we are not advocating that these are the only important variables for studying the cultural meanings of brands. Distinctions among cultural groups can be established by further dividing the human community using any meaningful criteria such as gender, age, class, occupation, or ethnicity (McCracken, 1986), as well as by paying attention to supralevel transnational cultural categories (e.g., Asianness, Cayla & Eckhardt, 2008). Furthermore, because social categories are hierarchically organized (Turner et al., 1987), and given that social identity goals are potential substitutes for one another (Braun & Wicklund, 1989; Wicklund & Gollwitzer, 1981), people can flexibly associate with culturally symbolic brands in a variety of situations. For instance, although both women and men evaluate more favorably brands that symbolize their own gender compared to brands that symbolize the other gender, women evaluate male-symbolic brands that symbolize America more favorably when their American identity is activated than when it is not (Torelli, Chiu, Keh, et al., 2010). That is because both men and women agree that such male-symbolic brands consensually symbolize America, thus they fulfill the salient cultural identity needs triggered by the activation of the superordinate American identity (that both men and women share). In other words, women can move up in their social categorization and connect to brands that fulfill this higher level social identity. Similar effects should be found in other contexts when supralevel identities are salient. For instance, among Latino immigrants in the United States, South Americans (e.g., people from Venezuela or Colombia) are in a minority position relative to Mexicans (Humes et al., 2011). Although South Americans might not perceive that Mexican brands (like Corona) symbolize their own culture, and hence might not be normally inclined to establish strong bonds with such brands, they might connect with these brands when reminded of the common superordinate identity (i.e., Latino) through an advertisement. A similar effect might occur when the heightened need to symbolize the South American identity (as when a South American foreigner is in a bar among a group of European Americans) can be substituted with the symbolizing of the superordinate "Latino" identity (i.e., that includes both South Americans and Mexicans). Further investigating these issues seems worthy.

In summary, the present chapter offers a framework to better understand the impact of the cultural meanings associated with consumer brands on brand perceptions and the fulfillment of identity goals. The discussions here illustrate the theoretical and practical significance of studying the cultural symbolism of brands for further understanding the formation of self-brand connections as well as for developing models of brand management in globalized markets.

REFERENCES

Aaker, J. L., Benet-Martinez, V., & Garolera, J. (2001). Consumption symbols as carriers of culture: A study of Japanese and Spanish brand personality constucts. *Journal of Personality and Social Psychology, 81*, 492–508.

Ahluwalia, R., Burnkrant, R. E., & Unnava, H. R. (2000). Consumer response to negative publicity: The moderating role of commitment. *Journal of Marketing Research, 37*, 203–214.

Allen, M. W. (2002). Human values and product symbolism: Do consumers form product preference by comparing the human values symbolized by a product to the human values that they endorse? *Journal of Applied Social Psychology, 32*, 2475–2501.

Alter, A. L., & Kwan, V. S. (2009). Cultural sharing in a global village: Evidence for extracultural cognition in European Americans. *Journal of Personality and Social Psychology, 96*, 742–760.

Avnet, T., & Higgins, T. E. (2003). Locomotion, assessment, and regulatory fit: Value transfer from "how" to "what". *Journal of Experimental Social Psychology, 39*, 525–530.

Balabanis, G., & Diamantopoulos, A. (2008). Brand origin identification by consumers: A classification perspective. *Journal of International Marketing, 16*, 39–71.

Batra, R., Ramaswamy, V., Alden, D. L., Steenkamp, J.-B., & Ramachander, S. (2000). Effects of brand local and nonlocal origin on consumer attitudes in developing countries. *Journal of Consumer Psychology, 9*, 83–95.

Betsky, A. (1997). *Icons: Magnets of meaning*. San Francisco: Chronicle Books.

Biederman, I. (1995). Visual object recognition. In S. M. Kosslyn & D. N. Osherson (Eds.), *Visual cognition: An invitation to cognitive science* (pp. 121–166). Cambridge, MA: The MIT Press.

Braun, O. L., & Wicklund, R. A. (1989). Psychological antecedents of conspicuous consumption. *Journal of Economic Psychology, 10*, 161–187.

Briley, D. A., Morris, M. W., & Simonson, I. (2005). Cultural chameleons: Biculturals, conformity motives, and decision making. *Journal of Consumer Psychology, 15*, 351–362.

Briley, D. A., & Wyer, R. S., Jr. (2002). The effect of group membership salience on the avoidance of negative outcomes: Implications for social and consumer decisions. *Journal of Consumer Research, 29*, 400–415.

Camacho, C. J., Higgins, T. E., & Luger, L. (2003). Moral value transfer from regulatory fit: What feels right is right and what feels wrong is wrong. *Journal of Personality and Social Psychology, 84*, 498–510.

Cayla, J., & Eckhardt, G. M. (2008). Asian brands and the shaping of a transnational imagined community. *Journal of Consumer Research, 35*, 216–230.

Chen, X., & Chiu, C.-Y. (2010). Rural-urban differences in generation of Chinese and Western exemplary persons: The case of China. *Asian Journal of Social Psychology, 13*, 9–18.

Cheng, S. Y.-y. (2010). Social psychology of globalization: Joint activation of cultures and reactions to foreign cultural influence. *Ph. D Dissertation*, University of Illinois at Urbana-Champaign.

Cheng, S. Y.-y., Rosner, J. L., Chao, M. M., Peng, S., Chen, X., Li, Y., Kwong, J. Y. Y., Hong, Y.-y., & Chiu, C.-Y. (2011). One world, one dream? Intergroup consequences of the 2008 Beijing Olympics. *International Journal of Intercultural Relations*, *35*, 296–306.

Cheng, S. Y.-y., White, T. B., & Chaplin, L. N. (2012). The effects of self-brand connections on responses to brand failure: A new look at the consumer–brand relationship. *Journal of Consumer Psychology*, *22*, 280–288.

Chiu, C.-Y., & Cheng, S. Y.-y. (2007). Toward a social psychology of culture and globalization: Some social cognitive consequences of activating two cultures simultaneously. *Social and Personality Psychology Compass*, *1*, 84–100.

Chiu, C.-Y., & Hong, Y.-Y. (2006). *Social psychology of culture*. New York: Psychology Press.

Chiu, C.-Y., & Hong, Y.-Y. (2007). Cultural processes: Basic principles. In T. E. Higgins & A. W. Kruglanski (Eds.), *Social psychology: Handbook of basic principles* (pp. 785–806). New York: Guilford.

Chiu, C.-Y., Mallorie, L., Keh, H. T., & Law, W. (2009). Perceptions of culture in multicultural space: Joint presentation of images from two cultures increases in-group attribution of culture-typical characteristics. *Journal of Cross-Cultural Psychology*, *40*, 282–300.

de Mooij, M. (2010). *Global Marketing and advertising: Understanding cultural paradoxes* (3rd. Edition). Thousand Oaks: Sage.

Erickson, G. M., Johansson, J. K., & Chao, P. (1984). Image variables in multi-attribute product evaluations: Country-of-origin effects. *Journal of Consumer Research*, *11*, 694–699.

Escalas, J. E.,& Bettman, J. R. (2003). You are what they eat: The influence of reference groups on consumers' connections to brands. *Journal of Consumer Psychology*, *13*, 339–348.

Fang, X., Singh, S., & Ahluwalia, R. (2007). An examination of different explanations for the mere exposure effect. *Journal of Consumer Research*, *34*, 97–103.

Greenberg, J., Porteus, J., Simon, L., & Pyszczynski, T. (1995). Evidence of a terror management function of cultural icons: The effects of mortality salience on the inappropriate use of cherished cultural symbols. *Personality and Social Psychology Bulletin*, *21*, 1221–1228.

Gürhan-Canli, Z., & Maheswaran, D. (2000). Determinants of country-of-origin evaluations. *Journal of Consumer Research*, *27*, 96–108.

Han, S.-p., & Shavitt, S. (1994). Persuasion and culture: Advertising appeals in individualistic and collectivistic societies. *Journal of Experimental Social Psychology*, *30*, 326–350.

Holt, D. B. (2003). How to build an iconic brand. *Market Leader*, 35–42.

Holt, D. B. (2004). *How brands become icons: the principles of cultural branding*. Cambridge, MA: Harvard Business School Press.

Hong, S.-T., & Kang, D. K. (2006). Country-of-origin influences on product evaluations: The impact of animosity and perceptions of industriousness brutality on judgments of typical and atypical products. *Journal of Consumer Psychology*, *16*, 232–239.

Hong, Y.-Y., Chiu, C.-Y., & Kung, T. M. (1997). Bringing Culture Out in Front: Effects of cultural meaning system activation on social cognition. In K. Leung, Y. Kashima, U. Kim & S. Yamaguchi (Eds.), *Progress in Asian Social Psychology* (Vol. 1, pp. 135–146). Singapore: Wiley.

Hong, Y.-Y., Morris, M. W., Chiu, C.-Y., & Benet-Martinez, V. (2000). Multicultural minds: A dynamic constructivist approach to culture and cognition. *American Psychologist, 55,* 709–720.

Humes, K. R., Jones, N. A., & Ramirez, R. R. (2011). Overview of race and Hispanic origin: 2010. *U.S. Census Bureau,* 1–23.

Insko, C. A., & Schopler, J. (1998). Differential distrust of groups and individuals. In C. Sedikides, J. Schopler & C. A. Insko (Eds.), *Intergroup cognition and intergroup behavior* (pp. 75–107). NJ: Lawrence Erlbaum Associates Publishers.

Internet World Stats. (2011). Internet Usage Statistics. In. http://www.internetworld-stats.com.

Johansson, J. K., Douglas, S. P., & Nonaka, I. (1985). Assessing the impact of country of origin on product evaluations: A new methodological perspective. *Journal of Marketing Research, 22,* 388–396.

Keh, H. T., Pang, J., & Peng, S. (2008). Understanding and measuring brand love. In J. R. Priester, D. J. MacInnis & C. W. Park (Eds.), *New frontiers in branding: Attitudes, attachments, and relationships.* Santa Monica, CA: Society for Consumer Psychology.

Keller, K. L. (1993). Conceptualizing, measuring, managing customer-based brand equity. *Journal of Marketing, 57,* 1–22.

Keller, K. L. (2007). *Building, measuring, and managing brand equity* (3rd. ed.). New Jersey: Prentice Hall.

Klein, J. G., Ettenson, R., & Morris, M. D. (1998). The animosity model of foreign product purchase: An empirical test in the People's Republic of China. *Journal of Marketing, 62,* 89–100.

Krauss, R. M., & Fussell, S. R. (1996). Social psychological models of interpersonal communication. In E. T. Higgins & A. W. Kruglanski (Eds.), *Social psychology: Handbook of basic principles* (pp. 655–701). NY: Guilford Press.

LaFromboise, T., Coleman, H. L., & Gerton, J. (1993). Psychological impact of biculturalism: Evidence and theory. *Psychological Bulletin, 114,* 395–412.

Lau-Gesk, L. G. (2003). Activating culture through persuasion appeals: An examination of the bicultural consumer. *Journal of Consumer Psychology, 13,* 301–315.

Lau, I. Y.-m., Chiu, C.-Y., & Lee, S.-l. (2001). Communication and shared reality: Implications for the psychological foundation of culture. *Social Cognition, 19,* 350–371.

Leclerc, F., Schmitt, B. H., & Dubé, L. (1994). Foreign branding and its effects on product perceptions and attitudes. *Journal of Marketing Research, 31,* 263–270.

Lee, A. Y., & Labroo, A. A. (2004). The effect of conceptual and perceptual fluency on brand evaluation. *Journal of Marketing Research, 41,* 151–165.

Leibig, N. K. (2005). Changing landscape for iconic brands. *Brandweek, 46,* 22–23.

Luna, D., Ringberg, T., & Peracchio, L. A. (2008). One individual, two identities: Frame switching among biculturals. *Journal of Consumer Research, 35,* 279–293.

Maheswaran, D., & Shavitt, S. (2000). Issues and new directions in global consumer psychology. *Journal of Consumer Psychology, 9,* 59–66.

McCracken, G. (1986). Culture and consumption: A theoretical account of the structure and movement of the cultural meaning of consumer goods. *Journal of Consumer Research, 13,* 71–84.

McGregor, H. A., Lieberman, J. D., Greenberg, J., Solomon, S., Arndt, J., Simon, L., & Pyszczynski, T. (1998). Terror management and aggression: Evidence that mortality salience motivates aggression against worldview-threatening others. *Journal of Personality and Social Psychology, 74,* 590–605.

Michaels, A. (2009). Muslim Europe: the demographic time bomb transforming our continent *The Telegraph, August 8, 2009.*

Morling, B., & Lamoreaux, M. (2008). Measuring culture outside the head: A meta-analysis of individualism-collectivism in cultural products. *Personality and Social Psychology Review, 12,* 199–221.

Morris, M. W., & Peng, K. (1994). Culture and cause: American and Chinese attributions for social and physical events. *Journal of Personality and Social Psychology, 67,* 949–971.

Ng, S. (2010). Cultural orientation and brand dilution: Impact of motivation level and extension typicality. *Journal of Marketing Research, 47,* 186–198.

Ortner, S. B. (1973). On key symbols. *American Anthropologist, 75,* 1338–1346.

Oyserman, D. (2009). Identity-based motivation: Implications for action-readiness, procedural-readiness, and consumer behavior. *Journal of Consumer Psychology, 19,* 250–260.

Reber, R., Schwarz, N., & Winkielman, P. (2004). Processing fluency and aesthetic pleasure: Is Beauty in the Perceiver's Processing Experience? *Personality and Social Psychology Review, 8,* 364–382.

Robertson, R. (1992). *Globalization: Social theory and global culture.* London: Sage.

Samiee, S., Shimp, T. A., & Sharma, S. (2005). Brand origin recognition accuracy: its antecedents and consumers' cognitive limitations. *Journal of International Business Studies, 36,* 379–397.

Sechrist, G. B., & Stangor, C. (2001). Perceived consensus influences intergroup behavior and stereotype accessibility. *Journal of Personality & Social Psychology, 80,* 645–654.

Shapiro, S. (1999). When an ad's influence is beyond our conscious control: Perceptual and conceptual fluency effects caused by incidental ad exposure. *Journal of Consumer Research, 26,* 16–36.

Shapiro, S., Macinnis, D. J., & Heckler, S. E. (1997). The effects of incidental ad exposure on the formation of consideration sets. *Journal of Consumer Research, 24,* 94–104.

Sharma, S., Shimp, T. A., & Shin, J. (1995). Consumer ethnocentrism: A test of antecedents and moderators. *Journal of the Academy of Marketing Science, 23,* 26–37.

Shavitt, S., Lalwani, A. K., Zhang, J., & Torelli, C. J. (2006). The horizontal/vertical distinction in cross-cultural consumer research. *Journal of Consumer Psychology, 16,* 325–356.

Shavitt, S., Lee, A. Y., & Torelli, C. J. (2008). Cross-Cultural Issues in Consumer Behavior. In M. Wanke (Ed.), *Social Psychology of Consumer Behavior* (pp. 227–250). NY: Psychology Press.

Shavitt, S., Torelli, C. J., & Wong, J. (2009). Identity-based motivation: Constraints and opportunities in consumer research. *Journal of Consumer Psychology, 19,* 261–266.

Shimp, T. A., & Sharma, S. (1987). Consumer Ethnocentrism: Construction and Validation of the CETSCALE. *Journal of Marketing Research, 24,* 280–289.

Shore, B. (2002). Taking culture seriously. *Human Development, 45,* 226–228.

Sperber, D. (1996). *Explaining culture: A naturalistic approach.* Massachusetts: Blackwell.

Stayman, D. M., & Deshpande, R. (1989). Situational ethnicity and consumer behavior. *Journal of Consumer Research, 16,* 361–371.

Steenkamp, J.-B., Batra, R., & Alden, D. L. (2003). How perceived brand globalness creates brand value. *Journal of International Business Studies, 34,* 53–65.

Swaminathan, V., Page, K. L., & Gürhan-Canli, Z. (2007). "My" brand or "our" brand: The effects of brand relationship dimensions and self-construal on brand evaluations. *Journal of Consumer Research, 34,* 248–259.

Torelli, C. J., & Ahluwalia, R. (2009). Cultural symbolism of brands: Effects on the evaluation of brand extensions. *Society for Consumer Psychology 2009 Winter Conference.*

Torelli, C. J., & Ahluwalia, R. (2012). Extending culturally symbolic brands: A blessing or a curse? *Journal of Consumer Research, 38,* 933–947.

Torelli, C. J., Basu-Monga, A., & Kaikati, A. M. (2012). Doing poorly by doing good: Corporate social responsibility and brand concepts. *Journal of Consumer Research, 38,* 948–963.

Torelli, C. J., & Cheng, S. Y.-y. (2011). Cultural meanings of brands and consumption: a window into the cultural psychology of globalization. *Social and Personality Psychology Compass, 5,* 251–262.

Torelli, C. J., Chiu, C.-Y., & Keh, H. T. (2010). Cultural symbolism of brands in globalized economy. *Paper presented at the Global Brand Management Conference,* Istanbul: Turkey.

Torelli, C. J., Chiu, C.-Y., Keh, H. T., & Amaral, N. (2009). Brand Iconicity: A Shared Reality Perspective. *Advances in Consumer Research, 36,* 108–111.

Torelli, C. J., Chiu, C. Y., Keh, H. T., & Amaral, N. (2010). "American = men? Gender and Cultural Dynamics in the Marketing of Male-Symbolic Brands to Women," in Darren W. Dahl, Gita V. Johar, & Stijn M. J. van Osselaer (Eds.), *NA—Advances in Consumer Research,* Volume 38, Duluth, MN: Association for Consumer Research.

Torelli, C. J., Chiu, C.-Y., Tam, K.-p., Au, A. K. C., & Keh, H. T. (2011). Exclusionary reactions to foreign cultures: effects of simultaneous exposure to cultures in globalized space. *Journal of Social Issues, 67,* 716–742.

Torelli, C. J., Keh, H. T., & Chiu, C.-Y. (2010). Cultural symbolism of brands. In B. Loken, R. Ahluwalia & M. J. Houston (Eds.), *Brands and brand management: contemporary research perspectives* (pp. 113–132). New York: Routledge.

Torelli, C. J., Ozsomer, A., Carvalho, S., Keh, H. T., & Maehle, N. (2009). A measure of brand values: cross-cultural implications for brand preferences. *Advances in Consumer Research, 36,* 41–44.

Torelli, C. J., Ozsomer, A., Carvalho, S., Keh, H. T., & Maehle, N. (2012). Brand concepts as representations of human values: Do cultural congruity and compatibility betweeen values matter? *Journal of Marketing, 76*(4), 92–108.

Trafimow, D., Silverman, E. S., Fan, R. M.-T., & Law, J. S. F. (1997). The effects of language and priming on the relative accessibility of the private self and the collective self. *Journal of Cross-Cultural Psychology, 28,* 107–123.

Triandis, H. C. (1989). The self and social behavior in differing cultural contexts. *Psychological Review, 96*, 506–520.

Triandis, H. C. (1995). *Individualism & collectivism*. CO: Westview Press.

Turner, J. C., Hogg, M. A., Oakes, P. J., Reicher, S. D., & Wetherell, M. S. (1987). *Rediscovering the Social Group: A Self-Categorization Theory*. Oxford: Blackwell.

Uleman, J. S., Winborne, W. C., Winter, L., & Shechter, D. (1986). Personality differences in spontaneous personality inferences at encoding. *Journal of Personality and Social Psychology, 51*, 396–403.

Varman, R., & Belk, R. W. (2009). Nationalism and Ideology in an Anticonsumption Movement. *Journal of Consumer Research, 36*, 686–700.

Wan, C., Torelli, C. J., & Chiu, C.-Y. (2010). Intersubjective Consensus and the Maintenance of Normative Shared Reality. *Social Cognition, 28*, 422–446.

Whittlesea, B. W. (1993). Illusions of familiarity. *Journal of Experimental Psychology: Learning, Memory, and Cognition, 19*, 1235–1253.

Wicklund, R. A., & Gollwitzer, P. M. (1981). Symbolic self-completion, attempted influence, and self-deprecation. *Basic and Applied Social Psychology, 2*, 89–114.

Winter, L., & Uleman, J. S. (1984). When are social judgments made? Evidence for the spontaneousness of trait inferences. *Journal of Personality and Social Psychology, 47*, 237–252.

World Travel & Tourism Council. (2011). Travel & Tourism 2011. In. http://www.wttc.org: World Travel & Tourism Council.

Zhang, Y., & Khare, A. (2009). The Impact of Accessible Identities on the Evaluation of Global versus Local Products. *Journal of Consumer Research, 36*, 524–537.

Zou, X. Tam, K.-P., Morris, M. W., Lee, S.-l., Lau, I. Y.-M., & Chiu, C.-Y. (2009). Culture as common sense: Perceived consensus versus personal beliefs as mechanisms of cultural influence. *Journal of Personality and Social Psychology, 97*, 579–597.

PART IV

Culture and Consumption

14

Culture and Materialism

RUSSELL BELK ■

Materialism is a construct that differs both within and between cultures. Not only are there individual and cultural differences in levels of materialism, but the meaning of the construct itself is likely to differ between people and between cultures. In addition, because cultures differ across time as well as space, the intersection of culture and materialism is a moving target. We know that in the current age of globalization and across the broad scope of human history, cultures have influenced one another materially, spiritually, and in their orientations toward life. Consider, for example, the difficulty or impossibility of separating postcolonial cultures from their colonial pasts, much less retrieving an accurate sense of their precolonial cultures. But fortunately the speed and pervasiveness of the current globalization of material culture provides a common denominator for gauging the appeal of certain material practices in different parts of the globe. Thus we might reasonably ask how appealing American television shows and French wines are to consumers in Mumbai and how appealing Bollywood movies and lassi are to consumers in New York and Paris. Appadurai (1996) refers to this global nexus as the social imaginary, and suggests that it involves global flows of people, media, money, technology, and ideas. To this list we should certainly add the global flows of products and services. To decompose material culture into its various manifestations and to superimpose the flows of people, objects, and ideas with diverse global origins and destinations would no doubt provide a detailed and useful understanding of the confluence of materialism and culture. But the task is far too large to attempt here. Instead we need to reduce this complexity by trying to assess general material orientations within individuals, regions, and nations. This we shall call materialism. To aid in making comparisons, it will be useful to focus on a small number of cultural differences including religions, resource distribution, economic conditions, and social conditions.

In this chapter I will first examine the concept of materialism and related constructs. Some of these related constructs are individual traits, values, and behaviors, including acquisitiveness, possessiveness, envy, avarice, compulsive hoarding, and compulsive buying. But others are inherently social, such as keeping up with the Joneses, cultural capital accumulation, social comparison, conspicuous consumption, and status seeking. This leads to a consideration of the various manifestations of materialism at the cultural rather than individual level. Both people and cultures can be materialistic and this tendency can change as the person goes through his or her life and as the culture goes through different historical periods and events. At the cultural level, rather than materialism the comparable terms are consumer culture (e.g., Fox & Lears,1983; Sassatelli, 2007; Slater, 1997), consumer society (e.g., Glickman, 1999; Goodwin, Ackerman, & Kron, 1997; Schor & Holt, 2000), or consumerism (Miles, 1998; Mukerji, 1983; Stearns, 2001). Certain periods are often singled out when cultures become more consumerist. For example the changes in the post-Mao era in China have involved so extensive and rapid a transformation in materialism and related consumption practices that it has been referred to as a consumer revolution (e.g., Davis, 2000; Li, 1998; Wu, 1999).

Like the construct of materialism at the individual level, the concept of consumer culture is often regarded as something quite negative (e.g., Barber, 2007; Kasser, 2002; Schor, 1998), although as we will see, this need not always be the case. Advertising, branding, and marketing are often criticized as being the causes of materialism and consumer culture (e.g., Klein, 2000; Lasn, 1999; Lears, 1994). Because we often see the spiritual and the material as being opposing forces, a special degree of opprobrium is apt to be unleashed when materialistic appeals and marketing mechanisms begin to be applied in promoting religion (e.g., Einstein, 2008; Miller, 2004; Moore, 1994; Twitchell, 2007). Others have objected more generally to the growing array of once seemingly free or innocent things that have been commoditized and offered on the market as additional objects of consumer desire (e.g., Cook, 2004; Radin, 1996; Zelizer, 2005). These too are taken as evidences of the growth of consumer culture.

In what follows I attempt to entertain both positive- and negative-value judgments about materialism and consumer culture, even though the literature is overwhelmingly negative. After examining materialism at an individual and cultural level I will turn to an appraisal of how materialism affects us and whether there are alternatives to becoming ever more materialistic.

INDIVIDUAL MATERIALISM

Meaning and measures of materialism

Ward and Wackman (1971) defined materialism as "an orientation which views material goods and money as important for personal happiness and social progress" (p. 422). They measured such materialism with items such as "It's really true that money can buy happiness," although the full scale was not reported. Csikszentmihalyi and Rochberg-Halton (1981) made a distinction between "terminal materialism" and "instrumental materialism." They describe terminal materialism as "a habit of consumption [as] an end in itself, feeding on its auton-omous necessity to possess more things, to control more status, to use more energy" (pp. 230–231). On the other hand, they describe instrumental mate-rialism as a condition "in which the possession of things serves goals that are independent of greed itself and have a specific limited scope within a context of purposes" (p. 231). It is clear from these definitions that the having orientation of terminal materialism is considered something bad, while the doing orientation of instrumental materialism is regarded as something good. This is roughly con-sistent with Fromm's (1976) discussion of having versus being, but is at variance with the view of Sartre (1943) who maintained that self-scrutiny of what we have is the only way we have of gaining a sense of who we are. Although Fournier & Richins (1991) cite Beaglehole (1932) and other instrumentalists to argue against the possibility of terminal materialism, I have instead argued that the rational consumer is a myth and that a large number of our possessions are valued for non-utilitarian reasons including the memories, self-extension, and magic we associate with them (Belk, 1991).

I began to consider materialism in the 1980s in several ways: in a series of con-ceptual papers focused on acquisitiveness, possessiveness, and collecting (Belk, 1982, 1983a, 1983b), in work investigating materialistic appeals in advertising (Belk & Pollay, 1985a, 1985b), in an effort to develop a scale to measure material-ism (Belk, 1984, 1985), and in considering material imperatives in the context of the American Christmas celebrations (Belk, 1989b, 1993). I measured material-ism as an individual trait, using subscales of acquisitiveness, possessiveness, and envy, and I defined materialism as:

> The importance a consumer attaches to worldly possessions. At the highest levels of materialism, such possessions assume a central place in a person's life and are believed to provide the greatest sources of satisfaction and dis-satisfaction (Belk, 1984, p 291).

Richins and Dawson (1992) developed a more transparent scale of materialism that also involved three components: success (how much people believe that what people own defines their success in life), centrality (how important people think that having luxurious and pleasurable possessions is in life), and happiness (how critical people think that having wealth and possessions is to happiness).

Other scales of materialism and related constructs have also been developed. Kasser and Ryan (1993) developed a scale to measure aspirations for financial success and subsequently revised it to also measure aspirations for social recog-nition and an appealing appearance (Kasser & Ryan, 1996). Cohen and Cohen (1996) developed a measure of materialistic values that involved reports of admiring those with expensive possessions, those who wear expensive clothes, and those who are pretty or handsome. Moschis and Churchill (1978) report a materialism scale for use with children and adolescents that involves attitudes toward possessions and money. Goldberg, Gorn, Peracchio, and Bamossy (2003) developed a "youth materialism scale" that is likewise intended for work with children and adolescents. They also developed a "parent materialism scale." Schor (2004) reports a "consumer involvement" scale for use with children, with items involving the importance of possessions, money, and brands, but reliability and validity data are not reported. Ronald Inglehart (1977, 1981) uses a different approach to measuring materialism using Euro-monitor questions asking people to prioritize what they think should be the aims of governments (e.g., focus on better security rather than higher wages).

Some attempt has also been made to refine materialism measurements to be more applicable across cultures. Ger and Belk (1990; 1996) revised the Belk (1985) materialism scales to be more usable across cultures. For example, items with culture-specific referents like borrowing a neighbor's lawnmower rather than buying one were omitted, while items related to tangibilization (e.g., I have a lot of souvenirs) were added. Still the results were less robust than desirable. Work with the Richins and Dawson (1992) scale in Asia, suggests that the scale's reverse wording provides measurement confounds (Wong, Rindfleisch, & Burroughs, 2003). Nevertheless, this has not stopped quantitative investigations of materialism in such non-North American cultures as Romania, India, Hong Kong, Japan, Singapore, Korea, Ukraine, Croatia, Iceland, Turkey, Thailand, Niger, and Northern European countries (e.g., Dawson & Bamossy, 1991; Dittmar, 1992, 2008; Ger & Belk, 1990, 1996; Wallendorf & Arnould, 1988; Wong et al., 2003). Qualitative investigation across cultures (Ger & Belk 1999) found that there are culture-specific ways in which materialism is understood (e.g., individually in the United States or in terms of family in Turkey) that reduce or prohibit the chances of creating a culturally universal measure of the construct. All those in the Ger and Belk (1999) study condemned materialism in the abstract as being shallow, unfulfilling, and selfish. Yet almost all went on to say that they would like a higher salary, a bigger house, a newer car, and so forth. Different cultures found different ways to justify these seeming inconsistencies. Those in the United States and Romania both said they deserved these things, but in the United States deservingness was based on hard work, while in Romania it was based on years of material deprivation under Ceausescu. Turks explained that they wanted things like colored televisions not for themselves, but for their children who would otherwise feel deprived relative to their peers. and Northern Europeans said it was the Americans who were the materialists because they spent their money on "stupid gadgets," while they themselves knew how to spend their money on worthwhile things like travel, art, and good food and wine, which they explained was not really materialistic at all. Given such complexities, it seems that materialism is likely best studied qualitatively, but there is very little research of this sort.

Although the materialism scales of Belk (1985) and Richins and Dawson (1992) have been the most heavily used in consumer research, both have been criticized either for having low reliability or as being reflections of other variables like social desirability or neuroticism (e.g., Mick, 1996; Solberg, Diener, & Robinson, 2004). Nevertheless, the correlation of these scales with each other and with criterion variables, suggests that they are measuring something meaningful regarding materialism.

Cultural comparisons and influences on materialism

Ger and Belk (1990, 1996) measured materialism in the United States, Sweden, Germany, Romania, Ukraine, India, Turkey, and New Zealand, in the late 1980s and in 1991 after the fall of communism in Eastern and Central Europe. The lowest levels of materialism were found in India, Sweden, and pre-unification Germany. In India a relatively fixed social class system at the time was likely more important in accounting for low materialism scores than the religious composition of the country, and in Sweden and Germany the social democratic governmental systems of the time made for relatively flat income distributions that also probably curbed materialistic aspirations. More surprisingly, the study found the highest levels of materialism in Romania and Ukraine, which we attributed to the social and economic turmoil and uncertainty that occurred following the collapse of communism and the new opportunities for status mobility that it provided. This interpretation was supported by the rise in materialism following reunification in Berlin and the higher levels of materialism there than elsewhere in Europe at the time. In this interpretation, when status is more fluid, people turn to material "marker goods" (Douglas & Isherwood, 1979) in an effort to claim a higher status position. An alternative interpretation would be that materialistic tendencies may increase in order to shore up feelings of self-worth in the face of uncertainty (Kasser, Ryan, Couchman, & Sheldon, 2004; Rindfleisch, Burroughs, & Wong, 2009). A still more extreme interpretation couched in Terror Management Theory is that we turn to materialism when thoughts of our mortality increase in an effort to deny death (e.g., Rindfleisch et al., 2009; Solomon, Greenberg, & Pysyczynski, 2004). But the devastating natural experiment of the 9-11 attacks and the subsequent decline of purchasing despite the encouragements of the US President and the UK Prime Minister to go out and buy, challenge this hypothesis as does work in an African context (Bonsu & Belk, 2003).

Inglehart measured materialism by having people prioritize their concern with: (a) maintaining order in the nation; (b) giving people more say in important political decisions; (c) fighting rising prices; (d) protecting freedom of speech. Those ranking the first and third values of order and low inflation highest are judged as most materialistic. Using Inglehart's measures of materialism, Abrahamson and Inglehart (1995) concluded that people in poorer countries are more materialistic than people in richer countries, although Ger and Belk's (1996) data challenge this generalization. Likewise Lindstrom's (2003) survey of global adolescents in eight countries found that the United States and India tied for the highest percentage (75%) who endorsed a statement that they wanted to be rich as a primary goal in life. However, using a combination of prior materialism scale items that were closest to Richins and Dawson's (1992) scale of materialism, Webster and Beatty (1997) did find that Thai consumers were indeed more materialistic than US consumers. Their data were collected just before the Thai Bhat collapsed during what was a heady period of economic growth for Thailand, further supporting the hypothesis that materialism increases during periods of increased social mobility.

Inglehart's measure of materialism is quite different from other measures of materialism, and his predictions have received only partial and often weak support. His major hypothesis is that countries with lower per capita incomes should be focused on satisfying lower order needs from Maslow's need hierarchy, and should thus be more materialistic than more affluent "postmaterialistic" countries. Measuring postmaterialists as those who value order and fighting inflation over political voice and freedom of speech, produced the following partial ordering of the proportion of postmaterialists by country using data from 2000: Australia (35%), Austria (30%), Canada (29%), Italy (28%), Argentina (25%), United States (25%), Sweden (22%), Netherlands (22%), and Puerto Rico (22%) (Inglehart, Basáñez, Díez-Medrano, Halmann, & Luijkx, 2004, p. 384). Postsocialist countries like Russia, Bulgaria, Hungary, and Estonia tended to be among the least postmaterialistic countries (i.e., the most materialistic) according to these measures.

Exposure to advertising, general media influence, parenting, and peer influence are other factors that have been found to affect materialism. For example, greater television viewing by children was found to be associated with higher materialism scores among these children, except in families that had strong communication patterns with their child (Moschis & Moore, 1982). Schor (2004) also found that the amount of television use is positively related to materialism as measured using her consumer involvement scale, but she also found that use of other media (e.g., videos, computers, video games) was an even stronger predictor. Richins (1992, 1995) found that more materialistic people are more likely to compare themselves to media images of celebrities and rich people, suggesting one possible reason for the correlations between media use and materialism. While such "stars" were once considered not to be objects of envy because of their extreme wealth, there is some evidence that they are now becoming objects of "benign envy" whom we try to emulate (Belk, 2011c). Gerbner's cultivation theory (Gerbner & Gross, 1976; Gerbner, Gross, Morgan, & Signorelli, 1980) suggests that those who watch more television will overestimate patterns such as the amount of crime, luxury, and wealth that is present in society. Studies in consumer research have found support for this prediction (e.g., Fox & Philliber, 1978; O'Guinn & Shrum, 1997; Shrum, O'Guinn, Semenik, & Faber, 1991; Shrum, Burroughs, & Rindfleisch, 2005), which offers a further reason for the relationship between media use and materialism.

Goldberg et al. (2003) found that children of more materialistic parents tend to be more materialistic themselves, as did Kasser, Ryan, Zax, and Sameroff (1995). Children whose parents had divorced have also been found to be more prone to materialism (Rindfleisch, Burroughs, & Denton, 1997), as are those from homes where possessions were stressed as a route to happiness (Roberts, Manolis, & Tanner, 2003). Kasser et al. (1995) report that teenagers with less nurturing mothers tended to be more materialistic, and Schor (2004) found that children who are more materialistic tend to fight or disagree with their parents more often about media use and purchases.

But peer influence is also important. In Lindstrom's (2003) survey of teens and preteens, American children were most likely to cite their clothes and the branded goods they owned as being keys to their identity and social status. Ritson and Elliott (1999) found that knowledge of current advertising was critical to being able to communicate with peers in a British high school. Wooten (2006) found that young, primarily African-American, men used ridicule to embarrass peers who did not wear locally popular brands of clothing. Banerjee and Dittmar (2008a) found that those adolescents who are less popular with their peers are more materialistic, evidently in an effort to garner peer acceptance based on what they have and due to enhanced perceptions of peer group pressure. This is consistent with Kasser et al. (2004) who provide evidence that feelings of insecurity are a major determinant of materialism. However, in testing Inglehart's (1981) theory that feelings of economic deprivation in childhood would result in greater levels of adult materialism, Ahuvia and Wong (1995) found a distinct lack of support for this hypothesis. This need not mean that insecurity is unrelated to childhood materialism, however. A major source of insecurity in childhood is peer acceptance based on judgments of a child's "coolness." "Coolness" is a measure of child and adolescent peer popularity and status and it is increasingly linked to the possession of expensive brands and possessions according to studies in North America and Europe (Banerjee & Dittmar, 2008b; Belk, 2006, 2010; Nairn & Griffith, 2007; Schor, 2004). Comparable notions of coolness exist among adolescents in Japan (Otacool, 2010) and Taiwan (Call Me!, 2005), and it seems likely that material notions of coolness are globalizing (Belk, Tian, & Paavola, 2010).

Related constructs and behaviors

There is some evidence that those who place greater value on their relationships with material things tend to place less value on their human relationships (Kasser & Ryan, 1993). Their relationships with others are shorter, they exhibit more conflict and aggression in these relationships, and they show a lower degree of trust (Kasser & Ryan, 2001). They are more likely to compete with others than to cooperate with them (Sheldon, Sheldon, & Osbaldiston, 2000), at least as suggested by creating a prisoner's dilemma in a laboratory situation. However, this perspective of seeing the world as a limited good society or zero-sum game is not culturally universal and may be relatively rare in contemporary societies (Foster, 1969; Belk, 2010).

O'Guinn and Faber (1989) found that compulsive buyers were more likely to be materialistic and scored especially high on the envy and nongenerosity components of the Belk (1985) measure of materialism. Dittmar (2005) found similar results using the Richins and Dawson (1992) scale. Although studies suggest that as many as 90% of compulsive buyers are women, Dittmar (2008) believes that the incidence of female buying compulsivity is overestimated due to sampling biases and that among young adults there is more male–female balance in this tendency. Faber (2004), on the other hand, suggests that women are socialized into shopping and may therefore experience problems in this realm, while men are socialized into aggression and gambling and are more likely to experience their own impulse control disorders in these realms. There is also some evidence that compulsive hoarders tend to be more materialistic (Frost & Steketee, 2010). The link here may well be because both materialism and hoarding can be obsessive–compulsive behaviors like compulsive gambling, overeating, and alcoholism. There is often a positive link between these various compulsive tendencies. For example, Faber (2000) reports that the most frequently reported cue to compulsive shopping is feeling overweight. Both buying and hoarding behaviors are relatively new entrants into clinical diagnosis and both can have an extremely disruptive effect on life, leading to problems of debt, feelings of insecurity, isolation, divorce, and various family problems. However, one key difference between most materialists and compulsive hoarders is also noted by Frost and Steketee (2010). Whereas materialists are apt to conspicuously display their material acquisitions out of pride and a desire to show off, compulsive hoarders are apt to hide their trove of possessions out of shame. There is no status to be found in hoarding; in fact just the opposite—the out-of-control possessiveness of hoarders is a major social stigma.

As might be expected given that one component of materialism is non-generosity (Belk, 1985), materialistic people are less willing to share with others. They also report feeling less empathy with others (Sheldon & Kasser, 1995) and place less value on affiliation with others (Kasser & Ryan, 1993). Materialistic people display a greater tendency toward Machiavellianism (McHoskey, 1999). Selfish as these correlates are, those scoring high on materialism also report lower self-esteem than less materialistic people (Kasser & Ryan, 1996).

Summary of individual materialism findings

Over more than 25 years of research on materialism as an individual difference, we have begun to learn a few things. Regardless of whether it is conceived of as a personality trait or a value, materialism is an important reality among contemporary consumers. While this the case in more affluent societies such those of North America and Northern Europe, it is, if anything, a stronger force in rapidly developing less affluent societies. There is some evidence that materialism increases in times and places of economic disruption and uncertainty. German reunification, the fall of European communism, and the rise of market capitalism in China and India are all cases in point, some of which will be examined in the next section. Materialism appears to involve undervaluing people and overvaluing things. Greater media consumption is also associated with greater materialism. But childhood parenting and peer experiences mediate the impact of media and advertising in inculcating materialistic desires. Compulsive buying and perhaps compulsive hoarding appear to be related to materialism. For adults pursuing conspicuous materialistic desires appears to be an effort to shore up low self-esteem, while for children materialistic tendencies seem directed toward trying to be cool, especially through consumption. In the next section I pursue these and other insights from a more societal perspective by looking at research and theory focused on the growth of consumer culture.

CONSUMER CULTURE: CULTURAL ASPECTS OF MATERIALISM

Historical changes in consumer culture

Although consumer culture is the counterpart of materialism at a more aggregate societal level, it is defined in quite different terms. Rassuli and Hollander (1986) suggest that four conditions must be met in order to qualify as a consumer culture: (a) a substantial portion of the population consume at a level that is considerably above the subsistence level; (b) exchange rather than self-production is the major source of consumer goods; (c) consumption is regarded as appropriate and desirable; and (d) people judge other people as well as themselves in terms of their consumption lifestyles. The first condition would seem to rule out much of the less affluent world, but it seems to be based upon a false belief in the Maslow (1954) hierarchy of needs model which suggests that consumers satisfy lower order needs like hunger and safety before moving on to higher-order needs like love, self-esteem, and self-actualization. There are counter-evidences to this hierarchy when consumers sacrifice "necessities" in order to afford "luxuries." For example, consumers in poor countries have been found to reduce their food consumption in order to afford a status-conveying refrigerator; nonfunctioning television antennas have been put up on favelas without electricity; and peasants have been found to sell their cows in order to buy candy for the children (Belk, 1988; Ger, 1992). Such transpositions of Maslow's hierarchy have been termed "Third World consumer culture" (Belk, 1988) and "leaping luxuries (Belk, 1999). Shrestha (1997) describes the dilemma of the poor in such societies:

> The poor are forced into a situation in which they either have to spend what little money or resources they have on senseless consumer objects rather than basic necessities in order to deflect total social humiliation or face the prospect of being teased and laughed at (p. 26).

Writing in postcommunist Yugoslavia, Draculić (1991) provides another explanation suggesting that there is a category of goods lying between necessities and luxuries that might best be labelled decencies:

> What is the minimum you must have so you don't feel humiliated as a woman? It makes me understand a complaint I heard repeatedly from

women in Warsaw, Budapest, Prague, Sofia, East Berlin: 'Look at us—we don't even look like women. There are no deodorants, no perfumes, sometimes even no soap or toothpaste. There is no fine underwear, no pantyhose, no nice lingerie. Worst of all, there are no sanitary napkins.' What can one say except that it is humiliating (p. 31)?

Other definitions of consumer culture incorporate some of these concerns by stressing that in a consumer culture our identity is tied up in the things we possess. For example, Stearns (2002) defines consumer culture as:

> A society in which many people formulate their goals in life partly through acquiring goods that they clearly do not need for subsistence or for traditional display. They become enmeshed in the process of acquisition—shopping—and take some of their identity from a procession of new items they buy and exhibit (p. ix).

Slater (1997) stipulates that a consumer culture is based on market-based capitalism, a system that produces unlimited desires, and one where status, identity, values, ideas, and aspirations are tied to the consumption of branded signs. This addition of status considerations is useful, but just as the definition of Rassuli and Hollander (1986) was found to be too restrictive, I question whether market-based capitalism is strictly necessary. There is ample evidence that consumers in the former Soviet Union and Eastern Europe were enticed by the status of having Western goods and knowledge of Western music, films, and popular culture, all before the collapse of communism (e.g., Bar-Haim, 1987, 1989; Kohak, 1992; Kozminski, 1992; Marling, 1994; Ostaszewski, 1992). Finally, Schudson's (1984) definition of consumer culture comes closer to definitions of materialism by emphasizing the sign character of goods rather than their mere acquisition and uses. He also takes a negative evaluative position in defining consumer culture as:

> A society in which human values have been grotesquely distorted so that commodities become more important than people, or, in an alternative formulation, commodities become not ends in themselves but overvalued means for acquiring acceptable ends like love and friendship (p 16).

There is an inversion here of Ciskszentmihalyi and Rochberg-Halton's definitions of terminal and instrumental materialism, in that the instrumental goals no longer have to do with doing states, but rather serve in a "grotesque" attempt to purchase human connections.

The consumer culture approach to materialism generally takes a more qualitative, historical, and cultural perspective rather than the more micropsychological approach of those studying materialism. For example, Schama (1987) analyzed how the rapid influx of money into the Netherlands in the seventeenth century when it became the shipping and finance center of the world, together with an influx of novel consumer objects from the New World, helped make it one of the world's first consumer cultures. He shows how the new wealth was expended on housing, furnishings, art, clothing, and fads like the tulip craze in which some bulbs cost as much as a house. The resulting uneasiness with such new consumption in a staunchly Calvinist society is displayed in Dutch art of the era including sumptuous still life paintings (Schneider, 1994), satirical paintings like those of Jan Steen (Chapman, Kloek, & Wheelock, 1996), and in the *memento mori* paintings that remind the viewer of the brevity of life (Bryson, 1990; North, 1997; Westermann, 1996). There is some controversy around the interpretation of just how much discomfort the Dutch actually felt, but by drawing on a variety of other historical sources, Schama (1987) is able to fill in a compelling portrait of the consumer culture of the Golden Age in Holland. For example, despite the ostensibly pious fashion for men to wear black fustian clothing from head to toe, conspicuous consumption was nevertheless accomplished through gold and silver buttons, fine stitchery, and elegant Belgian lace collars. Something similar appears to be happening today among the women of the Arab Gulf who remain ostensibly modestly covered in black from head to toe, but are nevertheless introducing touches of luxury through designer abayas, fine embroidery, brand name watches, sunglasses, and shoes, and Swarovski jewels decorating the outside of their abaya garments which cost hundreds and thousands of US dollars each and which may be part of a wardrobe of fifty or more such coverings, even though they go out of style within a few months (Sobh, Belk, & Gressel, 2010). In addition, beneath their abayas, these young women often wear fine designer brand Western clothing. At gender-segregated wedding receptions and other gatherings women often wear transparent abayas to show off their Western clothing to other women. The current trend is to hide less and less of the expensive clothing and accessories beneath the abayas when in public (Sobh & Belk, 2011).

As noted earlier, another recent historical time and place leading to consumer cultures involves the change from communism to capitalism in Eastern and Central Europe in the late 1980s and early 1990s. It appears that countries closer to Western Europe (e.g., Hungary) were able to transform to capitalist consumption patterns more quickly and less flamboyantly than more Eastern European countries where the change was more severe (Belk, 1997; Belk, Ger, & Lascu, 1993). The more eastern countries exhibited something similar to the stereotypically gauche behavior of nouveaux riches. However, all formerly Communist European countries experienced a rise of consumer culture as consumers suddenly had access to Western goods and media, freedom of the press, and for some, a substantial rise in income (e.g., Barker, 1999; Belk, 1997; Draculić, 1991; Drazin, 2001; Lovell, 2002; Neidhart, 2003). These revolutionary times and places remain a natural laboratory in which to study the rise of consumer culture and its impact on the people and the culture.

China's consumer culture

China is another such "laboratory" of consumer culture that has received schol-arly attention. Such attention has focused not only on contemporary post-Mao China, but also on China's earlier brush with consumer culture in its precom-munist "treaty port" cities, in particular Shanghai (e.g., Cochran, 2006; Dikötter, 2006; Gerth, 2003). One of the concerns in this earlier period was with the rapid adoption of foreign brands from the West and Japan, both of which were seen as imperialist invaders at the time. Although it was local Shanghai merchants who were selling these goods, they nevertheless advertised that they were patriotic in their support of national campaigns stressing buying local goods and rejecting the foreign (Zhao & Belk, 2008a). The "culprits" in the worship of foreign goods and the adoption of new consumer lifestyles were held to be women and it is women who were castigated in the press and popular discourse. The "modern girl" was singled out as an emblem of all that was bad about consumer culture (e.g., Bong, Tong, Ying, & Lo, 1996; Dong, 2008; Finnane, 2008; Hung, Li, & Belk, 2007; Jackson, 2005). But just as gender estimates of compulsive buyers may be biased toward women, so quite likely are the gendered criticisms of con-sumer culture in old Shanghai. In any case, this gendered criticism was rendered null and void in the decidedly nonconsumer culture of communist China, with its gender-neutral job practices and the unisex Sun Yat-sen outfits during the Cultural Revolution (Jackson, 2005; Roberts, 1997).

Post-Mao contemporary China has also received increasing attention as an emerging consumer culture. Although China is still officially a communist state, advertisers and marketers have found clever ways to invoke the symbols and ide-ological jargon of communism in order to sell products and advance consumer culture within "market socialism" (Zhao & Belk, 2008b). It is not the case that there was no consumer desire under the earlier communist China before Deng's reforms of 1978. But the "three bigs" of the 1960s and 1970s were simply a bicycle, a sewing machine, and a wrist watch (Croll, 2006). By the 1980s these desiderata had become a color television, refrigerator, and washing machine, and by the 1990s telephones (or cell phones), air conditioners, stereos, VCRs, and micro-waves were the new must-haves (Belk, 1989a; Croll, 2006; Tse, Belk, & Zhou, 1989). During the early 1980s there were still periodic government purity cam-paigns waged against the "spiritual pollution" of Western goods in China, but by the mid-1980s government propaganda banners glorifying the Chinese worker were being replaced by other banners championing the consumer and trumpet-ing new slogans like "To get rich is glorious" (Schell, 1984). Today, luxury goods makers of the world are eagerly anticipating that China will become their larg-est market. The proportion of Chinese who participate in the luxury market is debated (Chadha & Husband, 2006; Lu, 2008; Wang, 2008), but with 1.3 billion people even 5% represents a huge market.

Compared to the contested rise of consumer culture in Old Shanghai, after the waves of periodic government backtracking in the early 1980s and since the Tiananmen Square crackdown in 1989, the rise of China's economy and the rise of consumer culture have grown simultaneously and with little official opposition. There is concern elsewhere, however. A significant part of the new Chinese art movement, sometimes called cynical realism, is devoted to a critique of emerging Chinese consumer culture (e.g., Mallet, Artsi, Zi, Hongmei, & Hui, 2008; Ilan, Yun, & DuPriest, 2010). In works like those of the Luo Brothers and Wang Guangyi, iconic Chinese New Year babies (*nianhua*) are shown holding Big Mac hamburgers, cans or bottles of Coca-Cola and Pepsi Cola, and boxes of Pizza Hut pizzas. These are telling targets in light of the dramatic increase in obesity in China, due to both the influx of global junk foods and the one-child policy in China that has led to pampering and catering to the wishes of these only children (e.g., Davis& Sensenbrenner, 2000; Farquhar, 2002; Jing, 2000).

Materialistic places

Although the study of other consumer cultures like those of India, the Middle East, and Africa has begun (e.g., Mazzarella, 2003; Rajagopal, 2001; Stearns, 2001), the most concentrated research has focused on the United States, the United Kingdom, and several other European countries (e.g., Brewer & Porter, 1993; Cohen, 2003; Cross, 2000; Matt, 2003; Strasser, McGovern, & Judt, 1998; Twitchell, 1999). Rapidly developing economies like China, India, Brazil, Russia, and Indonesia may prove especially interesting to study. Just as individuals may behave in a materialistic way, so may nations, regions, and municipalities. This is beyond simply being a consumer culture, which refers to a culture with many materialistic consumers. Rather it refers to materialistic and conspicuous consumption by a nation, state, city, or other governmental entity. Similarly to the way we might stereotype the conspicuous consumption of nouveau riche consumers, we can see conspicuous consumption by nouveau riche nations. They build such lavish monuments to themselves such as luxurious national airlines, monumental national and commerical buildings, spectacular Olympic, World Cup, and regional athletic venues, and so forth. Consider, for example, the efforts of Dubai's Sheikh Mohammed al-Maktoum to build a city of superlatives:

Dubai has already surpassed that other desert arcade of capitalist desire, Las Vegas, both in sheer scale of spectacle and the profligate consumption of water and power. . .The biggest project, Dubailand, represents. . .forty-five major "world-class" projects [including] replicas of the Hanging Gardens of Babylon, the Taj Mahal, and the Pyramids, as well as a snow mountain with ski lifts and polar bears, a center for extreme sports, a Nubian village, Eco-Tourism World, a vast Andalusian spa and wellness complex, golf courses, autodromes, race tracks, Fantasia, the largest zoo in the Middle East, several new five-star hotels, a modern art gallery, and the Mall of Arabia. . .al Maktoum has a distinctive and inviolable criterion: everything must be "world class," by which he means number one in the *Guinness Book of Records*. Thus Dubai is building the world's largest theme-park, the biggest mall (and within it, the largest aquarium), the tallest building, the largest international airport, the biggest artificial island, the first sunken hotel, and so on (Davis, 2007, pp. 50–52).

Eclipsing the month of Ramadan in Dubai is the month-long Dubai Shopping Festival as well as a world-class tennis tournament, the world's richest horse race, the world's richest golf tournament, and much more (Junemo, 2004). The global financial crisis of 2008 has slowed, but not stopped this development. As might be expected there is a potential relationship between such civic ostentation and individual consumer ostentation within Dubai. As Junemo (2004) reports, "In Dubai this phenomenon even has a name, "Jumeirah Jane," describing the affluent Western women with a consumer lifestyle represented by mobile phone, sunglasses, a four wheel-drive car, and color-coordinated outfits" (p. 190). The Jumeirah name here refers to the Palm Jumeirah artificial island shaped like a palm tree and containing 2000 homes and many luxury hotels. Together with a second palm island, Palm Jebel Ali, these megadevelopments are adding 120 kilometers to Dubai's coastline.

DISCUSSION AND DIRECTIONS FOR FUTURE RESEARCH

As Wuthnow (1994) observed, we have stopped blaming the devil for all of the ills in life and have started blaming materialism. Studies converge on the conclusion that materialism, by all existing measures, is related to lower perceptions of well-being and greater perceptions of unhappiness. Although causal links for the associations found between materialism and unhappiness are unclear (Burroughs & Rindfleisch, 2002; Solberg et al., 2004), it is clear that Csikszentmihalyi and Rochberg-Halton's (1981) notion of a good (instrumental) materialism has not been considered in the literature on materialism. It may be possible to envision a relationship with material goods that is positive and leads to greater happiness, satisfaction, and well-being (Punset, 2007). For this to happen, the phenomenon of possessiveness needs to be separated from consumer object attachment (Belk, 1992; Kleine & Baker, 2004). In this case attachment to the things we own can mean holding onto them longer and more strongly, such that our disposable society tendency is lessened. If we keep our cars longer, wear our clothes longer, replace our furniture less often, and remodel or redecorate our homes less frequently, we would be enacting a positive type of materialism. Paraphrasing George Santayana, McClay (1995) observes that "American materialism is often really a strange form of idealism in which the things of this world, rather than being savoured for their intrinsic worth, are regarded as spiritual trophies" (p. 68). If so, we just might learn to embrace our success without feeling the necessity to keep proving our successfulness to ourselves with the latest trophies from the marketplace. We might learn to value things for their own sake and develop more faithful relationships with these things rather than quest for ever more trophies. These are areas that seem especially critical for future research as we recognize the increased ecological damage done by rampant consumption.

Collectors may offer an illustration of the difficulties of assessing the impact of materialism as well as in deciding just what is and is not materialistic (Belk, 1998, 2004). While collectors may seem materialistic in their passionate pursuit of nonessential goods, their devotion to their collections can be self-transcending and involve sacrifices as well as lavishing great care on these special possessions. Assessing materialism across cultures will also need to deal with these difficulties in deciding what is materialistic in different cultures and how its impact should be assessed.

A totally opposite perspective from becoming more attached to our possessions as a way to reduce materialism, is to become less attached to them. This is part of the Buddhist doctrine of nonattachment (Badiner, 2002; Belk, 2011a; Kaza, 2005; Rosenberg, 2004). One enactment of nonattachment is the growing sharing movement (Belk, 2010; Belk & Llamas, 2012; Botsman & Rogers, 2010; Orsi & Doskow, 2009). Besides reducing our environmental footprint, sharing fosters human connections, getting to know neighbors, and cooperating rather than competing. Hundreds of sharing organizations such as Sharability (www.sharability.org) and Neighborrow (www.neighborrow.com) are beginning to flourish as practical ways to build neighborhoods and reduce duplicate ownership. Others like the popular Couchsurfing (http://www.couchsurfing.org/) provide places to stay for free when traveling. and still others like Freecycle, ReUseIt, SwapTree, ToySwap, Landshare, Urban Gardenshare, Clothing Exchange, community-supported agriculture (CSAs), Skillshare, and many others, offer a variety of goods and services to share. Thanks to the Internet, we are rediscovering a sense of human community that has been all but lost (Belk, 2011b). Possessions are often a burden (Hammerslough, 2001) and sharing just may relieve us of some of this burden. The role of the Internet in facilitating sharing is just beginning to be researched and is also an important area for future research.

In a series of experiments, Tomasello (2009) demonstrates that starting at about age one, infants have an apparently natural tendency to cooperate by pointing to things that adults are looking for, sharing food, and expressing empathic concern with victims of property theft. What is more, the over justification of rewarding such behaviors tends to extinguish them, suggesting that these are innate rather than learned tendencies. It is only when they later encounter selfishness that children begin to gear their helpfulness and cooperation to their expectations of trust and reciprocity. This suggests that we have an innate tendency to cooperate and share, and it offers some hope for building communal identity and an aggregate sense of self through sharing rather than building individual identity through materialism.

In this chapter I have identified a number of factors that need to be considered in any effort to reduce individual, corporate, and cultural materialism. They include religion, social factors, cultural differences, economic conditions, resource distribution, childhood socialization, and individual difference factors. Each of these areas will benefit for future research considering the interaction of culture and materialism.

REFERENCES

Abrahamson, P. R., & Inglehart, R. (1995). *Value change in global perspective*. Ann Arbor, MI: University of Michigan Press.

Ahuvia, A., & Wong, N. (1995). Materialism: origins and implications for personal well-being. *European Advances in Consumer Research, 2*, 172–178.

Appadurai, A. (1996). *Modernity at large*. Minneapolis, MN: University of Minnesota Press.

Badiner, A. H. (Ed.). (2002). *Mindfulness in the marketplace: Compassionate responses to consumerism*. Berkeley, CA: Parallax Press.

Banerjee, R., & Dittmar, H. (2008a). Individual differences in children's materialism: The role of peer relations. *Personality and Social Psychology Bulletin, 34*(1), 17–31.

Banerjee, R., & Dittmar, H. (2008b). What is beautiful and who is 'cool'? In H. Dittmar (Ed.), *Consumer culture and socialization* (pp. 173–197), East Sussex, UK: Psychology Press.

Bar-Haim, G. (1987). The meaning of Western commercial artifacts for Eastern European youth. *Journal of Contemporary Ethnography, 16*(2), 205–226.

Bar-Haim, G. (1989). Actions and heroes: The meaning of Western pop information for eastern european youth. *The British Journal of Sociology, 40*(1), 22–45.

Barber, B. R. (2007). *Consumed: How markets corrupt children, infantilize adults, and swallow citizens whole*. New York, NY, USA: W. W. Norton.

Barker, A. M. (1999). Going to the dogs: Pet life in the new Russia. In A. M. Barker (Ed.), *Consuming Russia: Popular culture, sex, and society since Gorbachev* (pp. 266–277). Durham, NC, USA: Duke University Press.

Beaglehole, E. (1932). *Property: A study in social psychology*. New York, NY, USA: Macmillan.

Belk, R. W. (1982). Acquiring, possessing, and collecting: Fundamental processes in consumer behavior. In R. F. Bush & S. D. Hunt (Eds.), *Marketing theory: Philosophy of science perspectives* (pp. 185–190). Chicago, IL, USA: American Marketing Association.

Belk, R. W. (1983a). Acquisitiveness and possessiveness: Criticisms and issues. In M. B. Mazis (Ed.), *Proceedings, 1982 Annual Convention of the American Psychological Association Division of Consumer Psychology* (pp. 70–73). Washington, DC: American Psychological Association, Division 23.

Belk, R. W. (1983b). Worldly possessions: Issues and criticisms. In R. P. Bagozzi & A. M. Tybout (Eds.), *Advances in consumer research* (Vol. 10, pp. 514–519). Ann Arbor, MI, USA: Association for Consumer Research.

Belk, R. W. (1984). Three scales to measure constructs related to materialism: Reliability, validity, and relationships to measures of happiness. In T. Kinnear (Ed.), *Advances in consumer research* (Vol. 11, pp. 291–297). Provo: Association for Consumer Research.

Belk, R. W. (1985). Materialism: Trait aspects of living in the material world. *The Journal of Consumer Research, 12*(3), 265–280.

Belk, R. W. (1988). Third world consumer culture. In E. Kumcu & A. Fuat Firat (Eds.), *Marketing and development: Broader dimensions* (pp. 103–127). Greenwich, CT, USA: JAI Press.

Belk, R. W. (1989a). The benefits and problems of market socialism for Chinese consumers. In T. Childers, et al. (Eds.), *1989 AMA Winter Educators' Conference: Marketing theory and practice* (pp. 355–359). Chicago, IL, USA: American Marketing Association.

Belk, R. W. (1989b). Materialism and the modern U.S. Christmas. In E. Hirschman (Ed.), *Interpretive consumer research* (pp. 136–147). Provo: Association for Consumer Research.

Belk, R. W. (1991). The ineluctable mysteries of possessions. *Journal of Social Behavior and Personality, 6*(June), 17–55.

Belk, R. W. (1992). Attachment to possessions. In I. Altman & S. Low (Eds.), *Human behavior and environment: Advances in theory and research* (vol. 12, pp. 37–62). New York, NY, USA: Plenum Press.

Belk, R. W. (1993). Materialism and the making of the modern American Christmas. In D. Miller (Ed.), *Unwrapping Christmas* (pp. 75–104). Oxford: Oxford University Press.

Belk, R. W. (1997). Romanian consumer desires and feelings of deservingness. In L. Stan (Ed.), *Romania in transition* (pp. 191–208). Aldershot, UK: Dartmouth Publishing Company.

Belk, R. W. (1998). The double nature of collecting: Materialism and antimaterialism. *Etnofoor, 11*(1), 7–20.

Belk, R. W. (1999). Leaping luxuries and transitional consumers. In R. Batra (Ed.), *Marketing Issues in Transitional Economies* (pp. 39–54). Norwell, MA, USA: Kluwer.

Belk, R. W. (2004). The human consequences of consumer culture. In K. M. Ekström & H. Brembeck (Eds.), *Elusive Consumption: Tracking new research perspectives* (pp. 67–85). London, UK: Berg.

Belk, R. W. (2006). Cool shoes, cool self. In A. M. Dahlberg (Ed.), *Eyes just for shoes* (pp. 77–90). Stockholm, Sweden: Swedish Royal Armoury.

Belk, R. W. (2010). Sharing. *The Journal of Consumer Research, 36*(5), 715–734.

Belk, R. W. (2011a). Philosophies for less consuming societies. In K. Ekström & K. Glans (Eds.), *Beyond the consumption bubble* (pp. 205–220). London, UK: Routledge.

Belk, R. W. (2011b). The concept of giving (*Le concept de don*). In M. Bergadaá, M. Le Gall-Ely, & B. Urien (Eds.), *Giving and charitable practices (Don et pratiques caritives)* (pp. 19–33). Leuven, Belgium: De Boeck University Press.

Belk, R. W. (2011c). Benign envy. *Academy of Marketing Science Review, 1*(3–4), 117–134.

Belk, R., Ger, G., & Lascu, D.-N. (1993). the development of consumer desire in marketizing and developing economies: The cases of Romania and Turkey. *Advances in Consumer Research. Association for Consumer Research, 20*, 102–107.

Belk, R. W., & Llamas, R. (2012). The nature and effects of sharing in consumer behavior. In D. Mick, C. Pechmann, J. Ozanne, & S. Pettigrew (Eds.), *Transformative consumer research for human and earthly welfare: Reviews and frontiers* (pp. 625–646). New York, NY, USA: Routledge.

Belk, R. W., & Pollay, R. (1985a). Materialism and status appeals in Japanese and U.S. print advertising: An historical and cross-cultural content analysis. *International Marketing Review, 2*(4), 38–47.

Belk, R. W., & Pollay, R. (1985b). The Good Life in Twentieth Century Advertising. *The Journal of Consumer Research, 11*(4), 887–897.

Belk, R. W., Tian, K., & Paavola, H. (2010). Consuming cool: Behind the unemotional mask. In R. Belk (Ed.), *Research in consumer behavior* (vol. 12, pp. 183–208). Bingly, UK: Emerald.

Bong, B. C., Tong, C. P., Ying, W., & Lo, Y. (1996). *Chinese women and modernity: Calendar posters of the 1910s–1930s.* Hong Kong: Joint Publishing.

Bonsu, S. K., & Belk, R. (2003). Do not go cheaply into that good night: Death ritual consumption in Asante, Ghana. *Journal of Consumer Research, 30*(June), 41–55.

Botsman, R., & Rogers, R. (2010). *What's mine is yours: The rise of collaborative consumption.* New York: Harper Collins.

Brewer, J., & Porter, R. (Eds.). (1993). *Consumption and the world of goods.* London, UK: Routledge.

Bryson, N. (1990). *Looking at the overlooked: Four essays on still life painting.* London, UK: Reaktion Books.

Burroughs, J. E., & Rindfleisch, A. (2002). Materialism and well-being: A conflicting values perspective. *The Journal of Consumer Research, 29*(3), 348–370.

Call Me! (2005). *Call Me!* Taipei: Hermes,

Chadha, R., & Husband, P. (2006). *The cut of the luxury brand: Inside Asia's love affair with luxury,* London, UK: Nicholas Brealey.

Chapman, H. P., Kloek, W. T., & Wheelock, A. K. Jr. (1997). *Jan Steen: Painter and storyteller.* Amsterdam, the Netherlands: Rijksmuseum.

Cochran, S. (2006). *Chinese medicine men: Consumer culture in China and Southeast Asia.* Cambridge, MA, USA: Harvard University Press.

Cohen, L. (2003). *A consumer's republic: The politics of mass consumption in postwar America.* New York, NY, USA: Vintage.

Cohen, P., & Cohen, J. (1996). *Life values and adolescent mental health,* Mahwah, NJ: Erlbaum.

Cook, D. T. (2004). *The commodification of childhood: The children's clothing industry and the rise of the child consumer.* Durham, NC, USA: Duke University Press.

Croll, E. (2006). *China's new consumers: Social development and domestic demand.* London, UK: Routledge.

Cross, G. (2000). *All-consuming century: Why commercialism won in modern America.* New York, NY, USA: Columbia University Press.

Csikszentmihalyi, M., & Rochberg-Halton, E. (1981). *The meaning of things: Domestic symbols of the self.* Chicago, IL, USA: University of Chicago Press.

Davis, D. S. (Ed.). (2000). *The consumer revolution in urban China,* Berkeley, CA, USA: University of California Press.

Davis, D. S., & Sensenbrenner, J. S. (2000). Commercializing childhood: Parental purchases for Shanghai's only child. In D. Davis (Ed.), *The consumer revolution in Urban China* (pp. 54–79). Berkeley, CA: University of California Press.

Davis, M. (2007). Sand, fear, and money in Dubai. In M. Davis & D. B. Monk (Eds.), *Evil paradises: Dreamworlds of neoliberalism* (pp. 48–68). New York, NY, USA: The New Press.

Dawson, S., & Bamossy, G. (1991). If 'we are what we have,' what are we when we don't have? An exploratory study of materialism among expatriate Americans. *Journal of Social Behavior and Personality, 6*(6), 363–384.

Dikötter, F. (2006). *Exotic commodities: Modern objects and everyday life in China.* New York, NY, USA: Columbia University Press.

Dittmar, H. (1992). *The social psychology of material possessions: To have is to be.* New York, NY, USA: St. Martin's Press.

Dittmar, H. (2005). A new look at 'compulsive buying': Self-discrepancies and materialistic values as predictors of compulsive buying tendency. *Journal of Social and Clinical Psychology, 96,* 467–491.

Dittmar, H. (2008). *Consumer culture, identity and well-being: The search for the 'good life' and the 'body perfect'.* Hove, UK: Psychology Press.

Dong, M. Y. (2008). Who is afraid of the chinese modern girl?. In A. E. Weinbaum, L. M. Thomas, P. Ramamurthy, U. G. Poiger, M. Y. Dong, & T. E. Barlow (Eds.), *The modern girl around the world: Consumption, modernity, and globalization* (pp. 194–219). Durham, NC, USA: Duke University Press.

Douglas, M., & Isherwood, B. (1979). *The world of goods: Towards an anthropology of consumption.* New York, NY, USA: W.W. Norton.

Draculić, S. (1991). *How we survived communism and even laughed.* New York, NY, USA: Norton.

Drazin, A. (2001). A man *will* get furnished: Wood and domesticity in urban Romania. In D. Miller (Ed.), *Home possessions: Material culture behind closed doors* (pp. 173–199). Oxford, UK: Berg.

Einstein, M. (2008). *Brands of faith: Marketing religion in a commercial age.* London, UK: Routledge.

Faber, R. (2000). A systematic investigation into compulsive buying. In A. L. Benson, (Ed.), *I shop, therefore I am: Compulsive buying and the search for self* (pp. 27–53). Northvale, NJ, USA: Jason Aronson.

Faber, R. (2004). Self-control and compulsive buying. In T. Kasser & A. D. Kanner (Eds.), *Psychology and consumer culture: The struggle for a good life in a materialistic world* (pp. 169–187). Washington, DC, USA: American Psychological Association.

Farquhar, J. (2002). *Appetites: Food and sex in post-socialist China.* Durham, NC, USA: Duke University Press.

Finnane, A. (2008). *Changing clothes in China: Fashion, history, nation.* New York, NY, USA: Columbia University Press.

Foster, G. M. (1969). Peasant society and the image of limited good. *American Anthropologist, 67,* 293–315.

Fox, R. W., & Lears, T. J. J. (Eds.). (1983). *The culture of consumption.* New York: Pantheon.

Fox, W. S., & Philliber, W. (1978). Television viewing and the perception of affluence. *Sociological Quarterly, 19,* 103–112.

Fromm, E. (1976). *To have or to be?* New York, NY, USA: Harper and Row.

Fournier, S., & Richins, M. (1991). Some theoretical and popular notions concerning materialism. *Journal of Social Behavior and Personality, 6*(6), 403–414.

Frost, R. O., & Steketee, G. (2010). *Stuff: Compulsive hoarding and the meaning of things.* Boston, MA, USA: Houghton Mifflin.

Ger, G. (1992). The positive and negative effects of marketing on socioeconomic development: The Turkish case. *Journal of Consumer Policy, 15*(3), 229–254.

Ger, G., & Belk, R. (1990). Measuring and comparing materialism cross-culturally. In G. Gorn, M. Goldberg, & R. Pollay (Eds.), *Advances in consumer research* (vol. 17, pp. 186–192). Provo: Association for Consumer Research.

Ger, G., & Belk, R. (1996). Cross-cultural differences in materialism. *Journal of Economic Psychology, 17*(1) 55–78.

Ger, G., & Belk, R. (1999). Accounting for materialism in four cultures. *Journal of Material Culture, 4*(July), 183–204.

Gerbner, G., & Gross, L. (1976). Living with television: The violence profile. *Journal of Communication, 26*(2), 173–199.

Gerbner, G., Gross, L., Morgan, M., & Signorelli, N. (1980). The 'mainstreaming' of America: Violence profile no. 11. *Journal of Communication, 30*(3), 10–29.

Gerth, K. (2003). *China made: Consumer culture and the creation of the nation*, Cambridge, MA: Harvard University Press.

Glickman, L. B. (Ed.). (1999). *Consumer society in American history: A reader*. Ithica, NY, USA: Cornell University Press.

Goldberg, M. E., Gorn, G. J., Peracchio, L., & Bamossy, G. (2003). Understanding materialism among youth. *Journal of Consumer Psychology, 13,* 278–288.

Goodwin, N, Ackerman, F., & Kron, D (Eds.). (1997). *The consumer society*. Washington, DC, USA: Island Press.

Hammerslough, J. (2001), *Dematerializing: Taming the power of possessions*. Cambridge, MA, USA: Perseus.

Hung, K., Li, S. Y., & Belk, R. (2007). Glocal understandings: Female readers' perceptions of the new woman in Chinese advertising. *Journal of International Business Studies, 38*(November), 1039–1051.

Ilan, L., Yun, M., & DuPriest, B (Ed.). (2010). *East/west, visually speaking*. Lafayette, LA, USA: Paul and Lulu Hilliard University Art Museum, University of Louisiana, Lafayette.

Inglehart, R. (1977). *The silent revolution: Changing values and political styles among Western publics*, Princeton, NJ, USA: Princeton University Press.

Inglehart, R. (1981). Post-materialism in an environment of insecurity. *American Political Science Review, 75*(December), 880–900.

Inglehart, R., Basánez, M., Díez-Medrano, J., Halmann, L., & Luijkx, R. (Ed.). (2004). *Human beliefs and values. A cross-cultural sourcebook based on the 1999–2002 Values Surveys*. Coyoacan, Mexico: Siglo Veintiuno Editores.

Jackson, B. (2005). *Shanghai girl gets all dressed up*. Berkeley, CA, USA: Ten Speed Press.

Jing, J. (2000). Introduction: Food, children, and social change in contemporary China. In J. Jing (Ed.), *Feeding China's little emperors: Food, children, and social change* (pp. 1–26), Stanford, CA, USA: Stanford University Press.

Junemo, M. (2004). Let's build a palm island!': Playfulness in complex times. In M. Sheller & J. Urry (Ed.), *Tourism mobilities: Places to play, places in play* (Jr. 181–191). London, UK: Routledge.

Kasser, T. (2002). *The high price of materialism*. Cambridge, MA, UK: MIT Press.

Kasser, T., & Ryan, R. (1993). A dark side of the American dream: Correlates of financial success as a central life aspiration. *Journal of Personality and Social Psychology, 65,* 410–422.

Kasser, T., & Ryan, R. (1996). Further examining the American dream: Differential correlates of intrinsic and extrinsic goals. *Personality and Social Psychology Bulletin, 22,* 280–287.

Kasser, T., & Ryan, R. (2001). Be careful what you wish for: Optimal functioning and the relative attainment of intrinsic and extrinsic goals. In P. Schmuck & K. M. Sheldon (Eds.), *Life Goals and Well-Being: Towards a Positive Psychology of Human Striving* (pp. 116–131). Seattle, WA, USA: Hogrefe and Huber.

Kasser, T., Ryan, R., Couchman, C. E., & Sheldon, K. M. (2004). Materialistic values: their causes and consequences. In T. Kasser & A. D. Kanner (Eds.), *Psychology and consumer culture: The struggle for a good life in a materialistic world* (pp. 11–28). Washington, DC, USA: American Psychological Association.

Kasser, T., Ryan, R. Zax, M., & Sameroff, A. (1995). The relations of maternal and social environments to late adolescents' materialistic and prosocial values. *Developmental Psychology, 31,* 907–914.

Kaza, S. (Ed.). (2005). *Hooked! Buddhist writings on greed, desire, and the urge to consume.* Boston, MA, USA: Shambhala.

Klein, N. (2000). *No Logo.* Toronto, Canada: Vintage Canada.

Kleine, S. S., & Baker, S. M. (2004). An integrative review of material possion attachment. *Academy of Marketing Science Review, 1,* 1–39.

Kohak, E. (1992). Ashes, ashes. . .Central Europe after forty years. *Daedalus, 131*(Spring), 209.

Kozminski, A. J. (1992). Consumers in transition from the centrally planned economy to the market economy. *Journal of Consumer Policy, 14*(4), 26–35.

Lasn, K. (1999). *Culture jam: The uncooling of America.* New York, NY, USA: William Morrow.

Lears, J. (1994). *Fables of abundance: A cultural history of advertising in America.* New York, NY, USA: Basic Books.

Li, C. (1998). *China: The consumer revolution.* Singapore: John Wiley.

Lindstrom, M. (2003). *Brandchild.* London, UK: Kogan-Page.

Lovell, S. (2002). Soviet exurbia: Dachas in postwar Russia. In D. Crowley & S. E. Reid, (Eds.), *Socialist spaces: Sites of everyday life in the Eastern bloc* (pp. 105–121). Oxford, UK: Berg.

Lu, P. X. (2008). *Elite China: Luxury consumer behavior in China.* Singapore: John Wiley and Sons.

Mallet, D., Artsi, A., Zi, F., Hongmei, Y., & Hui, L. (2008). *Lets Consume!.* Beijing: Xin Dong Cheng Publishing.

Marling, K. A. (1994). *As seen on TV: The visual culture of everyday life in the 1950s.* Cambridge, MA, USA: Harvard University Press.

Maslow, A. (1954). *Motivation and Personality.* New York, NY, USA: Harper and Row.

Matt, S. J. (2003). *Keeping up with the Joneses: Envy in American consumer society, 1890–1930.* Philadelphia, PA, USA: University of Pennsylvania Press.

Mazzarella, W. (2003). *Shoveling smoke: Advertising and globalization in contemporary India.* Durham, NC, USA: Duke University Press.

McClay, W. M. (1995). Where have we come since the 1950s? Thoughts on materialism and American social character. In R. Wuthnow (Ed.), *Rethinking materialism: Perspectives on the spiritual dimension of economic behavior* (pp. 25–72). Grand Rapids, MI, USA: William B. Eerdmans.

McHoskey, J. C. (1999). Machiavellianism, intrinsic versus extrinsic goals, and social interest: A self-determination theory analysis. *Motivation and Emotion, 23*(December), 267–283,

Mick, D. (1996). Are studies of dark side variables confounded by socially desirable responding? The case of materialism. *Journal of Consumer Research, 23*(September), 106–119.

Miles, S. (1998). *Consumerism as a Way of Life.* London, UK: Sage.

Miller, V. J. (2004). *Consuming religion: Christian faith and practice in a consumer culture*. New York, NY, USA: Continuum International.

Moore, R. L. (1994). *Selling God: American religion in the marketplace of culture*. Oxford, UK: Oxford University Press.

Moschis, G., & Churchill, G. (1978). Consumer socialization: A theoretical and empirical analysis. *Journal of Marketing Research, 15*(4), 544–609.

Moschis, G., & Moore, R. L. (1982). A longitudinal study of television advertising effects. *Journal of Consumer Research, 9*(December), 279–286.

Mukerji, C. (1983). *From graven images: Patterns of modern materialism*. New York, NY, USA: Columbia University Press.

Nairn, A., & Griffith, C. (2007). Busted are cool but barbie's a minger: The role of advertising and brands in the everyday lives of junior school children. In K. M. Edström & B. Tufte (Eds.), *Children, media and consumption: On the front edge* (pp. 195–209). Göteborg, Sweden: International Clearinghouse on Children, Youth and Media.

Neidhart, C. (2003). *Russia's Carnival: The smells, sights, and sounds of transition*. Lanham, MD, USA: Rowman and Littlefield.

North, M. (1997). *Art and commerce in the Dutch golden age*. New Haven, CT, USA: Yale University Press.

O'Guinn, T. C., & Faber, R. J. (1989). Compulsive buying: A phenomenological exploration. *Journal of Consumer Research, 16*(2), 147–157.

O'Guinn, T. C., & Shrum, L. J. (1997). The role of television in the construction of consumer reality. *Journal of Consumer Research, 23*(March), 278–294.

Orsi, J., & Doskow, E. (2009). *The sharing solution*. Berkeley, CA, USA: Nolo.

Ostaszewski, K. (1992). The boldest social experiment of the twentieth century. In R. W. McGee (Ed.), *The market solution to economic development in Eastern Europe* (p. 229). Lewiston, UK: Lampeter, 229.

Otacool (2010). *Otacool 2: Worldwide Cosplayers*. Tokyo: Kotobukiya.

Punset, E. (2007). *Happiness: A scientific journey*. White River Junction, VT, USA: Chelsea Green Publishing.

Radin, M. J. (1996). *Contested commodities: The trouble with trade in sex, children, body parts, and other things*. Cambridge, MA, USA: Harvard University Press.

Rajagopal, A. (2001). *Politics after television: Hindu nationalism and the Reshaping of the public in India*, Cambridge: Cambridge University Press.

Rassuli, K. M., & Hollander, S. C. (1986). Desire: Induced, innate, insatiable? *Journal of Macromarketing, 6*(Fall), 4–24.

Richins, M. L. (1992). Media images, materialism, and what ought to be: The role of social comparison. In F. Rudmin & M. L. Richins (Eds.), *Materialism: Meaning, measure, and morality*. Provo, UT, USA: Association for Consumer Research, 202–206.

Richins, M. L. (1995). Social comparison, advertising, and consumer discontent. *American Behavioral Scientist, 38*, 593–607.

Richins, M. L., & Dawson, S. (1992). A consumer values orientation for materialism and its measurement: Scale development and validation. *Journal of Consumer Research, 19*(December), 303–316.

Rindfleisch, A., Burroughs, J. E., & Denton. F. (1997). Family structure, materialism, and compulsive consumption. *Journal of Consumer Research, 23*(March), 312–325.

Rindfleisch, A., Burroughs, J. E., & Wong, N. (2009). The safety of objects: Materialism, existential insecurity, and brand connection. *Journal of Consumer Research*, *36*(June), 1–16.

Ritson, M., & Elliott, R. (1999). The social uses of advertising: An ethnographic study of adolescent advertising audiences. *Journal of Consumer Research*, *26*(December), 260–277.

Roberts, C. (1997). *Evolution and revolution: Chinese dress, 1700s–1990s*, Sydney, NSW, Australia: Powerhouse Publishing.

Roberts, J. A., Manolis, C., & Tanner, J. F. Jr. (2003). Family structure, materialism, and compulsive buying: A reinquiry and extension. *Journal of the Academy of Marketing Science*, *31*(Summer), 300–311.

Rosenberg, E. A. (2004). Mindfulness and consumerism. In T. Kasser & A. D. Kanner, (Eds.), *Psychology and consumer culture: The struggle for a good life in a materialistic world* (pp. 107–125). Washington, DC, USA: American Psychological Association.

Sartre, J.-P. (1943). *Being and nothingness: A phenomenological essay on ontology* (H. E. Barnes, trans.). New York, NY, USA: Philosophical Library.

Sassatelli, R. (2007). *Consumer culture: History, theory and politics*. London, UK: Sage.

Schama, S. (1987). *The embarrassment of riches: An interpretation of Dutch culture in the golden age*. New York, NY, USA: Alfred A. Knopf.

Schell, O. (1984). *To get rich is glorious: China in the 80s*. New York, NY, USA: Pantheon Books.

Schneider, N. (1994). *Still life*. Cologne, Germany: Taschen.

Schor, J. B. (1998). *The overspent American: Upscaling, downshifting, and the new consumer*. New York: Basic Books.

Schor, J. B. (2004). *Born to buy: The commercialized child and the new consumer culture*. New York: Scribner.

Schor, J. B., & Holt, D. B. (Eds.). (2000). *The consumer society reader*. New York, NY, USA: The New Press.

Schudson, M. (1984). *Advertising: The uneasy persuasion: its dubious impact on American society*. New York, NY, USA: Basic Books.

Sheldon, K. M., & Kasser, T. (1995). Coherence and congruence: Two aspects of personality integration. *Journal of Personality and Social Psychology*, *68*, 531–543.

Sheldon, K., Sheldon, M., & Osbaldiston, R. (2000). Prosocial values and group assortation in an N-Person prisoner's dilemma. *Human Nature*, *11*(December), 387–404.

Shrestha, N. R. (1997). *In the name of development: A reflection on Nepal*. Lanham, MD, USA: University Press of America.

Shrum, L. J., Burroughs, J. E., & Rindfleisch, A. (2005). Television's cultivation of material values. *Journal of Consumer Research*, *32*(December), 473–479.

Shrum, L. J., O'Guinn, T. C., Semenik, R. J., & Faber, R. J. (1991). Process and effects in the construction of normative consumer beliefs: The role of television. *Advances in Consumer Research*, *18*, 755–573.

Slater, D. (1997). *Consumer culture and modernity*, Cambridge: Polity.

Sobh, R., & Belk, R. (2011). Gender privacy in Arab gulf states: Implications for consumption and marketing. In O. Sandicki & G. Rice (Ed.), *Handbook of Islamic marketing* (pp. 23–96). Cheltenham, UK: Edward Elgar.

Sobh, R., Belk, R., & Gressel, J. (2010). The scented winds of change: Conflicting notions of modesty and vanity among young Qatari and Emirati women. *Advances in Consumer Research, 37*, 905–907.

Solberg, E. G., Diener, E., & Robinson, M. D. (2004). Why are materialists less satisfied?. In T. Kasser & A. D. Kanner (Eds.), *Psychology and consumer culture: The struggle for a good life in a materialistic world* (pp. 29–48). Washington, DC, USA: American Psychological Association.

Solomon, S., Greenberg, J. L., & Pyszczynski, T. A. (2004). Lethal consumption: Death-denying materialism. In T. Kasser & A. D. Kanner (Eds.), *Psychology and consumer culture: The struggle for a good life in a materialistic world* (pp. 127–146). Washington, DC, USA: American Psychological Association.

Stearns, P. N. (2001). *Consumerism in world history.* London: Routledge.

Stearns, P. N. (2002). *The Battleground of Desire: The Struggle for Self-Control in Modern America,* New York: New York University Press.

Strasser, S., McGovern, C., & Judt, M. (1998). *Getting and spending: European and American consumer societies in the twentieth century.* Cambridge, UK: Cambridge University Press.

Tomasello, M. (2009). *Why we cooperate.* Cambridge, MA, USA: MIT Press.

Tse, D., Belk, R., & Zhou, N. (1989). Becoming a consumer society: A longitudinal and cross-cultural content analysis of print advertisements from Hong Kong, People's Republic of China and Taiwan. *Journal of Consumer Research, 15*(March), 457–472.

Twitchell, J. B. (1999). *Lead us into temptation: The triumph of American materialism.* New York, NY, UK: Columbia University Press.

Twitchell, J. B. (2007). *Shopping for God: How christianity went from in your heart to in your face.* New York, NY, USA: Simon and Schuster.

Wallendorf, M., & Arnould, E. J. (1988). 'My favorite things': A cross-cultural Inquiry into object attachment, possessiveness and social linkage. *Journal of Consumer Research, 14*(March), 531–547.

Wang, J. (2008). *Brand new China: Advertising, media, and commercial culture.* Cambridge, MA, USA: Harvard University Press.

Ward, S., & Wackman, D. (1971). Family and media influences on adolescent learning. *American Behavioral Scientist, 14*(3), 415–427.

Webster, C., & Beatty, R. (1997). Nationality, materialism, and possession importance. *Advances in Consumer Research, 24*, 204–210.

Westermann, M. (1996). *The art of the Dutch republic, 1585–1718.* London, UK: Weidenfeld and Nicholson.

Wong, N., Rindfleisch, A., & Burroughs, J. E. (2003). Do reverse-worded items confound measures in cross-cultural consumer research? The case of the material values scale. *Journal of Consumer Research, 30*(June), 72–91.

Wooten, D. (2006). From labelling possessions to possessing labels: Ridicule and socialization among adolescents. *Journal of Consumer Research, 33*(September), 188–198.

Wu, Y. (1999). *China's consumer revolution: The emerging patterns of wealth and expenditure.* Cheltenham, UK: Edward Elgar.

Wuthnow, R. (1994). *God and mammon in America.* New York, NY, USA: Free Press.

Zelizer, V. (2005). *The purchase of intimacy.* Princeton, NJ, USA: Princeton University Press.

Zhao, X., & Belk, R. (2008a). Advertising consumer culture in 1930s' Shanghai: Globalization and localization in Yue Fen Pai. *Journal of Advertising, 37*(Summer), 2008, 45–56.

Zhao, X., & Belk, R. (2008b). Politicizing consumer culture: Advertising's appropriation of political ideology in China's social transition. *Journal of Consumer Research, 35*(August), 231–244.

15

Culture, Self-Regulation, and Impulsive Consumption

AKSHAY RAO ■

INTRODUCTION

To resist temptation is an aspect of the human condition that has attracted the attention of poets, policy makers, and psychologists over the millennia. In Homer's *Odyssey*, the protagonist is urged to protect himself from prospective temptation when he encounters the Sirens, by ensuring that he is bound hand and foot to the mast of his ship. More recently, Thaler and Sunstein (2009) report that some gambling addicts have voluntarily added their names to a list that bars them from entering casinos (p. 233). And, the contemporary literature in psychology and marketing is rife with inquiries regarding the conditions under which individuals do and do not give in to temptation (Heatherton, 2011; Heatherton & Wagner, 2011; Muraven & Baumeister, 2000; Vohs & Faber, 2007).

In the consumption context, succumbing to temptation is generally manifested as engaging in impulsive consumption, i.e., ". . .when a consumer experiences a sudden, often powerful and persistent urge to buy something immediately" (Rook, 1987, p. 191). Three key elements of impulsive consumption therefore include: (a) an (irresistible) urge (b) to purchase (c) immediately. In other words, impulsive consumption is the manifestation of instant gratification in the material domain. Alternatively, giving in to the temptation to consume can be construed as a failure to resist temptation, or a failure to exercise self-control. Such a failure to exercise self-control, while desirable for marketers who benefit from impulse purchases, can have deleterious social consequences including obesity, addiction, poor financial decisions, and the like (Schroeder, 2007).

In this chapter, I will address the issue of self-control failure and its implications for consumption, broadly construed. I will examine the role of the *ability* and the *motivation* to exercise self-control, and how such ability and motivation may moderate the effect of environmental factors on self-control failure. I will introduce the notion of cultural differences as an individual difference variable that impacts the ability and motivation to exercise self-control, and thus develop the argument that self-control failure and its impact on consumption might be culturally mediated. That is, the factors that undergird self-control failure may sometimes be culture specific, and it is plausible that differences due to cultural norms and traits yield predictable differences in self-control failure-induced consumption, such as impulsive purchases, quantity decisions, reductions in price sensitivity, and the like. These differences might present opportunities for multinational corporations to design strategies that take cultural differences into account and profit from such nuanced strategies. These differences ought also to play a role in the formulation of public policies that are designed to influence prosocial behaviors among an increasingly culturally heterogeneous population in many countries around the world.

CONCEPTUAL FRAMEWORK

The literature on self-control is extensive, and employs a multitude of perspectives and approaches. To capture the entire waterfront on the topic and weave that literature into the discussion of consumption mediated by culture is beyond the scope of this chapter. I will therefore restrict myself to an approach shown in Figure 15.1. Unfortunately, a discussion of several other important dimensions of self-control such as the cognitive neuroscience literature that is beginning to generate fascinating insights on the neural underpinnings of culturally diverse populations will be relegated to the cutting room floor.

A big-picture view

As Figure 15.1 indicates, the failure to exercise self-control is often the consequence of stimuli or primes in the environment. I recognize that this is a relatively limited and static view of the world, since, in the interest of parsimony, I do not account for several other factors such as past experiences and knowledge of self-control failure. Presumably, to the extent that other factors are pertinent, they can be incorporated into the framework quite readily.

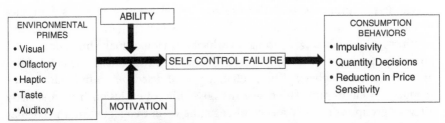

Figure 15.1 Selected antecedents, moderators and consequences of Self-Control Failure.

I classify the environmental cues according to their effect on the five human senses: olfactory, auditory, gustatory, visual, and haptic (touch). For instance, the smell of cigarette smoke for somebody wishing to quit smoking can serve as a powerful environmental cue to have just one; the sound of beer being poured can be a strong auditory cue for a recovering alcoholic; a small taste of dessert can result in "lapse-activated" causal patterns, that stimulate the reward centers of the brain (this is the equivalent of the "falling off the wagon" effect). Simple visual exposure to primary rewards such as erotic images or pictures of drugs can activate reward systems that yield cravings. Similarly, haptic (touch) experiences can have an impact on peoples' ability to exercise self-control.

Not all individuals are equally susceptible to self-control failure. Individuals differ in the ability and their motivation to exercise self-control, and the resultant variations in the exercise of self-control yield different behavioral consequences in the consumption domain. Chief among these consequences are the tendencies to respond to the urge to purchase and/or consume (display impulsivity), to do so to excess (quantity decisions), and to pay relatively higher prices (display lower price sensitivity), particularly when faced with the opportunity for immediate gratification.

I now drill down into the central components of the framework describe in Figure 15.1.

Elements of self-control

Engaging in self-control is a successful evolutionarily adaptation; the exercise of self-control is a desirable genetic trait (Heatherton, 2011). This trait allows individuals to be good group members, and ". . .belonging to a. . .group (has) considerable value, including access to shared resources, security from various threats, and even assistance with daily chores" (p. 364). For example, inhibiting one's natural impulses, such as the impulse to eat large quantities of food, so that there is a sufficient quantity of food available for the entire group, is one manifestation of the exercise of self-control. In many instances, the exercise of such self-control may diminish the availability of resources for the individual in the short run, so as to provide resources for other group members, and this sacrifice may be evolutionarily adaptive because the presence of sufficient numbers of group members may contribute positively to the longevity of the individual and his or her ability to propagate genes.

Heatherton proposes that the exercise of self-control requires four elements: (a) *self-awareness*, so individuals may reflect on their own identity relative to others; (b) *mentalizing*, a process by which individuals make inferences about how socially relevant others might evaluate their behavior (i.e., possessing a "theory of mind"; Gallagher & Frith, 2003); (c) *threat detection*, so individuals may monitor the environment to assess the possibility of exclusion from a socially relevant group (as a consequence of engaging or not engaging in a particular behavior); and (d) *self-regulation*, so that individuals may resist the temptation to do what is self-indulgent, and thus assure that they stay ". . .in the good graces of others" (p. 366) and are not excluded from the group. It is this last element, that of self-regulation (and its impact on self-control) when presented with consumption opportunities, that is particularly relevant to my story. (This focus is not to suggest that the other elements cannot be implicated in self-control failure. They can. I am simply focusing on self-regulation as the principal driving force in self-control failure because of its obvious and direct impact on consumption related self-control failure).

People need to regulate their emotions, their thoughts, and, most pertinent to our story, their behaviors. In the consumption context, failure to self-regulate can result in impulsive consumption, excessive consumption, and a willingness to pay relative high prices when presented with an opportunity to not defer consumption. As noted earlier, self-regulation failure leading to self-control failure can occur due to, among other things, environmental primes. However, whether or not such self-regulation failure occurs depends importantly on the individual's ability to self-regulate, and the individual's motivation to self-regulate, discussed below.

Ability to self-regulate

Not all individuals are equally susceptible to environmental primes. And, perhaps of greater interest, the same individual may be differentially susceptible to environmental primes, at different times of day or due to a host of factors that affect that individual's *ability* to engage in self-regulation. This ability is contingent on the availability of "self-regulatory resources" that facilitate the individual's attempts to not succumb to temptation (Baumeister, 2000; Hedgcock, Vohs, & Rao, 2013). When these resources are depleted, the tendency for self-control failure to occur is enhanced.

Self-regulatory resources can be depleted as a consequence of a variety of factors.[1] For instance, when individuals are asked to control emotions, make decisions, or overcome a desire, their self-regulatory resources may be depleted (Muraven & Baumeister, 2000). In one study, it was demonstrated that consumers faced with a demanding task (inhibiting responses to a sad video) suffered a reduction in self-regulatory resources that resulted in a failure to exercise self-control, manifested as an increase in consumption of ice cream, relative to a control group (Vohs & Heatherton, 2000). Other actions such as thought suppression tasks (e.g., asking subjects to *not* think of a white bear) can also deplete self-regulatory resources (Muraven, Tice, & Baumeister, 1998). The consequences of regulatory resource depletion and the resulting failure to exercise self-control are significant. Greater beer consumption (Muraven, Collins, & Nienhaus, 2002) and displaying greater racial bias (Richeson, Baird, Gordon, Heatherton,

---

1. A common trigger for self-regulation failure is negative mood (Tiffany & Drobes, 1990).

Wyland, Trawalter, & Shelton, 2003) are just some of the consequences of reduced self-control that have been documented in the literature. Many scholars have offered various explanations for why resource depletion occurs, including memory deficits (Richards & Gross, 2000), reduced attention (Muraven & Baumeister, 2000), and a decline in motivation (Muraven & Slessareva, 2003).

Various metaphors can be employed to describe the regulatory resource failure mechanism, but perhaps the most instructive metaphor is the muscle metaphor. According to this view, the regulatory resource is like a muscle. Overuse on a particular occasion results in weakness. Yet, regular exercise of the resource strengthens it. As Zhang, Winterich, and Mittal (2010) note, "All consumers have some (self) control resources, but using them reduces their availability and thus reduces self-control for the task at hand (Baumeister, 2002). Furthermore, practicing self-control can strengthen a person's self-control muscle and increase the general capacity for self-control in the long run (Muraven, Baumeister, & Tice, 1999)." (p. 946). In fact, Gailliot and Baumeister (2007) among others indicate that increasing the level of blood glucose by giving participants a glucose drink enhances their ability to engage in self-control, much like a glucose drink refreshes a tired athlete.

This muscle metaphor implies two consequences. First, multiple instances of regulatory resource depletion—making multiple decisions at one point during the day, for instance—can lead to decision fatigue, which might lead to poor decisions at a subsequent point in the day.[2] Second, regular attempts to enhance the regulatory resource through the exercise of self-control could be beneficial in the long run. Much like a muscle gets strengthened through daily exercise, people instructed to sit straight in their chairs for two weeks display greater self-regulation than a control group (Muraven, Tice, & Baumeister, 1998).

MOTIVATION TO SELF-REGULATE
Heatherton (2011) notes ". . .other important features of self-regulation, such as initiating self-regulatory efforts in order to reach personal goals (Shah, 2005)" (p. 365). In particular, ". . .people need to regulate behavior proactively, such as avoiding appearing prejudiced. . .people also self-regulate in order to promote positive goals (Higgins, 1997)" (p. 366). These goals have been discussed extensively in the "regulatory focus" literature, a topic to which we now turn.[3]

---

2. A popular press account suggests that President Obama is aware of the consequences of decision fatigue, and has therefore eliminated the opportunity for trivial decisions early in the day, such as sartorial choices. He only wears grey or blue suits, so as to not deplete regulatory resources early in the day, because such depletion might have adverse consequences for important decisions later in the day (http://www.huffingtonpost.com/emily-peck/barack-obama-decision-making-theory_b_1901070.html). See Vohs et al. (2008) for evidence that making choices impairs subsequent self-control because of resource depletion that adversely effects self-regulation.

3. There is potential for semantic confusion because of the use of the term "regulation" in both the self-control literature and the regulatory focus literature. However, recall, in the self-control literature, self-regulation is one of four dimensions (the others being

According to regulatory focus theory, individuals might subscribe to qualitatively different goals. Such goals include "promotion" goals (i.e., goals that emphasize the achievement of desirable outcomes) and "prevention" goals (i.e., goals that emphasize the avoidance of undesirable outcomes) (Higgins, 1997). These goals can be construed as the individual's *motivation* (to achieve a desirable outcome or to avoid an undesirable one) (Zhang & Shrum, 2009).

For example, an individual may be motivated to achieve success at work or at school and may display behaviors associated with the achievement of such a goal, while another may be motivated to prevent failure at work or at school, and may display (different) behaviors consistent with such a motive. While one stream of research views such goal orientations to be chronic (e.g., Zhu & Meyers-Levy, 2007), others have demonstrated that a promotion or prevention orientation can, on occasion, be situationally induced (Chen, Ng, & Rao, 2005).

Self-regulatory goals such as promotion or prevention, when activated, ought to serve as a valuable motivational resource that allows the individual to resist the temporary urge to indulge. For example, upon exposure to reward-laden stimuli such as chocolate cakes or cigarettes, individuals whose promotion goals are active might focus on their need to achieve a better figure or play harder successfully at a game of tennis, while individuals whose prevention goals are active might focus on their need to avoid the ill-health consequences of overeating or smoking. When the activation of the relevant motivational goals does not occur, self-regulatory failures and the consequent caving in to temptation is more likely to occur (Ramanathan & Menon, 2006; Shiv & Fedorikhin, 1999). Therefore, the accessibility of self-regulatory goals as a motivational device to help individuals engage in self-regulation is particularly germane to this discussion, since marketing communications might activate particular motivational goals.

One important implication of the notion that promotion or prevention goals might be chronic is the search for an underlying correlate of such a chronic trait. In other words, is there some observable feature about an individual (such as gender, age, or ethnicity) that might correlate with a chronic tendency to display a promotion or prevention orientation? Based on the work of cultural psychologists (e.g., Markus & Kitayama, 1991;Triandis, 1989), it has become apparent that Westerners tend to be relatively promotion oriented while Easterners tend to be relatively prevention oriented.

This individual cultural difference variable is central to the thesis of this chapter. Therefore, I turn to the conceptual underpinnings of the nexus between culture and self-control failure in the next section.

---

self-awareness, mentalizing, and threat detection) of self-control. A failure to self-regulate can result in self-control failure. In the regulatory focus literature, the term "regulatory focus" reflects an individual's goal orientation.

CULTURAL DIFFERENCES

The existing wisdom in cultural psychology draws from the seminal work of Hofstede (1980) according to whom an individual's geographic location (East versus West), or, in more sophisticated treatments, an individual's geographical origin (i.e., ethnicity embedded within a common culture, such as "Asian Americans"; see Shih, Pitinsky, & Ambady, 1999) is an important marker of cultural identity. People can be classified by their "self-construal" into two categories. Independents emphasize achievement and autonomy, a characteristic that is consistent with Western cultures and is associated with a regulatory focus of promotion, whereas interdependents emphasize the fulfillment of obligations within a social network, a characteristic that is consistent with Eastern cultures and is associated with a regulatory focus of prevention (Lee, Aaker, & Gardner, 2000). In effect, the individual's self-construal (whether they view themselves as independent Westerners or interdependent Easterners) may vary as a function of geographic longitude and/or ethnic origin, and this individual difference has implications for whether the individual is motivated by a promotion or prevention orientation (Aaker & Lee, 2001). These self-construals have important behavioral implications.

Empirical evidence on cross-cultural differences and self-control failure

Both conceptually and empirically, it has been argued and demonstrated that culture (the individual's self-construal) can have an impact on both the ability and the motivation to engage in self-regulation (Figure 15.2).

SELF-CONSTRUAL DRIVEN SELF-REGULATION FAILURE: ABILITY
The empirical evidence linking self-control with self-construal or cultural identity is limited. In the psychology literature, Seeley and Gardner (2003) examined

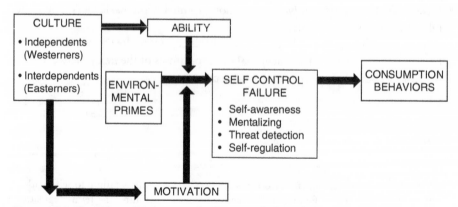

Figure 15.2 The Effect of Culture on the Framework described in Figure 15.1.

the possibility that resource depletion (the loss of ability) ought to occur less readily among socially oriented individuals such as "interdependent" Easterners. Self-control is argued to be fundamental to collectivist cultures, one of the most basic dispositional characteristics that define East Asians. Hence, Easterners, who are members of collectivist societies, are oriented to emphasize ". . .encouraging meeting the needs and expectations of others over the expression of one's individuality" (p. 105). Therefore, such individuals engage in self-regulatory effort more often in their normal lives, and, as a consequence, the self-regulatory "muscle" is likely better developed. That is, the ". . .repeated exercise of self-control may build self-regulatory ability over time, and moreover, that social orientation (self-construal) may encourage this exercise" (p. 114). For individualists, on the other hand, a lower level of obligation to others ought to result in a reduced tendency (and opportunity) to engage in and practice self-control. Consequently, interdependents ought to have a relatively large reservoir of regulatory resources and therefore a greater capacity to engage in self-control. Therefore, individuals who are from a collectivist society should display less regulatory resource depletion than individuals who are from an individualist society.

Consistent with this thesis, Seeley and Gardner (2003) observe that thought suppression (i.e., "don't think of a white bear") depletes resources to a greater degree among US subjects relative to Asian subjects. Specifically, they found that Asian subjects spent more time squeezing a handgrip (a measure of task persistence) following a thought suppression task, relative to their American counterparts. That is, because of the practice of self-control in their daily lives, Asian subjects were less subject to regulatory resource exhaustion.

Seeley and Gardner (2003) recognize that using subjects from different subsamples (Asian and US students) creates a concern regarding the presence of confounds. That is, a third (lurking) variable other than cultural identity-driven differences in regulatory resource availability might have caused the observed effect. To account for this possibility, Seeley and Gardner conducted a second study in which they *measured* self-monitoring. Again, they found that high "other directed" individuals (i.e., interdependents) performed better at a persistence task than low other directed individuals. In general, ". . .highly socially oriented (individuals) did not show regulatory impairment after an initial self-control task" (p. 113). However, the authors acknowledge that measuring self-monitoring does not eliminate the concern about confounds; as they note, ". . . a better test . . . might be to prime social orientation" (p. 114).

SELF-CONSTRUAL DRIVEN SELF-REGULATION FAILURE: MOTIVATION

Zhang and Shrum (2009) employ this notion of self-construal in combination with regulatory resource theory to assess whether chronically interdependent individuals, who tend to be prevention oriented, will, when in the presence of socially relevant others, engage in greater self-control than when alone. Conversely, they expect that individuals who are chronically independent, and who tend to be promotion oriented, will, when in the presence of socially relevant others, display less self-control than when alone. That is, ". . .acting on one's spontaneous feelings may itself be considered normatively appropriate in predominantly individualistic societies, and the presence of one's peers may further condone the behavior" (p. 840), while ". . .because impulsive consumption is often considered an unplanned and immature behavior that may reflect badly on the group in interdependent societies, people with an interdependent self-construal should be more likely to activate self-regulation goals, and thus suppress the impulsive urge, than people with an independent self-construal" (p. 839). In general, ". . .peer pressure increases the *motivation* to suppress impulsive consumption tendencies for *interdependents* but decreases it for *independents*" (p. 846, emphasis added).

This finding, along with the Seeley and Gardner (2003) study, suggests a conceptual link between self-construal and both the self-regulatory resources that are an element of the ability to engage in self-control, and the motivation to engage in self-control, on self-control failure. In other words, cultural differences might account for differences in both the ability and the motivation to engage in self-control, and chronic aspects of the individual that impinge on his or her ability to engage in self-regulate, might diminish the role of motivation in the manifestation of self-control.

Summary

The evidence on cross-cultural differences (as captured in the individual's self-construal) on the ability and motivation to engage in self-control and thus limit the tendency to display a failure of self-control is limited, but informative. It underscores two important conclusions.

First, by sheer force of practice, the self-regulatory resource is stronger among interdependent Easterners than among independent Westerners (Seeley & Gardner, 2003). That is, as the muscle metaphor would imply, the frequent exercise of self-regulation enhances the ability of Easterners to display self-control, and therefore those with an interdependent self-construal are likely to be chronically less likely to engage in impulsive consumption.

Second, regulatory focus induced self-construal, whether it is chronic or situationally primed, generates predictable differences in behavior that is enhanced in the presence of socially relevant others, but for different reasons (Zhang & Shrum, 2009). The presence of peers can stimulate self-control or suppress it, because the presence of peers interacts with one's self-construal such that pleasure-seeking goals are activated for promotion-oriented individuals, whereas prevention goals that emphasize maturity and restraint are activated for prevention-oriented individuals. That is, the natural tendency of people from a collectivist culture to engage in self-control can be enhanced in the presence of peers, while the natural tendency of people from an individualist culture to not exercise self-control can be enhanced in the presence of peers. Thus, in addition to differences in ability, the individual's motivation (captured in their regulatory focus driven goals) might vary across cultures, and is an important element in their tendency to engage in impulsive consumption.

As I will develop in the next section, for practitioners and theoreticians, these two conclusions are of nontrivial significance. The presence or absence of socially relevant others, and the activation of goals that can then appear to be difficult to achieve, can both impact the ability (resources) and the motivation (goals) to engage in self-regulation, which has consequences for subsequent self-control failure-induced consumption behaviors.

IMPLICATIONS AND OBSERVATIONS

The literature on self-control, self-regulation, self-construal, and the link with various types of consumption has a natural connection to some of the literature that addresses the general topic of impulsive consumer behavior. Early examinations of impulsive buying include Bellenger, Robertson, and Hirschman (1978), Kollat and Willett (1967), and Pollay (1968) among others, and defined impulse buying as unplanned purchases. Conceptual difficulties with this casual definition led to a more careful and psychologically rigorous examination of the construct that yielded the definition provided by Rook (1987, p. 191):

> Impulse buying occurs when a consumer experiences a sudden, often powerful and persistent urge to buy something immediately. The impulse to buy is hedonically complex and may stimulate emotional conflict. Also, impulse buying is prone to occur with diminished regard for its consequences.

As noted earlier, this definition of impulse buying captures several important elements associated with the failure to exercise self-control. There is an urge prompted by a stimulus, that demands immediate satiation reflected in the need for expedited delivery (Chen et al., 2005) through the act of consumption (Pollay, 1968).

As noted in Figure 15.1, in addition to impulsivity, the recent literature indicates that other consequences of the failure to exercise self-control on consumption include a preference for larger relative to smaller quantities, and a willingness to pay higher prices for immediate relative to deferred consumption, under some conditions.

Consequences for consumption behaviors

INCREASED IMPULSIVITY
Zhang and Shrum (2009) find that self-construal has an impact on impulsive consumption. Among subjects whose independent self-construal has been activated, peer presence increases impulsive beer consumption because the presence of others enhances preexisting dispositions such as the promotion goal of

experiencing pleasure. Conversely, for interdependents, the presence of peers enhances the activation of self-regulation goals (prevention goals that limit the tendency to engage in impulsive consumption that may be deemed immature and thus reflect badly on the group), and thus reduces impulsive beer consumption. In three studies employing both secondary and experimental data, the authors find support for the general thesis that independents are less likely to suppress the tendency to engage in impulsive consumption in the presence of peers, while interdependents were more likely to suppress the tendency to engage in impulsive consumption in the presence of peers. Perhaps more important, by manipulating the availability of self-regulatory resources, the authors demonstrate that interdependents lost the tendency to suppress their impulsive consumption. That is, when experimentally induced to not think of a white bear (thus draining self-regulation resources), interdependents displayed impulsive consumption even in the presence of peers.

QUANTITY DECISIONS

Indirect evidence for quantity decisions comes from a recent paper by Hedgcock, Vohs, and Rao (2012). In that study, we examined subjects' choice of healthy versus unhealthy snacks following a resource depletion task. I am going to employ calories consumed as a proxy for quantity to make the point that regulatory resource depletion results in the consumption of larger quantities.

We conducted two studies. The first employed functional magnetic resonance imaging to identify the neural correlates of self-regulatory resource depletion. The second study is more germane to the point I wish to make here, so I will describe it in some detail.

First, subjects were recruited as they exited the University of Iowa's recreational facility in which the gymnasium is located. They indicated a preference for healthy versus unhealthy (high caloric) snacks and drinks. Subjects then performed a regulatory resource depleting task pioneered by Baumeister, Bratslavsky, Muraven, and Tice (1998). They crossed out every instance of the letter "e" on a page from a textbook. Then, on the next page they encountered, they crossed out every instance of the letter "e" unless it was adjacent to another vowel or one letter removed from another vowel, forcing subjects to overcome the established pattern of crossing out every "e". Subjects were then exposed to other manipulations depending on condition, but these manipulations are not pertinent to my story. Then, their preference for healthy versus unhealthy snacks was measured again. In the control condition, in which no manipulations occurred to disrupt the effect of regulatory resource depletion, subjects displayed a significant increase in their preference for unhealthy snacks when their resources had been depleted.

This evidence of enhanced calorie consumption by subjects (who presumably were health conscious since they had just exited the gym) whose self-control resources had been depleted is strongly suggestive of the effect of depletion on quantity decisions. Further, in one of the manipulation conditions, we provided a motivational intervention (alerting subjects to "be mindful of the behaviors that you will need to do in order to reach your health *goals. . ."* (p. 491, emphasis added)) that had the desired effect; preferences for unhealthy (high caloric) snacks and drinks *declined* for subjects exposed to the motivational intervention. In other words, changing the level of motivation can have the desired effect on self-regulation, that then diminishes self-control failure driven quantity consumption decisions.

While this study is silent on whether culture ought to play a role in the effect of resource depletion on quantity decisions, it appears reasonable to speculate that, given the role of motivation in reducing the effect of depletion on quantity enhancement, culture will likely play a role. Since interdependent Easterners have relatively high levels of motivation, they are less likely to be suffer self-regulation decrements and thus are less likely to succumb to the temptation to consume larger quantities, than independent Westerners.

WILLINGNESS TO PAY

In a recent paper, Chen et al. (2005) employed a relatively subtle operationalization of impulsivity. Based on the argument that impulsivity is grounded in the desire for instant gratification, and impulsive consumption behavior ought therefore to be characterized by impatience (the desire for early relative to delayed delivery of a desirable product), the authors demonstrate variations in willingness to pay for expedited delivery of a desirable product as a function of the individual's self-construal (culture) and the individual's motivation (regulatory focus).

In several studies, the authors *prime* bicultural (Singaporean) subjects with one or another self-construal (independent or interdependent) by exposing them to visual icons from either Western (American) or Eastern (Singaporean) cultures.[4] Manipulation checks (questions that asked subjects to name politicians that came to mind) confirmed that subjects were thinking of exemplars from the culture that had been primed. Subsequently, subjects were primed to think in a promotion or prevention-oriented manner, and were then asked how much they would be willing to pay for expedited delivery of a book framed with a message that either matched their regulatory focus orientation (promotion/prevention) or was in conflict with that orientation.

The results from their studies were quite informative. It turns out that "(W) esterners are more apt to expend monetary resources to achieve a desirable outcome, whereas Easterners are more apt to expend monetary resources to avoid an undesirable outcome" (Chen et al., 2005, p. 299). The same outcome was observed for a measure of impatience, which is a proxy for impulsivity. This general finding is noteworthy because it adds nuance to the core argument, that interdependent consumers will generally exhibit greater patience. The effect can be reversed if interdependent consumers are confronted with a prospect that

---

4. The use of bicultural subjects and the employment of primes lends additional credence to these results, since the concern about confounds is eliminated.

increases the likelihood of an undesirable event which might be prevented if they display impatience. That is, achieving a prevention goal quickly is desirable for interdependents, and that motivation can yield enhanced impatience. The converse is true for independents. A roadblock on the path to a promotion goal will increase independent consumers' impatience to acquire a product that may eliminate that roadblock.

This finding is instructive in a larger sense. Consistent with classic perspectives on motivation, when goals are activated, yet cannot readily be achieved, individuals tend to pursue strategies that will overcome the hurdle, if such strategies are available to them. Even interdependent Easterners whose chronic ability and motivation at engaging in self-control is high, and whose impulsivity is low, can be induced to display impatience if goal achievement consistent with their self-construal is hampered. Prevention-oriented individuals who are faced with a hurdle to achieving a prevention goal might display impulsivity, contrary to their natural inclinations.

SUMMARY

The general conclusions that emerge from this relatively sparse literature on the nexus between culture (self-construal), ability and motivation on self-regulation, and its impact on consumption are as follows:

- Easterners (interdependents) have greater ability and motivation to self-regulate than Westerners (independents)
- consequently, the general tendency among Easterners (interdependents) will be to engage in relatively fewer impulse purchases, display a lower tendency to purchase large quantities, and demonstrate a lower willingness to pay for immediate gratification, but
- the lower willingness to pay tendency among Easterners (interdependents) may be reversed if their chronic (prevention) goal is activated and appears unlikely to be achieved unless they engage in immediate gratification.

I now turn to some speculations regarding the practical implications of the existing wisdom in the area.

Practical implications

It is convenient to examine the failure of self-control in the consumption domain along the familiar 4 Ps classification of marketing: the product, its price, promotion (i.e., advertising persuasion), and place (i.e., distribution).

PRODUCTS THAT FOSTER SELF-CONTROL FAILURE

There are many factors that can potentially have an adverse impact on an individual's ability and motivation to engage in self-control. For instance, in lapse-activated consumption, an individual's motivation to maintain a self-control regimen (such as dieting) can be damaged by a small indulgence (which then generates a strong activation in the brain's reward centers) that overwhelm the self-regulation mechanism. For instance, dieters who indulge in a small treat often tend to over-consume subsequently (Herman & Mack, 1975).

The research on dynamically inconsistent preferences is one stream of research that provides some insight into products that are likely to generate the urge for instant gratification. A "virtuous" product is one whose benefits are experienced in the distant future, but whose costs are experienced immediately (e.g., exercise), while a vice-laden or "vicious" product is one whose benefits are experienced immediately, but whose costs are experienced in the distant future (e.g., chocolate). Consumers display greater impulsivity when confronted with vices (e.g., alcohol; Acton, 2003) than when confronted with virtuous products (Wertenbroch, 1998). Seemingly, the motivation to engage in self-control is impacted adversely when tempting stimuli are encountered. In general, hedonic products ought to stimulate impulsivity to a greater degree than utilitarian products (Childers & Rao, 1992).

Are these effects likely to vary across cultural contexts? In many instances, the actor's cultural background can yield differences in self-control as demonstrated by Seeley and Gardner (2003) and Zhang and Shrum (2009). In particular, Easterners have a chronically higher ability to exercise self-control, but, as Chen et al. (2005) observe, self-control and associated impatience can vary *within* cultures due to variations in motivation. Consequently, the consumption goal associated with the product is likely to be an important determinant of the impatience displayed by actors from different cultures. For instance, a product that limits unsavory outcomes (i.e., fulfills a prevention goal) is likely to prompt impulsivity among Easterners, if they are not able to acquire it speedily, while a product that eliminates roadblocks to achieving a desirable outcome (i.e., fulfills a promotion goal) is likely to enhance impulsivity among Westerners, if they are not able to acquire it speedily.

Second, as Zhang and Shrum (2009) and Childers and Rao (1992) suggest, the salience of socially relevant others ought to play a role in the manifestation of self-control. In particular, because independents value uniqueness, and the presence of others ought to enhance preexisting dispositions (Zajonc, 1965), for products that are consumed in public (i.e., consumed in the presence of socially relevant others), their impulsivity should increase. This speculation ought to explain binge drinking on US college campuses (Zhang & Shrum, 2009). By the same token, interdependents ought to display less impulsivity for products that are publicly consumed, as opposed to those that are consumed in private (Childers & Rao, 1992). However, when prevention goals are activated, the salience of socially relevant others may enhance impulsivity for interdependents.

Cultures differ in time perception (Chen et al., 2005). Westerners tend to subscribe to a "linear-separable" notion of time (Graham, 1981) whereas notions of rebirth are dominant beliefs in the Orient. Consequently, Easterners likely subscribe to a "circular-traditional" perspective (Chen et al., 2005). This latter perspective is consistent with religious and spiritual beliefs (specifically, Hinduism, Buddhism, and Confucianism) that are dominant in Southeast Asia. Based on this reasoning, Easterners should discount the future less and display greater patience. Further, the literature on intertemporal discounting suggests that the manner in which people discount the future is nonlinear, i.e., "...the rate between any two adjacent periods is not the same" (Chen et al., 2005, p. 292). In fact, it has been demonstrated that the hyperbolic functional form is the best descriptor of discount rates (Read, Loewenstein, & Kalyanaraman, 1999). Chen et al. (2005) collected data to assess whether the *pattern* of discounting was consistent with the hyperbolic discounting functional form across different cultures. While both Western and Eastern primed subjects displayed hyperbolic discounting, the observed parameters differed. Western primed subjects displayed greater discounting of the future, reflected in a steeper slope. Therefore, Westerners are likely to be less attracted to financial products that have relatively long maturity periods, relative to Easterners.

PRICING CONSEQUENCES OF SELF-CONTROL FAILURE

Since impulsivity reflects a failure to self-regulate, there is a natural connection between diminished self-control and diminished price sensitivity, as reflected in a tendency to splurge (Vohs & Faber, 2007). In other words, in addition to a willingness to pay for expedited delivery (i.e., paying a premium for instant gratification) as demonstrated by Chen et al. (2005), it is feasible that diminished self-control will yield enhanced willingness to pay for products that stimulate the desire to engage in immediate consumption. Products that stimulate cerebral reward centers, such as hedonic products, are therefore likely to display relatively low price elasticity.

Again, price sensitivity variations across cultures ought to reflect the nature of the consumption experience. To the extent that socially relevant others are available (i.e., for products that are consumed in public), impulsivity and associated willingness to pay ought to be lower for Easterners and higher for Westerners. For instance, Kitayama et al. (2004) find that Asians justify their choice when socially relevant others are primed; consequently, since impulsivity is more difficult to justify (particularly for Easterners), willingness to pay ought to be relatively low for publicly consumed hedonic products in Asia.

PROMOTIONAL MESSAGES THAT FOSTER SELF-CONTROL FAILURE

Two aspects of messaging are relevant to our discussion. The first refers to the use of messages that activate goals. Chen et al. (2005) use a subtle message to suggest a promotion or prevention goal to facilitate a match or mismatch between subjects' self-construal and their regulatory focus. The substantive implication of their finding is that emphasizing the difficulty of achieving a desirable goal in Western contexts ought to enhance impulsivity for a product that will help counter that roadblock, while enhancing the possibility of an undesirable outcome in an Eastern context ought to enhance impulsivity for a product that will mitigate the likelihood of that undesirable outcome.

The second aspect refers to norms that are prevalent in a particular culture. In a working paper with Sharon Ng and Hakkyun Kim (Ng, Kim, & Rao, 2015), we demonstrate an interesting phenomenon. Westerners (native Canadians or Singaporeans primed with Western visual icons) by virtue of their independence, take actions as individuals, while Easterners (Chinese or Singaporeans primed with Eastern visual icons), by virtue of their interdependence tend not to take action as individuals, but do so as a group. Since messages consistent with self-construal will be most persuasive, messages that emphasize individual action are more likely to persuade Westerners, while messages that emphasize group action are more likely to persuade Easterners. More importantly, it is reasonable to speculate that *in*consistent messages (group action oriented messages to Westerners and individual action oriented messages to Easterners) will deplete self-regulatory resources and thus lead to self-control failure-induced consumption, much like other emotionally taxing outcomes such as negative moods (Tiffany & Drobes, 1990) yield resource depletion and self-control failure.

PLACE AND SELF-CONTROL FAILURE

The insight that bicultural subjects can be primed to behave in a manner consistent with their Western or Eastern cultural selves suggests a role for the store environment in priming consumers. As Chen et al. (2005) demonstrate, it is feasible to make one or the other culture more salient among bicultural consumers. (Further, even among Westerners, it is feasible to prime a prevention orientation, while it is possible to prime a promotional orientation among Easterners.)

As a consequence, bicultural consumers might display different levels of impatience depending on the self-construal that is primed by the store environment. Bicultural Singaporeans purchasing products from stores or locations that are consistent with their Eastern selves (e.g., Singaporeans purchasing fish from a wet market) may display greater patience, relative to when they purchase products from stores that are consistent with their Western selves (e.g., Singaporeans purchasing coffee from a Starbucks outlet). By the same token, online purchases (Chen et al., 2005) can prompt impulsivity through the display of culturally appropriate iconography depending on the cultural identity of the customer.

In summary, marketers may wish to take into consideration the existing scientific evidence regarding self-control and its failure, the differential impact of its failure across cultural contexts, and the profit implications of that failure, as they design strategies to maximize profits and sales. By the same token, public policy makers may wish to take into consideration the existing scientific evidence regarding self-control and its failure, the differential impact of its failure across cultural contexts, and the social welfare implications of that failure, as they design interventions and regulations to enhance consumer welfare.

CONCLUSIONS AND FUTURE RESEARCH

My focus has been on the important themes in the extant literature that provide a conceptual link to the focus of this volume and this chapter, that of the effect of cross-cultural variations on the ability and motivation to self-regulate, and the impact of the failure to self-regulate on consumption behaviors. Drawing from the literature on self-regulation failure due to variations in the ability and the motivation to self-regulate, I developed a link to the notion of self-construal that then permits the development of an understanding of cross-cultural differences in self-control failure-induced consumption. But, this review of the literature, while informative, raises several questions that would benefit from further scrutiny. I classify these questions into two categories: fundamental questions and applied questions.

Fundamental questions

Emerging accounts of human behavior that adopt an evolutionary perspective suggest that observed differences due to culture ought to be explained from an evolutionary standpoint. That is, since human behavior is *adaptive*, when a particular behavior is exhibited it ought to enhance the likelihood of the propagation of the genes of the organism that displays that behavior. In other words, much like morphological features such as skin pigmentation have been shaped by evolutionary pressures particular to latitude, the human brain's tendency to display a particular (culturally driven) behavior ought to reflect an inherited ability to solve problems that were confronted by that individual's ancestors from that culture.

There is limited evidence in the extant literature on this topic, and to the extent that it exists, it is speculative. For instance, Kitayama and Uskul (2011) observe that "...a cold and dry environment, combined with high residential or geographical mobility and low population density, which are often linked to nomadic or herding lifestyles...lends itself to a greater emphasis on independence over interdependence. On the other hand, a warm and humid environment, combined with low residential or geographic mobility and high population density, which are linked to a farming lifestyle, gives rise to a greater emphasis on interdependence over independence" (p. 423). But, what remains unclear is *why* a cold climate *causes* high mobility. Would it not be the case that climate *variability* would cause mobility? And, would it not be the case that a stable (and temperate) climate is more conducive to population stability?

Second, and consistent with the evolutionary meme, there are substantial regional differences within East and West. For instance, Western Europeans likely display different levels of independence relative to Eastern Europeans and the Latin countries. Similarly, Indians and Chinese consumers likely display markedly different patterns of consumption behaviors. *Why* do these regional differences exist? Simplistic allusions to recent history (e.g., Communism versus democracy or being subject to British colonial rule) are unsatisfactory, for these historical events account for a small fraction of the history of the peoples of these cultures. Surely thousands of years of acculturation could not have been so dramatically altered over the course of less than a century or two.

Third, an aspect left unaddressed in the literature is the potential effect of culture on other elements of self-control failure, such as self-awareness, mentalizing, and threat detection. In particular, self-awareness may arguably differ across cultures, as the meaning of the self might be culture specific;[5] mentalizing, which is subject to the assessment of socially relevant others, might be less important among independent Westerners, and therefore threat detection to assess the possibility of exclusion from a socially relevant group may also be less important a concern among independent Westerners.

Finally, do ethnically determined cultural variations persist following immigration, and if so for how long? For instance, second-generation immigrants (i.e., children of immigrants) likely tend to conform to the local culture to a greater degree than first-generation immigrants in public, but continue to adhere to the cultural norms of the original culture in private. *Why* do these differences in public versus private behavior persist? Are these differences evolutionarily adaptive in that they foster gene propagation? More specifically, if diversity in the gene pool is evolutionarily desirable (i.e., sexual congress between members of the same species who are ethnically dissimilar ought to yield better progeny who are more likely to propagate their genes into the future), should it not be the case that intermarriage between ethnically "distant" immigrants and natives will lead to more desirable progeny? This speculation suggests that children of ethnically and racially mixed marriages ought to display more self-control than children of ethnically and racially homogenous Western couples.

5. The emphasis on the self as a basis from which self-regulation and its failure can be analyzed is potentially problematic when conducting cross-cultural research, because the notion of the self might vary across cultures. For instance, traditional accounts in the literature in cultural psychology (e.g., Markus & Kitayama, 1991) conceive of the self as contextual, and defined in relation to socially relevant others. Consequently, because people in the East tend to be interdependent and people in the West tend to be independent (Hofstede, 1980), the definition of self may not be reliably applied in the same fashion in the two contexts. Cognitive neuroscience-based investigations confirm that Chinese participants show heightened activation of the medial prefrontal cortex when reflecting on themselves and their mothers, while Western subjects show enhanced activation in the medial prefrontal cortex only when thinking about themselves (Zhu Zhang, Fan, & Han, 2007). Similarly, Chiao, Harada, Komeda, Li, Mano, Saito, Parrish, Sadato, & Iidaka (2009) demonstrate with bicultural participants, that the medial prefrontal cortex activation is sensitive to whether participants were primed with individualistic or collectivistic values. In light of the existing evidence that extensive self-involvement produces medial prefrontal cortex activation, it is fair to speculate that the notion of the self is culture specific, and therefore, the neural correlates of self-regulation and associated impulsivity are likely culture specific.

Applied questions

Several important applied questions that pertain specifically to self-regulation failure are discussed here.

GLOBALIZATION EFFECTS

The effect of the Internet and social media on consumer behavior has been a matter of much inquiry (Riegner, 2007). Among the many alleged consequences of the Internet on the global economy (including expectations of reductions in average prices, price variability, competition and the like), one could ask several interesting questions about *how* the Internet, because it reduces search and other non-monetary costs of shopping, impacts self-control failure-induced consumption. Does an electronic shopping environment foster impulsive purchasing because of the frictionless nature of the shopping process, or does it inhibit impulsive purchasing because the search process is easier and reveals attractive options more readily, which in turn makes the decision process more difficult (Iyengar & Lepper, 2000)? And, do the forces of globalization dampen cross-cultural differences in consumer impulsivity because enhanced travel and communication result in a more homogenous population, or are these differences sufficiently embedded so that the differences are immune to relatively short-run changes in the technological environment?

WITHIN-COUNTRY VARIATIONS

Most cross-cultural research focuses on broad (i.e., East versus West) distinctions. In fact, most of the original cross-cultural research in marketing (e.g., Childers & Rao, 1992) examined difference between American subjects and subjects in an Asian (Thailand) country. Other studies have examined Japanese, Chinese, Korean, and Singaporean consumers as representative of the Asian culture. However, relatively little work has examined cultural differences within a country. That is, within the United States (a relatively homogenous country dominated by one religion, one language, and exposure to relatively similar media outlets) there exist multiple subcultures, including African Americans, Native Americans, Latinos, the Gay culture, and the like. These subcultures have persisted or developed over time and are likely to display different behaviors, particularly consumption behaviors. How do cognitions, emotions and motivations differ across these subcultures as they pertain to impulsive consumer behavior?

Concluding comment

The field of cross-cultural psychology is exploding (Kitayama & Uskul, 2011). The confluence of survey, experimental and cognitive neuroscience methods coupled with developing theoretical sophistication through the employment of multiple disciplinary orientations including biology and evolutionary perspectives augurs well for a field that is overflowing with interesting and important questions that would benefit from rigorous scrutiny. As global forces make for a smaller planet, understanding differences in cultures that inform and influence behavior is becoming an important priority, not just for multinational and transnational corporations, but also for governments and policy makers wishing to assure that their actions are not misinterpreted due to cultural mistranslations of intent or meaning. In the field of consumer behavior, the use of technology such as functional magnetic resonance imaging (see Hedgcock & Rao, 2009; Yoon, Gutchess, Geinberg, & Polk, 2006 for applications of this technique in consumer behavior research), analytical approaches that allow for examination of primary and secondary data, and theoretical perspectives from economics, psychology and anthropology should yield useful insights into the several knotty questions regarding cross-cultural differences in consumer impulsivity.

Over the last two decades, the study of cultural psychology has blossomed. The work of Markus and Kitayama (1991) as well as other distinguished scholars (Nisbett, Peng, Choi, & Norenzayan, 2001) has employed experiments to engage in systematic comparisons between Western (primarily North American) cultural contexts and Eastern (primarily East Asian) cultural contexts. More recently, it has become clear that the research "...can be united by its commitment to the hypothesis that it is behaviors and shared social representation in a collective, social context, *not* cognitive representations in the head per se, that ultimately matter most in understanding culture" (Kitayama & Uskul, 2011, p. 421, emphasis in original). Nevertheless, it is in the brain and its pathways that cultural practices and tasks reside. That is, the repeated employment of cultural routines (be they the tendency to be independent and promotion oriented among Westerners, or the tendency to be interdependent and prevention oriented among Easterners) ought to result in observable differences in the neural correlates of behavior among Westerners and Easterners. For instance, Westerners who are promotion oriented ought to display predictable differences in the manner in which they think of themselves, relative to Easterners. Neuroscientists aware of the plasticity of the brain (and the influence of nurture on creating neural pathways) note that "...neurons that are fired together will get wired together" (Kitayama & Uskul, 2011, p. 424).[6]

REFERENCES

Aaker, J., & Lee, A. L. (2001). 'I' seek pleasures and 'we' avoid pains: The role of self-regulatory goals in information processing and persuasion. *Journal of Consumer Research*, 28(1), 33–49.

6. In particular, mirror neurons (Iacoboni, 2009) allow for individuals to imitate others by accurately assessing others' neural processes. Such mirror neurons can be useful in the mentalizing process, and the development of empathy.

Acton, G. S. (2003). Measurement of impulsivity in a hierarchical model of personality traits: Implications for substance use. *Substance Use and Misuse*, *38*(January), 67–83.

Baumeister, R. (2002). Yielding to Temptation: Self-Control Failure, Impulsive Purchasing and Consumer Behavior. *Journal of Consumer Research*, *28*(March), 670–676.

Baumeister, R. F. (2000). Ego depletion and the self's executive function. In A. Tesser & R. B. Felson (Eds.), *Psychological perspectives on self and identity* (pp. 9–33). Washington DC, USA: APA.

Baumeister, R. F., Bratslavsky, E., Muraven, M., & Tice, D. M. (1998). Ego depletion: Is the active self a limited resource?. *Journal of Personality and Social Psychology*, *74*(5), 1252–1265.

Bellenger, D., Robertson, D. H., & Hirschman, E. C. (1978). Impulse buying varies by product. *Journal of Advertising Research*, *18*(December), 15–18.

Chiao, J.Y., Harada, T., Komeda, H., Li, Z., Mano, Y., Saito, D., Parrish, T. B., Sadato, N., & Iidaka, T. (2009). Neural basis of individualistic and collectivistic views of self. *Human Brain Mapping*, *3*, 2813–2820.

Chen, H., Ng, S., & Rao, A. R. (2005). Cultural differences in consumer impatience. *Journal of Marketing Research*, *42*(August), 291–301.

Childers, T. L., & Rao, R. A (1992). The influence of familial and peer-based reference groups on consumer decisions. *Journal of Consumer Research*, *19*, 198–211.

Gailliot, M.T., & Baumeister, R.F. (2007). The physiology of willpower: linking blood glucose to self-control. *Personality and Social Psychology Review*, *11*, 303–327.

Gallagher, H. L., & Frith, C. D. (2003). Functional Imaging of 'theory of mind'. *Trends in Cognitive Sciences*, *7*, 77–83.

Graham, R. J. (1981). The role of perception of time in consumer research. *Journal of Consumer Research*, *7*(March), 335–42.

Heatherton, T. F. (2011). Neuroscience of self and self-regulation. *Annual Review of Psychology*, *62*, 363–390.

Heatherton, T. F., & Wagner, D. D. (2011). Cognitive neuroscience of self-regulation failure. forthcoming, *Trends in Cognitive Sciences*, *15*(3), 132–139.

Hedgcock, W., & Rao, A. R. (2009). Trade-off aversion as an explanation for the attraction effect: A functional magnetic resonance imaging study. *Journal of Marketing Research*, *46*(1), 1–13.

Hedgcock,W., Vohs, K., & Rao, A. R. (2012). Neural correlates of self-regulatory resource depletion. *Journal of Consumer Psychology*, *22*(October), 486–495.

Herman, C. P., & Mack, D. (1975). Restrained and unrestrained eating. *Journal of Personality*, *43*, 647–660.

Higgins, T. E. (1997). Beyond pleasure and pain. *American Psychologist*, *52*(12), 1280–1300.

Hofstede, G. (1980). *Culture's consequences, international differences in work-related values*. Beverly Hills, CA, USA: Sage.

Iacoboni, M. (2009). Neurobiology of imitation. *Current Opinion in Neurobiology*, *19*, 661–665.

Iyengar, S., & Lepper, M. R. (2000). When choice is demotivating: Can one desire too much of good thing?" *Journal of Personality and Social Psychology*, *79*(6), 995–1006.

Kitayama, S., Snibbe, A. C., Markus, H. R., & Suzuki, T., (2004). Is there any free choice? Self and dissonance in two cultures. *Psychological Science*, *15*, 527–533.

Kitayama, S., & Uskul, A. K. (2011). Culture, mind and the brain: Current evidence and future directions. *Annual Review of Psychology, 62*, 419–450.

Kollat, D. T., & Willett, R. P. (1967). Consumer impulse purchasing behavior. *Journal of Marketing Research*, 4(February), 21–31.

Lee, A. Y., Aaker, J. L., & Gardner, W. L. (2000), The Pleasures and Pains of Distinct Self-Construals: The Role of Interdependence in Regulatory Focus." *Journal of Personality and Social Psychology, 78*(6), 1122–1134.

Markus, H. R., & Kitayama, S. (1991). Culture and the self: Implications for cognition, emotion and motivation. *Psychological Review, 98*(2), 224–253.

Muraven, M., & Baumeister, R. F. (2000). Self-regulation and depletion of limited resources: Does self-control resemble a muscle? *Psychological Bulletin, 126*(2), 247–259.

Muraven, M., Baumeister, R. F., & Tice, D. M. (1999). Longitudinal improvement of self-regulation through practice: Building self-control strength through repeated exercise. *The Journal of Social Psychology, 139*(4), 446–457.

Muraven, M., Collins, R. L., & Nienhaus, K. (2002). Self-control and alcohol restraint: An initial application of the self-control strength model. *Psychology of Addictive Behaviors, 16*(2), 113–120.

Muraven, M., & Slessareva, E. (2003). Mechanisms of self-control failure: Motivation and limited resources. *Personality and Social Psychology Bulletin, 29*(7), 894–906.

Muraven, M., Tice, D. M., & Baumeister, R. F. (1998). Self-control as a limited resource: Regulatory depletion patterns. *Journal of Personality and Social Psychology, 74*, 744–789.

Ng, S., Kim, H., & Rao, A. R. (2015). Sins of omission and sins of commission: The Impact of Implicit Theories of Agency on Brand Switching Intention Across Cultures," forthcoming, *Journal of Consumer Psychology*, January.

Nisbett R. E., Peng, K., Choi I., & Norenzayan A. (2001). Culture and systems of thought: holistic vs. analytic cognition. *Psychological Review, 108*, 291–310

Pollay, R. (1968). Customer impulse purchasing behavior: A reexamination. *Journal of Marketing Research*, 5(August), 323–325.

Ramanathan, S., & Menon, G. (2006). Time-varying effects of chronic hedonic goals on impulsive behavior. *Journal of Marketing Research, 43*(4), 628–641.

Read, D., Loewenstein, G., & Kalyanaraman, S. (1999). Mixing virtue and vice: Combining the immediacy effect and the diversification heuristic. *Journal of Behavioral Decision Making, 12*(4), 257–73.

Richards, J. M., & Gross, J. J. (2000). Emotion regulation and memory: The cognitive costs of keeping one's cool. *Journal of Personality and Social Psychology, 79*(3), 410–424.

Richeson, J. A., Baird, A. A., Gordon, H. L., Heatherton, T. F., Wyland, C. L., Trawalter, S., & Shelton, J. N. (2003). An fMRI investigation of the impact of interracial contact on executive function. *Nature Neuroscience*, 6(December), 1323–1328.

Riegner, C. (2007). Word of mouth on the web: The impact of web 2.0 on consumer purchase Decisions. *Journal of Advertising Research, 47*(4), 436–447.

Rook, D. W. (1987). The buying impulse. *Journal of Consumer Research, 14*(September), 189–199.

Schroeder, S. A. (2007). We can do better: Improving the health of the American people. *New England Journal of Medicine, 357*, 1221–1228.

Seeley, E. A., & Gardner, W. L. (2003). The 'selfless' and self-regulation: The role of chronic other-orientation in averting self-regulatory depletion. *Self and Identity, 2*, 103–117.

Shah, J. Y. (2005). The automatic pursuit and management of goals. *Current Directions in Psychological Science, 14*, 10–13.

Shih, M., Pitinsky, T. L., & Ambady, N. (1999). Stereotype susceptibility: Identity salience and shifts in quantitative performance. *Psychological Science, 10*(1), January, 80–83.

Shiv, B., & Fedorikhin, A. (1999). Heart and mind in conflict: The interplay of affect and cognition in consumer decision making. *Journal of Consumer Research, 26*(December), 278–292.

Thaler, R. H., & Sunstein, C. R. (2009), *Nudge: improving decisions about health, wealth, and happiness*, New Haven, CT, USA: Yale University Press.

Tiffany, S. T., & Drobes, D. J. (1990). Imagery and smoking urges: the manipulation of affective content. *Addictive Behavior, 15*, 531–539.

Triandis, H. C. (1989). The self and social behavior in differing cultural contexts. *Psychological Review, 96*(3), 506–520.

Vohs, K. D., Baumeister, R. F., Schmeichel, B. J., Wenge, J. M., Nelson, N. M., & Tice, D. M. (2008). Making Choices Impairs Subsequent Self-Control: A Limited-Resource Account of Decision Making, Self-Regulation, and Active Initiative. *Journal of Personality and Social Psychology, 94*(5), 883–898.

Vohs, K. D., & Faber, R. J. (2007). Spent resources: Self-regulatory resource availability affects impulse buying. *Journal of Consumer Research, 33*(4), 537–547.

Vohs, K.D., & Heatherton, T. D. (2000). Self-regulatory failure: A resource depletion approach. *Psychological Science, 11*(3), 249–254.

Wertenbroch, K. (1998). Consumption self-control by rationing purchase quantities of virtue and vice. *Marketing Science, 17*(4), 317–337.

Yoon, C., Gutchess, A. H., Geinberg, F., & Polk, T. A. (2006). A functional magnetic resonance imaging study of neural dissociations between brand and person judgments. *Journal of Consumer Research, 33*(1), 31–40.

Zajonc, R. B. (1965). Social facilitation. *Science, 149*(July), 269–274.

Zhang, Y., & Shrum, L. J. (2009). The influence of self-construal on impulsive consumption. *Journal of Consumer Research, 35*(February), 838–850.

Zhang, Y., Winterich, K., & Mittal, V. (2010). Power-distance belief and impulsive buying. *Journal of Marketing Research*, (October), 945–954.

Zhu, Y., Zhang, L., Fan, L., & Han, S. (2007). Neural basis of cultural influence on self-representation. *NeuroImage, 34*, 1310–1316.

Zhu, R., & Meyers-Levy, J. (2007). Exploring the cognitive mechanism that underlies regulatory focus effects. *Journal of Consumer Research, 34*(June), 89–96.